Eric J. Finnerty
9 Gable Close,
Abbots Langley,
WATFORD, Herts.

10th April 1984

# WORLD ATLAS OF RAILWAYS

*Research*
Rand McNally & Company

Concept, Design and Illustration by
QED Ltd.

*Art Director*
Roger Pring

*Designers and artists*
Alastair Campbell
Nicholas Farmer
Robin Gibbons
Elaine Keenan
Abdul Aziz Khan
Edward Kinsey
David Mallott
David Staples

*Contributing artists*
Moira Clinch
Sally Launder
Geoff Nicholson
Nigel Osborne
Jim Robins
David Worth

*Atlas Section*
Rand McNally & Company

Planning, Project co-ordination
Research and Editorial by
Chris Milsome Ltd.

*Editorial Director*
Chris Milsome

*Editor*
Chris Fayers

*Contributing authors*
O. S. Nock
John Bennett
Rory McPherson
Kenneth Cantlie

*Text editor*
Jeff Groman

*Editorial assistant*
Patricia Hayne

*Research*
Karen Gunnel
Pamela George

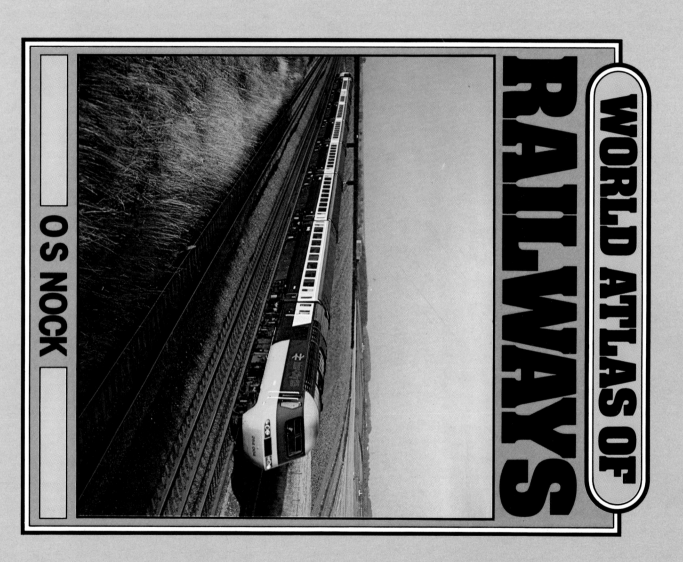

# WORLD ATLAS OF RAILWAYS

## O S NOCK

# Contents

## The development of railways

**The iron road**
page 8

Railway development 1700–1824
**Horse trains and iron rails**
page 10

Railway development 1825–1830
**Steam wins the day**
page 12

Railway development 1831–1850
**Worldwide expansion begins**
page 14

Railway development 1851–1880
**Opening up the West**
page 16

Railway development 1881–1913
**Achievements and disasters**
page 18

Railway development 1914–1922
**Networks in the Great War**
page 20

Railway development 1923–1945
**The fantastic streamliners**
page 22

Railway development 1946 and after
**The new age of railways**
page 24

Locomotive development 1800–1834
**Harnessing the power of steam**
page 26

Locomotive development 1835–1874
**Improving engine performance**
page 28

Locomotive development 1875–1905
**Compound locos and superheating**
page 30

Locomotive development 1906–1926
**The era of technological innovation**
page 32

Locomotive development 1927–1934
**The high point of steam**
page 34

Locomotive development 1935–1944
**Moving towards diesel traction**
page 36

Locomotive development 1945 and after
**Locomotive power now**
page 38

Rolling stock 1800–1875
**Cattle trucks to family saloons**
page 40

Rolling stock 1876–1924
**Traffic becomes specialized**
page 42

Rolling stock 1925 and after
**Freight improvements; commuter comfort**
page 44

Railway architecture
**Building on the grand scale**
page 46

**The paraphernalia of railways**
page 48

## How railways work now

**The eclipse of steam**
page 50

**Diesel motive power**
page 51

**Electric and hydraulic transmissions**
page 52

**Electric traction**
page 53

**High-speed trains**
page 54

**Permanent way: laying the track**
page 56

**Permanent way: smooth running**
page 58

**Bridge and tunnel construction**
page 60

**Passenger stock: early days**
page 62

**Passenger stock: modern improvements**
page 64

**Freight stock: specialization**
page 66

**Freight stock: automation**
page 68

**Modern signalling**
page 70

**Traffic and timetabling: main line**
page 72

**Traffic and timetabling: commuter**
page 74

**The science of freight handling**
page 76

**The great marshalling yards**
page 78

**The Conrail experiment**
page 80

## Great routes

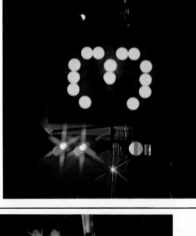

**Through the Alpine Fortress I**
page 82

**Through the Alpine Fortress II**
page 84

**Trans-Europe Expresses**
page 86

**The great British route: London to Glasgow**
page 88

**Rail versus air: a real contest**
page 90

**Paris-Lyon: tomorrow's way**
page 91

**Across Asia: the eastern goal**
page 92

**Across Asia: the great dream**
page 94

## Great expresses

Australia: crossing the arid continent
*page 96*

New Zealand: southernmost route
*page 98*

Japan's Shinkansen I
*page 100*

Japan's Shinkansen II
*page 102*

Crossing North America I
*page 104*

Crossing North America II
*page 106*

The Andes: highest in the world I
*page 108*

The Andes: highest in the world II
*page 110*

Mountain climbing: rack and pinion
*page 112*

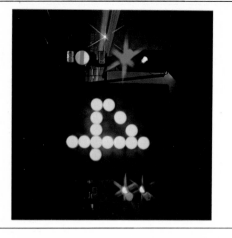

The Orient Express: the glory that faded
*page 114*

The Irish Mail: over a century of service
*page 116*

The Settebello: speed and luxury
*page 118*

The Aquitaine: pioneer of electric traction
*page 120*

The Chief: America in style
*page 122*

The Blue Train: pride of South Africa
*page 124*

The Canadian: transcontinental connection
*page 126*

The Rajdhani Express: India's fastest
*page 128*

## Atlas

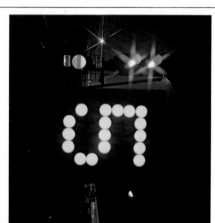

Europe
*page 130*

British Isles
*page 132*

France and the Alps
*page 134*

Central Europe
*page 136*

Italy
*page 138*

Northern Europe
*page 140*

Spain and Portugal
*page 142*

Western and Central USSR
*page 144*

Eastern and Central USSR
*page 146*

China, Japan and Korea
*page 148*

Japan
*page 150*

Southeast Asia
*page 152*

India and Pakistan
*page 154*

Western North Africa
*page 156*

Eastern North Africa
*page 158*

Southern Africa
*page 160*

Canada
*page 162*

United States
*page 164*

Central America
*page 166*

Northern South America
*page 168*

Southern South America
*page 170*

Australia and New Zealand
*page 172*

Legend and comparisons
*page 174*

## Railway systems

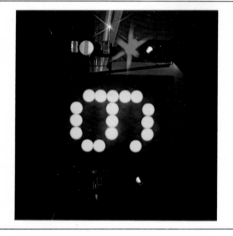

Europe: Scandinavia
*page 178*

United Kingdom and Ireland
*page 180*

Belgium and Luxembourg
*page 182*

Netherlands
*page 183*

West Germany
*page 184*

East Germany and Poland
*page 185*

Switzerland and Austria
*page 186*

Czechoslovakia and Hungary
*page 187*

Portugal and Spain
*page 188*

France
*page 189*

Italy, Yugoslavia, Albania
*page 190*

Romania, Bulgaria, Greece
*page 191*

USSR
*page 192*

Asia: Turkey and Middle East I
*page 193*

Middle East II and India
*page 194*

Pakistan and Far East I
*page 195*

Far East II
*page 196*

Africa: Northeast
*page 197*

West Africa
*page 198*

Central Africa I
*page 199*

Central Africa II
*page 200*

Southern Africa
*page 201*

Canada and United States
*page 202*

Central America
*page 204*

Caribbean and South America I
*page 205*

South America II
*page 206*

Australia and New Zealand
*page 208*

## Reference

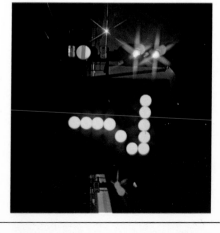

Chronology
*page 210*

Who's Who
*page 210*

Glossary
*page 216*

Bibliography
*page 218*

Index
*page 220*

Acknowledgements
*page 224*

# Introduction

Not so many years ago it was a widely held opinion in most parts of the world that railways were relics of the past. For medium-distance travel, the passenger train had been outstripped both in speed and general convenience by the private motor car; in commuter travel, city workers were beginning to prefer road congestion and the difficulties of parking to the gross discomfort, overcrowding and occasional breakdowns in local train services; while for long-distance travel the aeroplane showed an immense superiority in speed. Above all, rail travel in the popular mind was being outmoded. In the conveyance of freight, individual consignments of freight, struggling amid antiquated facilities and outworn legal regulations, railways could not match the rapidly developing road service provided by fast trucks. Only the handling of heavy freight and minerals in bulk remained with the railways, and that mainly because no one else wanted it. To outward appearances the picture was gloomy; and it would have become so in actuality had not far-sighted men begun to stress and develop the railways' priceless asset: speed for mass conveyance – both of vast numbers of passengers, and of vast tonnages of freight.

## The influence of geography

So there has come in Great Britain, France and Japan a great renaissance in railway activity. In the USA the development has been almost entirely in freight, and elsewhere in specialized traffic. Because it was the predominating influence of geography that led to the growth of railways in the first place, so, in this critical phase when so many outside influences are beginning to highlight the importance of railways in modern society, it is fascinating and immensely worthwhile to study the situation anew, on a worldwide basis, with aid of many maps. Going back to the earliest days, two of the first public railways in the world, the Stockton and Darlington, and the Baltimore and Ohio, were built to convey minerals from inland areas down to the sea for shipment. When the merchants of large industrial centres wanted quicker connection with their interests elsewhere, routes were chosen where geography made the going easiest and cheapest from the constructional point of view, and gave prospects of fast transit on a minimum of running costs.

Thus the broad conception of this book has developed, showing how geography as much as sociology and industry has dictated that geography was always on the side of the railway evolution. But it must not be imagined that geography was always on the side of the railway entrepreneurs and engineers. After the first modest beginnings, often with phenomenal financial success, business interests demanded the execution of bolder projects, and more direct connections. Contentment with roundabout itineraries following the contours of river valleys or coastlines (to secure easy gradients), and with low initial costs, began to evaporate, and engineers were faced with calls to cross mountain ranges, to span rivers, and to

traverse wide tracts of level, though unstable, marshland. This last-mentioned geographical hazard had been encountered earlier on one of the first railways, the Liverpool and Manchester, in crossing the notorious Chat Moss peat bog. The methods by which George Stephenson finally conquered this obstacle became the pattern for dealing with similar difficulties in many parts of the world.

Many of the engineering problems were entirely new. The established professional men had built harbours, lighthouses, roads and canals, but the introduction of the steam locomotive brought new parameters. There was a limit to the steepness of the gradients it could climb, and

LNER *Flying Scotsman*, restored in 1938.

while a military road for foot soldiers, pack horses, or even elephants would be taken up steep mountain sides, such a route was impossible for locomotives. The surveys to obtain a practicable gradient often had to be made in physical conditions of extreme difficulty: in the hill country at the foot of mountain ranges or in dense forests where the opportunities for obtaining long sights ahead, or of taking levels, were few. Nor could established concepts like the suspension bridge be used in the crossing of broad valleys or tidal waterways. New ideas for long-span bridges had to be formed.

## The development of techniques

It is an absorbing study to trace how the great principles of construction and early operation which developed in Great Britain, the USA and Europe, were gradually extended and adapted to geographical and other conditions elsewhere in the world. British conditions and prospects for expansion called for massively built, relatively straight and level railways and there was plenty of capital ready to be invested in such enterprises. In the USA, by contrast, railways were needed to open up the

virgin country. There was little money available; tracks had to be built as cheaply as possible with indigenous materials. Heavy industry was just setting up and could hardly afford large-scale imports. One outcome was the evolution of those masterworks of light civil engineering, the timber trestle bridges, so skilfully erected across many a deep valley or mountain torrent. Similarly, because of the infrequency of train services and the need to avoid high capital expenditure, the Americans developed the system of regulating traffic by telegraphic "train order", in contrast to the more comprehensive system of signalling and interlocking that was found essential on the much busier routes of Great Britain, France and other countries in western Europe.

As the railway networks spread so the natural geographical resources of the world became integrated with the overall picture. Conveyance of coal was the first task of railways in Great Britain and France, and although horses did much of the haulage in the very earliest days, coal was the locomotive fuel. In the USA, although there were great discoveries of coal in certain areas, the vastness of the country made its transport to other parts uneconomic, and the great majority of early American locomotives burned the indigenous fuel of the forests – wood. Thus environmental considerations were in evidence from the earliest days. The voluble reactionaries in Great Britain who opposed railways on principle secured the insertion of clauses in Acts of Parliament prohibiting the emission of smoke by steam locomotives, and to comply with this, coke had to be used in place of coal.

## Keeping pace with the times

Out of this deeply interesting historical foundation there emerges the majestic edifice of steady technical development; the evolution of codes of practice to ensure the safe running of trains at speeds that even our own grandfathers would not have dreamed of. The replacement of steam by diesel and electric traction is inevitable in the modern age. In recording it, and in recalling some of the grandest moments of the steam era, tribute is payed to one of the most wonderful and most human machines ever devised by man. The selection of great passenger trains for special mention is a blend of past and present, while in great mineral activities such as Hammersley, in northwestern Australia, Roberts Bank in British Columbia, and Richards Bay in Africa, outstanding examples of modern railways acting as mighty belt conveyors in a single-product industry have been included. These indeed are portents for the future, but equally so are the projects now under construction, for super-speed passenger lines in France, following the Japanese *Shinkansen*, and for the running of the ingenious Advanced Passenger Train at high speed over the existing tracks of the British railway network. In 1978, railways everywhere in the world are once again very much on the map.

*Evening Star*, the last steam loco produced by British Railways.

# The Development of Railways

# The iron road

Although, as the pages immediately following relate, there had been railways of a kind in many countries, to assist in the conveyance of wagons loaded with merchandise, and pulled by horses, even before the astonishing developments of the nineteenth century, it was the invention of the steam locomotive, and its successful use on the first *public* railway in the world, the Stockton and Darlington, that came as a predominating catalyst in the development of world transport. British engineers were to the fore in every facet of early railway pioneering; in the evolution of track, in tunnelling and railway bridge building as well as in locomotive experimentation and operation. If one studies the world chronology of railway inception in the momentous decade following the opening of the second great English pioneer work – the Liverpool and Manchester Railway, in 1830 – in most of them British engineers were consultants, contractors, or manufacturers of locomotives. In Europe alone railways were established in Austria, Belgium, France, Germany, the Netherlands and Russia before 1840; in the same decade railways in Canada and the USA were extending rapidly, and there had been a start in Cuba. Subsequently, it is remarkable to see the

The railway era really began with the commercial success of the Stockton and Darlington Railway, opened in 1825. A railway was inaugurated shortly afterwards in France, and Europe as a whole continued to lead the field in the introduction of railways. Although political upheavals prevented the satisfactory development of certain railway networks, specifically those in Poland, Germany and Austria. by 1869 every country in modern Europe had built the beginnings of a railway system.

Three factors helped to spread the railway worldwide: British enterprise (many foreign lines were built by British contractors); American enthusiasm for the new idea; and colonial possessions – the first colonial railway was opened in Jamaica in 1848.

The world's rail networks have only recently stopped expanding. This may be a temporary phenomenon caused by rationalization in the industrial nations, closing marginal lines built when the trains were unrivalled. Elsewhere construction continues.

Portugal 1856
Spain 1848
France 1832
Irish Republic 1834
United Kingdom 1825
Luxembourg 1859
Belgium 1835
Netherlands 1839
West Germany 1835
Denmark 1847
Norway 1854
East Germany 1839
Sweden 1856
Switzerland 1847
Austria 1838
Czechoslovakia 1839
Poland 1842
Finland 1862
USSR 1837
Italy 1839
Hungary 1846
Yugoslavia 1846
Albania 1947
Romania 1869
Bulgaria 1866
Grece 1869

New Zealand 1863

Indonesia 1864
Malaysia 1885
Kampuchea 1930
Vietnam 1885
Philippines 1888
Hong Kong 1910
Mongolia 1930
Taiwan 1891
China 1872
Japan 1872
Korea 1899
Ethiopia 1908
Saudi Arabia 1888
Pakistan 1904
Jordan 1891
Israel 1895
Lebanon 1895
Syria 1895
Turkey 1856
Tunisia 1876

Sudan 1875

Australia 1854
Thailand 1854
Burma 1877
Bangladesh 1862
Sri Lanka 1865
Mozambique 1886
India 1853
Tanzania 1894
Uganda 1903
Madagascar 1897
Kenya 1897
Swaziland 1964
Malawi 1907
Zimbabwe 1893
Botswana 1886
Namibia 1898
South Africa 1860
Zambia 1905
Angola 1898
Cameroon 1897
Nigeria 1901
Benin 1901
Ghana 1901
Ivory Coast 1903
Mauretania 1963
Liberia 1950
Guinea 1910
Iraq 1917
Iran 1920
Egypt 1854
Togo 1905
Volta 1934
Congo 1934

Senegal 1885
Mali 1904
Algeria 1862
Morocco 1876
Trinidad 1876
Colombia 1845
Jamaica 1837
Cuba 1837

Argentina 1857
Chile 1851
Uruguay 1869
Paraguay 1854
Brazil 1854
Peru 1851
Bolivia 1873
Guyana 1848
Surinam 1905
Venezuela 1877
Ecuador 1871
Panama 1855
Costa Rica 1890
Nicaragua 1890
Honduras 1869
El Salvador 1882
Guatemala 1880
Mexico 1850
USA 1830
Canada 1836

**Track mileage**

| by: | | |
|---|---|---|
| 1840 | 8,819 km | (5,512 mls) |
| 1860 | 194,753 km | (121,720 mls) |
| 1880 | 452,538 km | (282,836 mls) |
| 1900 | 790,551 km | (494,094 mls) |
| 1920 | 1,033,136 km | (645,710 mls) |
| 1940 | 1,255,876 km | (784,922 mls) |
| 1960 | 1,445,523 km | (903,451 mls) |
| 1975 | 1,418,228 km | (886,392 mls) |

1825-49
1850-74
1875-99
1900-24
1925-49
1950-77

steady increase in the extent of the world's railways, with regular increments of some 200,000 km (125,000 miles) every 20 years until 1960.

The rate of increase was of course not uniform in all countries; nor were the advances in technology, speed, or quality of service. The earliest and almost phenomenal increases in extent came in the industrialized countries, of which, in the nineteenth century, Great Britain was foremost, and an exporter of machinery, minerals and manufactured goods of all kinds to the whole world. The USA was only just emerging as a great industrial nation, while in Europe, France, Germany and Italy had all been torn by political and military upheavals. In all of them, however, railways came to play a great part in the subsequent consolidation. In the USA free enterprise and unbridled competition led to an enormous increase in railway activity in the last years of the nineteenth century. At the same time colonizing activities by the great nations of Europe led to the building of railways in many hitherto remote areas, quite apart from major, carefully planned projects like the building up of the Indian railway network.

or the great imperial ambitions of Cecil Rhodes in southern Africa. All initiated before 1900, one can trace beginnings, mostly on a modest scale, in Tunisia, in what is now Vietnam, Angola, Mozambique and Indonesia, while in the South American states there were railways flourishing long before 1900.

Success bred success. The provision of improved transport opened up the more remote communities, made their agricultural produce or mineral wealth available to wider, and hitherto unopened markets. This in turn demanded improved railway facilities, larger locomotives, better means of traffic regulation. There was more work for the manufacturers in Great Britain and elsewhere. Overseas railways needed coal to fire their locomotives. British-owned railways in South America purchased their coal from South Wales; at least one French railway had its own fleet of colliers to collect for itself at Cardiff the choice grades of Welsh steam coal that it favoured. New railways were built in South Wales to convey coal from the valleys to new ports, for shipment overseas. It was a booming reciprocal trade in some cases. Coal for locomotives was

exported from English east coast ports to the Baltic states in exchange for timber. Baltic pine was judged the finest material for railway sleepers. The expansion in world trade, which fostered the building of more railways, was aided to no small extent by the ability of railways to convey mail quicker than ever before. Where oceanic travel was concerned, as in the vital case of Anglo-American mail, it was sometimes quicker to put eastbound mail ashore at Queenstown (Cobh) in the south of Ireland, take it by train to Kingstown (Dun Laoghaire) on Dublin Bay, ship it across to Holyhead and thence by train to London rather than wait for the steamer to make her way into the Mersey, and dock at Liverpool. Even though the upheavals and reorientating of world trade after the First World War profoundly affected railway operations in many countries, expansion still continued elsewhere, as the routage graph opposite so vividly shows; and it is only after 1960 that the contraction in Great Britain and other highly industrialized areas there are magnificent new projects in hitherto remote areas of Canada, Australia and South Africa.

A cavalcade of rail: the *Rocket* of 1829; the broad gauge *Lord of the Isles*; an 1850s American 4-4-0; de Glehn's compound circa 1900; the 1937 LMS streamliner *Coronation Scot*; a 1941 GM diesel; Britain's new Advanced Passenger Train.

# Horse trains and iron rails

*Railway development 1700–1824*

**1700** The origin of railways for the exclusive use of vehicles with flanged wheels can be traced back to mining practice in medieval Germany; but the development of railways as a public means of transport took place entirely in Great Britain. In using the word public, however, and applying it to the conveyance of goods and minerals, activity has been recorded in both the sixteenth and seventeenth centuries. The influence of this development is evident from reference to similar work in the Ruhr coalfields of Germany as an *englischer Kohlenweg*. The rails were of wood, and laid exactly straight, and towards the end of the seventeenth century one reads that bulky carts were made with four so-called "rowlets" fitting the rails. These rowlets are taken to imply some form of flanged wheel, because it was claimed that their use made haulage so easy that one horse could draw four or five of these "bulky carts" laden with coal. No less celebrated a writer than Daniel Defoe told of coals being loaded "into a great machine called a Waggon", and run on an "artificial road" called a waggon-way.

*Right* This early colliery tramway in the north of England in 1773, shows a design of wagon that was still current 50 years later. The loaded wagon is relying upon gravity to propel it to the quay: the horse is there to pull the empty wagon back uphill to the mine.

*Left* Mine truck Agricola, 1556. *Below* Prior Park, 1750, near Bath, the family seat of Ralph Allen, Esq, with the tramway which it is claimed by many was the first railway.

**1726** Early in the eighteenth century mining interests in northeastern England led to the great combination known as the "Grand Allies", consisting of three hitherto independent groups of colliery owners. These were the Liddell family, of Ravensworth; the Montagu family and Thomas Ord, of Newcastle; and George Bowes. In 1726 they made an agreement to bring their interests together, and the arrangements concluded involved also the linking up of some of their collieries by wagon-ways to rationalize movement. The result was a remarkable development, including the construction of what was termed a "main line" from the River Tyne where the coals were shipped for a distance of 13 km (8 miles) inland. Traffic was so heavy that the "main line" was laid with a double track so that loaded and empty "trains" would not interfere with one another. The country through which the lines of the Grand Allies ran is hilly, and some engineering works of considerable magnitude were undertaken to provide an even gradient. There was an embankment at Tanfield 30 m (100 ft) high, and having a transverse width of 91 m (300 ft); but perhaps the most historic feature was the Causey Arch – the first bridge ever constructed for the exclusive purpose of carrying a railway. It was a single arch stone bridge built in 1727, having a span of 31 m (103 ft) and 7 m (22 ft) wide, to carry two tracks of 1,219 mm (4 ft) gauge, side by side.

Because these railways ran from inland regions to the banks of a navigable river it was possible to arrange the routes on a slightly falling gradient, so as to make the task of a horse easier when pulling loaded wagons. There was, however, then considered the need to keep the load horizontal when descending a gradient, and to do this the quaint expedient was adopted of making the leading wheels of the wagon of larger diameter than the trailing ones. Furthermore, in some wagons the leading wheels were spoked while the trailing ones were of solid wood. Flanges 2.5 cm (1 in) or 4 cm (1.5 in) deep were fixed to the inner faces of the wheels to provide an appropriate guiding effect. The wagons used in Durham and Northumberland had a primitive form of lever brake acting upon the rear pair of wheels. On the rail tracks running down to the rivers Tyne and Wear there was usually one horse to a wagon. Trains of wagons were not run.

There were places where the direction of the line had to be changed fairly abruptly, and because of the additional haulage effort that would have been necessary in pulling loaded wagons round a sharp curve turntables were adopted, consisting of circular tables that swivelled around a central vertical axis. These were the exact prototype of turntables that came to be used in countless British passenger stations for transferring the small four-wheeled carriages of the mid-nineteenth century from one track to another. On the early colliery wagon-ways there were places where the loaded vehicles would run by gravity. There the man in charge of the horse would transfer from front to rear, hitch a ride on the wagon, controlling the speed with the hand brake while the horse ran behind. At a later date in localities where horses pulled a train of three or more wagons, a special "dandy car" was provided for the horse to ride in, while at the same time the train was running downhill by gravity.

# 1750

An important development in the 1750s was the substitution of iron rails for wooden ones. Although there were other early and experimental uses of iron rails, one of the most important was that made on the wagon-ways of the Coalbrookdale Ironworks in Shropshire. These tracks were originally laid with fine quality oaken rails, but then, not only to improve their wearing quality, but also to use the products of their own furnaces, they covered the surfaces of these rails with cast iron. It is recorded that in the years 1768 to 1771 some 800 tonnes of cast iron rails were produced at Coalbrookdale. A contemporary development in the Sheffield area made use of iron plate rails with unflanged wheels to be used. It seems that the intention was to use wagons that were sometimes hauled along rail tracks, and at others on ordinary road or dirt tracks, and arrangements were made at certain places where the transfer from one to the other could be made. These plateways, as they were called, became very popular in South Wales.

Cast iron edge-rail near Belvoir Castle, England, still in use around 1900.

# 1789

The true turning-point in the early development of railway track was the invention, in 1789, of William Jessop's edge-rail, which was cast in 914 mm (3 ft) lengths. It was a beautifully conceived design to scientific principles; at the ends the base was flat where it rested on the track support, while in between the web portion below was deepened gradually to provide strength exactly in proportion with the distribution of stress caused by a load rolling along the upper surface. Instead of wooden cross sleepers the ends were supported on massive stone blocks sunk into the ground. Although so carefully and so correctly proportioned on theoretical grounds, Jessop's rail was inconvenient in that it could be manufactured only, in short lengths, and in Scotland about the end of the eighteenth century the first steps were taken towards the production of wrought iron rails, that could be rolled in much longer lengths. But many manufacturing difficulties had yet to be overcome, and the rails that supported the earliest experiments with steam locomotives in northeastern England were mostly manufactured in local foundries from cast iron and were in short lengths.

While the edge-rail first patented by Jessop was ideal for hauling short trains of coal wagons by horse the adventures of Trevithick with his first locomotive on the Penydarran plateway suggested to other pioneers that contact between a smooth wheel and a smooth rail would not give sufficient grip to enable a locomotive to haul a heavy load. On the Middleton colliery railway, near Leeds, a form of rail with projecting teeth at the side was installed to carry locomotives with a toothed wheel. The weight of the locomotive was taken on the head of the rail as in Jessop's arrangement, but the engagement of tooth with tooth prevented any slipping due to lack of adhesion on the rail surface. This ingenious design, by John Blenkinsop in 1812, was however expensive to make, and was suitable only for slow-moving trains. Of course at that time there was not yet any thought of speed on railways, and it was soon to be shown that this toothed wheel device was not necessary for heavy load haulage. It was, however, a fine example of contemporary inventiveness.

Richard Trevithick was a pumping engines designer for mines, but he also built the first loco ever to run on rails, at Pen-y-Darren, Wales, in 1804. In all he built 4 locos.

Richard Trevithick's Catch-me-who-can locomotive display in 1809. This was on a site which is near the present junction of Gower Street and Euston Road in London, and which is now occupied by the building of the National Union of Railwaymen. The exhibition was a financial failure and came to an abrupt end when the "train" fell off the rails.

all ahead of their time, being too heavy for the early rails, and suffering neglect from a public which failed to recognize their significance.

# 1813

In 1813 at Wylam Colliery, Northumberland, William Hedley produced the first locomotive to work satisfactorily on a smooth rail, the *Puffing Billy*. At that time George Stephenson was enginewright at the neighbouring colliery of Killingworth, and in 1814 he built his first locomotive. But Stephenson was far more than a clever engine mechanic, and he had the vision of a nationwide railway system. One thing that was causing endless trouble to these early pioneers was the track. Jessop's edge-rail was excellent in theory, but in practice there were many difficulties. The joints between successive sections of rail, whether resting on stone blocks or transverse baulks of timber, became uneven; the stone blocks sank into the ground, some deeper than others.

Stephenson/Losh locomotive, 1816, and Birkenshaw's patented malleable iron rails, 1820.

Therefore Stephenson with his friend William Losh patented a method of jointing the rails, by means of a scarfed, or overlapping joint whereby the ends of adjacent rails were secured together. This was patented in 1816, and solved the problem, so far as slow-running colliery railways were concerned. Then in 1820, at the Bedlington Ironworks, Northumberland, John Birkinshaw produced the first really successful wrought iron rail, rolled through a mill to the required shape. This rail was not only much stronger, and less liable to fracture than cast iron lengths, but it could be made much longer – namely 5.5 m (18 ft). Although Stephenson himself had a patent for another type of rail, he specified Birkinshaw's for the Stockton and Darlington Railway in 1825.

# Steam wins the day

*Railway development 1825–1830*

*Locomotion* No 1 was the first locomotive to be used on a public railway, the Stockton and Darlington Railway, in 1825. It was kept at work until 1858 and then mounted on a plinth at Darlington station, although it has recently resumed its travels.

**1825** The Stockton and Darlington, the first public railway in the world, was conceived as a coal carrier, to provide transport from the rich coalfields in the Bishop Auckland district of County Durham to tide water at Stockton. From there the coal was carried on, as an export, or by coastal conveyance, to other British ports. The businessmen of the northeast backed it strongly, but the great landowners and local farmers were implacable. One peer secured an alteration to the proposed route, because it ran through his fox covers! The surveyors were harried by farm hands armed with pitchforks and accompanied by fierce dogs. But through the sagacity of Edward Pease, the great merchant of Stockton, the professional influence of Nicholas Wood, a distinguished mining engineer, and the dogged commonsense of George Stephenson's pioneer engineering, the railway was built and opened to public transport in September 1825. Except for one isolated steam locomotive, the original motive power was by horses; and the horses worked all the passenger services.

To all the promoters, however, this was only a temporary expedient. George Stephenson was convinced that the future lay in steam traction, and the one unit on the line, the *Locomotion*, was undoubtedly the best that had been built anywhere in the world up to that time. But there were features other than motive power that made the Stockton and Darlington Railway a milestone for future development. The company was prepared to provide wagons for the transport of coal, or other traffic, but it was also prepared to convey goods in the consigner's own vehicles, if they were suitable to run on the railway tracks. Thus began a practice that developed to an almost embarrassing extent on the railways of Great Britain, and which was ended only when the railways were nationalized in 1948. So far as motive power was concerned, primitive as the *Locomotion* was, if it had not been "made to go", it is fairly safe to suggest that the whole development of railways would have been seriously, if not indefinitely, retarded.

The early success of the S & D was largely due to Stephenson, who not only engineered it, but also held out for locomotive haulage when the promoters would have been content with horse traction.

Eaglescliffe

Long Newton

Tees

Dinsdale

Sadberge

Skerne

Darlington

Aycliffe

Coatham Mundeville

East Thickley

From Shildon to the Stockton terminus, the line was locomotive operated. Stephenson's route down to the River Tees consisted of long straight sections connected by single, large-radius curves, although this involved constructing a long embankment from Dinsdale to Eaglescliffe, which strained the company's finances. West of Shildon was the first of 2 rope-worked inclines which took the wagons up to the colliery; at Shildon, the changeover point, the loco works were built.

The first line in America was the Baltimore and Ohio, begun in 1828. For a "first", it was on a grand scale; 608 km (380 miles) long, double track throughout, the Allegeny mountains to be crossed. The first 42 km (26 miles) were opened to traffic in May 1830.

# 1827

In the USA in the 1820s there was need for good communication between the developing lands west of the Allegheny mountains and the seaports of New York, Philadelphia, Washington and Baltimore. The first three cities opted for canals, and indeed the success of the Erie Canal between Buffalo and New York was intended to draw trade away from the others. Baltimore alone determined upon a railway, and no minor project at that. It was to be a double track right through from the city to the Ohio River at Wheeling, and in 1827 an application was made to the Legislature of Maryland for an Act incorporating the Baltimore and Ohio Railway Company. It is interesting that the term "railway" rather than "railroad" was adopted; today in the USA, of the many great, and still independent

companies, some are styled "railways" and others "railroads". Still more interesting is that the name "Baltimore and Ohio" survives today, because the B & O is one of the three great lines incorporated in the present "Chessie System".

Unlike the earliest railways in Great Britain and in parts of Europe, the incorporation of the Baltimore and Ohio was acclaimed by virtually universal rejoicing in Baltimore itself, and in the country through which it would run. It was regarded as a great popular venture, but a plunge into the unknown nevertheless. In 1827 no one knew whether the primitive locomotives, tracks and rolling stock then used on the earliest English railways would withstand the onslaught of the severe American winters, and the still more furious spring floods that followed the thawing of the snows. Still the merchants of Baltimore pressed on. It was perhaps indicative of their iron resolve that one of the first directors of the B & O was Charles Carroll, who in 1827 was the sole surviving signer of the Declaration of Independence. He was then more than 90 years of age, and in February 1828 was fit enough to turn the first spadeful of earth, with a silver spade, and to lay the symbolic foundation stone of the railway. Following the ceremony he said: "I consider this among the most important acts of my life, second only to my signing the Declaration of Independence, if even it be second to that."

The railway followed the course of the rivers where

possible, to make the gradients as easy as possible. It was not until May 1830 that the line was opened for passenger traffic over the first 42 km (26 miles) from Baltimore to Ellicotts' Mills. The motive power was by horses. The sharp curves made necessary by the rugged country in the valley of the Patapsco River suggested that steam locomotives would be impracticable. But Peter Cooper, an industrialist and inventor from New York, had made a large investment in Baltimore land, and it was important to him that the railway should succeed. That to him meant "speed" with the use of steam traction. He built a locomotive, the *Tom Thumb*, and in the summer of 1830

took the directors for a ride down the line as far as Carrollton, the home of Charles Carroll. The 21 km (13 miles) were covered in 57 minutes.

The more conservative among the railway supporters were still sceptical of the success of locomotives, and a race was organized and run on 28 August 1830 between the *Tom Thumb* and a horse. It was a close-running thing — neck and neck for most of the way — until the fan-belt slipped from the drum, and with the blower inoperative, steam pressure was dropped, and the horse forged ahead to victory. But though this victory was gained through a mishap to the machinery of the locomotive, the moral victory was with Peter Cooper.

# 1828

In France, the first railway, the St Étienne and Andrézieux, built in 1828, was also primarily a coal carrier, and was at first worked entirely by horses. Two, in tandem, were used to haul trains of six or seven wagons loaded with coal. But the provision made for passenger conveyance was more elaborate than on the Stockton and Darlington. They were quite commodious vehicles after the fashion of a stage-coach, covered over and with three separate compartments. But an even more elaborate affair was a double-decker. The lower deck had open sides to all three compartments, but with curtains that could be drawn to give protection against the weather. The upper deck was completely open.

The first line in America was the Baltimore and Ohio Railway.

The famous race between a horse and the *Tom Thumb* locomotive on the Baltimore & Ohio Railway.

The first locomotive built in the USA, *Best Friend of Charleston*, was constructed for the South Carolina Railroad in 1830.

# Worldwide expansion begins

*Railway development 1831–1850*

## 1831

It was the opening and the instant subsequent success of the Liverpool and Manchester Railway and the immense prestige gained by George Stephenson, with locomotives, and by his son Robert, in the civil engineering, that prompted the building of railways in many parts of the world. Though the Liverpool and Manchester was a relatively small project, even beside some of the railways engineered within the very next decade, the experience gained had been profound, particularly in surmounting the unexpected and severe difficulties of crossing Chat Moss, a desolate bog land, untouched and untraversed for centuries. There the problem had been to secure a stable foundation to carry the railway; tipping stones and gravel to form an embankment proved useless, the filling just slipped away. The

solution was found by building layers of brushwood and hurdles to form a core around which the orthodox filling could accumulate and bind.

When it came to building the first line between Amsterdam and Rotterdam in the Netherlands, F. W. Conrad, the engineer, was faced with a similar problem to that on Chat Moss, except that it extended for the greater part of the entire route. Practically the whole country to be traversed by the new railway lay below sea level, and was protected from complete inundation by the wonderful system of dykes, or embankments; and the ground was everywhere soft and spongy. Conrad used the same technique as that of George Stephenson, except that in most places he had to use many more layers of hurdles and brushwood before he could get a reasonably firm foun-

dation. Conrad had the first section of his line, that from Amsterdam to Haarlem, opened in 1839.

In 1834 Ludwig I of Bavaria gave his assent to the construction of the first railway to be built in any of the German states. It was named after the king himself, the *Ludwigsbahn*, and ran from Nürnberg to Fürth. This name set a fashion that has been followed ever since in countries where the language is German, or a dialect of it: simply *bahn*, "road", without any qualification. The opening date, by royal desire, had apparently been fixed long before the line was finished or even the equipment ordered. A German manufacturer, asked to supply the first locomotive, could not meet the delivery date required, and so the order was placed with the Stephensons. It was the first steam locomotive to run in Germany.

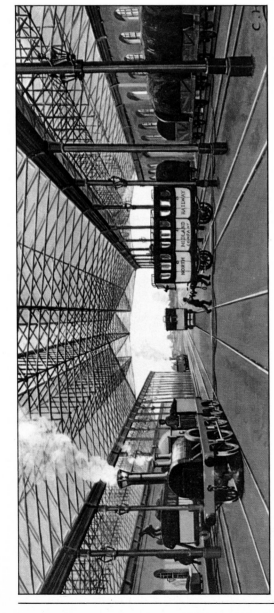

Derby North Midland station, an artist's impression, *circa* 1840.

The first railway tunnels were excavated with very unsophisticated equipment. Brunel's Box Tunnel on the Great Western Railway was started in 1836 and finished in June 1841. It was 3,000 m (3,280 yd) long, and up to 4,000 men and 300 horses were at work simultaneously. Weekly, one tonne of gunpowder, and one of candles, was used. The methods of tunnelling, illustrated *below*, had been established by the canal builders, and by Brunel's father, who built the first tunnel under the River Thames.

Brunel, the most revolutionary of the early rail engineers, enraged others by adopting a non-standard gauge of 2,133 mm (7 ft) for the Great Western Railway.

# 1837

In France railways had begun, as in England, with purely mineral lines in the St Étienne district, but the first to be a public common carrier was that which opened in 1837 between Paris and St Germain, a distance of 21 km (13 miles). From the outset it was intended to be steam worked, but the locomotives were not entirely reliable. Like the *Ludwigsbahn* in Bavaria this line enjoyed royal patronage, and was formally opened by Queen Marie-Amélie. The event was regarded more as a fashionable social occasion rather than the beginning of a new epoch in industrial development, and the venture-some action of the 55-year-old queen was looked upon with much disfavour. The conservative outlook of the day regarded the line as something of a plaything.

In the same year as the Paris–St Germain railway was opened came the first railway in Russia, again strongly influenced by British pioneer work, and again under royal patronage. The Tsar of Russia had been to England and visited some of the colliery lines in the north, and impressed with what he had seen he readily granted a concession to a company formed to build a railway over the 24 km (15 miles) from St Petersburg to Pavlovsk, where a new entertainment centre had been set up. The first loco-motives were obtained from England, one from Robert Stephenson and one from Timothy Hackworth, and in the depths of winter they had to be landed at the nearest port on the Baltic that was open, and then taken by sledge across the ice. The Tsar himself was present at the first steaming of the Hackworth locomotive in November 1836, and the engine was put through a baptismal ceremony according to the rites of the Greek Orthodox Church.

This first Russian railway was built to a rail gauge of 1,828 mm (6 ft), instead of that which was already becoming looked upon as something of a standard; but in England, in building the Great Western Railway, I. K. Brunel carried the question of gauge to a major confrontation by adopting no less than 2,123 mm (7 ft). He felt

that once the advantages of such a wide gauge, in its possibilities for speed, mass transportation of freight, and roominess of accommodation for passengers, had been demonstrated, all existing railways in Great Britain would be converted. But it did not work out that way. The Stephensons and their friends stood out firmly against any change, and the difficulties became so intense at places like Gloucester, where transfer from one gauge to the other had to be made, that a Royal Commission was set up, and in due course its recommendations went against the broad gauge of Brunel. But for his broad gauge lines Brunel built some magnificent engineering works, notably the great tunnel under Box Hill, Wiltshire.

# 1846

Despite the difficulties that had arisen in North America many lines were built in the early days with different gauges both in Canada and in the USA. In the latter the situation was not finally resolved until the end of the Civil War, when some lines in the southern states were converted to the European and North American standard of 1,435 mm (4 ft 8½ in). Some of the most interesting and picturesque work in the early days of American railroading was not over disagreements about gauges but in crossing the mountain ranges that lay between the eastern seaboard and the Ohio River. The ranges of the Alleghenies and of the Appalachians have none of the rugged, desolate and forbidding character of the Rockies. Indeed to see them from the air, densely covered with hundreds of kilometres of continuous forest land, it is difficult to appreciate that they do form a natural barrier that posed many problems for the pioneer railway engineers.

The Baltimore and Ohio, the first ever American railway, made its way beside the Potomac River to Cumberland, Maryland, amid a beautiful and often difficult terrain, and thence over the watershed to reach the Ohio River valley. At first, however, the main range of

the Allegheny mountains was considered impossible for a railway, and on the advice of William Strickland an extraordinary chain of communication was developed between Philadelphia and Pittsburgh, and brought into service in 1832. It was in some ways a primitive forerunner of the modern American piggyback principle, in that the whole journey was made in canal boats. These were constructed in halves, and it was in halves that they were hauled on rail-borne trolleys over the first 132 km (82 miles) from Philadelphia to Columbia, on the Susquehanna River. Then the two halves were joined, and proceeded by canal into the very heart of the mountains to Hollidaysburg. Then they were transferred once again to rail for cable haulage over the crest of the mountains, and down the far side to Johnstown. After that they reverted to canal for the rest of the journey to Pittsburgh.

It was a slow and cumbersome means of transit, and the all-rail route of the Baltimore and Ohio, although serving Pittsburgh directly, and only then by a roundabout route, was much quicker. So in 1846 the Pennsylvania Railroad Company was formed, following for much of the distance from Pittsburgh to Philadelphia this older composite transport system. But the crossing of the Alleghenies involved some spectacular engineering, especially in descending the eastern slopes by the great horseshoe curve below the Gallitzin summit, and it was not until 1852 that this great artery of modern railway traffic was first brought into use. American developments farther west came later.

# 1850

In the meantime the network in Great Britain was spreading rapidly. By the year 1850 one could travel from London to Edinburgh by train, although the present direct line from Peterborough to Doncaster was not yet completed. At first trains to the north travelled via Sleaford and Lincoln. There was already a rival route to Scotland, up the west coast. A great lengthwise merger of 1847 had produced the London and North Western Railway, which with its allies the Lancaster and Carlisle and the Caledonian made up a continuous line from London to Glasgow, with a northern offshoot into Edinburgh. The great central combination which produced the Midland Railway in 1844 had not yet secured an independent outlet to the south, and reached London by running powers over the Great Northern's line into King's Cross.

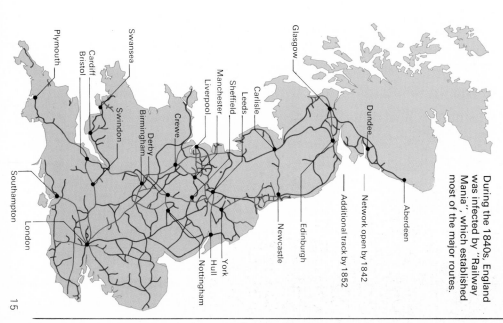

During the 1840s, England was infected by "Railway Mania", which established most of the major routes.

# Opening up the West

*Railway development 1851–1880*

**1854** Just as the Ohio River had been the goal of railways carried westward from the Atlantic, so the Mississippi proved the great obstacle to those building the lines westward from Chicago. The mid-1850s were exciting days in the race to reach out to the American West. First line to reach the river was the Chicago and Rock Island, in 1854, followed in 1855 by the Illinois Central, and the Chicago and Alton. In the following year the Chicago, Burlington and Quincy reached the left bank, and all this railway activity was looked upon with the greatest distrust by the steamboat men, who operated a profitable traffic on the great river. And distrust changed to violent action when the railway companies began to build bridges across the river. The Rock Island was the first to do this, from the city of that name to Davenport, Iowa, and the bridge was opened in April 1856. The steamboat men tried to serve court injunctions claiming that the bridges were a danger to navigation, and when these failed they used more subtly dangerous methods. In May 1856 a paddle steamer appeared suspiciously to go accidentally, but on purpose, out of control, and crashed into one of the piers bringing down the span, and herself taking fire. The steamer sank, and the owners claimed, and were granted, compensation. But the steamboat men were fighting a hopeless battle.

At this same time the first railways were being built out in the west – nothing except a few local lines at the start; but in 1861 the Central Pacific Railway of California had been incorporated, with the aim of building eastwards to forge a link with the eastern states. Then came the Civil War, and little could be done. But in 1862 Congress had launched the great scheme for building the Union Pacific Railroad, westward from the Mississippi. This great line, a vital artery of heavy east-west freight traffic, stands today as one of the very few railways anywhere in the world that has always been privately owned and yet was inaugurated by direct government action. During the war President Lincoln became most anxious about the isolated and undefended situation of the states on the Pacific coast. World opinion was sharply divided in its sympathies with the opposite sides in the war, and a descent was feared on California by those who favoured the southern states. So the most urgent encouragement was given to the construction of the Union Pacific Railroad. It was not until 1865, however, that the first rail was laid, in the Missouri valley. With this incentive work began in earnest from the western end also, by the Central Pacific. It became a great race, because the fares and freight rates on this transcontinental route would be proportioned according to the mileage owned by each company.

**1869** The construction of the line became one of the great epics of world railway building. Out on the prairies in wild undeveloped country, where the white man had scarcely penetrated, the survey parties and work trains were attacked by bands of Red Indians. The Union Pacific certainly had their fill of this kind of trouble, while the Central Pacific, forcing a way through tough country in the Sierra Nevada range, had the great handicap of obtaining all supplies by sea. There was no Panama Canal at that time, and everything had to be shipped to San Francisco round the very tip of South America – a voyage from Baltimore, or Philadelphia, of about 24,000 km (15,000 miles). The race to link up with the advancing construction gangs of the Union Pacific went on for four years, and eventually on 10 May 1869 at Promontory, Utah, the last spike was driven. The present main line takes what is called the "Lucin cut-off", and bypasses Promontory, but the place of the link up is a popular tourist spot, with two locomotives in period colours facing each other.

The construction of the Central Pacific and the Union Pacific provided the first east-west link from coast to coast in the USA, and although it was quickly followed by further developments this marked the first step in an important era in the development of the country as a whole.

One of the most spectacular terminal stations in London is St Pancras, *right*, built by the Midland Railway from 1868 to 1875. It is a monument to the Victorians' pride in the steam railway, and an indication also of the importance of railways in the Victorian economy: London's main stations were, when built, the largest buildings to have been erected since the cathedrals. Two of Victorian England's foremost architects designed it. The train shed is by William Barlow, with a clear span of 73.2 m (240 ft), the largest of its kind in Britain; the hotel fronting it is one of Sir Gilbert Scott's masterpieces.

Omaha
Columbus
Grand Island
Ogallala
Cheyenne
Laramie
Rawlins
Rock Springs
Ogden
Salt Lake City
*Rocky Mountains*
Winnemucca
Elko
Reno
Sacramento
San Francisco

# 1879

Along the deeply indented east coast of Scotland the firths of Forth and Tay presented serious obstacles in the path of any direct line of railway from Edinburgh to Aberdeen. The first step was the building of a great viaduct across the Firth of Tay, opposite to Dundee. Thomas Bouch was the engineer, a man whose work was inclined to be venture-some rather than like the solid, perhaps over-solid re-liability of the Stephensons and Joseph Locke. On the Firth of Tay, unfortunately, Bouch greatly underestimated the effect of the gale-force winds frequently experienced in that exposed area: not only that, but certain features of the detailed design were of highly questionable integrity—such as putting cast iron members into tension. Nor was the work inspected in progress.

British engineering has an enviable reputation for soundness of workmanship and a high sense of discipline. But in this one tragic instance not only had the basic design been a little incautious, but its execution was atrocious. The main columns were badly cast, having an uneven thickness of metal; the lugs, to which the tension members

The Tay Bridge disaster in 1879, one of the many artists' impressions of the scene.

were attached, fell off during casting and were re-attached by the process of "burning on". In the circumstances, it was nothing short of a marvel that the bridge lasted as long as it did. It was opened to traffic in May 1878, carrying a single line of railway. The end came on the evening of 28 December 1879 when a great gale was sweeping in from the North Sea and a passenger train from Burntisland to Dundee entered upon the bridge. It reached the high girders carrying the line over the navigable part of the Firth, and then the bridge collapsed, taking the train and all its passengers down into the deep water. There were no survivors. At the time Bouch had been commissioned to design a bridge for the crossing of the Forth; but his reputation was shattered.

# Achievements and disasters

*Railway development 1881–1913*

## 1885

The construction of the Canadian Pacific Railway, undertaken to honour a pledge made to the provinces of British Columbia and Vancouver Island that in return for their joining in the federation to form the Dominion of Canada a transcontinental railway would be built, proved to be one of the greatest individual tasks ever undertaken by a single railway company. Although the project was initiated by the government the company was privately owned, though at times the financial situation was so desperate that appeals for government aid had to be repeated several times. J. J. Hill, one of the original syndicate, had large interests in the USA, and to link up readily with these he urged that the line be carried to the south of Lake Superior and so through United States territory. But the general manager who he himself had introduced, W. C. Van Horne, was implacably opposed to this, and he was supported by the two Scots tycoons who made up the rest of the syndicate, George Stephen and Donald A. Smith. Hill resigned, and immediately set to work to promote a

rival transcontinental line in the USA from St Paul to Seattle, which became the Great Northern.

The all-Canadian route round the northern shores of Lake Superior involved some exceedingly difficult engineering, and although Van Horne, frequently taking command, as it were, in the field, pressed the constructional work forward at an unprecedented rate across the open prairies west of Winnipeg, the continuation of the line through the Rockies involved further tremendous difficulties. The first surveys had been made by the great veteran engineer Sandford Fleming, and to avoid unduly steep gradients and high constructional costs he had proposed going through the mountains by the Yellowhead Pass, a fairly long detour to the north. But Van Horne felt that such a route would leave a considerable stretch of Canadian territory near to the United States border open to rival railway infiltrations, and instructed his engineers to find a way through going as nearly as possible due west from Calgary. So the line was taken across The Great Divide near Lake Louise, then called Emerald Lake, and down the Kicking Horse Pass. Engineering difficulties were not ended when Field was reached, because finding a way through the tremendous barrier of the Selkirk Mountains was even more difficult. Operationally the ascent from Beavermouth to the Rogers Pass – named after the dynamic American engineer who found it – is the worst on the whole line, and today requires the use of up to 13 diesel locomotives to haul the heaviest mineral trains up the incline.

When competitive lines to the Canadian Pacific were surveyed, and plans made for further routes to the west coast, the Yellowhead Pass route was adopted, and the Canadian National Railways operates a transcontinental service that way. The two routes come abreast of each other at Kamloops and then run on opposite sides of the Fraser River for the rest of the way to Vancouver. At first when they are running through canyon country the scene is most dramatic, with rival trains passing along ledges cut in the rock walls, but they pass out of sight of each other as Vancouver is neared.

## 1889

On 12 June 1889 there was a terrible accident near Armagh, on the Great Northern Railway of Ireland. It was an accident that highlighted two fundamental weaknesses in operation on the railways of the United Kingdom at that time. Both these weaknesses were appreciated, and many of the railway companies had already begun to take the necessary safeguards against them; but disaster struck on a line that was not so equipped. The first point concerns signalling. Earlier practice was to work trains on a time interval basis, allowing a second train to go forward a specified number of minutes after the preceding one had passed. This system was subject to misjudgement and misunderstanding, and the principle of "absolute block" working was being substituted. In this a second train was not allowed to proceed until positive advice by telegraphic bell signal had been received from the next block post that the preceding train had passed clear.

The second point concerned the brakes. While brakes were in use operated on all vehicles by a valve on the

locomotive, the earlier form left the rear part of the train unbraked if it should in any circumstances become detached from that coupled to the locomotive. From Armagh a very heavy excursion train was dispatched for Warrenpoint. It had to climb a heavy gradient and the small engine could not make it and stalled. It was decided to divide the train, take the first half up to the top of the gradient, and then come back for the rest. But the hand brake on the guard's van could not hold the detached portion on the gradient. That detached portion began to run back downhill. In the meantime a second train, starting 20 minutes after the excursion, was climbing the gradient. The runaway gathered speed, and at 64 km/h (40 mph) came into a frightful collision with the second train. Seventy-eight passengers were killed and 250 injured. Shocked by this terrible occurrence a Regulation of Railways Bill was rushed through Parliament making the absolute block system compulsory on all passenger lines in the UK, and also the fitting of automatic continuous braking systems.

For his part in the completion of the CPR, Queen Victoria made Van Horne a Knight Commander of the Order of St Michael and St George, in 1894.

The Canadian Pacific route represented the first direct link across Canada from east to west. Services started on 28 June 1886.

The east and west sections linking Port Moody to Montreal were joined at Craigellachie in Eagle Pass, British Columbia, on 7 November 1885.

Completion of the line within ten years was a condition of British Columbia entering the Confederation on 20 July 1871.

From Montreal to Vancouver, 4,633 km (2,879 miles) the journey today takes three days, half the journey time in 1886.

First sod was cut at Fort William on 1 June 1875. 1,126 km (700 miles) was under construction by October 1880.

Left The interior of the signal box of the South Eastern Railway at London Bridge station in 1886. Below The accident at Armagh in 1889. The caption reads: "Wreck of train on side of embankment 70 ft high at Armagh". The rear half of an excursion train slipped on the gradient and collided with the following train, killing 78 passengers.

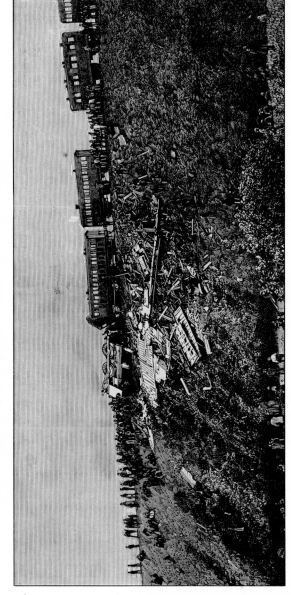

**1892** The findings of the Royal Commission on railway gauges in Great Britain, unfavourable to Brunel's 2,133 mm (7 ft) gauge, were somewhat watered down by the subsequent parliamentary legislation, which, while discouraging its use did not preclude any further extensions. But after the death of Brunel in 1859, and the retirement as locomotive superintendent of Daniel Gooch, Great Western enchantment with the broad gauge began to diminish rapidly. Mixed gauge was laid in on many important routes so that both broad and narrow gauge trains could run, and other lines were converted. By the beginning of the year 1892 the only part of the line remaining wholly broad gauge was that from Exeter to Truro— 160 km (100 miles) on the main line and about 114 km (71 miles) on various branch lines, such as from Newton Abbot to Kingswear, and from Truro to Falmouth. The remarkable decision was taken to convert the whole of this extensive area in a single weekend. All broad gauge locomotives and rolling stock had to be evacuated from the area and worked to Exeter or beyond, where there was mixed gauge track, and then a work force of 4,200 men moved down to Devon and Cornwall. The men were organized into gangs of 20, and each gang had 1.6 km (1 mile) of plain line to convert. The business of moving the men and all their heavy tools and equipment was complicated by all trains from the further ends of the line being standard gauge, because once the men had been conveyed to their places of work the broad gauge carriages had to be evacuated from the western areas — otherwise they would have been trapped and immovable. No time could be wasted in moving men about from place to place during the operation and accommodation was arranged adjacent to the job to be done. Sleeping arrangements were organized in goods sheds and station buildings; and where nothing else existed tents were pitched beside the line. The whole operation went very smoothly. Fortunately the weather was fine; the last through broad gauge train left Paddington for Penzance on Friday 20 May, and on Monday 23 May the full service was recommenced with standard gauge trains.

**1900** The technique of spiral tunnelling, which needed consummate skill and precision in the preliminary and final surveys, was used to remarkable effect in easing the gradients on the Canadian Pacific main line in the Rocky Mountains — climbing the Kicking Horse Pass in British Columbia — and was used again spectacularly in Switzerland on the Bern-Lötschberg-Simplon line at Blausee-Mitholz, in climbing from Frutigen to Kandersteg on the great line opened in July 1913.

Despite the speed and efficiency of spiral tunnelling, the endeavour was often extremely hazardous. For example, in the building of the Lötschberg Tunnel, which began in 1906, over 3,000 workers were involved. In 1908, 30 men were killed when a workers' hostel was destroyed in an avalanche; and only four months later, 25 men were drowned when water burst into a section of the tunnel blocking over 1 km (0.6 mile) of its length and causing its course to be diverted, resulting in a total increase of over 800 m (2,625 ft). Where the disaster had taken place, a wall 10 m (33 ft) thick was built to seal it off. Rock temperatures of up to 34°C (93°F) were encountered.

The world precedent for spiral tunnelling had been set by Louis Favre, engineering the Gotthard line. It was conceived as a major international main line on the highway from Germany through Switzerland and into Italy. The St Gotthard Pass had been a highway for centuries, albeit impassable in the winter snows; but the task of building a major railway over the same route set a number of unprecedented problems. It was not so much the driving of a great tunnel under the pass itself, from Göschenen to Airolo, but the exceptional steepness of the approach valley to north and south. On both sides of the deep valley up which the railway had to be carried were high mountains and into these Favre took the line on a series of spiral locations to gain height. The actual gradient of the railway is about 1 in 40, and this was achieved by having no fewer than three spiral tunnels on the ascent from Erstfeld to Göschenen.

Cape Town · Beaufort West · Kimberley · SOUTH AFRICA · Mafeking · Gaborone · BOTSWANA · Bulawayo · RHODESIA · Livingstone · Lusaka · ZAMBIA · Tenke · Bukama · Lualaba · Kongolo · Kindu · Ubundi · Kisangani · Aketi · Mungbere · Bondo · ZAIRE · Congo · SUDAN · Wau · Kosti · Khartoum · Atbarah · Wadi Halfa · Aswan · Luxor · EGYPT · Cairo · Dar es Salaam · TANZANIA · Moshi · Voi · Nairobi · KENYA · UGANDA · Tororo
···· Navigable river

Rhodes never envisaged the Cape-to-Cairo as only a rail line; river navigation was also to form a part. He proposed a route west of Lake Tanganyika, using the Congo and Nile. Today it is possible to travel from Cape Town to Zaire in this way. Since the opening of the Tazara line (see p.200), an alternative route via East Africa is possible, though either way there is a gap in the through route, there being no railways out of Sudan into Zaire or Uganda.

*Above* An 1870s standard gauge loco, superimposed upon a broad gauge loco and coach, shows the two advantages Brunel claimed for his Great Western Railway: greater roominess inside vehicles, and greater stability, enabling higher speeds.

*Left* Replacing the broad gauge track with standard gauge in Devonport station.

**1910** In the lengthy ranges of the Andes, extending high and continuously from north to south of the South American continent, with their crests little more than 160 km (100 miles) from the Pacific Ocean, are to be found the highest railway summits in the world. The highest of all, the Antofagasta (Chile) and Bolivia, was one of the first. It was a British enterprise, as it is still British owned today. It reaches the remarkable altitude of 4,826 m (15,835 ft) on its Collahuasi branch. The company was formed in 1888 to take over certain concessions granted by the two governments. The line was built on the 762 mm (2 ft 6 in) gauge and continued thus with a productive length of 1,230 km (769 miles) through its period of greatest prosperity in the early 1900s. Initially its traffic was in nitrate from Bolivia down to the sea at Antofagasta, but in later years traffic has been in tin and copper. By 1928 the line was converted to metre gauge and powerful articulated locomotives of the Beyer-Garratt type purchased to operate mineral trains on the heavy gradients. At the time of the conversion of the gauge a third rail was laid on many sections, but the final conversion, which involved some 320 km (200 miles) of line, mostly in waterless, desolate country, took no more than six days.

Further north, the Central Railway of Peru has been claimed as the most spectacular in the world, reaching 4,829 m (15,845 ft) on the European standard gauge. The choice of this gauge in Peru was remarkable, because the broad gauge standard generally in South America is 1,676 mm (5 ft 6 in) with metre gauge for the feeder lines. The climbing of the main range of the Andes begins at Callao, and has already attained a height of 860 m (2,820 ft). Then comes a tremendous ascent to the summit of the line in the Galera tunnel. This point is only about 64 km (40 miles) from Chosica, but with a difference in altitude of 3,923 m (12,870 ft), the average inclination would be 1 in 16.5, but for the ingenious and spectacular engineering that intervenes. The actual gradient presented to the locomotives is about 1 in 25, but height is gained here not by direct tunnelling but by a series of zigzags up the side wall of the valley.

The trans-Andine railway, which forms part of a continuous line of communication between Buenos Aires and Valparaiso, formerly had separate Chilean and Argentinian sections, but between 1923 and 1939 it was operated first by a joint administration and then by the British-owned Buenos Aires and Pacific Railway. It is metre gauge, and includes some rack sections in climbing to its summit level of 3,186 m (10,453 ft) near Las Cuevas. If the weather is fine there is a sight here of the highest mountain in all the Americas, the 6,959 m (22,834 ft) Aconcagua. The trans-Andine passenger train takes about 12 hr to cover the 386 km (240 miles) from Valparaiso to Mendoza, the railhead of the Argentine 1,676 mm gauge line.

# Networks in the Great War

*Railway development 1914–1922*

## 1914

Until 1914 railways had played small, but significant, parts in warfare, in the confused campaigns in the Mississippi basin during the American Civil War, and in the working of patrols with armoured trains in the later stages of the Boer War. But in 1914 much of the normal pattern of international travel on the continent of Europe had been disrupted. The important chain of communication between England and Germany was necessarily severed and not at any time afterwards to be restored in its old form. Tracks were destroyed to hinder troop movements, bridges were blown up, particularly in Belgium during the first weeks of the campaign in the west, and locomotives and rolling stock hurriedly withdrawn to avoid their falling into enemy hands. Then, with the overrunning of much of the industrial areas of northeastern France, and the total loss of manufacturing facilities in Belgium, the French and British governments were faced with difficulties in providing replacement for consumable spare parts on rolling stock that had been withdrawn in time. The heavy industries in both countries were rapidly switched to direct

Germans rebuilding a railway bridge in Northern France, maintaining vital rail links with the Front.

First World War, German troops leaving home.

production of armaments, and the railways found great difficulty in obtaining raw materials to manufacture, in their own works, the spares that were needed. A British purchasing mission went to the USA, and arranged for large quantities of steel plate, bars, ingots, and other material, to be shipped to the United Kingdom. The formation of a Railway Operating Division in the British Army proved invaluable in getting reinforcements and munitions to the forward zones in the battle areas. Track was lifted from sections of the home railways made temporarily redundant by the suspension of tourist and other peacetime activities. Many British locomotives were sent abroad for use with the Railway Operating Division. The neutrality of Switzerland made it a place whereby the repatriation of prisoners-of-war could be arranged and Constance, on the German-Swiss frontier, was a centre through which much of this unusual traffic passed. In the campaigns in the Middle East much of the guerrilla activity against the Turkish armies, so dashingly organized and led by T. E. Lawrence, centred upon disruption of the Hedjaz Railway, and the destruction of troop trains. Among the Arabs Lawrence became known as "Destroyer of Engines".

## Railways in the western battle areas

Although the Allied battle line from the North Sea to the Swiss frontier swayed backwards and forwards to some extent during the four years of the war, despite the numerous and terribly costly offensives the line remained stable enough for the pattern of railway operation to assume a fairly constant form. Two major routes of the Northern Railway of France were completely severed, namely those to Arras and Lille, and that leading into Belgium. The Eastern main line towards Nancy and Strasbourg was purely a route furnishing reinforcements and munitions for the French line of battle. The Northern main line to Boulogne and Calais became almost entirely a British Army supply route. In Great Britain itself, the establishment of the main base of the Grand Fleet at Scapa Flow in the Orkneys imposed an unusual and severe task. Huge battleships were then coal fired, and because best quality steam coal was needed, this had to be hauled from South Wales, via Crewe, Carlisle, Perth, Inverness to the most northerly railhead, at Thurso. It was a tremendous operation needing the redeployment of many locomotives.

| | |
|---|---|
| ■ | Central Powers in December 1915 |
| ★ | Principal railway centres |
| ◆ | Principal ports |

*Below* A mammoth French Mle 93-06 rail gun weighing 178 tonnes, and with a firing elevation of 40°. Horizontal traverse was not possible except by moving the gun around a curve in the rail track. It was capable of firing a shell of 348 kg (766.5 lb) over 27,500 m (29,965 yd).

A considerable number of new locomotives for the French railway system were manufactured in Scotland. The British Railways Operating Division had built up a total man-power of over 18,000 by the end of the war, covering a rail network of over 1,300 km (800 miles).

## 1916

The early conquests of the German and Austrian armies in the First World War, which put Serbia, Romania and most of Belgium into the hands of the so-called Central Powers, provided a remarkably complete railway network that was generally immune from attack from the Allied forces. Aerial attack at that time was almost non-existent. The map shows how the overrunning of Belgium in the early stages of the war provided an additional outlet to the North Sea at Zeebrugge, while the similar action against Serbia opened a direct line to Bulgaria and Turkey. The network itself was entirely of prewar construction, but when linked together under a largely unified wartime direction, was ideally suited for the movement of troops and supplies, both from the central areas to the battlefronts and from one front to another if necessary. In the early stages of the war, the Russian forces were still in existence on the Eastern Front; but their collapse in the autumn of 1916 relieved the Central Powers of much railway movement through Poland and eastern Hungary, though the war in the Balkans was increasing.

# 1919

The peace conference of 1919 and the treaties that ratified its recommendations not only redrew much of the map of Europe, but they led to a regrouping of many of the old-established railway facilities. The total dismembering of the Austro-Hungarian Empire had the most profound results of any, with the great reduction of the extent of Austria itself, and the formation of the new autonomous states of Czechoslovakia and Yugoslavia. To the north Poland gained independence. The existing railways did not suit the new countries and many new lines were needed to assist in the building up of new national unities. In Germany the railways were nationalized, and from 1923 it was only in France, with the restoration of the Alsace-Lorraine lines, that the administrative situation remained unchanged.

In Great Britain the coalition government returned to power with a huge majority in the so-called "Khaki election" of 1918, imposed legislation upon the former private railways forming them into four large groups.

The reasons for the British grouping arose directly from circumstances arising during the war. From its outbreak in 1914 the entire network of Great Britain and Ireland had been put under government control, and administered by the Railway Executive Committee, formed of a consortium of general managers of the leading railways. The interests of individual railway companies were subjugated to the national interest, but the interests of the owners — the shareholders — were safeguarded at the outset by a guarantee of a continuance, for the duration of the war, of dividend payments equal to those of the year 1913. During the war, however, strong representations were made by labour interests for uniformity of wage rates, which had previously been negotiated on a company rather than a national scale, and there had been great disparity, for example, between English and Scottish rates. New national scales were negotiated and paid in the later stages of the war; but it was realized that these could not be sustained by certain companies when the railways were decontrolled and handed back to their owners. The solution seemed to be to group the "rich with the poor", at the same time aiming at the continuance of some aspects of rationalized working that had been found advantageous during the war.

The British postwar situation, with a government-imposed grouping, but under private ownership, with nothing in the way of subsidies, was therefore notably different from that in all the former belligerent countries where reorganization immediately brought national ownership. After the brief postwar boom the new era was to lead the railways of Britain into a time of acute financial difficulty. The years immediately following the grouping, in 1923, witnessed much confusion and frustration, while companies that had previously been rivals, and their staffs, tried to settle down together.

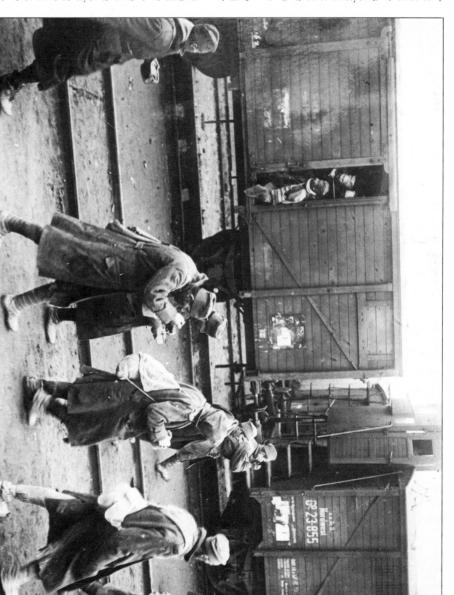

*Above* Serbian prisoners arrive at their destination in Hungary. *Below* Russian prisoners cross a bridge on the German strategic railway after the Battle of Tannenberg. *Right* Picture taken at Rethondes after the signing of the Armistice in 1918.

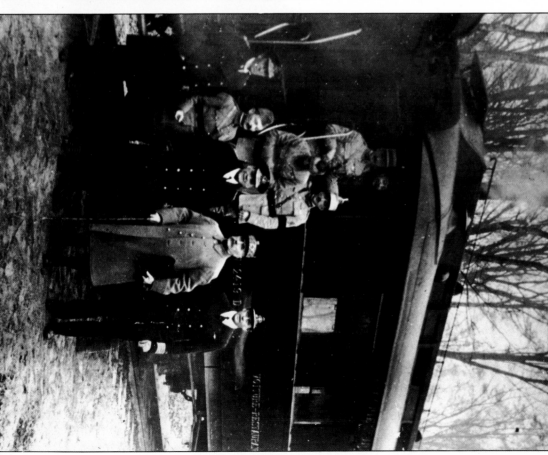

# The fantastic streamliners

*Railway development 1923–1945*

## 1923

The grouping of the former British main line railways into four large companies, still privately owned and entirely self-supporting, taking effect from 1 January 1923, was in many ways typical of the worldwide attitude towards railways in the period of reconstruction after the First World War. The outlook was towards greater comfort for the passenger, greater safety, and improved standards of punctuality. At first there was little thought to do more than fully restore prewar standards of speed. Although this was done in Great Britain by 1923–4, on the Continent of Europe, after the ravages of war, most countries were still lagging behind. But what railway managements all over the world did not seem to foresee, still less to plan to combat, was the extent and seriousness of the growing competition from road transport, both for passengers and freight. Around the great cities with their rapidly increasing populations much attention was given to commuter traffic. The most careful studies were made of traffic flows in relation to the capacity of the lines, and around London in particular certain junction layouts were changed in order to avoid delay from conflicting movements. While electrification was envisaged, in many areas some extremely ingenious replanning of commuter services was accomplished successfully while retaining steam – notably in and out of Liverpool Street in London, terminus of the former Great Eastern Railway. On those services passenger accommodation remained in three classes, while the former "second class" had largely disappeared in most other regions of Great Britain.

A most important trend, that could be seen in countries all over the world, was the beginning of a move away from coal as a steam locomotive fuel; while elsewhere the

attention of locomotive engineers was drawn to the need for firing with coal of quality much below the choicest steam grades. This trend originated during the First World War, with the cutting off, by hostile naval action, of British exports of coal. The South American railways, then mostly British owned, were hit particularly hard, and had to improvise. Then, when restoration was in hand after the war there came the disastrous coal strike of 1926, which again cut off supplies. After that second experience the changeover to oil firing became permanent. In the USA the change was equally definite, on railways serving the Midwest and western states that were adjacent to large indigenous supplies of oil. In the USA certain heavily graded mineral lines had been electrified, but there was considerable difference of opinion as to the best traction system to adopt. Except in the newly developing countries there was not a great deal of new railway length built. The "grouping" in Great Britain produced some rationalization of routes, short connections to facilitate interrunning between what had been separate company lines; but some of the most significant works, in developing the world's railway network, were in Australia. Connection between states of New South Wales and Queensland had been made in 1888, by a roundabout route that involved a change of gauge at the border station of Wallangarra. In 1930, however, the North Coast Line of the New South Wales Railways was completed on the standard gauge throughout and running through 113 km (70 miles) of Queensland territory to a terminus in South Brisbane. Even in 1925 the journey between Sydney and Brisbane took 25 hr, whereas after the completion of the new line the time was brought down to 15 hr 30 min. During this period much electrification was carried out.

*Above* This view of one of the Rio Grande Western's 4-6-6-4 locomotives shows both the size, and frequent ugliness, of American steam engines.

*Below* The first Southern Railway express engines were the King Arthur class 4-6-0s. One of the new engines leaves Waterloo, July 1926.

*Left* Two years after the Grouping a former North Eastern Railway Z class Atlantic leaves Darlington.

*Below* 1927, a party of Germans views the hump in the mechanized shunting yard at Wath (LNER).

# 1930

While electrification was being hailed as the motive power of the future, and committees in Great Britain and elsewhere were trying to establish the standard systems to be adopted, there was much important development in steam locomotive design, particularly in France, Great Britain and the USA. While speeds were gradually creeping up, the aim of locomotive engineers generally was to increase thermal efficiency to convey heavier loads without a proportionate increase in fuel consumption, especially on railways still entirely dependent on coal. There was also a move, noticeably strong in the USA, to increase the speed of through freight trains, aided by the development of the huge articulated locomotives from the Mallet compound type, by improved suspension, into units capable of sustained fast running. But when the worldwide depression of the 1930s began to affect, most seriously, railways in the advanced countries of the world, effective competition with the road hauliers was found to be seriously handicapped. This was evident particularly in Great Britain, because of legislation framed in economic, political and international conditions totally different from those of the 1930s. The railways of Britain were common carriers, and they found that all the choicest and most remunerative traffic was being taken by the new competitors, leaving them with sectors that no one wanted. Appeals for revised legislation fell on stony ground. Public sympathy was with the road hauliers, while in rural passenger transport, the convenient, friendly motor bus was making its way into the heart of village communities, took the bulk of the business from the country branch lines, which were coming to be considered old fashioned and whose services were often inconvenient.

The publicity departments of railways worked hard. The speed of a few prestige trains in Great Britain, France, Germany and the USA was pushed upwards, and for a time the honour of having the fastest start-to-stop run anywhere in the world was held by the Canadian Pacific, which was then waging intense, but highly unremunerative, competition with the Canadian National Railways for the inter-city traffic between Montreal and Toronto. In Great Britain there was mild competition, at no more than moderate speeds, for the maximum length of non-stop run on the Anglo-Scottish services, and while the London Midland and Scottish had a daily run, made all the year round, of 478.8 km (299.25 miles) between Carlisle and London (Euston), the London and North Eastern, during the summer tourist season ran the Flying Scotsman non-stop in both directions over the 628.4 km (392.75 miles) between London (King's Cross) and Edinburgh. The Great Western booked the lightly loaded Cheltenham Flyer over the favourable 123.6 km (77.25 miles) from Swindon to Paddington in 65 min. But while this average from start-to-stop of 114.2 km/h (71.4 mph) was not representative of the service provided as a whole over that route, it was a splendid publicity "boost", especially when, as one special feat, the journey time was cut down to 56¾ min, an average speed of 130.72 km/h (81.7 mph).

By the early 1930s however, despite the prevailing depression, the supremacy of steam as a railway motive power was being challenged, not by electricity but by the diesel engine, of which one of the earliest successful examples in railway traction was on the Buenos Aires Great Southern Railway. The use of diesel power on the railways was soon spread throughout the world.

An American development that became of strategic importance in the Second World War lay in the mechanization of marshalling yards. Means for the efficient sorting and resorting of the wagons of freight trains had been developed early in Great Britain, notably on the London and North Western Railway at Edge Hill, Liverpool, and arrangements for centralizing and power operating the points had been adopted subsequently. But it was the Americans who eliminated the need for hand-operated wagon brakes, by introduction of the so-called "car retarders", or rail brakes. Some large yards were so equipped in the early 1920s, and in Germany the great yards at Hamm were similarly furnished, later to become a familiar and frequent target in the Second World War. British yards at March (Cambridgeshire) and Hull were also equipped, enabling these important centres of traffic to be operated with a greatly reduced workforce. Although the weekly length of track involved and the

*Right* Many spectacular photographs were taken of bomb damage to Britain's railways. Most of it was superficial, as

shown in this picture of Liverpool Street station. *Above* A crash could be more devastating, causing much damage.

# 1939

In the last years before the Second World War there was a great worldwide improvement in passenger train services. It was not so much the spectacular few streamlined trains, but the general average. This was particularly true on the great American railways running east from Chicago like the Pennsylvania and the New York Central, whose fast running with start-to-stop speeds of 105–113 km/h (65–70 mph) were made with heavy overnight sleeping car expresses. In France the standards went equally high, and again with heavy trains, while in Great Britain the number of trains maintaining average speeds of 96 km/h (60 mph) or more was exceptionally high in relation to the size of the country. Despite their financial difficulties which in Great Britain meant low or non-existent dividends for the shareholders, railways were in excellent physical condition, and everywhere proved an invaluable tool of basic

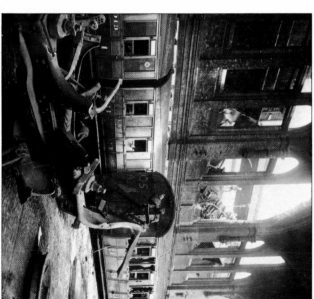

introduction of high-speed streamlined trains in the 1930s Great Britain and France passenger facilities were immediately reduced and timings much decelerated, and as the aerial war developed there was sustained and relentless bombing of railway targets in Germany. Marshalling yards naturally came in for much attention, but in Berlin, but criticized somewhat for the cramped nature of the passenger accommodation. In the USA a series of Zephyr services, with streamlined railcar trains, were introduced between Chicago and cities in the Midwest, in competition with which were a series of Rockets, on the Chicago, Rock Island and Pacific Railroad. In Great Britain the response to this movement was entirely with steam and principally on the London and North Eastern Railway with the Silver Jubilee in 1935, and the Coronation in 1937. These trains provided start-to-stop average speeds slightly over 113 km/h (70 mph), but brought immense publicity and prestige by their peak rates, which on one special test produced the highest speed ever attained by a steam locomotive, namely 203 km/h (126 mph). This was achieved by the famous *Mallard* locomotive of LNER, on 3 July 1938, on a run between Grantham and Peterborough.

The speed of a few prestige trains in Great Britain, France, Germany and the USA was pushed upwards, and for a time the honour of having the fastest start-to-stop run anywhere in the world was held by the Canadian Pacific, Hamburger of the German Railways was one of the first, and was a to-car diesel railcar train running to and from Germany, as elsewhere, the organization for repair was highly efficient, and this offensive, though cumulatively serious, did not have so crippling an effect on railway movement as the strategic bombing of the French railways immediately prior to the Allied invasions of 1944, in which a great number of viaducts were destroyed, and very seriously hindered the forwarding of supplies to the battle areas. In the USA wartime traffic threw an immense burden upon the lines leading to the west coast, and to assist in carrying a far greater number of trains than that for which they were equipped, the technology of modern signalling in the form of Centralized Traffic Control (CTC) was applied to great advantage. Although large-scale production of diesel-electric locomotives had begun, steam carried the main burden of wartime traffic in the USA, with passenger train speeds little reduced from those achieved in peacetime.

resultant revenue was quite small, it was undoubtedly the strategy on the outbreak of the Second World War. In that helped to keep railways in the public eye, even though it did not help the overall financial position. The Flying

# The new age of railways

*Railway development 1946 and after*

**1950** The first ten years after the end of the Second World War saw great changes on the railways of the world. Much of it was in the unwelcome form of retraction of facilities and reduction of worked track in face of a rapidly worsening economic situation. Yet in many countries there were notable advances in technology. Apart from the USA, whose land had not been invaded, or their cities subjected to aerial attack, the railways of Great Britain were practically alone among those of the most heavily involved belligerent nations in having their tracks and workshops intact at the end of the war. Damage had been repaired, although the standards of maintenance of track and rolling stock had, by *force majeure*, been very much reduced. But the fact that the railways of Britain were still operating meant that they received nothing in the way of financial aid towards recovery, such as that made available to those on the Continent of Europe, and elsewhere, through "Lend-Lease" and so on, that enabled the rapid restoration of services to be made.

In Great Britain, because of circumstances that were not very widely understood, the prestige of railways had sunk very low, and nationalization was hailed by many people as the panacea for all ills. Then when the necessary legislation had been passed by Parliament, and the situation deteriorated rather than improved, the blame for the worsening financial position was shifted on to the steam locomotive. At the beginning of the 1950s, however, no funds were available to permit of a change to electric or diesel traction on a big scale, and apart from commuter routes the railways of Britain remained steam worked.

Ironically, railways in the USA itself were soon facing an unexpected and unprecedented situation. All over the country commercial air services were being introduced, while there was a great increase in the operation of large trucks on the highways. Businessmen began to transfer their patronage from the long-distance luxury express trains to air services, which even with the aeroplanes available in the 1950s, were immeasurably quicker than the fastest trains.

**1963** In Britain it was very different. The increasingly large deficit on railway operation was a charge on the national exchequer. In 1955, to try and halt and reverse the process, Parliament voted funds for a large-scale modernization plan, of which one of the principal features was the elimination of steam traction. Large sums were spent on new rolling stock, improved signalling and construction of huge marshalling yards. The existing electrified lines were extended, and work commenced on electrifying the main line from London to Birmingham, Liverpool and Manchester. Contracts were placed for many hundreds of diesel locomotives, as a first step towards the replacement of some 18,000 steam locomotives. But still the adverse financial trend was not halted. In 1961 a distinguished industrialist, Dr Richard Beeching, was appointed Chairman of the British Transport Commission, later reconstituted as the British Railways Board, and he subjected the entire network to ruthless analysis as to which routes and which facilities were profitable, with a view to closing altogether the unremunerative lines and developing others. The plan, although highly controversial, was actually carried through from 1963.

**1976** Altogether contrasting was the situation in Japan where the great prewar plan of a new high-speed national network was consummated, in its first phase, by the opening of the New Tokaido line in 1964. In the USA the railway situation deteriorated alarmingly. The privately owned railways were hamstrung with outdated legislation, which the Federal government persistently refused to revise. Most railways cut their passenger services to the minimum that legislation would permit, and would have abandoned them altogether, if they had been allowed to. To relieve the railways themselves of the responsibility of operating passenger services the National Railroad Passenger Corporation (Amtrak) was set up by Act of Congress in 1970 and a network of long-distance passenger routes chosen for development. These included all except two of the remaining passenger routes in the USA. In the meantime, by the application of modern technology, great and successful efforts were made to win back some of the freight traffic lost to long-distance trucking enterprises. In Great Britain, in 1976, a massive programme of accelerated service was introduced between London (Paddington) and Swansea, and between Paddington, Bristol and Weston-super-Mare, with a large new fleet of diesel-powered High Speed Train sets (HST), having 4,400 engine horsepower and scheduled to run at 200 km/h (125 mph) over lengthy stretches of both routes. The important feature of these new services is their uniformity of high speed throughout the day and the frequent intervals at which they run.

There is a maximum distance for the route length of inter-city passenger services (*below left*). Beyond 600 km (370 miles), it is quicker for the passenger to fly. In the USA, air travel (blue) shows a continuing supremacy over rail (green). However, many European cities are close and inter-city trains still perform an important function.

Railways are occasionally branded as an outmoded transportation concept, fit only for a museum of industrial archaeology, but the figures belie this. The diagram, *below*, shows how the total amount of traffic, world-wide, has increased in the 30 years since 1948: freight traffic has multiplied almost 4 times, and passenger traffic has more than doubled.

figures in thousand million passenger kilometres
*passenger mile equivalents in italics*

figures in thousand million
net tonne kilometres
*net ton mile equivalents in italics*

| Year | | |
|---|---|---|
| 1976 | 241 | 151 |
| 1974 | 217 | 141 |
| 1972 | 198 | 124 |
| 1970 | 172 | 107 |
| 1968 | 157 | 98 |
| 1966 | 109 | 68 |
| 1964 | 80 | 50 |
| 1962 | 54 | 34 |
| 1960 | 49 | 31 |
| 1958 | 41 | 26 |
| 1956 | 45 | 28 |
| 1954 | 47 | 29 |
| 1952 | 55 | 34 |
| 1950 | 51 | 32 |
| 1948 | 66 | 41 |

| Year | | |
|---|---|---|
| 1976 | 16 | 10 |
| 1974 | 17 | 10 |
| 1972 | 14 | 9 |
| 1970 | 17 | 10 |
| 1968 | 21 | 13 |
| 1966 | 27 | 17 |
| 1964 | 29 | 18 |
| 1962 | 32 | 20 |
| 1960 | 34 | 21 |
| 1958 | 37 | 23 |
| 1956 | 26 | 16 |
| 1954 | 27 | 17 |
| 1952 | 20 | 13 |
| 1950 | 15 | 10 |
| 1948 | 11 | 7 |

figures in thousand million passenger kilometres
*passenger mile equivalents in italics*

| Year | | |
|---|---|---|
| 1976 | 6,603 | 4,106 |
| 1972 | 5,400 | 3,355 |
| 1968 | 4,642 | 2,884 |
| 1964 | 4,008 | 2,490 |
| 1960 | 3,338 | 2,074 |
| 1956 | 2,823 | 1,754 |
| 1952 | 2,258 | 1,403 |
| 1948 | 1,804 | 1,121 |

| Year | | |
|---|---|---|
| 1976 | 1,447 | 899 |
| 1972 | 1,184 | 735 |
| 1968 | 1,069 | 664 |
| 1964 | 959 | 596 |
| 1960 | 866 | 538 |
| 1956 | 784 | 487 |
| 1952 | 707 | 439 |
| 1948 | 640 | 398 |

*Above* Ex-LNER *Sir Nigel Gresley* preserved. *Left* Modern Amtrak stock, USA. *Below left* Interior, Bern station, Switzerland.

*Right* A night express leaves London Euston *Below right* Union Pacific Co-Co and booster unit push freight over hump in Los Angeles.

# Harnessing the power of steam

*Locomotive development 1800–1834*

**1800** It is no exaggeration to assert that the invention of the steam locomotive changed the face of the world. By paving the way towards unprecedented speed in transport it put the finishing touch upon the developments of the Industrial Revolution. It was the indirect, and highly competitive, association of two men, both ingenious mechanics, that first blazed the trail. In 1765 James Watt, mathematical instrument maker at Glasgow University, had to repair an instructional model of a Newcomen Cornish beam engine, and hit upon the idea of using a separate condenser as a means for effecting a very great economy in the use of steam. His innovation created such interest that eventually he went into partnership with Matthew Boulton, an industrialist in the West Midlands. The firm of Boulton and Watt prospered exceedingly, in the building of stationary steam engines, but it was when they began to receive orders for pumping engines in the Cornish tin mines that the practice developed by Watt had its first and only influence on the future of rail transport. One of the young men who saw the Watt engines installed in Cornwall was Richard Trevithick, and while Watt was timorous and self-effacing, albeit a superb mechanic, Trevithick was bold and confident to the point of rashness.

Watt used steam at comparatively low pressure; Trevithick at once began to build engines using much higher pressure, and instead of condensing the steam after use he exhausted it into the atmosphere: his first engine was nicknamed "Capt. Dick's Puffer".

From stationary engines used in the Cornish tin mines, Trevithick turned to rail traction, but not before he had made experiments with a locomotive on the roads in Cornwall, to the alarm of the populace. In 1803 a demonstration in London led to the "road carriage" getting out of control, and tearing down the railings outside a private house. He became associated with industrial activities in South Wales and then there came the famous wager that led to the building of the first steam railway locomotive. The bet, between two prominent iron masters, challenged Trevithick's "tram wagon" as it was called, to haul a load of 10 tonnes over the 15.6 km (9.75 miles) from Pen-y-Darren to Abercynon Basin on the Glamorganshire Canal. That Trevithick won the bet for his sponsor is a matter of history, and now interest centres round the design of the locomotive. It had but one cylinder, and to carry the drive over dead centre there was an enormous fly-wheel. The piston, through the conventional crank-connecting rod mechanism, rotated a small pinion wheel which drove a large gear wheel. This engaged with gears mounted on the same axles as the road wheels of the locomotive. Its performance was a triumph but the locomotive had many shortcomings.

**1814** Although Trevithick himself took very little part in the development of his locomotive after this first experiment, those who followed profited by its failures. It frequently broke down, and its relatively great weight compared with the horsedrawn wagons broke many rails. Matthew Murray, of Leeds, for example, suggested having two cylinders working cranks at right-angles to each other. This eliminated the "dead centre" position, and dispensed with the huge fly-wheel. This suggestion was incorporated in Blenkinsop's locomotives put to work on the Middleton Colliery railway near Leeds, in 1812. It had been thought that the contact between a smooth rail and a smooth wheel tyre would not provide a good enough grip to enable a locomotive to haul a heavy load, and Blenkinsop had, in 1811, taken out a patent for a toothed rail laid to one side of the running rail, in which a gear mounted on the axle of the locomotive worked as a pinion in a rack. Locomotives of this type, hauling trains of coal trucks, achieved a certain degree of reliability, though progress was slow and the geared arrangement expensive. One of the Blenkinsop engines was purchased by Blackett, for trial at Wylam Colliery, Northumberland, and the outcome was that the toothed rail arrangement was considered unnecessary, and by the

time this engine was at work George Stephenson was beginning to come into the picture. With financial backing from Lord Ravensworth he built his first locomotive for the Killingworth Colliery in 1814. It had many shortcomings, and the second Killingworth locomotive, in which Isaac Dodds was the joint patentee with Stephenson, was a vast improvement. The noise of exhaust, about which many complaints were made was practically silenced by turning the exhaust steam into the chimney, where it performed a second function, that of sharpening the draught of the fire, and increasing the rate of steam production. Then the complicated gear drive was superseded by connecting the crosshead directly to the driving wheels through the connecting rod. In this locomotive, Stephenson and Dodds together had reached nearly all the fundamental points of the orthodox, classic, steam locomotive, in 1815: two cylinders, simple direct drive, exhaust turned from cylinders into chimney to increase draught on the fire. The partners had, in the second Killingworth locomotive, incorporated a synthesis of all the best features of the pioneer work of Trevithick, Blenkinsop, Matthew Murray, and Blackett, and the way was clear to introduce steam locomotive haulage on the projected Stockton and Darlington Railway.

The world's first ever railway locomotive was built by Richard Trevithick and tried out on the Pen-y-Darren tramway, in South Wales, on 21 February 1804.

An early atmospheric stationary engine.

William Hedley was the first to build a locomotive running on smooth edge-rail, in 1813: the *Wylam Dilly*. Here, *left*, it is seen much later, after rebuilding into the form of the *Puffing Billy*, 1815.

# 1827

The celebrated *Locomotion*, engine No. 1 of the first public railway in the world, incorporated all the best features of the Killingworth colliery locomotives, but the working conditions on what was virtually a main line, by comparison, were much more severe and the *Locomotion* was found incapable of steaming continuously for any length of time, and stops had to be made to raise steam. In the meantime, George Stephenson was away and engaged with the surveys and estimates for the Liverpool and Manchester Railway, so that to his faithful assistant Timothy Hackworth, in charge on the Stockton and Darlington, and to that painstaking and very able man fell the task of making the pioneer locomotives reliable work units. In 1827 he built the *Royal George* locomotive at Shildon Works. It was much larger than any of the previous engines built by Stephenson, and had six wheels coupled by arranging the flue from the firebox to the chimney in the form of a U, instead of a single large pipe, and so presented an increased area of flue tube in contact with the water. Hackworth was also the inventor of the blast pipe, a narrowing cone through the nozzle of which the exhaust steam passes at high velocity and creates an intense draught on the fire. The *Royal George* steamed very freely, but it was a curious thing to look at. Because of that return flue the firedoor was at the chimney end of the boiler, and the fireman rode on a separate tender propelled in front of the engine, while the driver was at the rear end, where there was a second tender carrying the water supply tank. The greatly improved performance of the *Royal George* was in many ways a turning-point in railway history, because until then in the later 1820s there were many who felt that locomotives could not be made sufficiently reliable, and that cable traction would be the only preferable alternative.

On the Liverpool and Manchester Railway, construction of which was nearing completion, the directors decided to stage a competition, the Rainhill trials, for the best type of locomotive to work the line. Although Hackworth had done so much to pull the Stockton and Darlington Railway round from failure, George Stephenson and his son, Robert, felt that his *Royal George* type of locomotive was rather clumsy and slow, and in entering a locomotive for the competition they introduced some further novel features, particularly in the way it [was arranged]. To promote rapid evaporation by increasing the hot surfaces in contact with the water, the flue from the firebox to the chimney was split up, so that the hot gases of combustion instead of passing through one large tube passed through a nest of much smaller ones. This feature was incorporated not by a fellow engineer but by the suggestion of the secretary of the company, Henry Booth. As the first of its kind it gave much trouble in the constructional stage, because great difficulty was experienced in fitting the tubes to the boiler ends without leakage occurring. But Robert Stephenson persevered, and eventually turned out a first-class job. The engine was the ever-famous *Rocket*, which steamed very freely.

Hackworth also entered the competition, and at his own expense built a four-wheeled engine, the *Sans Pareil*, having the return flue type of boiler. But the conditions of competition staged at Rainhill did not require such a massive engine as the *Royal George*, and the *Sans Pareil* had only one tender, propelled in front. The driver stood on a small platform jutting out at the rear. Hackworth's engine was sound enough in conception but he was rather let down by some of the suppliers of parts. One of the cylinders was badly cast and burst at one point, and then the feed pump supplying water to the engine's boiler failed, and of course put an end to the engine's participation. The third competitor, the *Novelty* of Braithwaite and Ericsson, made some spectacular runs, but broke down frequently, and eventually the *Rocket* of George and Robert Stephenson was the only one of the three to stay the course. Not only did it win the competition, and ensure that the *Rocket* type became the first standard engine type of the Liverpool and Manchester Railway, but it became a world prototype, incorporating all those basic features of design that were perpetuated for more than a hundred years in locomotives of increasing size all over the world, culminating in the gigantic "Big Boys" of the Union Pacific Railroad, which were built in 1941.

*Top* The successful entrant at the 1829 Rainhill trials was the Stephensons' loco *Rocket*.
*Centre* The exacting nature of the Rainhill trials defeated the *Novelty*.
*Bottom* The *Sans Pareil* was the only serious rival to the *Rocket*; but it was crippled when a cylinder failed.

The *Planet* was built in 1830 by Robert Stephenson. It was the first locomotive with inside cylinders situated beneath the smokebox, the drive being via a cranked axle just ahead of the firebox.

# 1830

When it came to day-to-day working on the Liverpool and Manchester Railway, the *Rocket* type did not prove entirely satisfactory, and Robert Stephenson obviated the trouble from jerky and rough riding by introducing the *Planet* type in 1830, which had the cylinders between the frames, situated beneath the smokebox. All the machinery became largely concealed; but while this produced a much smoother riding engine, a problem of another type was introduced, that of a driving axle that had to incorporate two cranked features between the frames. The problems were, however, of manufacture rather than of principle, and locomotives with inside cylinders became very popular in Britain. The *Planet* type followed the *Rocket* type in having only a single pair of driving wheels, though situated at the rear instead of at the leading end of the locomotive. A single pair of driving wheels was favoured for passenger trains, because it afforded a greater freedom in running; but the four wheels coupled type, as in the *Locomotion* and the *Sans Pareil*, was more suitable for goods trains, as providing greater adhesion in hauling a heavy load, and locomotives of this latter type were among the first exported from Great Britain to North America. They were, however, not to have any lasting influence in that continent.

In the USA the first ever railway, the Baltimore and Ohio, had from its inception in 1827 relied upon horse traction; but in 1830 a New York industrialist and inventor, Peter Cooper, had made a large investment in Baltimore and Ohio land, and in his determination to see the railway succeed he set to work to produce a steam locomotive. Working in the Mount Clare shops at Baltimore, with scrap iron, borrowed wheels, and using gun barrels for boiler tubes, he built America's first home-made railroad steam locomotive, the *Tom Thumb*. It had a vertical boiler with the chimney extending directly from the boiler end, and although having many defects arising from the primitive methods used in its construction, it paved the way to success, and was followed by locomotives of the same general type, built by the firm of Davis and Gartner. The *Atlantic*, built by the same partners in 1832, was the first of the so-called "grasshopper" type, again with vertical boiler, and the cylinders acting through large rocking shafts on the top of the boiler.

In the pioneer days of American railroading some strikingly original forms of steam locomotive were tried, none of any lasting success, but of great interest historically. The first locomotive ever to run in America, as distinct from the indigenous *Tom Thumb*, was imported from England by the Delaware and Hudson Canal Company in 1829. It was a typical English four-wheeler of pre-*Rocket* days, and named the *Stourbridge Lion*. While Peter Cooper's *Tom Thumb* was going through its teething troubles on the Baltimore and Ohio Railroad, a much larger engine of the vertical boiler type was put to work in December 1830 on the South Carolina Canal and Rail Road Company. This was named the *Best Friend of Charleston*, and goes down in history as the first locomotive to operate a regularly scheduled passenger run in the USA. Another notable American locomotive of early days, more in the contemporary British style, was the *De Witt Clinton* of 1831, that began work between Albany and Schenectady. This was an 0-4-0 with a horizontal boiler, and chimney at the leading end after the style of the *Locomotion* on the Stockton and Darlington Railway. While American manufacturers were making their first essays in locomotive building, the Stephenson inside cylinder 0-4-0 type, developed on the Liverpool and Manchester, had a limited phase of popularity, and the firm of Robert Stephenson and Company of Newcastle supplied some locomotives of characteristic appearance in 1831, including the *John Bull*, to the Camden and Amboy Railroad.

The first train to run in New York State was hauled by the locomotive *De Witt Clinton*, in August 1831. It reached 24 km/h (15 mph).

# Improving engine performance
## *Locomotive development 1835–1874*

**1835** By 1835 the steam locomotive had passed beyond the stage of a questionable "gimmick". The Liverpool and Manchester Railway was proving a very profitable investment, worked entirely by steam, and men like Robert Stephenson having settled the fundamentals of working were becoming involved in finer points of performance. Speeds were increasing rapidly, more rapidly than development of the track, and the safe riding of locomotives became a point of much importance. The jerky action and rough riding of locomotives of the *Rocket* type with outside cylinders, led to the production of Stephenson's famous *Patentee*, with inside cylinders, and this formed the prototype of many British locomotives exported to pioneer railway enterprises in Belgium, France, Germany and Russia. It came to be popular on the earlier British railways, and was exported to Canada and the USA. In North America, however, it was not successful. There was a great difference between the lavishly engineered, solid tracks of England, and the pioneer lines in America where, with little supporting capital, tracks were laid on meandering courses in river valleys, up steep hillsides, and all with an absolute minimum of constructional cost. The short, rigid wheelbased locomotives of conventional European type took unkindly to these sinuous, lightly laid tracks of America and derailments were frequent. A new conception of locomotive chassis design was therefore evolved on the simple principle of a three-legged stool or three-point suspension, which will stand on any rough ground. Thus came the American, or 4-4-0 locomotive, in which the driving wheels on either side, with compensating levers to the axle boxes, and the pivot point of the leading four-wheeled bogie. It was so successful that the American became the standard type of locomotive for

hauling both passenger and freight traffic all over North America, lasting in popularity for upwards of 50 years.

In the meantime a distinguished English engineer, Thomas Russell Crampton, who at one time worked on the Great Western Railway at Swindon, Wiltshire, was applying his own inventive mind to the problem of providing a smooth and safe-riding express locomotive. He conceived the idea that if the large diameter driving wheels were placed at the extreme rear end, the centre line of the boiler could be made low, thus securing greater steadiness of riding. A few of these picturesque stern-wheelers were put into service in England and Scotland, but it was in France particularly that the type found great favour, and so many of these engines were built that "Prendre le Crampton" became a common phrase for "going by train". But even in the 1840s thoughts of some inventors were turning to alternatives to steam as the motive power, in avoidance of using coal and coke, emission of smoke and sparks, and the puffing noise. Thus came the ill-starred experiment with the so-called "atmospheric system" of traction, in which a large pipe was laid in the middle of the track; the traction unit had a piston which fitted into the pipe, and the air in front of the piston was exhausted, thus drawing the traction unit along. The trouble was that the connection between the traction unit and the piston had to pass through a longitudinal joint in the pipe, normally sealed by a leather flap, but pushed aside by the movement of the piston connection, and resealing afterwards. Because the flap was made of leather, quick deterioration destroyed its sealing value. A vacuum could not be created ahead of the piston, and the system became useless.

It was natural that the early primitive steam locomotives working on the colliery lines in northeastern England should burn coal; but when plans were laid for more and more public railways, running through the green

shires of the Midlands, those who opposed the building of railways managed to get restrictive clauses inserted into the Acts of Parliament authorizing them to prohibit the use of locomotives that did not consume their own smoke. At that early stage in the development that meant using coke instead of coal, and incurring the additional cost. This, however, could be regarded as no more than a temporary measure, and much experimenting was undertaken with coal-fired locomotives to reduce the emission of smoke to an acceptable level. In North America no such restrictions applied, but in areas distant from the coalfields locomotives were built that burned wood. This in turn brought problems with the throwing out of sparks. Many of the early American railways ran through densely forested country, and sparks whether from wood or coal could cause serious forest fires. Sparks also occasionally set fire to the great timber trestle viaducts. While a major conflagration could lead to the complete loss of a viaduct, a smouldering insidious fire could lead to weakening of bridge members and result in a collapse while a train was crossing. Various spark-arresting devices of strange and picturesque appearance were fitted to the tall chimneys of early American locomotives, and given such names as "diamond stacks" and "balloon stacks" – depending on their shape. The first spark arresters were developed in the early 1830s and pioneered by such engineers as Matthew Baird. In all, over 60 types were tried on American wood-burning locomotives and became standard by the 1860s.

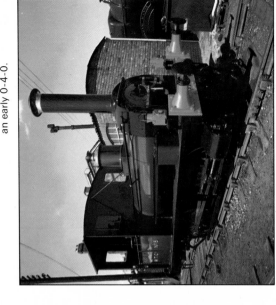

WTC No 5 Shannon loco, an early 0-4-0.

*Left* The atmospheric railway system of Jacob and Joseph Samuda. The cylindrical tube had a flanged slot at the top which was closed by a continuous flap of leather sandwiched between thin iron plates. The flap was hinged to the flange on one side and was free on the other, so that it could lift to allow the passage of the arm connecting the piston and the carriage. Air was expelled from the tube in front of the train thus creating movement by air pressure on the rear of the piston.

## 1859

In Great Britain while experiments were in progress to obviate the use of coke there were interesting developments in the boiler itself. Robert Stephenson himself introduced what was known as the "long-boiler" type, in conjunction with a relatively small firebox. The object was twofold: by having a long barrel, and making the products of combustion pass a considerable way before being exhausted, the fuel would be more completely burned; the long boiler would act as a large reservoir for steam, ready for use, while the small grate would need less coal to keep the fire bars covered, while the locomotive was standing. It seemed an ideal type of boiler for freight trains, which spent a good deal of their time standing or shunting and using relatively little steam. The solution to the coal burning problem came ultimately in a very simple form – namely the firebrick arch, built transversely across the firebox. The flames and gases from the forward part of the grate were drawn back and round the rearward edge of the grate of the arch, by the draught from the smokebox, and except at the times when the locomotive was being fired, gave a clear exhaust from the chimney. This arrangement was first used on the Midland Railway in England in 1859, and thereafter the firebrick arch became a universal feature.

Locomotives of the 2-2-2 type, with outside frames, were at one time popular for passenger work in Great Britain, with variations, some with double frames, and both exported to Europe. Nevertheless, important variations must be noted, both English: the "Jenny Lind" type which had outside framing for the leading and trailing wheels, and inside frames for the single pair of driving wheels. On the London and North Western Railway, Southern Division, J. E. McConnell used inside frames only for a notable series of 2-2-2 express locomotives, nicknamed 'bloomers'. Before the end of the period, however, locomotives of the 2-4-0 type were coming into general use for passenger work, with notable examples in France, Belgium, Holland and Germany, in addition to those of Great Britain. In France, so long using the Crampton stern-wheeler type, the change to four coupled wheels was accompanied on the Paris, Lyon and Mediterranean by use of the "long-boiler"; but as the locomotives in question tended to pitch when running at speed, the 2-4-0 arrangement was changed to the 2-4-2, a type which at a later date in the USA became known as the Columbia. While the 4-4-0 or American type with outside cylinders, leading bogie and three-point suspension remained the standard design for general service all over the USA, larger locomotives were being introduced for heavier freight duties, and the Mogul (2-6-0), and the Consolidation (2-8-0) were coming increasingly into service. Speeds were not high, and competition in speed for such important traffic as that between New York and Chicago had scarcely begun to play a major role.

The Englishman Robert Fairlie patented an early design of articulated locomotive, and a few were built in the 1860s and 1870s. The 28-tonne *Snake* was imported into New Zealand about 1873.

*Above* Steam locomotive wheel notation, though perhaps a mystery to the uninitiated, is in fact a remarkably simple system. A distinction is made between driving and trailing wheels.

2-2-2 / *1-1-1*
4-4-0 / *2-2-0*
0-6-0 / *0-3-0*
4-6-0 / *2-3-0*
4-6-2 / *2-3-1*
2-8-4 / *1-4-2*
2-10-0 / *1-5-0*

● Power transmission
*Continental European notation in italics*

*Right* The moving principles of Walschaert's valve gear. Such mechanisms, though apparently complicated, operate purely to ensure that steam is let into and out of the cylinder to provide motion to the piston. Orange: high pressure (live) steam; yellow: medium pressure steam; blue: low pressure steam; green: steam under compression.

## 1863

The opening of the Metropolitan Railway in 1863, the first purely Underground line in the world, involved the design of locomotives that literally consumed their own exhaust steam. No exhaust, however clear, could be permitted in the tunnels, and to meet this requirement a remarkably successful range of tank engines of the 4-4-0 type was introduced. The exhaust steam was diverted from the top of the blast pipe into a large pipe on either side entering into the side tanks and was discharged upon the surface of the water. At one time no fewer than 120 of these locomotives were in service in the London area.

An interesting phase in the development of the steam locomotive came to centre around lines of substandard gauge, principally in the USA, but a focus point of world attention came to be the 600 mm (1 ft 11½ in) gauge Festiniog Railway, in North Wales. Eminent engineers of the day stated that it would be impossible to design steam locomotives to operate satisfactorily on so narrow a gauge. After building some small locomotives of the 0-4-0 type that were limited in their haulage capacity, C. E. Spooner, engineer of the Festiniog Railway, decided to try one of Robert Fairlie's patent double engines, which were in effect two tank engines arranged back to back on a single frame. Each engine unit, with its cylinders and running gear, was carried on a swivelling bogie, and having ball and socket joint connections for the steam pipes below the smokebox at each end. These locomotives had two inside fireboxes, with doors alongside, stoked by the fireman who rode on one side of the central platform, the driver riding on the other. The first of these engines, named *Little Wonder*, was put into service in 1869, and was an outstanding success. Several engines of the same type were added subsequently, and one is still working on the Festiniog Railway today. Locomotives of the same general type, but much larger, and for the 1,435 mm (4 ft 8½ in) gauge were built in England for service in Mexico, Russia, South America and Sweden.

By 1874 the speed of passenger trains was becoming an important consideration in Great Britain. The British Post Office, for example, had definitely specified an average speed of 68 km/h (42 mph) overall between London and Holyhead for the Irish Mail, and to maintain such an average inclusive of the lengthy stops needed for postal traffic at such stations as Rugby, Stafford, Crewe and Chester, involved running at over 96 km/h (60 mph) on the open stretches of line. By the 1870s, indeed, speeds up to about 113 km/h (70 mph) were being reached on favourable stretches, not only with the Irish Mail, but on the Great Northern line from London (King's Cross) on the steep, though well-aligned descents of the west coast main line north of Lancaster. At that time, both on scheduled speed and in maximum speeds attained, the leading railways of Great Britain stood alone in the excellence of their performance, though this supremacy was not to last for many more years. While every credit must be given to the locomotives and their designers, this standard of running could not have been attained without a track that was solidly built to the highest standards and thereafter scrupulously maintained.

# Compound locomotives and superheating

## *Locomotive development 1875–1905*

**1875** By 1875 the steam locomotive had passed well beyond its trial and experimental stages and was the predominant asset in the worldwide development of land transport; but its overall efficiency, in terms of work done in hauling a train in relation to the latent energy in the coal, or other fuel consumed, was very low, something less than 8 per cent. The attention of engineers in Great Britain, France, Germany, Austria and the USA became directed towards the improvement of this low return for the fuel consumed. Theoretical studies were made of the stages in which steam was produced, and used, and by common consent the use of two-stage, or compound expansion of the steam, appeared to show the best prospects for improvement. It was an attractive theoretical concept, first put into practice by Anatole Mallet, who in 1875 built a small tank engine for the Bayonne and Biarritz Railway. Instead of being admitted simultaneously to two cylinders, steam was admitted only to the one high-pressure cylinder, and after expanding in that, it passed into the one low-pressure cylinder to complete its expansion before exhausting to the atmosphere. By this means Mallet was able to secure a greater pressure range over the whole expansion of the steam than if it had been passed through only one cylinder. Because the steam was at a much lower pressure on entering the low-pressure cylinder, it had to be made of much larger diameter, to ensure that each cylinder had a roughly equal thrust on the piston. Had this not been so the motion imparted to the locomotive as a whole would have been irregular and conducive of rough and dangerous riding.

Mallet's precepts were quickly taken up by other engineers, first by A. von Borries of the Prussian State Railways, who in 1880 built two locomotives of his own design. One of the problems immediately confronting designers of compound locomotives was that of starting. In a conventional two-cylinder locomotive using single expansion, and cranks at 90 degrees to each other, if one cylinder happened to have its crank and connecting rod on

of steam. But a further factor that handicapped these three-cylinder locomotives was that the two pairs of driving wheels were not coupled. This did not help when starting when one pair might slip independently of the other, and thus cause a lack of synchronization in the flow of steam. The Webb three-cylinder express compounds of which there were 100, in five separate classes, did a great deal of hard work, but it might have been done much more easily had the two pairs of driving wheels been coupled. Webb's whole achievement as an engineer was unfortunately criticized because of the failure of his compound engines.

A very important trend that came to affect all aspects of locomotive design, maintenance and their work out on the line was the general introduction of steel instead of wrought iron as the basic material of construction, and also of rails. With harder rails, and harder tyres on the wheels, both locomotives and coaching stock could run more freely. In Great Britain it was so remarkable to find

locomotives of good reputation, which in the 1870s were rarely exceeding 113 km/h (70 mph), speeding up to well over 130 km/h (80 mph) in the 1890s. Although claims of very high speed had been made for the Empire State Express in the USA, these have never been fully authenticated, and the climax in speed achievement took place in the Race to the North in 1895, when competition between the east coast and west coast routes from London to Scotland led ultimately to an all-out race between the sleeping car expresses leaving Euston and King's Cross at 20.00 hrs for Aberdeen. The west coast record of 512 min for a run of 870 km (540 miles) with three intermediate stops, each to change locomotives, remained unsurpassed on the world's railways for many years to follow. It is perhaps significant that all the fastest start-to-stop runs, on both sides, were made not by compounds but by single-expansion engines, 2-4-0 type on the London and North Western, and 4-4-0 on both the Caledonian and the North Eastern railways.

*Above* Light locomotives built by H. K. Porter, Pittsburg Pa. *Left* A locomotive of the Erie Railroad Company in 1908 demonstrating a design which was to be considerably developed. It was truly gigantic and weighed 155 tonnes. *Below Rob Roy*, Midland and GWR, built in 1873 by Nelson & Co.

dead centre, the second crank would turn the wheel and start the motion. But in a two-cylinder compound engine, if the high-pressure cylinder was on dead centre the engine would not start. Von Borries designed a special starting valve that allowed a small amount of steam to pass directly into the low-pressure cylinder on starting, and allowed the engine to get away in all circumstances. Many locomotives of this type were built for service in Germany, while an adaptation of it was successfully used on the North Eastern Railway in England. One of the best known, yet unfortunately the least successful, of the compound systems used in England was that of Francis William Webb on the London and North Eastern Railway. Webb was chief mechanical engineer on the London and North Eastern for a period of 32 years and helped to a very high standard of workmanship. But for some reason, never fully explained, Webb chose to employ three cylinders – two very small high-pressure ones outside, exhausting into one huge low-pressure cylinder between the frames. It was a curious arrangement, not helped by the low-pressure cylinder, despite its size, being too small to take the exhaust without somewhat restricting the flow

**1885** Although larger locomotives were being introduced, as prototypes, to the very end of the nineteenth century the 4-4-0 type remained a world favourite for passenger work. In America outside cylinders were universal, and the traditional American of earlier days was the same, though greatly enlarged, as the pioneers designed in the first place to run on lightly laid track. The celebrated *999* of the Empire State Express, for which a maximum speed of 179 km/h (112 mph) was claimed, was of this type. In France, Germany and Austria, the various types of compound had outside cylinders, but in Great Britain, followed by Holland and Belgium, inside cylinders were generally preferred. Much store was set upon a neat and compact outward appearance, and these traditions were reflected in British locomotives exported to India, Australia and South America. Locomotive development on the Caledonian Railway must be specially mentioned because there particular attention was paid, by Dugald Drummond, to the design of the steam passages leading to and from the cylinders to ensure a free flow of steam. Drummond's locomotives were notably fast runners, and produced a high output of power.

Compound locomotive development in Austria and France took different ways. In Austria Karl Gölsdorf had to provide for severe hill climbing on main lines through the Alps, and used a two-cylinder system at first. With the cylinders outside, and of different sizes, these locomotives looked curious when seen from the front; but the 2-8-0 type designed specially for the Arlberg Tunnel route in the Tyrol acquired a very high reputation, and some were still in service 70 years after their first introduction, though transferred to other areas after the electrification of the Arlberg line. In France the major development was due to one of the pioneers of steam locomotive compounding – Alfred de Glehn – who was technical head of the Société Alsacienne, Belfort. He used four cylinders, two high-pressure outside and two low-pressure inside. The system was applied first on 4-4-0 locomotives of the Northern Railway of France, and though his experimental prototype had the two pairs of driving wheels uncoupled as in F. W. Webb's system, this engine, built in 1885, remained the only one of its kind. All subsequent de Glehn compounds

had the two pairs of driving wheels coupled. The de Glehn compounds were complicated engines to drive, and their outstanding success was due to the French custom of allocating each engine to one driver only, who not only had exclusive charge of it in traffic, but who went into the repair shops and worked as a fitter on the engine when the time came for overhaul.

**1904** The de Glehn system of compounding, as applied to the Atlantic express locomotives of the Northern Railway of France, came prominently to the notice of British travellers on the boat trains between Paris, Boulogne and Calais, and the purchase by the Great Western Railway of three for comparative trials in England led, under G. J. Churchward, to a successful development, not with compound, but with four-cylinder single expansion locomotives. This range of 4-6-0 locomotives, that in 1923–7 led to the famous Castle and King classes, included a number of de Glehn design features. At the same time, Great Western boiler design was being derived largely from American practice with tapered barrel and a high raised Belpaire (or flat topped) firebox. In 1904, older Great Western locomotives were prominent in making new speed records, including the first authenticated instance of a speed of 160 km/h (100 mph) by the engine *City of Truro*, and the running of a stretch of 113 km (70 miles) at an average of 130 km/h (80 mph) by the 4-2-2 engine *Duke of Connaught*. These two locomotives were responsible, in succession, for running an Ocean Mail special from Millbay Docks, Plymouth, to London (Paddington) – a distance of 394 km (246.5 miles) in 225 min, inclusive of a 2 min stop at Bristol to change engines. This run, with its overall average of nearly 106 km/h (66 mph), was the fastest ever up to that time.

An important development was then in progress in Germany. Hitherto locomotives had used the steam just as it was boiled – saturated steam as it is termed. Dr Wilhelm Schmidt was applying the principle of superheating to certain locomotives of the Prussian State Railways. After formation the steam was heated further before use. This had the advantage of considerably increasing its volume, and thereby its capacity to exert power in the cylinders. Of course in getting more steam, additional heat, and thereby

more coal, had to be used; but the advantages far outweighed the cost, and although by the turn of the century the practice was only in its infancy, superheaters were to become a universal item of equipment on nearly all new locomotives from about 1912 onwards.

With the twentieth century came the era of extremely large locomotives. In Great Britain the 4-4-2 and the 4-6-0 types began to supersede the 4-4-0 for passenger work, while in America the transition from the traditional outside cylinder 4-4-0 was very rapid. The intervening stages of the 4-4-2 and 4-6-0, known in America as the Atlantic and the Ten-Wheeler, respectively, quickly gave place to the Pacific or 4-6-2. In the USA compounds were built on the Vauclain and the tandem system, both being generally favoured to the systems then popular in Europe because they allowed the cylinders to be mounted outside the frames. Both employed four cylinders. In the Vauclain system the high- and low-pressure cylinders were mounted in two pairs, one on each side of the engine. The high-pressure cylinder was immediately above the low-pressure cylinder, and their pistons were connected to a common crosshead. In the tandem system one high- and one low-pressure cylinder were mounted on a common horizontal axis, and the pistons for each cylinder were built in line in the USA. The Vauclain system derived its name from Samuel Matthews Vauclain, who became superintendent of the Baldwin Locomotive Works in 1890 and eventually became chairman of Baldwin in 1929. He also designed engines for railway systems in many other parts of the world, including heavy goods engines for Brazil and engines for Japan.

Adams Radial locomotive, preserved today in immaculate working condition on the Bluebell Railway, England.

# The era of technological innovation

## Locomotive development 1906–1926

**1907** By the end of the nineteenth century it seemed that railway administrations in all parts of the world aimed to have the smallest locomotives that would work the traffic, while within a matter of ten years the pendulum had swung strongly to the opposite way. Heavier and much more luxurious rolling stock was being built; dining and sleeping cars were being added to many of the principal trains, and while the urge to accelerate services had lessened, there was no deceleration. In all countries very much larger locomotives were built, and for the first time – in Great Britain at any rate – size and weight began to approach the maximum that the lines would take. Civil engineers placed limits upon the maximum axle loads that they were prepared to accept; but in Great Britain the crisis in this respect was postponed by the introduction of superheating. Smaller locomotives thus equipped could do greatly superior work to their predecessors of equivalent size and overall weight. Certain locomotives of a size exceptional by previous standards and of the 4-6-0 type were built by the Caledonian and by the London and South Western Railways, but for sheer size in Great Britain Churchward's Pacific *The Great Bear*, on the Great Western Railway, surpassed all. This was only the second locomotive of the type to be built in Europe, the first being on the Paris-Orléans Railway in 1907. *The Great Bear*, completed at Swindon in 1908, was virtually an experiment and exercise in boiler design, in readiness for future requirements, which in fact did not materialize.

The problem of maximum axle loading in locomotives was becoming much more acute on the Continent of Europe. The massively built and well maintained British main lines were mostly capable of taking axle loads up to 18 or 19 tonnes, but this was not so in Holland, for example. In the early 1900s, traffic across that country, particularly in conveying the Anglo-German mails, was becoming increasingly heavy, and the elegant British-built 4-4-0s of the State Railway could not cope with the trains single-handed. Larger locomotives were needed, and that in the ordinary way would have meant heavier axle loads, which the civil engineers could not permit, because of the nature of much of the foundations on which the lines were laid. The matter of engine balancing became critical. In any locomotive the revolving cranks and reciprocating rods and pistons set up a degree of imbalance, which, if not compensated for, can give rise to unsteady and unsafe riding. So, a degree of balance was provided by putting compensating weights in the wheels. These, while resulting in a smooth riding engine, impart a "hammer blow" effect on the track that increases in seriousness as the speed rises. On some British 4-4-0 locomotives the hammer blow at 113 or 120 km/h (70 or 75 mph) was equal to 50 per cent of the static axle load, giving a total load on the track of 28 or 29 tonnes. If, however, four cylinders are used instead of

two, and all four drive on to the same axle, the movements of the pistons, cranks and rods exactly compensate each other and there is no hammer blow at all. On the Netherlands State Railways the civil engineers were prepared to accept heavier axle loads on larger locomotives providing they were built with four cylinders. A very fine range of powerful 4-6-0 locomotives were built.

In the USA the equipping of all freight trains with the continuous automatic air brake enabled very long and heavier trains to be safely controlled when descending steep gradients, and the size and power of the locomotives needed to haul such trains on level track and adverse gradients had to be increased accordingly. For this the Mallet articulated compound type proved suitable, and it was enlarged to unprecedented length and tractive power. Some of the largest built in the period 1906–15 were 2-6-6-2s for the Chesapeake and Ohio, weighing 270 tonnes, and 2-8-8-2s for the Southern Pacific, weighing 265 tonnes. With such large boilers and fireboxes the rate of coal consumption was far greater than that which could be sustained by a single fireman, and mechanical stokers were introduced whereby coal from the huge tenders could be fed directly on to the firegrate and distributed evenly over its wide area. The stokers were so designed that the rate of feed could be regulated by the fireman according to the needs of the journey. These giant locomotives were four-

cylinder compounds, and the low-pressure cylinders carried on the forward articulated engine unit were often as large as 101 cm (40 in) diameter. The working of American freight trains did not require any fast running, and that these compound Mallets became rather unstable at any speed over about 48 km/h (30 mph) was then of no consequence: no higher speeds were needed. This instability was later shown to be due to an uneven distribution of the weight between the front and rear engine units, correction of which enabled more recent articulated locomotives to be run safely up to 113 km/h (70 mph) with the express freight trains of the 1930s.

This electric locomotive was introduced on Switzerland's Emmenthal-Burgdorf-Thun Railway as early as 1910.

*Left* The Great Eastern 0-10-0 No 20 *Decapod* was built by James Holden to achieve high acceleration. It failed because it was too heavy for existing track.

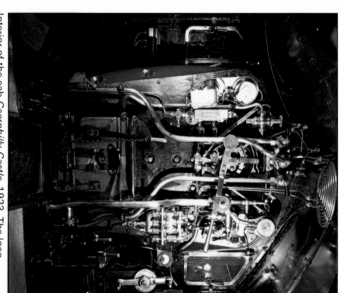

## 1912

One of the most important advances in this period was in the technique of locomotive testing. From an early date in the history of railways, dynamometer cars had been used by which the pull exerted by a locomotive could be measured – a sophisticated version of the simple spring balance. But such measurements taken while a locomotive was working a service train were necessarily subject to all the incidentals of daily railway operation, checks because of adverse signals, and suchlike; and in the USA plant was set up at Purdue University, Illinois, and at the St Louis Exhibition of 1904, on which locomotives could be tested under laboratory conditions, as it were. The wheels were supported on rollers, and the driving wheels could be made to rotate the test plant rollers against an applied load. This could be varied according to requirements, and the task of hauling a train of any load and at any speed simulated. The behaviour of the locomotive, steam production, coal consumption and all other workings could be observed in the carefully regulated atmosphere of a laboratory, instead of in the rough and tumble conditions of service on an ordinary route.

At the conclusion of the St Louis Exhibition in 1904, the test plant on which the working of a number of dissimilar American locomotives had been demonstrated, was removed and set up on a permanent basis at the principal locomotive works of the Pennsylvania Railroad, at Altoona. In Great Britain modern dynamometer cars were built by the Great Western, North Eastern, London and North Western and Lancashire and Yorkshire Railways, but it was only the Great Western that followed the American example and built a stationary testing plant. In the period now under review this was not used to a great extent, reliance being placed upon tests with the dynamometer car on service trains. On the London and North Western Railway, in November 1913, during tests with one of the four-cylinder 4-6-0 locomotives of the Claughton class, the highest output of power registered with a British locomotive was attained, namely 1,669 hp at a speed of 113 km/h (70 mph). This was not surpassed until considerably larger locomotives were in service after the First World War.

By the year 1912 the era of the "mixed traffic" locomotive was beginning. With the acceleration of freight services the need was felt for units that could haul a fast freight train but could also be used in medium-speed passenger services. Valve gears were being improved, and locomotives with coupled wheels of no more than 1,676 mm (5 ft 6 in) diameter were able to make speeds up to 113 km/h (70 mph) economically. This trend, and the locomotives that were coming into service in Great Britain as a result of it, was particularly advantageous when railways could not agree among themselves as to the motive power had to be supplied for serving the battlefronts in the First World War. Mixed traffic locomotives

Interior of the cab *Caerphilly Castle*, 1923. The locomotive is preserved in the Science Museum, London.

were ideal for both troop and munition trains. But the bringing of railways under government control both in Great Britain and France, due to the war emergency, led those with overall responsibility to look towards a far greater degree of standardization of locomotive design than had been thought desirable previously. Committees were set up, and new standard designs drafted. In France events moved rather faster than in Great Britain, because one sector of the French railway network was actually owned by the state; and the government took the standard Pacific engine design of that railway, and a 4-6-0 mixed traffic type, and placed large orders. Some were placed in Britain, because certain normal manufacturing facilities in France were in enemy hands. Arrangements were made for these new locomotives to be allocated also to the privately owned railways of France in the hope that they would subsequently be adopted as a standard. In Great Britain at the end of the war, the Minister of Munitions, then Winston Churchill, was anxious to place large orders for new locomotives, to avoid the large-scale unemployment that it was feared would result from the sudden end to the demand for munitions. This project never materialized, partly because the then separately independent British railways could not agree the then separately independent British individual locomotive designs and specifications that should be ordered.

## 1923

Just as the increasing size and weight of locomotives had brought Continental engineers together in the earlier 1900s, so also in Great Britain, after the end of the war, locomotive and civil engineers were associated with scientific and university interests in the researches of the Bridge Stress Committee. The responsibility of this committee was to examine the effects that different types of locomotives had upon a variety of underline bridges. The outcome was to emphasize the beneficial effects of locomotives having three or four cylinders, and equally to underline the damaging effect of certain designs having only two cylinders inside. This confirmed the correctness of the policy of all four of the large groups set up by the Railways Act of 1921, the provisions of which took effect from 1 January 1923. Notable multi-cylindered express passenger locomotives of the 1920s were the Gresley three-cylinder Pacifics of the LNER, the four-cylinder 4-6-0 Lord Nelson class of the Southern, and the three-cylinder 4-6-0 Royal Scot of the LMSR. Meanwhile the Great Western policy of building four-cylinder 4-6-0s for the heaviest passenger traffic continued with enlargements from the Churchward Star class of 1907 to the King of 1927 with the high nominal tractive effort of 18,280 kg (40,300 lb). The continued use of loose-coupled, unbraked vehicles on the majority of British freight trains meant that loads could not be greatly increased, and no significant increase in the size or power of freight locomotives took place in Great Britain throughout this period.

In France the allocation of government-ordered locomotives to some of the private railways did not have the desired effect. The Northern, and the Paris, Lyon and Mediterranean had always followed a strongly individual practice, and the new locomotives of the State Railway type were regarded as no more than temporary assistance and were transferred elsewhere after a short time. The Northern brought out a splendid new design of Pacific which did magnificent work on the very heavy English boat trains, while the PLM brought out a huge 4-8-2 for working over the steeply graded central section of the main line from Paris to Marseille, between Laroche and Dijon, where the line passes through the Côte-d'Or mountains. In the meantime the American Mallets were getting larger than ever, and in 1923 the Denver and Rio Grande Western took delivery of some compound freight engines of the 2-8-2 type that had grates of 9 m² (96.5 ft²) and a tractive effort of 48,353 kg (106,600 lb). The diameter of the low-pressure cylinders was no less than 1 m (39 in) and the total weight of engine and tender was a staggering 332 tonnes.

This graceful 4-4-0 was built in 1913 by the North British Locomotive Co. in Glasgow, Scotland, to the order of the South India Railway. The tender cab is somewhat unusual, indicating that the engine was expected to run backwards frequently.

# The high point of steam

*Locomotive development 1927–1934*

**1927** The years from 1927 until the outbreak of the Second World War were among the most momentous and productive in the entire history of the steam locomotive. In the mid-1920s it had reached practically to the limit of physical size in Great Britain, France and North America, and the multi-faceted challenge of increased haulage requirements, the competition looming up from newer forms of motive power, and the economic conditions of the times, presented engine designers with the urgent need to effect the basic improvements in the day-to-day performance of the machine itself, taking the term "performance" in its very broadest sense. The situation attained by 1927 was graphically portrayed at the time of the centenary celebrations of the Baltimore and Ohio Railroad, when a great pageant of locomotives was staged. At that time the Pacific type (4-6-2) was giving place to the 4-6-4, or Hudson, for the heaviest express passenger traffic, because a four-wheeled truck at the rear was advantageous in supporting the ever-larger fireboxes that were becoming necessary. Even so, the 4-6-4 was not considered large enough on some North American railways, and the 4-8-4 was being introduced. In the year of the Baltimore and Ohio centenary the Northern Pacific

took delivery from Alco of some huge 4-8-4s, while across the border the Canadian National were also using the type, in their celebrated Confederation class. At one time it was thought that eight coupled wheels would be restrictive upon the maximum speed a locomotive could attain; but 4-8-4s have been run regularly at 130 km/h (80 mph) and at even higher speeds.

Another important feature of then current American practice was the almost universal abandonment of multi-cylinder layouts. One of the last designs to have anything but the simplest two-cylinder arrangement of the machinery was a series of very large freight locomotives built by Alco for the Union Pacific in 1926. These were of the 4-12-2 wheel arrangement, with three cylinders, and a valve gear of the conjugated type introduced by Sir Nigel Gresley, on the Great Northern Railway of England, and standardized on all his principal designs for the London and North Eastern Railway. But by 1930 two cylinders only were used in North America, and on freight locomotives having tractive efforts approaching 45,359 kg (100,000 lb) the cylinders were necessarily very large. On a class of 2-10-2 built by Baldwin for the Reading Railroad in 1931 the cylinders were 77 cm (30.5 in) diameter by

78 cm (32 in) stroke. Another important American development of the period was to design the main frames and their cross-stretchers as a single one-piece steel casting, instead of building them up from flat members. The cylinders were also included as part of this all-embracing "bed". One of the first instances of this development was in a class of 4-8-4 passenger locomotives for the Southern Pacific built in 1930. These large units had a booster engine on the four-wheeled trailing truck beneath the firebox which increased the tractive effort from 27,200 to 32,660 kg (60,000 to 72,000 lb) when it was put into operation.

*Left The Royal Scot,*
*c. 1927, preserved today.*
*From the class of the*
*same name, these three-*
*cylinder 4-6-0s were*
*designed to run on the*
*LMS London to Carlisle*
*route non stop, a*
*distance of 478 km*
*(299 miles).*

# 1930

It was remarkable that while American practice had swung so pronouncedly to the simplest of all machinery layouts, with two cylinders only, and all the running gear outside, and the four "grouped" railways of Great Britain were using three-cylinder, or four-cylinder single-expansion types for their principal express services, all of the French railways retained an unshakeable preference for the four-cylinder compound, mostly continuing to use the de Glehn arrangement of cylinders. This was a complicated arrangement, both in the proliferation of the machinery and in the skill needed to drive it efficiently. But French railway traditions were more than equal to the need, and some outstanding work was performed around 1930. French expertise in all matters connected with four-cylinder compound locomotives was epitomized on the Paris-Orléans Railway, after the electrification of the sections leading out of Paris. Steam locomotive men feared that with acceleration of service and increased haulage capacity of the electric locomotives, unfavourable comparison would be made upon the standards of running south of Orléans. A very careful and scientific study was made of one of the existing Pacific engines, and certain weaknesses in the design of 20 years earlier were laid bare. The young engineer charged with this investigation, André Chapelon, recommended a redesign of the cylinders, improvement in the internal steam passages, and enlargement of the superheater. One engine was altered in accordance with his findings, and on test it was found that the capacity was increased by no less than 50 per cent, while at the same time having the locomotive running more freely. The features embodied in what became known in France as the "P. O. Transformations" became a yardstick for locomotive improvement throughout the Continent of Europe.

In England Sir Nigel Gresley embodied Chapelon principles in a large new 2-8-2 design for use in heavy passenger service on the east coast main line between Edinburgh and Aberdeen, where increase of train loads had made double-heading a regular necessity while older types of locomotive had to be used. But one of the most important developments in Britain in the early 1930s was the mandate given to the new chief mechanical engineer on the London Midland and Scottish Railway to "scrap and build": to replace the somewhat heterogeneous stock of locomotives inherited from the constituent companies of the Grouping in 1923, with standard new designs of as few different classes as possible. Associated with this programme was the aim to obtain greater monthly distances from each locomotive. In total contrast to the continuing French practice of allocating one locomotive, and one driver only, to each locomotive, the LMSR aim to secure maximum utilization involved the use of individual locomotives by several different crews in the course of a single journey. There was one instance of six different crews manning a locomotive on successive stages of a 467 km (290 mile) working. To meet such service requirements a locomotive of extreme simplicity for handling and outstanding reliability was needed, and W. A. Stanier, the chief mechanical engineer of the LMSR, provided such a locomotive in the mixed traffic 4-6-0 officially classed 5P5F, but known colloquially as the "Black Five".

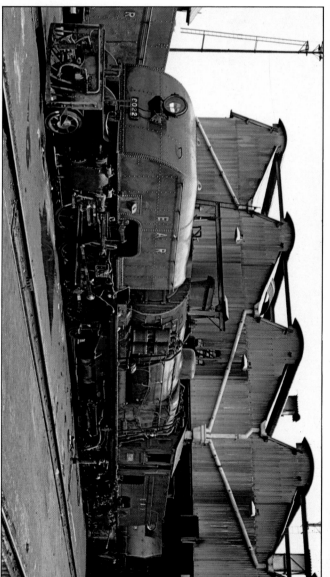

*Left King George VI,* built by GWR, pictured in the late 1950s at Bath spa, England. *Above* Nord Pacific-Bréville series, experimentally rebuilt with Cossart valve gear. *Right* 60 class Garratt 4-8-2 + 2-8-4 outside Nairobi shed.

# 1934

Thus in the early 1930s major developments in locomotive design had taken place in Great Britain, France and the USA, while elsewhere the process of evolution was a reflection of the practice of one or another of the leaders, adapted to suit local conditions. From that time, however, a very distinctive development in two directions became evident on the sub-standard gauge railways of the world, and particularly in southern Africa. Hitherto the 1,067 mm (3 ft 6 in) gauge had been considered to impose a limitation upon size and the intrinsic merits of design; but on the South African Railways new locomotives of the 4-8-2 type were introduced which for characteristics of height, size, width and performance surpassed many of the medium-speed units operating in Europe on the 1,435 mm (4 ft 8½ in) gauge. But the most remarkable development in Africa was in respect of the Beyer-Garratt articulated type. This type, on a sub-standard gauge line with severe curvature and a serious limitation on maximum axle loads, was shown in 1921 to have a considerable advantage over the Mallet articulated type in a series of comparative tests on the Natal main line of the South African Railways. The Garratt, with two separate but identical engine units, and one huge boiler carried on a cradle slung between the two, proved an ideal locomotive for a sharply curved sub-standard gauge line. The boiler could be built to ideal proportions for free steaming, short barrel and large diameter, which was clearly impossible on the Mallet. The latter was very successful on the relatively straight standard gauge lines of the USA.

In India, another area of intensive utilization of steam locomotives, much was done by the Indian Railway Conference Association (IRCA) to standardize on locomotive design for the several once-independent railways that one by one, as their original concessions expired, were coming under national ownership and control. The IRCA produced three classes of Pacific, XA, XB and XC, for various conditions of passenger service on the broad gauge engine. At the same time those railways that in the early 1930s still remained independent, notably the Bengal Nagpur, pursued an individual line, and the BNR favoured the de Glehn four-cylinder compound system in some large Pacific engines. Very powerful articulated locomotives of the Beyer-Garratt type were introduced for coal train working in Bengal.

In express passenger service the introduction of high-speed diesel powered railcar trains in both Germany and the USA spurred steam locomotive designers to apply a degree of external streamlining to locomotives allocated to prestige high-speed trains. This was done to remarkable effect on the London and North Eastern Railway in 1935, when a new high-speed service was to be introduced to mark the Silver Jubilee of King George V. With a knowledge of what Chapelon had achieved in France, with internal streamlining of all the ports, passages and valves to facilitate the freest possible flow of steam, and experience from his large 2-8-2 engines on the Edinburgh-Aberdeen route, Sir Nigel Gresley modified considerably the design of his standard Pacific engines, one of which had already attained a maximum speed of 173 km/h (108 mph). But with an eye to its publicity value, and to the saving of a little coal by reducing air resistance, the new Pacific engines designed for the Silver Jubilee service were streamlined externally. It was not true streamlining, but a form of aerodynamic screening copied from the external shape of some high-speed Bugatti railcars then operated on certain routes in France. This external streamlining, coupled with a silver-like finish that complied with the name of the new train, was most sensationally successful in its appeal to the public, and when the Silver Jubilee train attained a speed of 180 km/h (112.5 mph) on a preliminary demonstration run, its success as a commercial proposition was assured, in giving a service in the even four hours over the 429 km (268 miles) between London (King's Cross) and Newcastle. This train was, however, as yet, a once-off, travelling up from Newcastle to London in the morning and returning at 17.30 hrs.

# Moving towards diesel traction

*Locomotive development 1935–1944*

## 1935

Technical opinion in the advanced countries of the world was much divided in the late 1930s upon the relative merits of steam and diesel traction. In the USA in particular, while railways operating prestige transcontinental services such as the Burlington, the Rock Island, and the Union Pacific were moving towards diesel traction, some of the greatest of all American railways of that era, such as the New York Central, the Norfolk and Western, and perhaps the greatest of them all, the Pennsylvania, remained solidly with steam. The policy was to run massive trains at speeds of 120–130 km/h (75–80 mph) on level track, rather than attempt to emulate the spectacular very high speeds of the diesel-hauled streamliners. An exception was that of the Milwaukee Road, which between Chicago, Milwaukee and St Paul was in competition with the streamlined diesel trains of the Burlington. The Milwaukee reply was to introduce the super-high-speed steam-hauled "Hiawatha" expresses, for which special streamlined locomotives were designed.

For working the high-speed Silver Jubilee express of the London and North Eastern Railway, introduced in September 1935, Sir Nigel Gresley built a new range of Pacific locomotives – class A4 – with important modifications from his previous standard A3 series. Apart from the striking form of external streamlining, and the silver-grey livery that attracted so much attention from the public, the internal steam passages and the valve ports were fully streamlined. This afforded the freest possible flow of steam, while the use of a higher boiler pressure – 17.58 kg/cm$^2$ (250 lb/in$^2$) against 15.47 kg/cm$^2$ (219 lb/in$^2$) – smaller cylinders, and larger valves all contributed to a very free-running engine. Whereas the A3 class had to be pressed beyond their natural limit to attain speeds of more than 160 km/h (100 mph), the A4s ran up to 177 km/h (110 mph) and more with ease.

The form of streamlining on the LNER A4 Pacifics was very effective in deflecting the exhaust steam clear of the cab. This was at a time when the increased girth of locomotive boilers was causing difficulties on some types, with steam beating down and obscuring the look-out ahead from the cab. On the huge articulated freight locomotives of the Southern Pacific Railroad that worked over a route including lengthy tunnels on single-line sections, the locomotive was turned "back to front" as it were, and the cab placed at the leading end so as to provide a clear look-out. The locomotives in question were oil burners, and the fuel supply was piped from the large tender attached to the smokebox end of the engine. A notable range of locomotives of this general type operated on the heavily graded coastal route north and south of Oakland, California, as well as on other similar routes in the United States.

In the USA the fastest regular running in the steam era was made by Hiawatha trains on the Milwaukee Road, which attained speeds of more than 160 km/h (100 mph) between Chicago, Milwaukee and St Paul. When these trains were first introduced in 1935, and the formation was relatively light, special streamlined locomotives of the Atlantic type were used, built by the American Locomotive Company. But the service grew so much in popularity that much larger locomotives became necessary to haul the heaviest trains, and a class of 4-6-4s of similar appearance, styling and colouring was introduced in 1938. They had a tractive effort of 22,815 kg (50,300 lb) compared to the 18,144 kg (40,000 lb) of the Duchess class on the English LMS.

## 1937

What was probably the zenith of British express passenger locomotive development was reached in 1937 with the introduction by Sir William Stanier of the LMS Princess-Coronation class of Pacific, originally streamlined for the Coronation Scot train, but later developed into a standard type for heavy express working on the Anglo-Scottish west coast route. In their non-streamlined final form they were known as the Duchess class. Very powerful and free-running locomotives, they hold the British record for the maximum recorded performance in continuous "all-out" steaming, at a rate of 18,144 kg (40,000 lb) per hour from the boiler. They have also been timed at speeds up to 185.5 km/h (114 mph), although the record for British locomotives, and the maximum attained anywhere in the world with steam, was by the LNER A4 Pacific *Mallard* in 1938. When pressed to its limit, 203 km/h (126 mph) was reached on a special test run. These locomotives were capable of pulling up to 20 passenger coaches.

One of the most significant developments in the history of railway traction came in the later 1930s from the Electro-Motive Corporation of General Motors in the USA. Under the direction of Richard Dilworth the highly successful 567 diesel engine, designed and well-nigh perfected by Charles F. Kettering and his son Eugene, was built into a standard main line diesel-locomotive. Using all standard components, they could be managed by a single crew, without the expense of multiple manning that was necessary when heavy trains were double or triple headed by steam locomotives. While some of the American

*Below* This line-up of former LNER locomotives, at King's Cross shed in 1949, emphasizes the unusual shape of the streamlined A4 class Pacific 60033 *Seagull*.

*Above* The London Midland & Scottish *Coronation Scot* streamliner was introduced in 1937. It is seen here leaving Euston for Crewe on a test run on 29 June.

*Left* Period Penn Central locomotives pictured today on yard duty. The bull-nosed loco comes from a class of 4,800 hp units which once pulled the eastern section of the Broadway Limited.

In 1941, ALCO built a class of 4-8-8-4 Mallet-type articulated locos for the Union Pacific Railroad. They were the largest and heaviest steam engines ever built: together, engine and tender weighed 534 tonnes. Although designed primarily to work the heavily-graded section through the Wasatch Mountains, they were also capable of speeds of up to 130 km/h (80 mph).

railways such as the Burlington and the Rock Island introduced special streamlined diesel unit trains, Dilworth decided that the most profitable field for diesel traction was in direct replacement of steam, and his handsomely styled and gaily painted "first generation" locomotives began to do that most successfully.

Following the spectacular — but transient — success of the diesel-powered Zephyr trains in the Middle West of the USA, the development of the General Motors locomotives began the movement that was soon to sweep across the railways of North America like a prairie fire. This consisted of 1,800 hp units that could be made up into multiples of as many as four, to provide a locomotive of 7,200 hp with the completely standard 567 engine. The first passenger locomotive for long-haul duty was introduced in 1937, and the freight variation followed in 1939. The outstanding value of the diesel freight locomotive, in heavy-grade service, lay in the high power output at low speed, roughly double that of a steam locomotive of equal nominal tractive effort.

# 1938

In France a remarkable development of the 4-6-4 type was interrupted by the outbreak of hostilities in 1939. After the general amalgamation to form the French National Railways in 1938, a central office for studies and design had been set up, and M. de Caso produced a plan for a super-high-speed 4-6-4 that would haul trains of 200 tonnes at a speed of 169 km/h (105 mph) on level track. Eight were eventually built, remarkably so during the German occupation. Three were three-cylinder single expansion machines, and the other five were four-cylinder compounds in the characteristic French style. They were never used for high speed, but in heavy-load haulage they did much splendid work, until the lines they worked were electrified.

In 1938 the German State Railways had introduced a powerful 2-10-0 for general freight service, known as class 50. A large number were put into service. But with the onset of war, and the need to economize in use of materials, an "austerity" version was produced. Known as class 52, or in Germany the *Kriegslok*, every part that could be dispensed with was discarded. Sections that could be made lighter or more economical were redesigned. None but the basest of materials were permitted. As a result, whereas the class 50 with its tender weighed 148 tonnes, the 52 *Kriegslok* itself weighed only 120 tonnes. During the war, in Germany itself and in the countries then under German occupation and control, no fewer than 10,000 of these "austerity" locomotives were built.

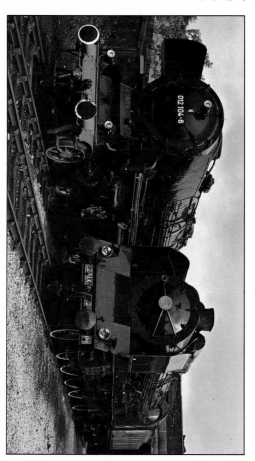

Chapelon compound and Kriegslok locomotives preserved.

# 1941

It was in this same period that the articulated locomotive began to reach its ultimate size and tractive power. In the USA this took the form of an extension to the Mallet principle of having two "engines" carried beneath one huge boiler. The rearward "engine" was carried on the main frame, while the forward one was articulated and gave a degree of flexibility to the locomotive as a whole. While the general trend was away from the original Mallet concept which was that of a compound locomotive, in a few notable instances — particularly on locomotives designed for relatively slow and heavy freight work — the compound principle was retained.

The ultimate in steam locomotive construction for heavy fast freight service came in 1941, with the building by Alco of the celebrated 4000 class, 4-8-8-4 type, for the Union Pacific Railroad. They were the largest and heaviest steam locomotives ever built. The engine alone weighed 350 tonnes and the huge tender another 197 tonnes. This vast assemblage of 547 tonnes may be compared to the 162 tonnes of an LMS Duchess 4-6-2. The Union Pacific 4000 class locomotives were nicknamed "Big Boys", but their tractive effort of 61,400 kg (135,400 lb) was not the highest achieved in the USA. They were essentially fast running locomotives, used mainly between Ogden, Utah and Green River, Wyoming. Detailed to heavy priority freights, they performed invaluable service during the Second World War.

At this time the British firm of Beyer, Peacock, of Manchester, was continuing to develop the Beyer-Garratt type of articulated locomotive for use in difficult terrain and substandard gauge lines in the countries of the British Commonwealth. The development of this type of locomotive was by no means complete by the end of the particular period covered here, although one of the most successful designs ever produced here, by Beyer, Peacock, the 4-6-4 + 4-6-4 of the 15th class for the Rhodesia Railways, was first introduced in 1939. These were mixed traffic units, used alike on heavy freights and on mail trains. Although coupled wheels are no more than 144.78 cm (4 ft 9 in) diameter, these locomotives run very smoothly at express speed on the 1,067 mm (3 ft 6 in) gauge, and their excellent tracking qualities enable them to take curves without any appreciable reduction from the maximum allowed speed of 88 km/h (55 mph). These engines have an all-up weight of 179 tonnes, and a tractive effort of 21,544 kg (47,496 lb). Another remarkable Beyer-Garratt design was that of the EC3 class on the Kenya and Uganda Railway, on which the maximum axle load was then limited to 11.75 tonnes, on the metre gauge, against 23 tonnes on the main lines of Great Britain. The EC3 had the wheel arrangement 4-8-4 + 4-8-4, and the designers packed such power into the limitations imposed by gauge and track that these engines had a tractive effort of no less than 20,910 kg (46,100 lb). They were used essentially as heavy freight haulers.

The high-speed service offered by the Hiawathas became so popular that relief trains often had to be run. The Atlantic locos built specially to inaugurate the service in 1935, and shown here, were thus replaced within 4 years by larger 4-6-4 locos able to haul twice the load.

# Locomotive power now

*Locomotive development 1945 and after*

**1948** An outstanding event influencing the design of steam locomotives was the nationalization of the British Railways as from 1948, and the decision of the newly formed Railway Executive Committee that, for economic reasons, reliance must continue to be placed on steam traction for some years to come. In 1948 a series of interchange trials between express passenger, mixed traffic and heavy freight locomotives of the four previously privately-owned companies, having shown no designs markedly superior to any other, the Railway Executive Committee decided to produce a series of new standard designs for future quantity-production that would embody the best of the regional types. The first of these was the class 7P7F mixed traffic Pacific, of which the first was No. 70000 named *Britannia*, and completed at Crewe in 1951. The Pacific, followed by 4-6-0s in various power classes, and new standard tank engines for short-distance traffic, achieved a considerable degree of success in the short time before the launching of the British Railways Modernization Plan of 1955, a major point of which was the elimination of steam traction throughout Britain. The new standard locomotives of 1951 and subsequently, of which 999 were built, were therefore not fully developed, and included traits in their performance

the greatly reduced turn round time necessary with diesel-electric locomotives, as compared with steam. While on certain specially regulated duties like those of the Santa Fe between La Junta and Los Angeles, a very high percentage utilization could be obtained from steam locomotives, such results were not generally practicable. The swift replacement of steam locomotives by diesels in the USA had repercussions all over the world, and led commercial rather than technical interests to press for similar "revolutions" elsewhere, and nowhere more strongly than in Britain. This eventually led to the launching of the British Railways Modernization Plan of 1955, and the elimination of all steam traction on that system by 1968.

Cutaway of the steam locomotive *Britannia*, British Railways No 70,000. While no one locomotive can be said to be typical, as so many variations were produced, this model exemplifies the strong traditional lines

reflected in post-1945 production. This series of locomotives represented, along with the 9F 2-10-0's, the last steam traction built in the UK – and some of the noblest. Their passing remains a sadness to all enthusiasts.

*Above* Southern Pacific locomotive, about 1951. The four-unit diesel engine had a total rating of 6,000 hp.

The first main line diesel-electric train in Britain leaves Euston in 1948.

that were not eliminated before it was decided that all future development was to be concentrated on non-steam forms of traction. Most successful of all the new standard designs was that of the 9F 2-10-0, primarily designed as a freight engine, but proved so versatile in ordinary service as to be used in express passenger traffic, and attaining speeds up to a maximum of 145 km/h (90 mph).

In the USA the elimination of steam traction was more rapid even than in Britain. The diesel-electric locomotive has traction characteristics definitely superior to those of steam, on units of nominally equal tractive power, when working hard up a severe gradient at speeds of 32 km/h (20 mph) or less, and its introduction came in areas where bad gradients existed. On some of the eastern lines in the USA where gradients are less exacting, extensive trials were conducted between diesel-electric locomotives and the latest steam designs, notably on the New York Central, but elsewhere steam was swept away, involving in many areas the replacement of relatively new locomotives that had run no more than a small part of their economic life. Two factors tended to hasten the end of steam traction in the eastern United States because of severe and recurring labour troubles in the coal industry, and the second was

## 1955

In France, and to a lesser extent in other countries on the Continent of Europe, the drive towards modernization was no less strong, but to electric rather than diesel traction. The mountainous regions of the Alps were favourable to the generation of hydroelectric power, while equally in these countries the large-scale importing of fuel oil was undesirable. Consequently much of the funds made available for reconstruction after the war were directed towards electrification. Leaving out of account certain obsolete systems, three forms of electric traction current supplies were in use in 1950: 1,500 volts dc in France and the Netherlands; 3,000 volts dc in Belgium and Italy; and 15,000 volts ac at $16\frac{2}{3}$ cycles in Germany, Austria and Switzerland. These systems were continued in the first reconstructions made after the war, notably on the Paris-Lyon-Marseille line of the French National Railways. One of the most notable developments, derived from the practice of the Bern-Lötschberg-Simplon Railway in Switzerland, was the adoption in France and elsewhere of electric locomotives in which all axles were powered. Earlier conceptions that some non-powered guiding wheels were needed fore and aft on locomotives used in high-speed service were dispelled, first by Swiss experience and then by the remarkable performances of the new French locomotives, two of which attained a maximum speed of 330 km/h (206 mph) on test.

In the USA, while certain routes over which very heavy mineral traffic was conveyed had been electrified for upwards of 30 years, all postwar development was in diesels; but while it was the so-called "first-generation" nose-cab type that had been first in sweeping steam aside, as the diesel conquest continued to its conclusion the "second-generation" type predominated. This was a less elegant but more serviceable design with the walkways giving access to the engines out in the open, and affording much easier maintenance. Locomotives of this type, from both General Motors and the American Locomotive Company (Alco), virtually took over the entire freight working in the USA, operating trains of unprecedented length. On heavy gradients, such as the Sierra Nevada, additional units were cut in at the mid-point of lengthy trains, radio controlled by the engineer on the head-end unit. In Britain the introduction of diesel traction was not so clear cut. The policy of British Railways had been to give trial to a variety of makes and transmissions, and on

the Western Region, for example, all the new power first introduced had hydraulic rather than electric transmission, the former being generally favoured in West Germany, for use on non-electrified lines.

The culmination of steam traction on the railways of the world came to be seen in India and southern Africa. Economic conditions in India, since the attainment of independence, compelled the restriction of imported fuel to a minimum, and with ample supplies of coal available development of the steam locomotive continued. New standard designs for both the broad and the metre gauge, derived from experience with those used in imperial days, continued to be built in large numbers, until it was possible to extend electrification and import sufficient oil to make diesel traction an acceptable alternative. Today the indigenous manufacture of both electric and diesel-electric locomotives is proceeding satisfactorily. In southern Africa the development of the Beyer-Garratt articulated locomotive continued to reach colossal proportions. On the Kenya and Uganda Railway, improved standards of track and road bed permitted of the use on certain routes of locomotives with a 21-tonne axle load, and advantage was taken of this to introduce the exceptionally powerful 59 class, having the 4-8-2 + 2-8-4 wheel arrangement, an all-up weight of 252 tonnes and the very high tractive effort of 37,807 kg (83,350 lb). They are the most powerful locomotives ever to be built for metre gauge track, and they haul freight trains of more than 1,000 tonnes on 1 in 50 gradients between Mombasa and Nairobi.

Electric traction in France, and Britain, and subsequently in many other countries, took a new turn after experiments in France showed that by using 25,000 volts, alternating current, at the commercial frequency of 50 cycles per second, considerable savings could be made in the cost of installation; and in the electrification schemes embodied in the British Railways modernization plan this form of traction supply has been standardized, except on the Southern Region, where large areas were already equipped with the "third rail system" of pick-up, instead of an overhead line. The locomotives used on the London Midland Region, operating the most intense main line express passenger service in the world, are carried on two four-wheeled bogies and develop 5,000 hp. They are capable of hauling a 12-car train of 420 tonnes up a gradient of 1 in 100 at 145 km/h (90 mph).

## 1978

Today the newest forms of railway traction are moving away from the locomotive-hauled train, for high-speed passenger service. In 1964 the New Tokaido Line of the Japanese National Railways was opened, with the so-called "bullet trains" running at speeds of 210 km/h (130 mph) on a specially designed track. The service has proved so popular that today there is one of these trains every 15 minutes from Tokyo to Osaka from 06.00hrs to 21.00hrs. The same general principle is used in the British high-speed train (HST) sets now operating on the Western Region, except that these latter have a 2,200 hp diesel driving unit at each end, whereas the Japanese trains are electric. The Western Region HST sets, running at a maximum speed of 200 km/h (125 mph), provide the fastest and most intense diesel operated service in the world, between London and Bristol, and between London and South Wales. In France construction is now going ahead with an entirely new high-speed line between Paris and Lyon, on which high-speed trains of the unit type, like the Japanese "bullets" and the British HST's, will run at speeds of up to 300 km/h (185 mph). In France the latest electric locomotives are of 8,000 hp, and can run at 200 km/h (125 mph).

*Above left* Steam express in India today. *Left* Regional Transportation Authority locomotive arrives at La Salle Station, Chicago, USA.

*Above* After withdrawal, the world's steam speed record holder *Mallard* was restored for display in Britain's National Railway Museum.

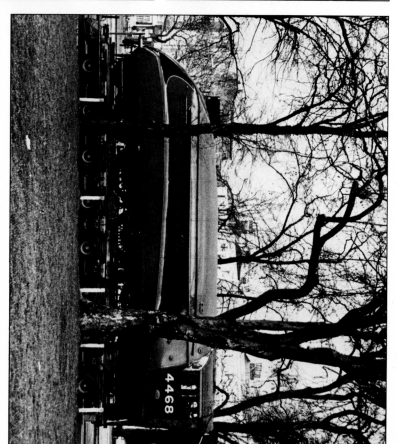

*Below* British Rail's High Speed Train (HST) power unit, containing a 2,250 hp diesel engine. Each trainset has one at each end.

# Cattle trucks to family saloons

*Rolling stock 1800–1875*

**1800** The earliest form of vehicle for conveyance on rails was the colliery tram, or cauldron wagon, designed for carrying coal. It was a four-wheeler, of such a size that it could be pulled by a single horse on one of the rough cart tracks of the day. When such wagons were fitted with flanged wheels and ran on the early form of edge-rails, it was found that a single horse could pull three or four of these wagons, and the type was in general use when the first locomotives were tried out in northeastern England. In early trials men climbed aboard these wagons, for the ride, and when the Stockton and Darlington Railway was opened in 1825 many of those participating, men and women alike, rode in the traditional cauldron wagons. The earliest passenger vehicles varied according to the class of traveller. First class carriages were built to look like the familiar stage-coach, while for third class passengers nothing more than an open truck was provided. Between these two extremes was the second class – an open truck with seats and a canopy over the top to give some protection against the weather. Recalling how passengers travelled on the outside seats of the old stage-coaches, it was not surprising that thoughts turned to double-deck railway coaches, and some quaint examples were built in France and the USA. But in Great Britain the reduced headroom provided from the outset, passing under bridges and through tunnels, precluded the use of double-deckers in the early stages. Indeed, double-decker coaches in Britain have never raised any interest.

Although conditions of rail travel in the pioneer days were not greatly different from those on a stage-coach, at any rate for the outside passenger, the addition of smoke, steam and red-hot cinders from the locomotive chimneys introduced new hardships, particularly as many more people than ever before were travelling. A general outcry against rail travel conditions in Great Britain led to the passing of Gladstone's famous Regulations of Railways Act of 1844. This Act laid down as a legal necessity that on every line of railways there should be at least one train every day on which properly covered-in third class accommodation was provided, at a fare of one penny per mile, and serving every station on the line. The so-called "Parliamentary trains", despite the covered-in carriages, were not the height of luxury. On the first class carriages luggage was usually stacked on the roof, and was sometimes set on fire by sparks from the engine. On the goods

**1850** At an early stage of development larger vehicles were introduced on to the American railways for much the same reason as the traditional 4-4-0 locomotive was adopted. The short wheelbase wagons and passenger carriages did not ride well on the sharply curved and lightly laid tracks, and vehicles for both passenger and goods, carried on two four-wheeled bogies, were much preferred. Thus originated the American passenger car. There were entrances only at the ends; the inside was completely open, without any of the divisions that made a British, or a European, car into a series of compartments. Usually they had a high clerestory roof. Whereas an English passenger train might consist of 12 or 15 four-wheeled carriages, an American train would have no more than three or four of these large bogie cars. For third class passengers there would be little difference in comfort – or lack of it: bare boards was the rule for all. Third class carriages were often in the form of a primitive, unlit, open saloon car with rough wooden benches across the centre, the only ventilation being provided by a few doors. The British four-wheeler of the mid-nineteenth century was a basic feature of operation, and so far as size was concerned the same applied to passengers, parcels, mails, or even horses. They were light, and could be pushed easily by human effort. At the larger stations locomotives were not used for shunting. On each of the tracks there were small turntables, large enough to take one four-wheeler. If it were necessary to transfer a vehicle from one line to a parallel track, it was pushed to a turntable; then the table was rotated through 90 degrees, and the vehicle pushed across the connecting rails on to the turntable for the next track, and then turned until it was in line. These turntables were an inbuilt feature of most early British railway stations, and their existence explains the reluctance of many railway managements to introduce large coaches.

*Top* The Experiment, the first passenger coach, horse drawn, Stockton & Darlington Railway, 1825. *Above* Bodmin and Wadebridge carriage, c. 1845, in National Railway Museum, York. *Right* Captain Powell's transferable carriage, from an old print. A typical eccentric scheme dreamt up for the existing world of railways.

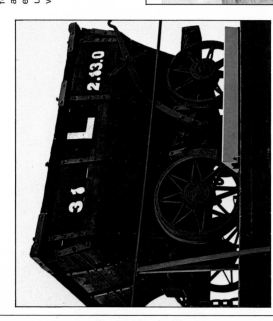

trains cattle were carried in open cage-like vehicles, and the drovers travelled with the animals. While conveyance of coal had been the basic traffic of the earliest railways in the northeast of England, when railways were opened in the rural shires farther south, it was considered *infra dig* to carry coal. When such business was offered to one railway manager he is said to have exclaimed with much indignation: "What, coal by railway – they'll be asking us to carry dung next!"

*Above* Early wagon from Stockton and Darlington Railway. Such designs were an inevitable result of the transfer from road to rail.

*Right* Stock on the Liverpool and Manchester Railway, 1831. One example of innumerable contemporary engravings of the period.

# 1875

A characteristic feature of many British railways in this period was the family saloon. This was usually a four-wheeler that could be chartered on payment of so many first class fares and would be conveyed from anywhere to anywhere. It would be attached to advertised train services, though there would be times of lengthy wait for the next connection at a junction. The accommodation was that of a drawing room, with an adjoining compartment for family servants travelling in attendance. Sometimes in the case of wealthy patrons there would be horseboxes in addition, and these included accommodation for the grooms. At times of the shooting season in Scotland trains from England often included ten or more of these family saloons, many with horseboxes attached. The epitome of comfort and convenience was to be seen in the Royal saloons built especially for Queen Victoria.

At this early stage in railway development the arrangements for braking were primitive. The British passenger train of the 1860s and 1870s had brake vans at the front and rear in which the brakes were applied by the guards, by hand. There was a whistle code, whereby the driver whistled for the brakes to be applied. It is remarkable to recall that by that time passenger trains were regularly running at 96 km/h (60 mph) or more. In America trains had a front and rear brakeman, and on freight trains, which were usually made up of a series of closed box cars, the brakeman would often be seen running along the top of the cars while the train was at speed, applying or releasing the brakes as required. On British freight trains when a severe descending gradient was being approached, it was necessary to stop, for the hand brakes to be applied on a specified number of vehicles before the descent was begun. British freight trains were manned by a single guard, in addition to the locomotive crew, and there was no facility for the work of a travelling brakeman to be done. Because of the conveyance of most freight in box cars, the American goods train presented a more uniform appearance than its British, or Continental, counterpart in the latter part of the nineteenth century.

Coaches have not changed very much over the years in their basic construction, which is essentially a box on a rigid frame spring-mounted on wheels. The actual accommodation has, however, been tempered by a changed society.

*Top* A saloon carriage of the London, Brighton and South Coast Railway, 1873.
*Above* An artist's impression of the new Pullman car introduced on the Great Northern Railway in 1879.
*Below* Plan views of first class carriage on the Moscow and Koorsk Railway around 1880.

# Traffic becomes specialized
*Rolling stock 1876–1924*

**1874** In the last years of the nineteenth century there was a marked transformation in the size and comfort of passenger rolling stock in Great Britain, Continental Europe and in colonial territories. The influence came from the introduction to certain English railways of the American Pullman car. It was a movement that found little favour at first. British railway managements were rather horrified at the size and length of these cars and feared that their inclusion in trains of conventional coaching stock would cause havoc in the case of a derailment or a collision. But the move to provide better accommodation for the lower classes, pioneered on the Midland Railway, gradually gathered impetus. Although the Pullman car as such was adopted on no more than a few railways, longer coaches, carried on two four-wheeled bogies began to come into more general use in the 1880s and 1890s in Britain. At the same time the four-wheelers, designed to suit the old station turntables, had given place to six-wheelers on most of the main lines, and these vehicles were built to quite remarkable lengths, particularly in certain postal vans in service on the east coast route from London (King's Cross) to the North. Even so, at the time of the exciting race to Aberdeen in August 1895, the 20.00 hrs sleeping car express from King's Cross was composed entirely of six-wheeled coaches, including sleeping cars of that size.

On the Continent of Europe a great variety of passenger coaching stock was in use, ranging from the luxurious sleeping cars of the Wagons-Lit company to cramped ill-lit compartment vehicles that were not inaptly nicknamed "dog-boxes". All the older vehicles were built entirely of wood, and the inclusion of more modern steel-framed bogie coaches in the same trains was at times disastrous. This situation prevailed throughout the period up to 1924, and travelling even on "rapides" running to sharp time schedules was apt to be hazardous. In the USA, with railways still providing the premier means of land transport, the large bogie vehicles were advanced to provide increased luxury for those who could pay substantial supplements over the ordinary fares, and in addition to including restaurant and sleeping cars on the night trains, lavishly appointed club cars, lounges and facilities for businessmen were added. For railway officers travelling on official business and entertaining guests, the so-called "business cars" were introduced. These were very large vehicles, including four or more sleeping compartments, a business lounge, private dining room, and usually a stern-walk observation platform, with a first class chef in constant attendance. In Great Britain the corridor carriage came into general use on the principal express trains, and as on the Continent of Europe, but unlike North America, the corridor was at one side of the vehicle, from which entry was made into individual compartments. In America the coaches remained open, with access to seats from a central gangway.

The developing traffic in all parts of the world led to the construction of many special vehicles for freight. The advantages of bulk transport were realized, but with coal, for example, huge bogie wagons carrying 30 tonnes, or more, however excellent on the run, were not entirely convenient because of the difficulty of getting them into the collieries for loading. They were used mostly by the railways themselves for locomotive coal. A problem so far as vehicles for special traffics were concerned was that they were loaded in one direction only, and had to be returned empty. In Britain a great number of collieries and individual coal merchants had their own private wagons, and the liability of the railways to haul these put further restriction upon movement and the most economical use. Apart from coal, there were a great number of miscellaneous private wagons in circulation. Some of the most interesting and specialized of freight wagons were those specially designed for perishable goods, such as refrigerated vans for meat in transit across continents, or taken from ships bringing imports from far overseas. Some British companies made a speciality of running express fish trains from northern ports direct to the larger cities. The wagons used, although four-wheeled, were designed for running up to 96 km/h (60 mph) and were fitted with the continuous automatic brake, as on passenger trains. Vans were also fitted for conveying fruit, fresh vegetables, and spring flowers in bulk. Because of the relatively short journeys involved in transporting these perishable goods from one part of Britain to another, it was not thought necessary to install special refrigeration equipment in the majority of these vehicles.

*Left* WCJS postal van built in 1883 and restored to its original livery for the PO Centenary in 1938. *Below* Iron covered goods wagon.

*Lower* First class coach for South India Railways.

*Left* Victorian mail sorting carriage – a travelling post office.
*Below* Third class coach for Metropolitan Railway.

# 1900

Postal business required the provision of special vans. Travelling post offices were attached to many express passenger trains, and both Britain and the USA introduced several exclusively mail trains. In Britain, at a great number of points mail was collected and set down, without the train stopping, by means of the mechanical pick-up apparatus. Mail was thus delivered to many relatively small communities lying on or near the main train routes. The special mail vans included post letters, for which convenience a small extra charge was made. Although these vans had gangway connections, these were not for the purpose of connecting up to the corridor of the passenger section of the train. The gangways were set to one side, instead of centrally. This was done so that the entrances at each end of a mail van would be clear of the tables running from end to end, and used for sorting mail.

Another specialized traffic on the British railways was that of milk. The large six-wheeled vans with slatted sides have been likened to "prisons on wheels", and into these were loaded in large numbers the once-familiar milk churns. From the rural districts of the West of England, and from west Wales, special trains at almost passenger train speed were run to London and other large city centres. More recently, however, the milk has been conveyed in glass-lined tank cars. Another familiar feature of British railways was the so-called tarpaulin-bar wagon. This was an open four-wheeler, which had a central horizontal bar. It would be used for any consignment that needed covering in transit, and a tarpaulin was passed over the central bar and fastened at the two sides, giving the assembly the look of the gable of a house. Flat trucks were also used on to which special consignments were loaded and secured. These included small private conveyances, vehicles, and containers, brought to the railway goods yards on road vehicles, and there transferred to the railway wagon. This practice, which began in the early 1900s, was the beginning of what developed into the modern technique of the container train.

*Left* A third class carriage in Brittany, France, at the beginning of the 20th century. *Below left* The restaurant car of a French luxury train at the turn of the century. *Top right* Interior of GER first class carriage around the turn of the century. *Centre right* The overhead monorail system between Barmen and Elberfeld-Vohwinkel, this section of the line passes along the river Wupper.

*Below* Stock built for the Great Argentine Railway. *Bottom* Model of coach made for the Bengal-Nagpur Railway in Bengal, 1924, showing the considerable facilities provided for civilized travel.

BENGAL NAGPUR RAILWAY

# Freight improvements: commuter comfort

*Rolling stock 1925 and after*

## 1925

From 1925 onwards there came a greater specialization in freight rolling stock to provide more efficient service and less damage in transit. In North America the universal employment of centre couplers involved buffing and snatching shocks when trains were starting, or being braked. The standard box car was gradually developed to enormous size, up to 27 m (85 ft) long and 5.5 m (18 ft) high, and the improvement in braking techniques enabled long trains of them to be controlled safely. In the USA refrigerator cars, nicknamed "freezers", are used for the transport of great quantities of citrus fruits from California eastward, and at specific points on the long journey the examination of brakes, running gear, and the servicing of locomotives, is supplemented by examination of the cars' icing equipment. The trains are put on to what are termed icehouse tracks. Oil is another traffic that requires special cars, while the massive transport of coal, in enormous bogie gondola cars from which the entire load can be dumped on to a conveyor belt in a few seconds, forms the lifeblood of railways like the Norfolk and Western and the Chesapeake and Ohio. In Great Britain conveyance of coal used to be a very profitable but exceedingly slow business, in lengthy trains of four-wheeled unbraked wagons, rarely travelling at more than 40 km/h (25 mph) and involving much tedious marshalling and remarshalling, and the subsequent return of empty wagons to specific collieries, or other owners. Today the "merry-go-round" principle is used for conveyance of coal, to regular standing orders. The trains are made up of large bogie hopper wagons, equipped with continuous air-brakes, and the diesel-electric locomotives remain coupled during the loading process and then convey them to the power station, running intermediately up to 80 km/h (50 mph) or more. The locomotive remains coupled during the unloading.

On the Continent of Europe freight vehicles have been developed as long wheelbase four-wheelers, that have excellent tracking qualities, and which can be run at speeds up to 80 km/h (50 mph). Through the activities of the International Union of Railways (UIC), a great deal of standardization of size, couplings and brake equipment has been achieved, making convenient the interchange of

vehicles over the railways of Europe. A number have been built to run on the more restricted British loading gauge, thus facilitating the working of through loads to and from the Continent, by one or other of the ferry boat services. Road congestion in all the advanced countries of the world has led to arrangements for delivery of new motor cars by train. In the USA advantage has been taken of the height available for loading to build three-deck automobile carriers, and one "trailer", as they are known, is loaded with 15 automobiles. In Britain and on the Continent two decks is the maximum that can be accommodated. The integration of transport services by road and rail has taken two forms. In Britain long flat trucks are loaded at freight terminals with three containers, where they are lifted from the road vehicles by special overhead cranes. In the USA with the advantage of extra height, the entire road vehicle, including its wheels, is loaded on to the railway flat truck in what is termed a "piggyback" operation. Although primitive forms of such a system had been in use in the USA for many years, it was only in the 1950s that it became economically attractive and developed into the sophisticated operation seen today.

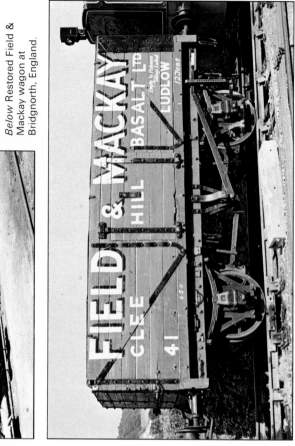

*Top* London-Paris night ferry of Cie Internationale des Wagons Lit, at Gare du Nord, Paris.

*Above* Breakdown train near Waverley, Edinburgh.

*Left* Third class, 4-wheeled wooden RENFE coach at Lorca, Spain.

*Below* Restored Field & Mackay wagon at Bridgnorth, England.

*Left* A simplified automatic air brake showing the principle of two compressed air tanks operating in opposition to each other, to operate the brake cylinder. With the brake on the air is discharged out of the main system, isolating the main compressed air tank, thereby bringing the auxiliary compressed air tank into play to apply the brake. With the brake off the main tank is again fed into the system, supplying the auxiliary cylinder and discharging the air from the brake cylinder, releasing the brake shoe.

**Brake on**

Brake valve — Pressure regulating valve — Main compressed air tank — Auxiliary compressed air tank — Brake cylinder

Brake pipe

Air discharged

3-way valve
piston moved to left by compressed air from auxiliary air tank

**Brake off**

Compressed air — Atmospheric pressure

piston moved to right by compressed air from main air tank

Air discharged

*Above right* Modern double-decker commuter stock on SNCF, France.

*Lower* Peruvian diesel railcar – for rail or road transportation?

*Below* Restaurant car of Iran National Railways in Tehran station.

*Below* British Rail EMU of late 1950s, refurbished 1977, on Western Region.

*Right* Modern stock of Trans-Europe Express.

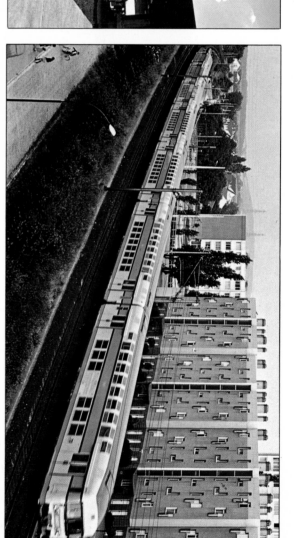

# 1964

So far as main line passenger service is concerned, one of the most important developments is the addition of air conditioning. The discomfort of long-distance inter-city or trans-continental travel, in the USA in particular, with the accompaniment of draughts from open windows, dust, and smoke from heavily fired steam locomotives, is now receding into memory; and it is only when the air conditioning plant on a modern car fails temporarily that discomfort returns, in the form of stifling heat, because the windows cannot be opened. The general tendency in most parts of the world today is to make passenger accommodation on long-distance trains more like that of an airliner. This is partly because of the shortening of journey times, and the growing practice of taking "snack" meals, rather than the elaborate menus of a full restaurant car service. On an increasing number of modern trains arrangements are being made to serve "packaged" meals to every passenger at his seat, again in airline style. The coaching stock now being designed for the new super-high-speed service in France from Paris to Lyon, and beyond, will have passenger seating with no greater space between seats than in a modern airliner. Prior to this present trend vehicles of great luxury were introduced on some routes in Europe, notably the "Grand Confort" coaches on some French trains, such as the all-first class Mistral, Capitole and Aquitaine. In the USA advantage was taken of the height available to build coaches having seating on an upper deck, and baggage space, washrooms, and so on, below. The same principle has been used in the "dome" observation cars run on many American long-distance trains. In Japan, where there is more passenger travel per head of population than anywhere else in the world, the practice of seat reservation by computer has been carried to an all-embracing extent, on the super-high-speed *Shinkansen* bullet trains, in that the act of booking a ticket also confers a reserved seat on a particular train. There are so many of these that if the next train, at the time of booking, is full, one can be fairly sure of getting on to the next following, 15 minutes later. Knowing the number of his coach by the seat reservation, the passenger can wait on the platform in exactly the right position for him to enter the train when the doors open.

The problem of the commuters is acute in all large cities, and in the USA and Canada many double-deck cars of breathtaking size have been built for service around Montreal, Chicago and elsewhere. In North America, however, the intensity of service required is not to be compared with that of London. The need for station stops of no more than 30 seconds would completely preclude the use of double-deck cars such as those used around Chicago, on which all passengers entrain or alight through one door on each side of one of these huge vehicles. Non-corridor compartment stock, with individual doors to every compartment, seems the only solution to a traffic situation such as that existing on the Southern Region of British Rail. On the so-called "rapid transit" lines now operating around cities in many parts of the world, the multiple-unit electric stock, with wide opening sliding doors, is designed to take a high proportion of standing passengers. It has been found that even though there are only two wide openings on each side of a carriage, the designed interior, to make possible easy movement of passengers, and the limitation of the length of individual cars, makes possible rapid station stops even in the rush hours, and to close the doors despite crowding inside. It is only in certain Indian cities that commuters cluster so thickly round doors that they cannot be closed!

# Building on the grand scale
*Railway architecture*

The arrival of the railways demanded innovative and inventive construction in the fields of mechanical and civil engineering. But the one structure that was totally new, and symbolized to the general public the power and prestige of the railways, was the station. Although in its early days the station was a relatively crude affair, matching the locomotives and stock that arrived and departed, very soon, with the rapid expansion of services, stations were being constructed on a grand scale.

At important termini, the demand for a roof span to encompass a great number of tracks and platforms led to the increasing use of cast iron — one of the most striking innovations of nineteenth-century architecture. Throughout Victorian Britain, and also in many other parts of the world, stations of impressive and enduring grandeur were built, combining imposing façades with miracles of train shed construction.

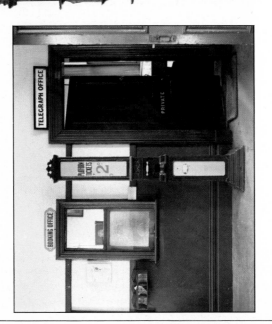

**Britain**
Before the 1830s the finest existing ancestor of the railway station was the Palm House at Kew, London, built between 1844–8. This collaboration of architect and engineer, Decimus Burton and Richard Turner, proved to be typical of many such projects and underlines the contrast between the Victorians' confidence in their technological skills and their conservatism regarding architectural style. This led to an alternation of Classical or Gothic façades that rarely related to the amazing great shed behind them. It is strange that the Crystal Palace, built at the same time as King's Cross station, London, did not inspire complete stations in iron and glass. It did, however, provide an object lesson in prefabrication and the two great arched sheds at King's Cross resembled

*Left* Booking office, Worth Valley Railway, Yorkshire, England. *Above* St Enoch's Underground Station, Glasgow. *Below* Antwerp Station. *Right* Gare de Lyon, Paris.

technically at least the transept of the original Crystal Palace, although they were made of laminated wood (later replaced by steel).

Lewis Cubitt planned King's Cross station the year before the Great Exhibition of 1851 was to give the greatest boost to passenger travel that Britain has ever known. Hundreds of thousands of travellers left their homes for the first time and flocked to London by train. The general confidence in rail travel gained by this enterprise led to the building of many new imposing stations.

The exterior of Paddington station, London (1852–4), is hidden by Philip Hardwick's Great Western Hotel and it is the spatial grandeur of the interior and the attempt by its builders, Wyatt and Brunel, to relate the platform buildings and shed with an unusual design of ornamental metalwork that make it one of the finest early stations.

The most astonishing Gothic façade still remains at St Pancras, London (1868–74), designed by Giles Gilbert Scott. He collaborated with W. H. Barlow who constructed the shed which spans 73.2 m (240 ft) and is 30 m (100 ft) high (see pages 16–17).

## Outside Britain

The rest of the world took Britain's lead for some years and nearly all stations continued to show two methods of construction, one for façades and the other for sheds. In Stuttgart (1911–14), for instance, Paul Bonate and F.E. Scholer produced one of the finest station exteriors of its time. Unbroken masonry wall surfaces and plain rounded arches provided a traditional approach to design that was very different from Hamburg station (1903–6), in which an attempt had been made by the builders, influenced by the Paris Exhibition of 1889, to construct a station in a more genuinely modern manner. In an attempt to improve design, competitions were held in Germany in 1903 for Basel station and in 1907 for Darmstadt. This practice was followed in other countries and the most notable competition winner was Eliel Saarinen who in 1904 won the competition for Helsinki station which he built between 1910–14. This complex and highly original structure is his principal early work. In size and monumentality it rivals

*Above* Interior of Grand Central Station, New York. *Below right* Tunnel keeper's house, Clayton Tunnel, Sussex, England.

Stuttgart and is the most outstanding railway station of the pre-1914 period. In New York traditionalism still ruled and the Pennsylvania Railway Station, built in 1906–10 and now demolished, was a vast building obviously modelled on the Tepidarium of the Baths of Caracalla in ancient Rome.

Eventually a nostalgia for styles of the past was replaced by an enthusiasm for new forms of expression, offered by new materials such as concrete, and a sense of identification with the twentieth century. Florence station (1934–6) was built in the "International Style" which was prevalent in Europe between the wars and is identified by its assymetrical composition of cubic and rectangular shapes devoid of mouldings, smoothly rendered, and relieved by large windows arranged in horizontal bands. It was the most advanced station in the world before the Second World War. It remains to be seen whether any station built in the remainder of this century will surpass Rome's outstanding Termini station, built in 1951.

Wherever in the railway world the traveller may find himself, he is sure to discover many interesting stations, from the grandiose city terminus to the often highly individualistic, but no less architecturally interesting, country stopping places. On these pages we have attempted to illustrate some of this diversity.

*Above* Aerial view of Bern station. *Below* Modern Dutch station.

# The paraphernalia of railways

Apart from an architectural form, railways have helped to create a whole world of paraphernalia and related ephemera. Each railway company has moved through a series of images, each expressing its individuality through uniforms, badges, tickets, and a host of other detail. Indeed each railway engine, especially in the days of steam, had its own trappings, which when the day of doom struck made many a collector happy, and many a dealer rich. The nameplate of a famous locomotive may well fetch over £1,000 today. While much of the past has been lost, the public in many countries has been left with a fine representative sample in a multitude of museums and railways preserved by enthusiasts. Meanwhile the paraphernalia continues to be generated.

Apart from the paraphernalia of the railways themselves, there are also its first cousins the postage stamp, the cigarette card, and especially the model locomotives built to a variety of scales. To these, too, the enthusiast rushes. Many a country has taken its railway system as a source of national pride and has issued a variety of postage stamps. But probably the most meaningful remembrance of the glories of the railway era is symbolized by the model train. While model racing cars now compete for interest, the sheer glamour of the locomotive and its rolling stock shines through and the child's love of his clockwork engine can turn into the grown-up's desire for the most finely detailed model locomotive – often at considerable expense.

*Above* Railways have provided a theme for many nations' stamps.

*Left* Plaque commemorating the opening of a new stretch of the *Shinkansen* in Japan.

*Left* Manufacturer's plate from German locomotive.

*Above* Brass locomotive model made in Japan.

*Below* Variety of US model stock.

*Below* Tōkyō Express on the Imperial Railway, Japan. One of a set of cigarette cards published by the Imperial Tobacco Co Ltd, circa 1896.

# How Railways Work Now

# The eclipse of steam

The steam locomotive was unquestionably the simplest, cheapest and most reliable form of motive power ever devised for railways; but its cheapness related mainly to first cost. After the Second World War, when the immediate rehabilitation of British Railways was in hand, and economic considerations were uppermost, R. A. Riddles, the member of the Railway Executive responsible for mechanical and electrical engineering, said that investment would first be made in the form of traction that gave the most tractive effort per pound sterling. At that time a diesel locomotive cost two and a half times that of a steam locomotive of equal tractive power. On a longer term view, however, steam locomotives had many disadvantages in the new era then opening out. Fuel was a major problem. Although railways in many parts of the world were using alternatives, coal was still the most generally used, and its cost was rapidly increasing. Furthermore, with the introduction of coal cutting machinery in the mines, the form in which it was received on the railways was not ideal for locomotive firing, and troubles were frequently experienced with inadequate steam production. There was also the question of labour availability, because even the smallest steam locomotive needed two men in constant attention, and changing attitudes towards working conditions after the Second World War were tending to make work on a steam locomotive unattractive.

Quite apart from the actual manning and running of steam locomotives, their percentage availability was relatively low. While much had been done in the 1930s to reduce the work content of daily servicing, by the introduction of such devices as self-cleaning smokeboxes, hopper ashpans and streamlined processes of attention at running sheds, the fact remained that one could rarely schedule duties taking up more than about ten hours out of 24, and then only with the closest attention to all matters of servicing. The average utilization was much less. With steam locomotives spending a considerable time "on shed", space and housing were becoming uneconomical.

By contrast, the diesel locomotive started with several evident advantages, once the initial cost had been covered.

It needed very little in the way of daily servicing, and its first cost could be balanced by its much higher availability – roughly double that of steam. This meant that many fewer locomotives would be needed to work the traffic. With much less time spent "on shed", a great economy in space could be made – in fact locomotive depots began to take the form of roadside filling stations, so little was the time that individual units were out of traffic. The most difficult problem to be faced was in covering the time of transition from one form of motive power to the other, because in one respect diesels, if not properly cared for, could become a far greater liability than steam. It was vitally necessary to keep steam and diesel servicing facilities separate. Diesels should not be housed, or serviced, amid the inevitable dirt of a steam shed.

The power to weight ratio of non-steam locomotives is often quoted to their advantage. In North America

particularly the performance characteristics of a diesel-electric showed up to remarkable advantage over steam on severe gradients. At speeds below 32 km/h (20 mph) the power to pull is roughly double that of a steam locomotive of nominally equal tractive power, whereas at 80 km/h (50 mph) and over the advantage, if any, would lie with steam. On the Euston-Glasgow route, electric locomotives of 80 tonnes total weight develop 5,000 hp, whereas the largest and most modern steam Pacifics, with an all-up weight of 160 tonnes, developed around 2,000 hp.

Steam today: *Above left* Barry scrapyard. *Above right* Taj Express, Delhi. *Below* Nairobi station, locomotive No 2423 simmers in the sun.

# Diesel motive power

The diesel heavy-oil engine starts with a big theoretic advantage over steam in its much higher thermal efficiency, and in its use of a lower grade of fuel than is necessary for the ordinary motor car. Although not to the same extent as the petrol engine, the diesel is a quick-running engine compared with the reciprocating steam locomotive, which drives direct on its "road" wheels. A steam express passenger locomotive with driving wheels of 2 m (6.5 ft) diameter will be making about 300 rpm when running at 113 km/h (70 mph), whereas the normal engine speed of diesels extends from about 750 rpm upwards. But again, while the steam locomotive has a variable-speed engine, with a working range from 0 up to 300 rpm or more, the engine itself in a diesel locomotive needs to be kept running at approximately constant speed, and there must be interposed between the engine and the road wheels some form of transmission gear, as with a petrol engine. Before describing the various types of diesel engine that have been used in rail traction, the two principal types of diesel engine in general use should be mentioned. The great majority are the relatively slow-running marine type, exemplified by the Sulzer, General Motors, and General Electric designs, which have an engine speed of about 800 rpm. But the other type, the Napier quick-running aero type "Deltic" engine, has had an outstandingly successful record in a small specialist application on the railways of Great Britain.

Among transmissions, the simplest is mechanical, though the power to be transmitted precludes the use of a purely manual gearbox, as on a motor car. One of the most successful early applications in Britain was on the former Great Western Railway, which in collaboration with the AEC of Southall, builders of London's buses, introduced diesel powered railcars in the 1930s, with a precisely similar type of engine an transmission to that then in use on the buses. This included the well-tried Wilson gearbox, which is the best-known application of epicyclic change-speed gearing to locomotives and railcars. This utilizes the so-called "sun and planet" type of mechanism, and can be built with either a four- or five-speed arrangement. The

*Below* British Rail diesel mechanical shunter. *Below right* West German diesel hydraulic loco.

The diesel engine cycle might be mistaken for that of the petrol engine, but the spark of the latter is missing. The power stroke depends on the compression taking place which provides the condition for ignition. Fuel is injected into the cyl-inder into which it enters in an atomised state. Multi-cylinder diesel engines provide the power plant for mechanical and hydraulic transmissions to the wheel, and for conver-sion into electric power in diesel-electric systems. The main dis-advantage of diesel systems is the high weight involved.

gear changing was effected by compressed air cylinders, although in retrospect the traditional locomotive engine-men, used to steam, were puzzled at first over the matter of changing gear. These railcars were introduced at a time when private cars were the exception rather than the rule among railways employees of British Railways. There is a story told of the driver who felt ashamed to go home and tell his wife that he had "been trying to drive a blue pencil motor bus". However, all the drivers became expert enough in a very short time.

Mechanical transmissions, however, could be used only for relatively small power units, and it was electric transmission that became the most usual in the very rapid changeover from steam to diesel traction in the USA, in the years just after the Second World War. Before proceeding to a description of electrical transmission, it must be explained that a so-called diesel-electric locomotive is really an electric locomotive in all its traction characteris-tics, but one that carries its own powerhouse. A diesel-electric locomotive is entirely self-contained, as with steam, needing only supplies of fuel and water, to be taken at intervals according to the built-in capacity of its fuel and water tanks.

*Above* 35 class diesel hydraulic, Nairobi.

*Right* Wheel notation used for diesel and electric stock, with all their variations, appears more mysterious than that used for steam locos. Numbers are given for carrying axles, letters are used for driving axles: A=1, B=2, C=3. Axles which are in-dividually driven are suffixed 'O'. This system is also used on the Continent of Europe for class-ifying steam locos.

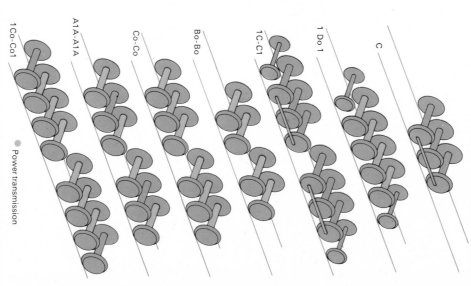

C

1 Do 1

1C-C1

Bo-Bo

Co-Co

A1A-A1A

1Co-Co1

● Power transmission

# Electric and hydraulic transmissions

Radiator cooling fan | Diesel engine | Turbocharger | Exhaust | Electrical control cubicle

Traction motor | Radiator | Power lines to traction motors | Battery box | Generator | Exciter

In a diesel-electric locomotive there is no physical connection between the engine and the road wheels. It should more correctly be called an electric locomotive that carries its own power generating station. In most designs the generator, and the diesel engine that drives it, are mounted on a common foundation, built as a single entity, while the electric traction motors are quite separate and carried directly on the driving axles of the locomotive. On the Peak class 1-C-C-1 of Britain Rail, for example, there are six traction motors, three on each bogie. These locomotives have the Sulzer double-bank type of diesel engine, whereas the earlier British diesel-electric locomotives had the added complication of having to carry steam generators. They were introduced at a time when all main line passenger coaching stock in Britain was steam heated, and the auxiliary electrical generator, coupled to the main generator and part of the engine unit, had to have additional capacity to feed the steam generator when it was required. While the output of the main generator could be varied according to the immediate demands for power from the traction motors, the output from the auxiliary generator had to be kept constant.

The transmission of power between the main generator and the traction motors is controlled by the driver, by a handle operating the power controller. This operates the traction motor contactors, regulates the diesel engine speed, and varies the excitation current of the main generator according to requirements. All these controls are interconnected and electrically interlocked one with another, actuated by the movement of the one driving handle.

In West Germany the hydraulic system of transmission is favoured, and for a time this system was standard on the Western Region of British Rail. German manufacturers have also exported locomotives of this type to many parts of the world. The transmission is different from that of diesel-electric locomotives in that there is direct mechanical connection between the engine and the road wheels. The diesel engine crankshaft is connected to the fluid transmission unit through a device called a Cardan shaft, which consists of a telescopic shaft with a universal joint at each end. There is a separate diesel engine for each bogie of the locomotive, and the transmission unit is mounted so that its drive wheel is on the centre line of the bogie, in the case of a locomotive with two four-wheeled bogies. From this drive shaft Cardan shafts extend fore and aft to the final drive on the axle of the road wheels. The hydraulic form of transmission has the advantage that there is less weight actually carried on the bogie, but the usage of diesel-hydraulic locomotives on British Rail is now virtually at an end, those on the Western Region being phased out.

When diesel-electric locomotives were first installed it was thought that the effect on the track would be less severe than with steam: that the smooth action, in contrast to the fluctuation of load due to the rotation of heavy parts, would be beneficial. In fact there was no advantage, because of the heavy weight of traction motors carried low down on the actual bogie axles, which caused a pounding action not previously experienced. In the very successful "all-adhesion" electric locomotives introduced in Switzerland at the end of the Second World War, the traction motors are not mounted on the bogies. These types of locomotive have been used in other railway systems, the Swiss having always been world leaders in this field.

*Top* SD 40 units 5581 and 5745 stand with a freight train in Vancouver depot yard.
*Above left* Basic layout in a diesel-electric locomotive, with the power flow from power unit to traction motor.
*Right* British Rail class 56 in erecting shop; the ventilator grill is being lowered into position, with one of the bogies in the foreground.

*Right* Lowering the diesel engine into a British Rail High Speed Train power car.

# Electric traction

Series E 410 electric locomotive built for German Federal Railways. This is a multi-current locomotive designed to run under all four of the main European current systems. This Bo-Bo loco-motive has a 4,300 hp one-hour rating and a starting output of 6,800 hp, which for a mere 84 tonnes weight is a considerable achievement. Multi-current equipment carried is increased by the need to cope with the different systems, though this has been tempered with the introduction of thyristor controls. Never-theless the mechanical parts had to be designed to be as light as possible to accommodate the con-siderable weight of electrical equipment. Other particulars include a total length of 16,950 mm, an hourly output of around 3,200 kW (more on later models), a continuous power output at between 89 and 145 km/h of 3,000 kW, a maximum tractive effort of 28,000 kg and a maximum speed of 150 km/h (93 mph).

There is a considerable diversity of electric traction systems on the railways of the world, largely because of the different eras in which the various countries made major investment and consequent standardization. The four systems now in widespread use in Europe are: (1) 1,500 volt dc in the Netherlands and earlier French lines. (2) 3,000 volt dc in Belgium, Poland, Italy and Czechoslo-vakia. (3) 15,000 volt ac at $16\frac{2}{3}$ cycles, in West Germany, Norway, Sweden, Austria and Switzerland. (4) 25,000 volt ac at 50 cycles, standard in Britain for all except the third rail dc system of Southern Region; it is standard for new works in France, and is being generally adopted in all countries installing main line electric traction today, notably in Hungary and India. The 3,000 volt dc system is used in Brazil, Chile and South Africa.

The 25,000 ac system has the advantage of being considerably cheaper to install, requiring lighter overhead conductor wires and lighter supporting structures. It was first adopted on a large scale in France, in preference to the previous standard 1,500 volt dc system, after extensive trials and close comparison of costs with a line largely used by heavy freight between Valenciennes and Thionville. The particular attraction of the system lay not only in the reduced initial cost of the lineside equipment, but that the development of static devices for converting alternating to

*Below shows the construction of an electric locomotive at the Swedish firm of ASEA, who have con-tributed much to the development of modern electric motive power.*

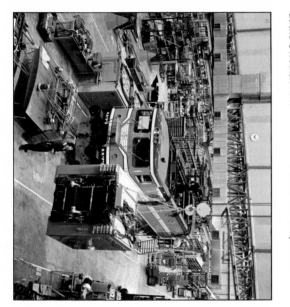

direct current made it possible to operate the overhead line at the industrial frequency of 50 cycles per second, and at high voltage, and yet retain the advantage of the direct current traction motor for driving the axles of locomotives and the motored axles of multiple-unit trains. In Europe the existence of four different systems of overhead line electrification is now no obstacle to the working of many international services without the need for changing locomotives, or power units, at national frontiers. The French Railways have introduced powerful electric loco-motives carrying four pantographs, each of which can be raised, as required, to suit the supply voltage and type of overhead wire design. They can pass from one traction system to another without stopping. Power is shut off on the approach to a frontier point, and the train allowed to coast until under the wires of the new network. Then the appropriate pantograph is raised.

The latest French electric locomotives working on the Eastern Region main line from Paris to Nancy and Strasbourg include a feature of control that enables the driver to pre-set and automatically maintain the speed he requires. The route includes numerous changes in gra-dient, while the maximum speed permitted is constant over long sections. The pre-setting device can be set, for example, to correspond with a line maximum speed of, say, 145 km/h (90 mph). Once this is done the locomotive will maintain that speed whatever the gradient. The fastest French running today, however, is performed over lines equipped with the 1,500 volt dc system, from Paris to Bordeaux and Paris to Toulouse. The locomotives working the 200 km/h (125 mph) trains on these routes are of approximately 8,000 hp. In Britain on the Euston-Glasgow route, with the aim of simplifying the drive between motors and axles, one series of 100 locomotives was built with the motors axle-slung, as on diesel-electric types. But lengthy experience, and a tendency to poor riding, led in later designs to a return to the previous use of frame mounted motors with a flexible drive.

Pantograph *Dutch/Belgian*

Pantograph *French*

Main switch ac

Circuit breaker

Pantograph *German/Austrian*

Pantograph *Dutch/Belgian*

Control equipment and field-weakening of motors

Control gear

Traction motor ventilator

Signalling equipment

Main transformer

Smoothing choke

Traction motor ventilator

Electronic motor rectifiers

Starting and braking resistances

High tension control equipment

Auxiliary machinery

Electronic controls

Brake rigging

Lateral beams

Traction motors

Rubber ring flexible drive

# High-speed trains

*Above* Part of the new Rome-Florence high-speed line, the Italian answer to modern regional inter-city transit.
*Left* Fiat tilting rolling stock designed for the new high-speed services.

*Above* RTV 31 Hovertrain on test at Earith, England, in 1971. The project was unsuccessful as the manufacturers, Tracked Hovercraft Ltd, failed to receive enough government backing. *Above right and right* The French monorail prototype, which was also an ill-fated endeavour.

**Hydraulic system**
1 Tilt jack
2 Pressure line : left tilt
3 Pressure line : right tilt
4 Control valve
5 Accelerometer
6 Pump
7 Accumulator
8 Reservoir

In the railway context, "high speed" must necessarily be a relative term, and relate to something that travels a great deal faster than anything else on the particular line; but here we are referring to trains that run at more than 160 km/h (100 mph). There are still not many places in the world where the speed is achieved, having regard to the total of railway length. However, speeds are increasing and the marked trend is to ever increase both maximum and overall speed. This urge to accelerate is affecting all the advanced countries of the world with new style trains being introduced in Italy, Canada and the Soviet Union, in addition to those of France and Britain. It is therefore extremely important to have a full appreciation of the manifold factors that are involved, quite apart from the vital primary need to provide constant tractive power in a form that will make the higher speeds attainable and capable of being sustained – all with an economic use of fuel. Engineers of today are widely aware of all the different technological disciplines that must be satisfied, including the need for an economic use of fuel, before a super-high-speed service can be offered to the travelling public, and they are unlikely to fall into the traps that ensnared their predecessors of more than 100 years ago, who developed the steam locomotive to feats of speed before the track was ready to take it safely, and before the means of stopping it were adequate.

Two quite distinct ways of introducing high-speed trains are in progress today, the first by building special purpose new railways, such as the Japanese *Shinkansen* and the French TGV, and the second by upgrading existing lines. From the engineering rather than the financial viewpoint the second method is by far the more difficult, especially on such old-established railways as those of Britain. The cost of realigning curves and remaking difficult junctions to

permit of uninterrupted high speed can be prohibitive, while in mountainous country the physical circumstances could well make the project impossible. It is to meet these conditions that the principle of the so-called "tilting" train has been developed. The first production units of the British Advanced Passenger Train are expected in service in 1978, and by utilizing a mechanism that causes the train to adjust itself to the curves by a tilting action of the body in relation to the bogies, it can safely negotiate existing curves at far higher speeds than are permissible with conventional rolling stock. Maximum speeds of up to 250 km/h (155 mph) are planned.

The braking on all high-speed trains, and the difficulties that arise on a "mixed" railway like those of Britain, are highlighted when a direct comparison is made of the signalling arrangements on the Euston to Crewe section of the West Coast Main Line and what is proposed for the Paris-Lyon TGV line in France. On the Euston-Crewe line the four-aspect colour light signals are spaced, on an average, about 1,100 m (1,200 yd) apart. The lead-up to a red signal is first a double yellow, and then a single yellow, so that the distance from the first warning to the red, where the train must stop, is 2,200 m (2,400 yd). This provides a safe margin for trains travelling at a maximum of 160 km/h (100 mph), consisting of ordinary coaching stock hauled

The tilting mechanism associated with all ultra high-speed trains today is shown *above* in the Italian Fiat model. The hydraulic system, which effects a maximum tilt of 9°, is that developed for the British Rail APT. Other systems exist in operation or development in North America, France and the USSR, but there is no doubt that a considerable spread will occur, though operation of such trains while utilizing existing track nevertheless demands the highest standards, which will be attainable only with complete reconstruction.

by electric locomotives. The diesel powered HSTs are equipped with special braking equipment, which enables them to stop from 200 km/h (125 mph) in the same distance taken by ordinary trains from 160 km/h (100 mph). On the French TGV line, by contrast, the distance between signals is to be exactly double that between Euston and Crewe, and the normal stopping distance allowed is to be four sections, or 8,780 m (9,600 yd). Nevertheless, the trains will be equipped with brakes to permit of an emergency stop in 3,750 m (4,100 yd), from a speed of 274 km/h (170 mph). The line can be signalled in this way because it will be used exclusively by the TGV trains.

Another important point to be considered in the running of very high-speed trains is that of passenger comfort. Again it is not the comfort 'in flight', as it were, although the passenger has yet to experience the sensation on a considerable curve when the tilting feature of the Advanced Passenger Train, or its overseas counterparts, comes into play. In the ordinary way the passenger is not aware of curves when the speed is precisely that for which the cant of the track has been designed. It will be the sensation in the train when the brakes are applied on sight of an adverse signal. Up to now the effect on a diesel-powered HST when braked hard from 200 km/h (125 mph) is not noticeably different from that in an ordinary train in similar circumstances from 153 or 160 km/h (95 or 100 mph), though the initial rate of deceleration is necessarily higher. From 250 km/h (155 mph) it may be noticeable. A further consideration is that of the signal sighting at such speeds, with colour light signals already coming up, on the Euston-Crewe line, every 25 seconds at 160 km/h (100 mph), and with audible signals in the cab to mark each location. This can be compared with the more secluded atmosphere in the cab of a Japanese *Shinkansen* train with no visible or audible signals, and only the speed direction to observe. Also the *Shinkansen* train does not have to provide for other classes of traffic in addition to the 160 km/h (100 mph) 'flyers'. On the French TGV line, at 290 km/h (180 mph) the signal locations will be passed at intervals of about 28 seconds, which will compare closely with British Rail's Euston-Crewe system.

A model of the Japanese linear motor train. This scheme, like others in the UK and Germany, has failed to continue development with any reasonable momentum, but many think it is the motive power (if that is the correct description) of the future. Operation depends on electrification or in some cases hovering devices, motion then taking place by linear means.

*Left and right* The French TGV prototype on test, destined for the new Paris-Lyon high-speed line. The basic prototype was powered by a gas turbine, as was the British APT, but likewise in the production overhead electric power will be used for economic reasons. The mock-up on the left is being pressure-tested by the passing of an in-service train.

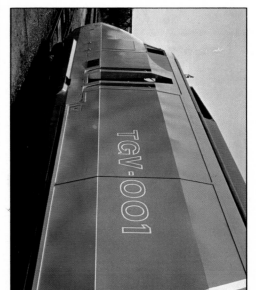

*Left* The British Rail APT-P power car fitted for overhead electrical pick up. The livery is still provisional. The power car will be in the centre of the trainset providing limited access between the two sections. This is to prevent extensive buckling. *Below left* The APT-E prototype set. Here the power unit is at the end as in this early prototype gas turbine motive power was used.

It is interesting to compare the locomotive power on the high-speed lines. As mentioned previously, the latest electric units on the Euston-Glasgow route are of 5,000 hp and they haul trains of up to 12 coaches on the fastest timings. The Western Region HST trains of seven passenger coaches are powered by two 2,200 hp diesel units, for running at 200 km/h (125 mph) on level track. On the Japanese *Shinkansen* trains, which consist of 16 cars, every axle in the train is motored, making up a total of 16,000 hp. The designed speed on the later sections is 257 km/h (160 mph), but the distribution of power throughout the train gives a very smooth ride, and almost imperceptible braking. On the French TGV trains, which will have eight cars and six bogies out of 13 motored, the combined horsepower of the two power units is 8,500. It is considered that this is not excessive considering the speeds to be run; but the designers hope that a certain amount of power will be saved at the very high speeds by the elaborate streamlining of the nose and tail of these trains. The weight of the eight passenger coaches of these trains is 405 tonnes, compared to the maximum of 610 tonnes hauled by the CC6500 class 8,000 hp electric locomotives at 200 km/h (125 mph) on the Paris-Bordeaux route.

# Permanent way: laying the track

Ditch to intercept run-off from above
Side ditch
Side drain
Track
Ballast
Lower drain
Lower intercepting ditch

Pipe drain to catch water permeating ballast

Although it is possible to run trains over a lightly-engineered track formation, any line over which it is hoped to run trains at speed, and/or locos and vehicles with a heavy axle loading, has to be fully prepared.
Standards recommended for main lines by the American Railway Engineering Association are shown, *left*.

Two types of clips are shown *below*, both used extensively today, and both of which can be used in conjunction with concrete or wooden sleepers, and different types of base plate. The accent is on strength and flexibility, but ease of installation is also a major factor.

*Below* Track is maintained to high standards in certain countries, but in many parts of the USA this is not the case and derailments are frequent.

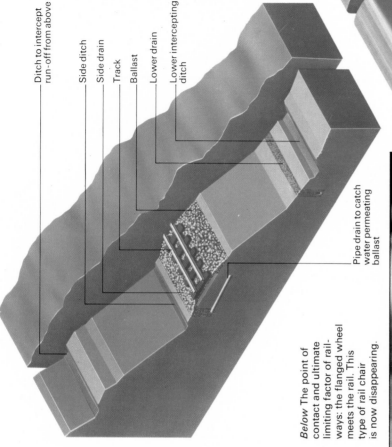

*Below* The point of contact and ultimate limiting factor of railways: the flanged wheel meets the rail. This type of rail chair is now disappearing.

New railways for heavy modern traffic are being built in Iran, France and Japan, and have recently been completed in Australia. Also on certain British main routes what is virtually a new railway has been built over the tracks of one more than 100 years old. The very heavy utilization of refurbished British and French routes, and their success in carrying fast and frequent traffic at unprecedented speeds, has provided an invaluable fund of experience for the building of new railways. The problems in laying out and building new railways in countries like Iran and in the remoter parts of Australia differ considerably, because even with today's modern equipment there are difficulties of terrain, of procuring indigenous labour, and of climate, that can well dictate much of the form a new railway will take. The traffic forecast can also play a major part. For example, a new line in the style of the Japanese *Shinkansen* would not be engineered if the principal traffic was likely to be in heavy minerals.

A major consideration is the economic factors involved in alternative methods of construction. While it is clearly desirable to avoid heavy gradients as far as possible, because this will lessen operating costs on a completed line, with modern motive power this is not so important as in the days of steam traction. The spectacular civil engineering of some of the early British lines, through relatively easy country, was due to the limited tractive power of early locomotives and their inability to climb a gradient at good speed with a paying load. It is interesting to compare the approximate relative costs of laying a new railway by

hand, as might be considered in a country having an abundance of local labour, and by mechanized methods. In the simple preparation of the roadbed, removing topsoil, trimming sides and cutting drainage slopes, the difference for an 18 m (60 ft) length of single track would be between 150 man hours by hand, and four man hours by machine. It can be imagined what the difference would be if deep cuttings or high embankments had to be formed. On new lines the ballasting is often done in two stages, one-third of the total volume being put down in advance of track laying and two-thirds afterwards. In the actual laying of the track itself, the difference in cost can be relatively small where labour is cheap, but mechanical laying is four to five times as fast, and would therefore cause less interference to the laying of the bottom ballast. On double- or multiple-track routes where a closely adjoining track is available for railborne appliances, replacement of old track can be expeditiously effected by laying completely prefabricated track direct from transporter vehicles alongside.

The most remarkable example of new railway construction in recent times is that of the new Frenchline from Paris to the southeast, which is being planned for continuous running at 300 km/h (185 mph). All the preliminary work was preceded by comprehensive aerial surveys, and with particular regard to the environment, great care has been taken to avoid towns and villages.

Because there will be an abundance of power built into the new electric trainsets, gradients as steep as 1 in 29 are included. Although the line has been engineered to provide a notably straight course, and consequent freedom from speed restrictions on account of curves, the inclusion of such steep gradients has meant that in hilly country tunnels are avoided, although there are several lengthy viaducts. By use of modern earthmoving equipment, construction has proceeded rapidly, and with the surveys providing for convenient "cut and fill" techniques, the spoil excavated from relatively shallow cuttings has been readily moved to form the contiguous shallow embankments in the undulating countryside.

The underlying reason for the construction of the new French line, an addition to the network of the national railways, was that the existing main line of the former Paris, Lyon and Mediterranean Railway was at times approaching traffic saturation point. The new line, with its anticipated acceleration of service, is expected to attract much extra traffic. The Japanese *Shinkansen* lines were built for similar reasons. In contrast, however, some of the most interesting lines built recently in Australia have been entirely private commercial enterprises, connected with long-range projects for the export of coal and iron ore. The cost of a first class main line railway, through harsh and barren country, has been no more than one part of the capital investment in mining plant, mechanized handling equipment at the mines and port of shipment, and provision of houses, shops and recreational facilities to attract workers to an otherwise unattractive part of the country.

The evolution of track itself has passed through several stages to arrive at its present standard of excellence and general reliability. The one-time highly favoured British "chaired" track is now obsolete, though considerable lengths of it will no doubt remain in service for many years, on secondary, and slower running lines. It arose from the concept of the great pioneer engineer Joseph Locke, who propounded the idea of a rail that was shaped like a dumbbell, having the same sized heads and which could be turned over when the upper edge was worn, thus doubling its life. It was not successful, because the undersurface resting in the cast iron supporting chair became damaged with the constant pressure of traffic. But although the equal headed rail was abandoned the bullhead type survived, and until the end of the Second World War remained the British standard. Nearly everywhere else in the world the Vignoles, or flat-bottomed rail was standard; but a British investigation towards a future standard favoured the flat-bottomed rail, because it had a greater lateral stiffness for the same weight per metre, and was thus likely to need less work in maintaining a good line. This was an important feature at a time when labour was scarce, and the cost of it steadily rising.

On most overseas railways up to the end of the Second World War, flat-bottomed rails had been spiked directly to the cross-ties, or sleepers as they are known in Britain; but a

feature of British track had always been a slight inwards inclination of the rails toward each other to give a centring effect and to counteract quickly any tendency of locomotives or rolling stock to yaw from side to side. To achieve the same effect with flat-bottomed rails involved the insertion of slightly tapered bedplates between the sleeper and the foot of the rail. At the same time the need was felt for a more positive form of anchor than the simple dog spike used in America. Great ingenuity was shown among British manufacturers in the design of spikes, or clips which had a spring feature, and these have been used in great quantities on the modernized high-speed routes in Britain, and are now becoming favoured on some of the most heavily used railways in the British Commonwealth. Sleeper design has also become a specialized job. A rectangular section of timber is of course the simplest, and is still almost universal in North America, where ample supplies of suitable wood are available. In Europe, and particularly in Britain, reinforced concrete is generally superseding wood, which previously was of Baltic pine. Concrete sleepers can be designed in a shape to provide strength in conformity to the distribution of stress due to passing traffic, and it has been used with conspicuous success on the high-speed electrified line from London (Euston) to the north. The French railways are also adopting concrete sleepers, but in a different form. Whereas the British design consists of a continuous concrete member, the French has two concrete blocks, one beneath each rail, connected by a steel tie-bar. This design is also giving excellent service on high-speed routes.

An essential of all track, and particularly where continuous welded rails are used, as on most high-speed routes in Britain, is a solid and well maintained bed of ballasting. This is usually provided by granite chippings of regular size solidly packed beneath and around the sleepers and having an outer frame of considerable width beyond the sleepers. With such adequate and well maintained ballasting no trouble is experienced with continuous welded rails, which do not have the freedom to expand longitudinally with changes in temperature; the stresses due to temperature change are taken up internally. Another essential of good track is a carefully designed system of drainage, and close attention to areas where the subsoil is clay. There is a tendency for clay to work up and impregnate the ballast, but this is counteracted by the insertion of a thick "blanket" of finely powdered granite between the clay and the bottom of the ballast. Experiments have been made in France and Britain with the so-called "slab-track" used on parts of the Japanese *Shinkansen* lines. Instead of the ballast there is first a base slab of concrete extending to the full width of the ordinary sleepers, and on top of this is a paved slab. This latter takes the place of the rails and their baseplates. One of the great advantages of this design is in tunnels, in the reduction in depth it makes possible. It was installed to useful effect in certain tunnels in the approach to Glasgow from the south, when the line was electrified and the rails needed to be lowered from their previous height to give space above for the overhead electric wires.

*Left* New concrete slab track laid beside traditional way. The absence of ballast is clearly visible.

The most advanced method of track laying, utilizing a continuous concrete bed, is still under development in the UK. PACT (Paved Concrete Track), *below*, has already been used to overcome the problems of under-bridge electrification where ballast bedding provides insufficient clearance. 40 m (130 ft) of PACT can be laid by a 'paving train' in one hour.

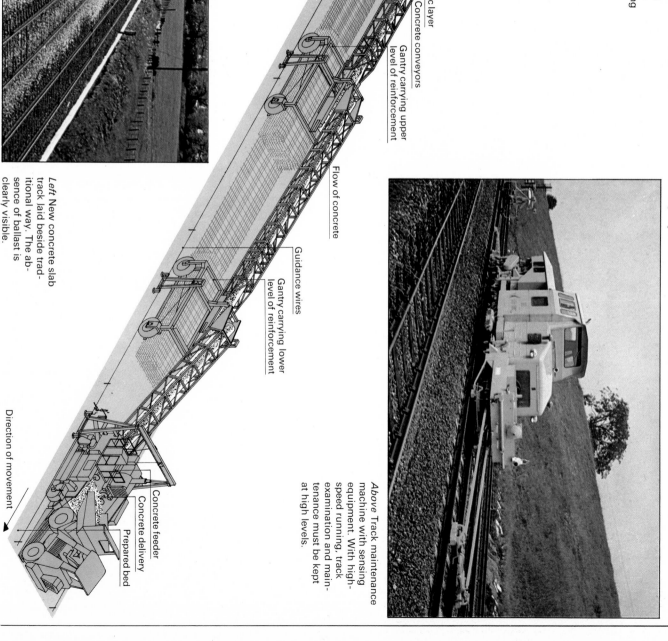

Finished concrete bed ready for track laying

Slipform paving machine

Fabric layer

Concrete conveyors

Gantry carrying upper level of reinforcement

Flow of concrete

Guidance wires

Gantry carrying lower level of reinforcement

Concrete feeder

Concrete delivery

Prepared bed

Direction of movement

*Above* Track maintenance machine with sensing equipment. With high-speed running, track examination and maintenance must be kept at high levels.

# Permanent way: smooth running

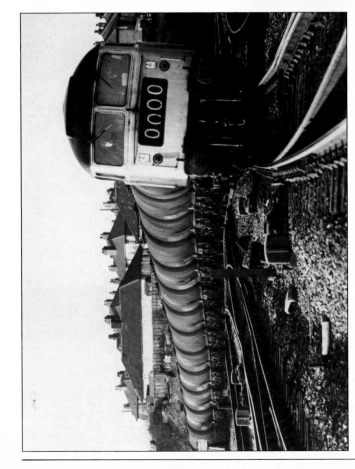

*Left* An empty oil train pulled by class 47 loco leans to the cant of the main line curve while leaving Hunslet oil terminal, Yorkshire, England. *Right* Welded rail joint showing original fish-plate holes.

*Right* The frog or nose point of a crossover.

*Below left* A very worn blade on a set of points in a US yard. *Below right* Series of crossovers on the entrance to a German station.

The need to reduce the cost of track maintenance and at the same time provide a road of consistently high quality on which speeds of 160–200 km/h (100–125 mph) can be run with complete safety has led to the design of many ingenious machines for such tasks as ballast cleaning, checking alignment, and, when repairs are needed, for changing sleepers without disturbing unduly the adjoining sleepers and ballast. In former days the alignment was checked by the gauger getting down on to his knees and simply looking along the rails. These men, with a lifetime of experience, were consummate experts at the job, and with two or three plate-layers to hand with their crowbars, any slight irregularities in line were quickly corrected. Today there is neither the time nor the labour for this skilled task. Nowadays one of the greatest boons to track maintenance is the automatic self-levelling and tamping machine, the word "tamping" meaning the packing of the ballast round the sleepers. Many variations of this machine are used throughout the world, one of which has an alignment feature combined.

In keeping with the great advances in the basic design of track on what is termed "plain line" – that is where there are no points, crossings or other intersections – have been the developments in switches, and in the method of their operation. As in so many aspects of modern railway equipment and working, it is often a question of line capacity. For example, at the branching of two first class main lines, one route will probably be straight and the other involve a diversion. Even with the most advanced type of junction switch in use until recently, a speed restriction to about 72 km/h (45 mph) would have been called for on the diverging route. But today what are called "high-speed turnouts" are installed, enabling the divergent line to be taken at 113 km/h (70 mph). These are also used on certain quadruple track sections to enable a train to change tracks at 113 km/h (70 mph).

In heavily worked areas, particularly within city boundaries where there is an intense commuter traffic and much complicated track work, the wear on the rails is often severe on the crossing noses in a switch layout. It is also a characteristic of the power units of multiple-unit suburban trains, with the electric motors carried on the bogies, to be very hard on the track. In consequence it has become the practice for the most vulnerable parts of switch layouts, crossing noses in particular, to be made of high wear-resisting cast manganese steel, instead of from ordinary rail steel. Over many years it has been found that for standard rails a medium manganese steel gives the best service in heavy high-speed traffic. The operation of points and crossings is actually the job of the railway's signal and telecommunications engineer, in that he provides the apparatus to move the points; and where this is electric, as in all modern installations, he designs the electric circuits for the control, with appropriate interlocking with the signal control circuits. The principles of interlocking are referred to in more detail on pages 70–71. A modern electric point-operating machine has three functions. Before the points can be thrown the facing point lock must be withdrawn. The provision of a facing point lock is a legal requirement at all points over which passenger trains run in the facing direction. Then when the lock is withdrawn the points are moved over, and the lock reinserted, securing the points in their new position. The last function is the setting up of electric detection to prove that the switch blade has gone fully home, and is fitting snugly against the stock rail. Only when this is proved is it possible to clear signals for a train to pass over the points. The electric point machine completes all these functions in about three seconds.

*Right* Locomotive washing plant, UK. The thoroughness of such behind-the-scenes operations is not fully appreciated by the commuter.

**1** Indian metre gauge
**2** South Africa
**3** United Kingdom
**4** Europe (Bern Conference)
**5** North America

| | rail gauge | maximum height | maximum width |
|---|---|---|---|
| 1 | 1,000 mm *3'3"* | 3.429 m *11'3"* | 2.591 m *8'6"* |
| 2 | 1,067 mm *3'6"* | 4.140 m *13'7"* | 3.048 m *10'0"* |
| 3 | 1,435 mm *4'8½"* | 3.861 m *12'8"* | 2.819 m *9'3"* |
| 4 | 1,435 mm *4'8½"* | 4.280 m *14'0½"* | 3.150 m *10'4"* |
| 5 | 1,435 mm *4'8½"* | 4.724 m *15'6"* | 3.277 m *10'9"* |

These examples reflect the wide variety of existing loading gauges. Interesting differences to note are the large dimensions permitted on South African Railways, where the rolling stock is taller than in the UK although the gauge is narrower, and the great size of North American stock. Those shown are no more than a representative selection of the world's loading gauges. Perhaps the two most notable ones not illustrated are that of the Indian broad gauge which permits a maximum width of 3.6 m (12ft), and the Russian loading gauge. Russian engines can be the largest and most impressive in the world, permitted as they are to be more than 5.2 m (17ft) above rail level.

*Right* South African Railways 4-8-4 at Kimberley shed showing huge size of loading gauge as compared with rail gauge.

*Top* Vehicle used for lifting derailed trucks back on to the rails in a US yard.
*Above* Vehicle above in operation. Such derailments are common in the US where high capital costs have led to a lack of maintenance, even on main lines. On some railway systems speed limits are kept low to avoid accidents. This is the major problem in providing faster services.

# Bridge and tunnel construction

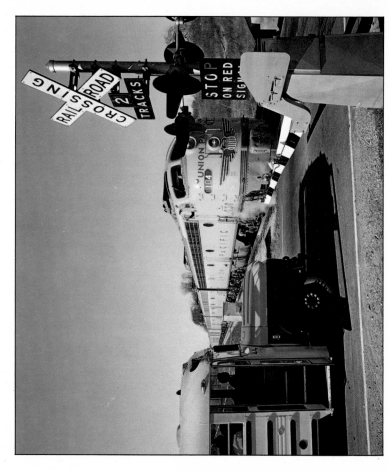

## Bridges

The provision of relatively straight track to serve the needs of modern high-speed railways, has meant the construction of long bridges and tunnels over and through geographical obstructions. On these new railways the appearance of the bridges is notably different from the masonry arched viaducts of the pioneer lines, or the timber trestles of North America. On the Japanese *Shinkansen* line between Tōkyō and Osaka, for example, there are eight bridges more than 457 m (500 yd) long, the longest being the Fujigawa, no less than 1,508 m (1,650 yd), within sight of Mount Fuji. The foundations of these bridges are mostly in the form of pneumatic caissons 15.5–18 m (17–20 yd) in depth, on which piers of reinforced concrete are built. The superstructure varies, but where steel trusses are used they are made continuous, from one end of the bridge to the other. Erection takes place by the cantilever method, extending stage by stage outwards from the completed part of the steelwork which is anchored to the piers. On the *Shinkansen* lines the standard length of span, from one pier to the next, is 59 m (65 yd).

In certain locations pre-stressed concrete girders are used. These are of remarkable design and provide complete support for a double track high-speed railway, with its ballasting and roadbed with a total width of top platform of about 11 m (36 ft). The girder portion, providing the strength to carry the weight of the trains, consists of four deep beams approximately beneath the running rails. The total length of this cast, pre-stressed concrete unit is 23 m (25 yd). These bridges, with their sleek, modern

*Above* Construction of the Overvaal Tunnel in South Africa, well illustrates the scale of works necessary in tunnelling. While techniques have improved enormously over the years, working conditions can often be harsh. *Right* A level crossing in the United States, one example of many different approaches to the problem when road meets rail. Nevertheless, one of the major sources of railway accident statistics is found at the crossing gate, or lack of it.

appearance are wholly in keeping with the external décor of the *Shinkansen* lines. While new railways are being built covering new locations, ingenious work is often involved where old bridges have to be strengthened, or renewed to meet the needs of present-day traffic. Where complete renewal is necessary and a new location is available, straightforward modern techniques can be used, a remarkable example of this being provided by the Rajahmundry bridge on the Howrah-Madras line of the Indian Railways, 900 m (1,000 yd) downstream of the original bridge, with the piers in water about 12 m (40 ft) deep. Here the foundations are on massive concrete wells sunk to a depth of 30 m (100 ft) below low water mark to ensure sufficient grip in the river bed, even in conditions of maximum erosion during high floods – always a hazard on Indian railways. This great new bridge, which has a total length of 2.8 km (1.75 miles), carries a roadway built to Indian national highway standards on the upper level, with the double line railway inside the 12 m (40 ft) high K-type trusses, which form the superstructure of the bridge. These girders were erected by the cantilever method.

## Tunnels

Tunnelling, despite all modern aids to excavation and subterranean survey, still involves very much of a plunge into the unknown, and methods have to be varied according to the nature of the soil and rock encountered, sometimes after excavation has proceeded some way. In good ground, a favoured way of cutting through mountains and hillsides is known as the "bottom heading and half section" method. A pilot heading is driven along the bottom line of what will be the finished tunnel, as a means of access and a way for the removal of spoil. When this has

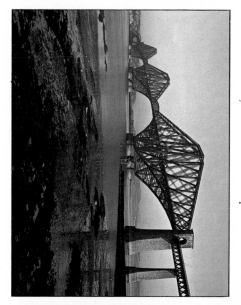

been driven an adequate distance, excavation to the full size begins in the upper half section. Then arch shuttering is put in to support the concreting of the top arch, until this is set. With the upper half section complete and the top arch in place side cutting on either side of the bottom heading is carried out, working outwards to the full width of the tunnel, until the side walls are ready to be concreted. In bad ground twin headings at the bottom inside of a single heading on the centre line of the tunnel are cut. When this is done, a heading is driven along the line of each side wall, so that massive side walls at the lowest level can be got into place at an early stage, providing protection against ingress of water or shale, and support for the shuttering when the time comes to install the top arch. In some of the long tunnels on the *Shinkansen* line the side heading method had to be used for part of the bores where the ground was considered too treacherous for any other method to be used.

Another method used where there is a prospect of good ground throughout is known as the "top heading and bench cut". Excavation begins with a heading in the upper half of the tunnel, which is enlarged out to the full profile and the top arch fully concreted. Then, using bulldozers, the lower half is excavated out to the full width, and the side walls put in. In recent years, however, when the task of carrying railways beneath waterways has arisen, excavation beneath the river or canal bed has been avoided altogether by use of the "submerged tube" method. In Rotterdam when the Métro was projected, it was at once known that excavation for the underground

sections in the style of London or Paris would be quite impracticable: the excavations would immediately fill with water. Therefore a channel was dug on the line of the proposed Métro, allowed to fill with water, and then the prefabricated tunnel sections were lowered into it. The tubes were constructed with sealed ends, and when lowered into the water and butted accurately together, connection between adjoining tubes was made. The same "submerged tube" form of construction was used for the Bay Area Rapid Transit line, at San Francisco, in passing beneath the bay to Oakland. The tube is 6.4 km (4 miles) long and it is possible for trains to travel between the two centres in as little as 8 min.

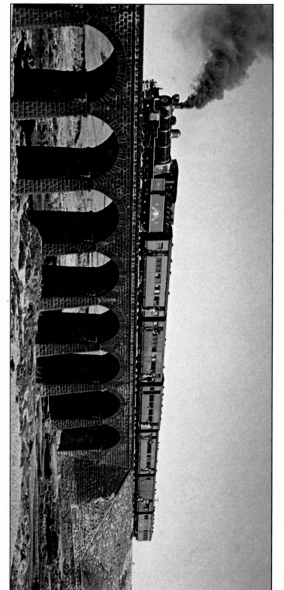

*Top* Stone viaduct in India. *Above* Bridge on the Kuranda-Cairns line in Queensland, Australia. *Above left* Forth railway bridge, Scotland. *Right* Modern viaduct in Spain built to massive proportions.

# Passenger stock: early days

Roof

Ceiling ventilation ducts

Fluorescent lighting

Luggage shelves

Luggage racks

Underfloor ventilation ducts

Saloon heating ducts

Double glazed tinted windows

Adjustable seating

Corner doors with wide access

Toilet

Steel shell construction

Bogies with air springing and disc brakes

This cutaway of the Mark III, the latest coach model running on British Rail, bears comparison with its predecessors on page 41. The essential structure remains the same, with obvious improvements, and a longer wheelbase. Heating and ventilation as well as actual seat comfort achieve a high priority today, but perhaps the greatest single difference is the capability of the Mark III to travel at speeds in excess of 160 km/h (100 mph).

*Below* High Speed Train with Mark III coaches.

Until recently there was a marked contrast between the basic layout of passenger accommodation in European and North American carriages. In Europe, including the practice of Great Britain with that of Continental countries, the separate compartment type was favoured, each compartment entered from a side corridor. At one time British carriages of this general type had individual doors to each compartment on the side away from the corridor, but latterly there was a change towards the Continental style with entrance doors only at the ends. For day travel this style of carriage was used for all classes. By contrast North American railways used almost exclusively the open saloon, originating from the early so-called "colonist" carriages, used for conveying immigrants from their ports of arrival. In North America this type has now been developed to a high standard of comfort and amenity, with adjustable seats able to take up a reclining position for night travel.

In the nineteenth century, timber was the universal material for carriage construction, both for bodies and underframing, and when the change to steel began many railways that built their own carriages retained wooden bodies, while adopting steel underframing. There was a difficult period on many railways when trains were made up of a mixture of wooden and steel carriages. The former suffered severely in times of collision or derailment, becoming crushed between the stronger steel carriages. Wooden carriages were also a high fire risk, particularly before the days of electric lighting.

Today, the open saloon type of passenger carriage is becoming widely adopted on the Continent of Europe, and is universal in new construction on British Rail. While

Water tank

Drawbar and coupling

Foam lined gangway

some passengers prefer the seclusion of separate compartments, the open saloon offers so many advantages in modern travel, in which the journey times are being progressively reduced. To the businessman the tables are a convenience, on which papers, books, or documents may be studied *en route*, or impromptu discussions or conferences held with colleagues; while on many trains a trolley service of drinks and snacks is provided for those who do not wish to walk several coaches to a buffet car. On the fast Inter-City trains of British Rail there is often insufficient time to take a full restaurant car meal. For others, travelling *en famille*, the four seats with table between is ideal for picnic meals, and other incidentals of an excursion outing. On the Continent of Europe on some of the TEE services providing luxury as well as high-speed, the traveller can choose between compartment or open saloon carriages at the time of seat reservation. On the frequent Inter-City services of British Rail, seat reservation is usually unnecessary, but it is essential on most Continental express trains, and on some obligatory.

The provision of dining cars on long-distance trains became an attractive accompaniment to travel around 1900, and serving of breakfast, lunch, or dinner became something of a ritual with conductors specially selected for the task, and taking as much pride in their service as the head waiters in fashionable restaurants. Echoes of this age in railway travels are to be seen on some prestige trains on the Continent of Europe, but for the most part railway meals are nowadays simpler, taken in greater haste, often from the bar counter of a buffet car. Nevertheless, the counter service "steak and chips" breakfast on Australian inter-state express trains, taken in 20 to 25 minutes, is not so far removed from the slick movement required in the restaurant car of the prewar Cornish Riviera Express, when in the height of the holiday season the conductor served three sittings of lunch between London and Ply-

*Right and below left Construction of the Mark III in British Rail engineering works. Below right interior of the Mark III coach.*

mouth! In the modern trains of open saloon type stock, certain parts of the train are set aside for the service of meals, and available only to those passengers requiring them. At one time a walk from one's seat to the restaurant car provided a welcome diversion during a long journey, but an advertised amenity of many prestige trains today is that meals are served to every seat, if required.

The evolution of the sleeping car has followed different paths in many parts of the world. In Europe little was done in early days to provide any additional comfort for night travel, whereas the much longer continuous journeys made across the American continent led to forms of seclusion in the early "colonist" or saloon carriages, including blinds that could be lowered on either side of the central gangway, behind which passengers could to some extent undress. In Britain, when sleeping cars were introduced, for first class passengers only, they provided completely private compartments for one, whereas on the Continent of Europe even the first class sleepers on the prestige international trains included two berths, one above the other in a "compartment". This form of accommodation is still in use today. In Britain "third class" (now second class) sleepers were introduced in 1928, and these have two-tier bunks in a compartment. The accommodation consisted of no more than a "bed" with pillow and blankets, at each level.

Much has been done in recent years to improve the smoothness of the ride. In earlier days certain British railways famed for the smoothness of travel achieved their high standards by close and meticulous maintenance of the bogies. More recently, faced with the need to minimize the work content of railway work, new and advanced designs of bogie have been introduced that give an excellent ride over long periods, at much higher speeds than previously, with a minimum of attention. The methods of suspension have been the subject of constant research.

# Passenger stock: modern improvements

*Above* New stock on the Wuppertal Monorail, Ruhr, West Germany.

*Left* Older type of Dutch DMU at Utrecht station.

*Below* Modern stainless steel EMU – northeast United States.

*Above* Modern suburban EMU on Moorgate-Hatfield line, north London.

*Above left* New London Transport electric train entering Paddington.

The great distances traversed by transcontinental trains in North America, and also in Australia, led to a demand by wealthy patrons for a luxury of accommodation beyond that of the ordinary first class carriage and its associated dining and sleeping saloons. Cars including private suites were introduced, while more generally available bar-lounges, club carriages and observation saloons were run on certain trains. In Britain, both from Manchester and Bradford, from which at one time there was a high-class daily commuter traffic for businessmen living at seaside resorts and travelling daily, there were club carriages, entry to which was open only to members of a travelling club. Cars of this kind were attached to certain express trains between Manchester and Blackpool, Manchester and Southport, and Bradford and Morecambe. They each had their own regular stewards, and all the facilities of a first class city club.

Modern tendencies in the highest class main line service are all toward airline style in passenger accommodation. The technical features that have developed to provide a comfortable ride in conditions of very fast running are to a large extent epitomized in the new stock now being built

for the Paris-Lyon TGV (*très grande vitesse*) line in France. On this line it has been decided to adopt powered trainsets, in preference to locomotive-hauled stock, with no more than moderate axle loading, considered essential for stability at 300 km/h (185 mph). The coaches are articulated, with bogies between the car bodies, which make possible a reduced height and therefore lower resistance to their passage through the atmosphere. To provide for rapid acceleration, six bogies out of the 13 in each trainset are powered. The trains themselves consist of eight passenger cars with a power unit at each end and will provide seating for 375 passengers.

An important accompaniment of the introduction of very fast new trains is a more complete understanding of the relationship between wheel and rail. For some time a roller test plant has been in operation at Pueblo, Colorado, USA, on which track conditions can be simulated, and the reaction of vehicles passing over it observed under advantageous laboratory conditions. This test plant, and one also recently brought into operation near Munich, West Germany, provides a parallel activity to that of stationary locomotive test plants, in that the unit to be examined can be run at maximum road speed, without moving from the test bed. In the case of the Pueblo and Munich effects of such track features as curves and transitions, together with defects such as kinks and hollows, can be studied. It is not necessary to have a complete vehicle for satisfactory tests to be made. A truck can be loaded to correspond with the loaded or unloaded weight of a coach. Furthermore, when new designs are proposed incorporating novel features, prototypes can be built and tested before mass production is started.

The introduction of new rapid-transit commuter services in many cities of the world has been accompanied by some notable advances in the technology of rolling stock design. Some years ago, in an attempt to minimize noise when passing through tunnels, rubber-tired vehicles were introduced on a new underground line of the Paris Métro. Like other urban rapid-transit projects, the trains themselves were of the multiple-unit "set" type, but unlike other applications of pneumatic tires such trainsets could not be steered, and means for guidance had to be provided in the form of additional wheels, on vertical axles, in contact with the vertical side of the concrete trough in which the main wheels ran. Also, further additional wheels were needed, to be brought into operation when these unusual trainsets had to be switched on to other routes, when entering a maintenance shop or storage yard. They had, therefore, three times as many wheels as on a normal trainset. This type of train has been used on only one of the Paris Métro lines, but it was adopted for the Montreal subway, and has been installed on the Marseille rapid-transit line.

Some of the latest techniques in car production for

rapid-transit lines are embodied in new cars for the Paris Métro. Until recently, aluminum as a material for car bodies, while attractive from the viewpoint of weight reduction, has been impracticable because of its higher cost over steel; but now, with major progress in aluminum assembly techniques, French manufacturers have for the first time been able to achieve lower constructional costs for aluminum, and large orders have been placed, not only for Paris, but for several other cities. The older lines of the Paris Métro impose restrictive space conditions, which are nonexistent on the notable "express" underground routes of the RER (regional express metro), which allow locomotives and trains of main line dimensions to run through the new tunnels. However, the body design of the new cars for the older Métro lines incorporates much structural ingenuity to provide additional space for passengers. An outstanding feature is the use of three pairs of sliding doors on each side of the car, which when fully opened provide space for entering equal to one-third of the total length of the car. As in all rapid-transit cars there is a large amount of space for standing passengers.

For the commuter services on certain of the main lines around Paris, some very handsome new double-deck passenger cars are now in use, hauled by electric locomotives. The set of cars and the locomotive make up a two-directional trainset, in the same way that steam locomotives were used on earlier commuter trains. The locomotive is not uncoupled, and while hauling the cars in one direction it propels them in the reverse. The car furthest from the locomotive has a driving cab, from which the locomotive is remotely controlled. This was also practiced with steam, but the fireman had to remain on the locomotive at all times, and when propelling he and the engineer were at opposite ends of the train.

*Right* Tiny diesel railcar of ENAFER, Peru.

*Below* Air-conditioned double-deck stainless steel EMU for long haul work, comprising 2 × 2 car and 1 × 4 car units; Central Station, Sydney.

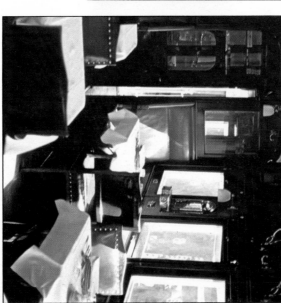

*Below* Local passenger train passing through Ellis Park station, South Africa. Hillbrow in background.

*Right* Interior of dining car, Benguela Railways, Angola; note the wood paneling and luxurious style.

# Freight stock: specialization

*Top left* German ferry wagon in the UK. *Above left* Illinois Central boxcar, USA. *Above* Wellington harbour, New Zealand, an important railhead in modern-day freight terms. *Top right* Missouri Pacific Railroad bulk carrier, Los Angeles. *Above right* Tipper truck manufactured in the UK for export. *Right* Detail of back-eye truck couplings in US yard. *Below* Santa Fe boxcar.

The modern freight car is very much a specialist vehicle, and in no respect more so than in carrying the mineral for which the earliest railways were built – coal. The British Rail hopper wagons of today, used on the "merry-go-round" coal trains, are in size, though not in the sophistication of their equipment, the baby brother of some of the gigantic gondola cars used in other countries. The New Zealand railways, for example, although operating on the 1,067 mm (3ft 6in) gauge use large bottom-discharge, cylindrical shaped wagons that carry a payload of 42 tonnes, while in the USA, the Chesapeake and Ohio, one of the greatest coal carriers in the world, has thousands of large gondola cars capable of carrying 90 tonnes of coal. These are used in the export coal trade from Newport News, where stationary turn-over car dumpers are at work capable of handling 30 cars an hour, 2,700 tonnes of coal per hour from each dumper. The Canadian Pacific has a remarkable coal operation from the Crowsnest Pass, British Columbia, for export to Japan, from Roberts Bank near Vancouver. There the 100-tonne coal cars are discharged on to conveyor belts one by one without them being uncoupled one from another in the long train. The couplings, including the continuous airbrake connections, are so designed that each car is rotated about the horizontal axis of its couplings. The mechanized handling equipment moves the whole train forwards one car length after the coal has been discharged, and the vehicle rotated back to its normal position.

Discharge through bottom hoppers, or by the rotating process, is not always possible, especially in the conveyance of waste products in industrial plants, such as blast furnaces and steel works. In the USA, and more recently in South Africa, side-dumping wagons are used. The bodies resemble an extra-massive version of an ordinary gondola car, but are supported on four huge compressed air cylinders. If it should be required to dump to the right-hand side of the line, air is applied to the two cylinders on the left-hand side and the extending of their pistons tilts the body to the right – pivoting about this centre line of the vehicle. For dumping to the left, the tilting is provided by the cylinders on the right-hand side.

The covered wagon, or box car in the USA, has now been built to great size. It may be nothing more than a "box", designed to carry general merchandise, but many designs include highly specialized equipment for carrying perishable goods or even newsprint, which needs particularly careful carrying when in large quantities.

The conveyance of automobiles and road trucks has become another specialized part of rail freight business. In Britain and on the Continent of Europe, the cars are loaded in two tiers, while the extra height of the North

American loading gauge enables three tiers to be used. On the latest American car transporters, 15 cars are carried, five on each deck. In Britain, however, whatever limitations in height are imposed by the loading gauge are made up for in length. The articulated principle has been applied to produce a four-unit articulated wagon, each unit of which carries seven cars. With articulation intermediately only five bogies are needed to support the four units, and fully loaded with 28 automobiles the assemblage weighs as much as 93 tonnes. These remarkable vehicles are designed to be run at 120 km/h (75 mph) if necessary. In the USA, because of vandalism, the side protection of multiple transporters has been found necessary, and in the latest designs the whole surface, except the ends, is completely covered in. At inland stations where automobiles are delivered, both to private purchasers and distributing agencies, special ramps are installed to permit easy unloading on the upper decks. The export of automobiles from Japan sometimes leads to unusual railway sights in North America: the passage of a heavily loaded westbound train of American automobiles, heading for San Francisco, is followed by an equally long eastbound train loaded with their Japanese counterparts.

The introduction of special-purpose vehicles has grown to a remarkable extent in the USA where strenuous efforts are being made to win back traffic that had been lost to the road hauliers. In no respect has this trend been more noticeable than in the co-operation between the railways and individual manufacturers for delivery of their products. In a joint conception of the Southern Pacific

Railroad and General Motors, the ingenious "vert-a-pac" car carrier was evolved, specially to convey new cars from plant to distribution centres. The "vert-a-pac", as its name suggests, carries cars in a vertical position. On each side of a vehicle of maximum box car dimensions there are 15 doors, which are hinged at the bottom; when opened they form an inclined ramp on to which an automobile is driven. It is then secured for transit on to this ramp, and

*Below* Loading piggyback trailers on to a Union Pacific train in Argos Yards, Seattle, USA, using a mobile crane. Piggyback transport is

of growing importance in North America where ocean shipment is not included and simple container flexibility is required.

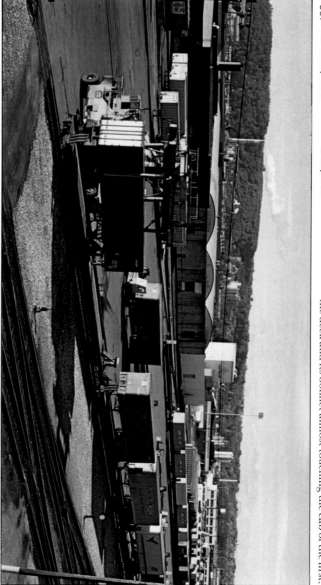

when the door is shut the automobile is in a vertical position inside the vehicle. Loading takes place on both sides, and with a full complement 30 automobiles can be loaded into this one vehicle and ensconced in a totally enclosed box car. Another special vehicle is that known as the "stackback" flat car, used widely in the US for transporting heavy trucks, which are delivered from the builders with nothing more than the chassis and the driver's cab. It was on the Louisville and Nashville that the ingenious idea of stacking them in an inclined position originated. The first in the line is positioned with its front wheels about 60 cm (2 ft) above the level of the platform with the flat deck in the rear of the driver's cab inclined downwards. The second truck then has its front wheels on the deck and its bonnet almost touching the cab of the first.

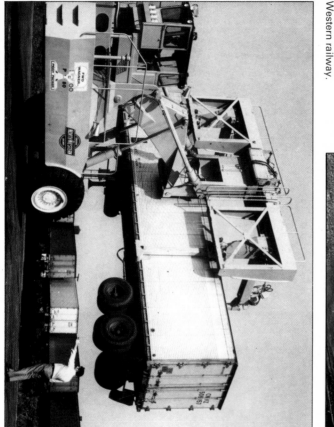

*Below* "Piggy packer" vehicle, which can lift 40-tonne trucks, working on Chicago & North Western railway.

*Right* Canadian National car transporter with a particularly graphic device. Over long distances car transportation achieves greater importance, though even in the United Kingdom Motorail has created a growing market.

*Above* Piggyback car — not as neat as a container car, but just as effective.

*Below* British Rail Motorail train running by south Devon coast near Dawlish, England.

# Freight stock: automation

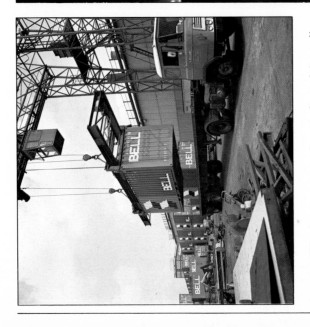

*Above left* Loading containers after manufacture. *Above right* Harwich at night, loading containers. *Right* Oil train from Milford Haven to London moving through Sonning Cutting. *Below left* Container train, administered by Intercontainer, an international co-ordinating body. *Below right* US oil tanker.

A major difficulty that at one time confronted Australian railways when it came to interchange of traffic between the different states was that at every state boundary except one, that between Victoria and South Australia, there was a change of rail gauge. In one or two major cases this has been partly resolved by the building of new standard gauge lines, but this does not apply everywhere and on certain through runs, in particular those concerning the State of Victoria, special vehicles are used on which the bogies are changed at the point where there is a change of gauge. The vehicles are lifted bodily from one set of bogies and lowered on to a second set for the altered gauge. At the frontier between New South Wales and Victoria it is not unusual for 20,000 vehicles to be bogie-changed annually.

These difficulties lead to the modern concept of the container train, which is being developed extensively in Europe. So far as railway working generally, the idea of a sealed container that can be transferred from rail to ship, and then back to rail again, is not a new one, because it was practised for very many years in the days of steam haulage on the Continental boat train services from London, across the English Channel to France. The modern rail concept is to have a fixed-formation set of flat cars for each schedule service, and not to alter that formation, even though a full complement of containers is not available on the particular day. For example a nightly service from Garston Docks, Liverpool, to Glasgow, would contain a set of 20 flats, each capable of carrying three containers – 60 to a train. If, however, by loading time the traffic of the day has produced only 47 containers, the train would be dispatched with some of the flat cars not fully loaded. The working of these trains is given top priority in the night hours. Then, express passenger trains are run at considerably lower speeds than in the daytime, and the container trains, or "freightliners" as they are called, running continuously at 120 km/h (75 mph), are equally fast. A fully loaded 20-flat container train would represent more than 1,000 tonnes, or roughly double that of a heavy night passenger train, and on the heavy gradients in the north of England and Scotland two 5,000 hp electric locomotives are needed to maintain the fast scheduled speeds.

The conveyance of livestock needs specially equipped freight trains. In former days sheep and cattle were transported in single-deck four-wheeled wagons, with open caged sides; but this traffic has largely ceased. In other countries, however, it is still a major item, and the modern concept of the high-capacity bogie wagon has been applied to this traffic. Large double-decked sheep vans are run on the Iraqi State Railways, and even larger ones in the USA. The Atchison, Topeka and Santa Fe introduced double-decked stock cars that were adjustable.

Specialized vehicles are used for the bulk conveyance of materials in powder and pellet form. On British Rail, while the private owner's wagons of former days are no longer to be seen as individual loads in freight trains, contracts have been arranged with large industrial concerns for the running to regular timetables of daily nominated freight trains carrying a single product. The Rugby Portland Cement Company has a fleet of large four-wheeled cylindrically shaped wagons, which have a gross laden

*Below* Bogie of US oil tanker showing spring-ing and braking arrangements. Such tankers may carry up to 70 tonnes of oil products apiece, which require considerable stability.

*Left* Snowploughs, Maine Central, Bangor, USA.

*Right* The Automatic Train Control plate from a truck, which details, for an electronic eye to read, full information regarding destination, etc. This system is not entirely successful as the plates become dirty, thus confusing the auto-matic reading. Many marshalling yards have installed hybrid computer equipment to deal with some sorting work.

*Below right* Canadian Pacific caboose at the end of a coal train.

weight of 50 tonnes and are run at speeds up to 96 km/h (60 mph). Considerably larger are the 100-tonne bogie vehicles operated for the Blue Circle Cement group. These carry a maximum payload of 78 tonnes, and are also run at speeds of 96 km/h. Their appearance is striking, with the cylindrical bodies inclined in sections to facilitate the easy flow of the material when loading. All these large vehicles impose an axle load of about 25 tonnes on to the track. This can be accepted only on trunk main lines because it is of the same order as that of locomotives. Another special vehicle on British Rail is a 100-tonne bulk powder tank wagon used for conveyance of raw material needed for detergent manufacture. In tune with the actual containers themselves, whether it be consignments loaded into containers, or minerals and materials conveyed in bulk, is the design of the bogies to permit of safe and steady running up to 96 km/h (60 mph). Every effort is made to reduce unsprung weight, to incorporate load-sensitive dampers and to equip them with disc or clasp brakes. All British fast freight trains are fitted with the Westinghouse automatic air brakes permitting of the safe and smooth control of the heaviest trains in the most adverse circumstances.

In North America, although there have recently been a number of amalgamations reducing the number of com-panies and setting up large combines such as Conrail, the Burlington Northern, and others, there are still a vast number of different owners and an equally great variety of cars. With the approach to computerizing the operational process was necessary to eliminate the human recording of wagon types, ownership and destination of individual loads as freight trains came into the reception sidings so that they could be correctly routed. This is now done by computer, but the computer has to know such information

CONRAIL

*Above* Zillertalbahn, Austria, showing how the standard gauge wagons are transported.

as destinations and weights. To do this the system of Automatic Car Identification has been introduced. A colour-coded panel is fixed to every freight vehicle in major railway service. It is a rectangle 60 cm (24 in) high and 25 cm (10 in) wide and includes 14 horizontal strips of colour in combinations of red, blue, black and white. By varying the relation of adjacent colours, a very large number of codes can be obtained, and when decoded identify the type of vehicle and the owning railway. As a train enters the reception sidings at a marshalling yard, it passes a photoelectric scanner, which registers the code on the side of the vehicle and transmits the information to the computer in the control tower, from where the point setting for train marshalling is set up.

# Modern signalling

Approach to Rotterdam station.

The function of modern signalling is primarily to ensure the safe movement of trains, but equally, by giving clear and unmistakable indications, to give drivers confidence to run at the maximum speeds permitted by the physical characteristics of each section of line. While originally semaphore signals were devised and installed to tell drivers when to stop, today modern signalling is the one feature of railway technology without which it would be impossible to run high-speed services, or intense commuter programmes. The modern signal is the day colour light type, which, unlike the old semaphore signals, gives essentially the same indication to the driver by day and by night. The code of indications varies in different countries, but the underlying philosophy is generally the same. The code used on British Rail for what is termed "multi-aspect signalling" is the oldest, first introduced in 1925, by far the simplest, and is second to none in its record of safe operation. At junctions it tells the driver what route he is to take, whereas the standard code in North America instructs the driver at what speed he should travel. This latter method involves a considerable proliferation of signal lights, but is very effective in operation. On the Continent of Europe, systems of colour light signalling are of more recent origin and vary from country to country, some involving a blend of the British "geographical" and the North American "speed" aspects.

The fundamental safety feature underlying all modern signalling is the track circuit. Each line of railway is divided into a number of sections, insulated from each other, into which an electrical feed is made at one end. Connected across the rails at the other end is a relay, which acts as a multi-purpose switching device. If there is no

train, or vehicle, in the particular section, the relay is energized, and certain contacts made. If the electrical feed along the rails is in any way interrupted, by the presence of a train, or the misfortune of a broken rail, the relay is de-energized. The contacts of the track relay control the signal indication at the entering point to the track circuit, and by other contacts enable the whereabouts of all trains to be shown on the illuminated cabin diagrams. The track relay, which is a highly sophisticated instrument with upwards of 80 years' research and development behind it, is at the heart of the interlocking that performs a number of vital functions. It prevents conflicting signals being displayed; keeps following trains on the same line at a safe distance apart while the interlocking of units in electrical circuits prevents the clearing of signals until the line ahead is correctly set through points and crossings; and prevents the establishment of a line-up of points that would intersect the line-up of another, and so give rise to what would become a "collision course".

The safeguards against the chance of a signalman's error are now so complete as to make modern systems virtually accident proof as far as track relay systems are concerned. With the modern push-button control consoles, there is nothing physically to prevent a signalman pushing a wrong button; but the interlocking in the system is such that if he did so the function concerned would not respond. There would be no answering indication light to show that all had correctly worked, and he would realize that he had inadvertently tried to set up a potentially dangerous

situation. At the present time, however, there is no corresponding safeguard for the driver, although a great deal is done to help him. It is considered that the control of the running of the train should not be taken out of his hands except if he is ignoring the warnings given by a signal, and by warning apparatus in his cab. The question as to how and when warnings should be given and direct control applied have been the subject of much debate, with differences of viewpoint in various parts of the world. On British Rail it is now standard practice on main lines to give an audible warning in the cab at every signal on colour light multiple-aspect routes, and at the "distant" or warning signal where semaphore signals remain. In multiple-aspect territory on the approach to a green (clear) signal, a bell is rung briefly in the locomotive cab, while on approach to a first warning double yellow, or a final warning, single yellow, a horn is sounded. In the case of the clear indication, no action is required from the driver, but at the warning the horn continues sounding until an acknowledging lever is operated. If the driver acknowledges promptly it is taken as an assurance that he is alert, and full control of the train remains in his hands. Should he fail to acknowledge after a brief time, the brakes are automatically applied and the train stopped. Varying degrees of cab warning and control are used in other countries.

*Left* Modern four aspect and junction signals, British Rail.

*Above* Manual signal box preserved on the Bluebell Line, UK.

Point switches numbered

Fulwell Junction

Washing sidings

Shackleton Junction

Train on this stretch (orange)

Signal

Twickenham Station

Number of train on stretch

Lights for every signal which light if driver telephones (hand set not shown)

Strawberry Hill station

Strawberry Hill crossing

Computer address

Signals activated – train approaching (yellow)

Full controls for level crossing

Strawberry Hill level crossing monitor screen

The regulation of traffic on important routes has been greatly improved by the concentration of control at a few large centres, instead of having a chain of small signal boxes along the line. The modern panel British Rail signal box controls anything up to 160 km (100 miles) of high-speed main line in addition to all the local working around a large station or junction. The whereabouts of all trains are indicated by lights on the illuminated track diagram, while a system known as "train description" pinpoints the position of individual trains by displaying their numbers in illuminated characters on dark rectangles at key positions on the diagram. These numbers progress from one rectangle to the next as the train proceeds on its journey. At junctions or among the diversity of routes around a large station, the routes are set by the signalmen. Unlike the earlier days of mechanical signalling, there is now no need to operate each individual function separately. A complete route is set up by the pressing of two push buttons. The system is known as "entrance-exit". The signal immediately before a junction may lead to a number of different routes and first the entrance button is pressed; then the signalman selects the button at the exit of the route he requires. If the interlocking is free, because no conflicting movement is signalled, the pressing of the exit button sets up the whole route. When all the points in the route are correctly lined up, and have been detected, the signal at the entrance to the route clears automatically and the traffic is able to proceed.

On the busiest routes of the London Underground, the practice of route setting has been carried a remarkable stage further. Dealing with nothing other than multiple-unit passenger trains working to an intense timetable, the operation for a whole day's running is controlled by an instrument called a "programme machine". In simple terms, all the signal and point operation required for the service set out in the timetable is, as it were, put on to tape, and as the trains pass through the various junctions, such as Camden Town, or Earls Court, the tape is advanced one step and automatically sets the route for the next following train. In the traffic control centres the regulators watch the progress of the trains, but have no need to intervene except in cases of late running, or emergency. It is a remarkable example of automated traffic control. On the Victoria Line of the London Underground the trains themselves are automatically driven, except that the driver presses two buttons simultaneously to close the doors and start the train, once the "right away" is given from the platform.

*Above* A general view of the interior of the Feltham signal box in southwest London. The main display is on the left, angled in five panels. The main panel featured on this page (above) is the second from the left. The small television screens which monitor all level crossings on this section are visible at the base of the panels. The main control desks are to the right, and hidden behind them are computer printout machines giving information regarding traffic flow, timetable changes and cancellations.

*Above* The public address control at Feltham. From this panel a controller can give messages over the public address systems of all the stations on the section. Not only can recorded messages be played announcing trains, but also the whole system can be overridden and direct address effected using the microphone which is visible. This is necessary when train delays occur.

*Above* The supervisor's desk at Feltham. Clearly visible are the key switches for entry into the computers used to control operations and the keyboard for addressing the computer. Of interest are the 'signal address' and 'description' panels which give details of any train present at any signal point. The code given in the description panel is that carried on the locomotive. The first digit gives the class of train, the letter indicates the destination, and the final digits constitute a train number.

# Traffic and timetabling: main line

The planning of a passenger timetable on a line carrying a variety of traffic usually involves striking a balance between the immediate demands of traffic flows, and what is practicable in the way of speed. Clearly, the coaching stock should be worked to the best advantage, securing maximum utilization, but an ideal backward and forward movement of a rake of coaches might not fit in with the traffic flows, and some runs might be no more than lightly loaded. On the other hand it has been demonstrated many times that the introduction of regular interval services between important centres throughout the day breeds traffic. Undoubtedly trains running in the off-peak periods will sometimes be sparsely loaded, and in early days it was often the practice to work these with fewer coaches. But the fixed formation trainset presents no problems with coach marshalling, and the time and labour saved thereby amply compensates for the under-utilization of the seating accommodation in off-peak hours. On the busiest inter-city services on British Rail, trainsets shuttling between major cities on single journeys of 160–240 km (100–150 miles) do not leave the terminal stations at either end. There is no question of their being worked as empty stock to some stabling yard. In many cases these inter-city trains are in the terminal platforms for little more than half an hour, before leaving again often fully loaded for the return trip.

The intensity of stock utilization today creates its own problems. The attractions of a fast, frequent service will be dimmed somewhat if there are times when the equipment of the coaches is faulty, quite apart from major considerations such as the quality of the ride. But in addition to engineering maintenance, which on coaches providing an intense daytime inter-city service has to be carried out at night, there are points that are small so far as the overall planning is concerned, but are important from the viewpoint of public relations. Nothing can be more irritating or repellant to passengers entering a carriage at the start of their journey than to find old newspapers and other debris left by the occupants on the incoming journey, and however briefly a trainset may rest in a terminal station platform between incoming and outgoing trips, time must be allowed for platform staff to clear the train's interior.

Provision for maintenance of the track also governs the timetabling of intense high-speed passenger services. On the electrified line of British Rail northward from London (Euston), the traffic today is enough to justify an hourly service throughout the day from London to Liverpool and to Manchester, and a half-hourly service to Birmingham.

This series of diagrams explains the workings of a *timetabling graph*, of which the section *below* is seen as representing a small part. One of the axes of such a graph ought to have 24 hours marked out along it, not 3 as here. Such a graph would also, normally, cover a greater route length than the 120 km (75 miles) here. The line is single track, with passing places at all stations except C.

Crowded passenger train in India: the answer to high passenger densities.

Perhaps the reason for its sudden haste between stations C and D is that a faster train is following it, not stopping at all stations, which therefore has to overtake it. As seen *below*, the slower mixed train is scheduled to wait half an hour at station D, perhaps to shunt, while the fast passenger train will wait only 2 minutes, at the station, overtaking the slower mixed train at the same time.

Trains going in the other direction will appear as lines sloping the opposite way. On a single-track line, as here, they can only cross diagonal lines sloping the other way at those stations with passing loops. Two trains moving the other way are shown *above*: one non-stop from E to A crosses the mixed at B without stopping; and a slower, all stations, train. Note that just before 13.00 hrs, there are 3 trains in station D.

Travelling through the Rockies in a leisurely style.

As the time scale moves from left to right, horizontally, the train, *above*, is travelling from A to E. The steeper the diagonal line between stops, the faster it is travelling. The longer the horizontal line at a station, the longer it stops. This, therefore, is a slow train, perhaps mixed, averaging less than 60 km/h (37 mph) between stops, except between stations C and D where it manages 100 km/h (62 mph).

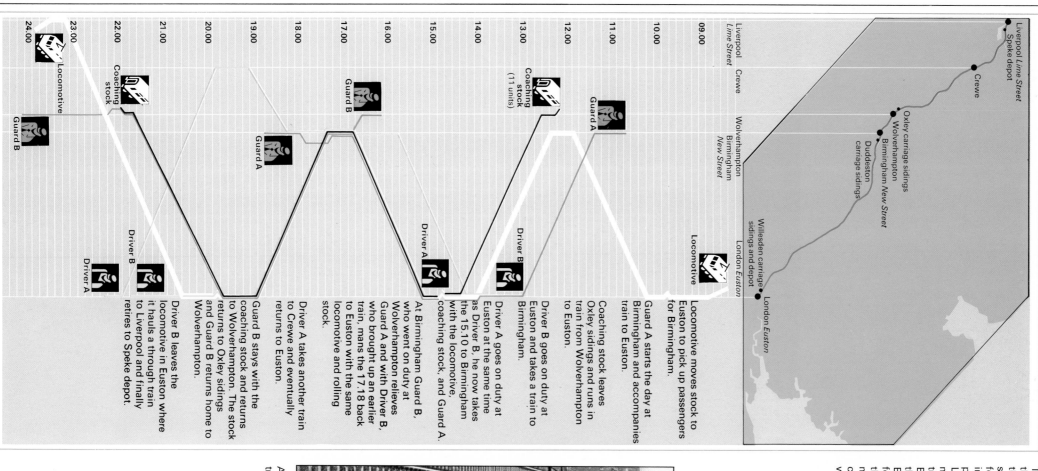

**Time axis (left):** 24.00 · 23.00 · 22.00 · 21.00 · 20.00 · 19.00 · 18.00 · 17.00 · 16.00 · 15.00 · 14.00 · 13.00 · 12.00 · 11.00 · 10.00 · 09.00

**Station axis (top):** Liverpool *Lime Street* / Speke depot — Crewe — Wolverhampton / Birmingham *New Street* — London *Euston* / Willesden carriage sidings and depot

**Map labels:** Liverpool *Lime Street* · Speke depot · Crewe · Oxley carriage sidings · Wolverhampton · Birmingham *New Street* · Duddeston carriage sidings · London *Euston* · Willesden carriage sidings and depot

Diagram labels: Guard A · Guard B · Driver A · Driver B · Coaching stock (11 units) · Coaching stock · Locomotive

Locomotive moves stock to Euston to pick up passengers for Birmingham.

Locomotive leaves Birmingham and accompanies train to Euston.

Guard A starts the day at Birmingham and accompanies train to Euston.

Coaching stock leaves Oxley sidings and runs in train from Wolverhampton to Euston.

Guard B goes on duty at Euston and takes a train to Birmingham.

Driver B goes on duty at Euston and takes a train to Birmingham.

Driver A goes on duty at Euston at the same time as Driver B, he now takes the 15.10 to Birmingham with the locomotive, coaching stock, and Guard A.

At Birmingham Guard B, who went on duty at Wolverhampton relieves Guard A and with Driver B, who brought up an earlier train, mans the 17.18 back to Euston with the same locomotive and rolling stock.

Driver A takes another train to Crewe and eventually returns to Euston.

Guard B stays with the coaching stock and returns to Wolverhampton. The stock returns to Oxley sidings and Guard B returns home to Wolverhampton.

Driver B leaves the locomotive in Euston where it hauls a through train to Liverpool and finally retires to Speke depot.

Driver A takes the locomotive in Euston where it hauls a through train to Liverpool and finally retires to Speke depot.

---

The diagram, *left*, follows the movements, throughout their working day, of the staff and equipment used for a single return working of a locomotive-hauled passenger train between London (Euston) and Birmingham. Although the trains are the 15.10 Euston–Birmingham and the 17.18 Birmingham–Euston, the diagram shows, for the rest of their day, the different paths of the men and equipment who come together briefly to work these trains.

Every hour also there are fast trains serving other northern destinations, in addition to which there are, at slightly longer intervals, trains to Scotland. To provide an adequate time interval for small items of track maintenance and the working of trains which intersect the high-speed main lines, the regular interval trains are grouped in "flights", leaving London at 40 minutes past each hour, until 10 minutes past the next hour, thus leaving a full half hour free for local movements and other essential maintenance work to be carried out on the line.

The intensity of regular passenger train working in Britain has no counterpart elsewhere, because even the *Shinkansen* lines in Japan are dealing with a fixed-interval service of one particular class of train. In France today, the very fast inter-city services are planned to enable a traveller from the provinces to make a visit to Paris, have a full afternoon for business, and return by a train reaching his home destination before midnight. French passenger train travel at its greatest intensity is seen at seasonal holiday periods, when a vast number of extra trains are run from Paris to resorts in Switzerland, on the Côte d'Azur, and in Spain. In the days just before Christmas, for example, it is not unusual in the six hours before midnight for about 60 long-distance trains to be dispatched from the Gare de Lyon alone. Only six or seven would be regularly scheduled services; the rest are extras. But such is the reserve organization available that this intense provision

A London–Birmingham train leaving Euston.

can be worked punctually, with most trains covering between 120 and 130 km (75 and 80 miles) in the first hour out of Paris, and serving such diverse destinations as Athens, Rome, Nice, Grenoble, Milan, Interlaken and Genoa.

In France the prestige passenger train services entering and leaving Paris have to be interwoven with the commuter traffic, which is intense in the peak hours, though on all the principal routes approaching the city there are four tracks from distances of about 32 km (20 miles) inwards. On the main route from Paris to the south-east, particularly over the 316 km (195 miles) southwards to Dijon, the line, although quadruple-tracked for most of the way, is at times being worked to full capacity; because of this the new TGV line is being built to cope with this intensity.

# Traffic and timetabling: commuter

The operation of an intense commuter service presents a totally different set of problems from those posed by main line working. Paramount is the inescapable fact that a very large amount of rolling stock has to be available to cater for the morning and evening peak periods, but which is necessarily idle or much under-utilized during the rest of the day. There is also the problem of stabling, because the great volume of stock needed for the morning peak cannot be accommodated in the precincts of the city terminal stations; it has to be worked outwards to suburban centres before standing by during the off-peak hours. Because of the under-utilization of much of the stock on the basis of a 24-hour assessment, the working of commuter services tends to be uneconomic, despite progressive increases in fares. The nature of the stock essential for such a service, whether it be the non-corridor compartment type of the Southern Region of British Rail, the underground type, with as many as three pairs of sliding doors a side, or the huge double-decker coaches of Chicago, makes it quite unsuitable for any other kind of duty in the off-peak hours. Today, however, while the situation in the immediate environs of great cities is acute, and likely to remain so, the acceleration of main line services with the latest forms of motive power has resulted in many more city workers commuting from further afield. In earlier days many businessmen travelled to London daily from Brighton, Eastbourne or Worthing, and today travellers commute daily from as far afield as Peterborough (122 km; 76 miles) and Bath (171 km; 107 miles).

A criticism directed at many commuter services is that while trains may run at frequent intervals, the overall time from outer residential stations to the city centre is relatively slow, because of the frequent stops. This is a criticism that could well be levelled at the latest extension of the London Underground to Heathrow international airport, from

we find that in the half hour 18.00–18.30 A1 has reached Staines, B1 is nearly in Brentford, C1 and D1 are between Richmond and Twickenham, and B2, A2 and E1 are on their way to Richmond, the latter having just left Waterloo. This progression can be followed through with other sets appearing on the scene. The operation shown here represents movements on one section of line out of Waterloo during the evening peak and later evening, and well illustrates the complexity of traffic movements which must be planned.

The intensity of stock utilization on a fast commuter service is geared to passenger demand and does not simply involve the continuous running of stock to the train's end from a city terminus to the suburban centres and then back again. The diagrams along the bottom of these two pages represent trains running on British Rail's Waterloo–Windsor line for the 6½-hour period between 18.00 and 00.30 hours on a weekday. Each train is represented by a ball coloured according to the train's order of departure and is coded according to its place of destination eg C – Windsor (see first panel) and its order of running eg C2 – second train to Windsor. Trains which at some point split in two, usually an eight-car set splitting in two, with each half going to a different destination, are indicated – C2a, C2b, etc.

The block of small panels (above right) indicate the individual routes of each train set in chronological order of departure from Waterloo. A double line indicates a return journey, while further lines show additional journeys by the same set in the time period covered. As mentioned above where sets split, this is also shown. Thus if we start with the small panels at A1 and refer to the first of the larger panels

The train routes of the Waterloo to Windsor line from 18.00 to 00.30 hrs are shown in chronological order of departure.

High-density rush hour traffic has been building up for some time from the Waterloo terminus.
● 18:00 hrs to 18:30 hrs
Train departures from Waterloo

During this period, the number of trains has more than doubled – indicating higher commuter demand.
● 18:31 hrs to 19:30 hrs
Train positions at 19:30 hrs

The route becomes more congested as travellers have been reaching their destinations for some time.
● 19:31 hrs to 20:30 hrs
Train positions at 20:30 hrs

Train positions at 18:30 hrs

L Waterloo · K Wimbledon Park · M Richmond · S Teddington · H Strawberry Hill · U Hampton Court · B Brentford · C Windsor · E Twickenham · V Staines · P Shepperton · J Chessington · W Ascot · G Woking · Y Dorking · A Guildford · X Aldershot · N Basingstoke · F Reading which the trains entering the central area must necessarily take their turn among the swarm of other tube trains. A striking attempt has been made to overcome this problem in Paris, by the construction of new deep-level express lines. By the use of these lines a great deal of the congestion at main line termini has been relieved by diversion of commuter trains to the new deep-level underground lines. The new network is known as the Regional Express Métro, and its outstanding feature is the provision of no more than a few spaced stations in the central area, in contrast to the closely spaced stations of the original Paris Métro, and on the London Underground. For example, the distance between the stations Auber and Défense is 7.2 km (4.5 miles), and the time allowed only 6.5 minutes inclusive of a 20 second intermediate stop at Étoile. The track and rolling stock are fully up to main line standards, though even on the Regional Express Métro provision is made for a large number of standing passengers at the peak periods. The total seating accommodation of a three-car train is 40 first class, 160 second class, seated, and 638 second class passengers standing.

One of the most remarkable modern examples of complete railway timetable integration is that now in operation on the Netherlands State Railways. Connecting all the major cities, such as The Hague, Rotterdam, Amsterdam, Utrecht, Zwolle, Eindhoven and Maastricht, there is a half-hour service of fast electric trains, so that a traveller can arrive at a city station and be sure that within half an hour at the most there will be a fast train. The service may require a change of trains en route, but the connecting service will arrive within a matter of minutes, and therefore the continuation of the journey will be equally fast. To the outermost centres, such as Leeuwarden, Groningen, and Vlissingen (Flushing), there is a one-hour service of fast electric trains. In the operation of such a network everything depends upon strict punctuality, and all trains entering the Netherlands from surrounding countries, and all goods trains, are subjugated to this basic national electric train network. So regular, standardized and punctual is the operation, that it is regulated by computer program to suit the planned timetable. At the large centres the traffic supervisors keep no more than a watching brief, and manual intervention takes place only when some unusual circumstance arises, or when some train from outside the country approaches one of the frontier stations at a time outside its timetabled path. The only passenger trains that are locomotive hauled are vices in the Netherlands are all of the multiple-unit type. electric trains operating the half-hourly and hourly ser-the international through services.

*Left* Double-deck commuter coach, Burlington Northern, waiting in Chicago Union Station.

*Below* When railways were first built, their terminals were on city edges, but as these have grown, the termini have become relatively more convenient. This diagram shows how important the main lines have become for short-distance commuting, even in Paris with its Métro.

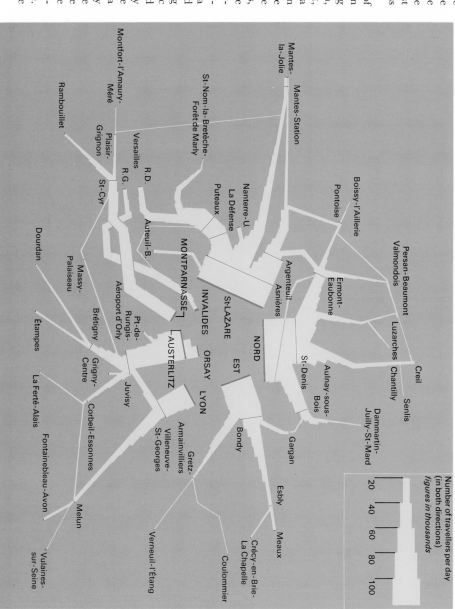

Number of travellers per day (in both directions) *figures in thousands*

Train positions at 21:30 hrs

Train positions at 22:30 hrs

Train positions at 23:30 hrs

Train positions at 00:30 hrs

20:31 hrs to 21:30 hrs

21:31 hrs to 22:30 hrs

22:31 hrs to 23:30 hrs

23:31 hrs to 00:30 hrs

By this time the number of rush hour trains has begun to diminish as the pressure is taken off Waterloo.

From 21.30 onwards there is a gradual build-up of trains returning from the suburbs to Waterloo.

A limited number of trains are leaving Waterloo on their final journeys and many more are in the sidings.

The last train has departed from Waterloo and the whole route has become virtually deserted.

# The science of freight handling

The great variety of consignments handled by the freight department of a modern railway makes essential a scientific study of traffic flows and the demands of commerce. In all parts of the world the problem of using tracks to the best advantage is severe and continuing, and whether the railway is an intensively used "mixed" line, like most of the trunk routes of British Rail, or the principal main routes in France and West Germany, or consists of lengthy stretches of single line as on some of the great transcontinental routes in North America, the ultimate aim is similar, though on a different scale: to run the longest freight trains it is practicable to operate to secure minimum line occupation.

Marshalling, and the subsequent classification after a long run to some distant distributional centre, is an expensive business, to be avoided wherever possible. While in Britain particularly today, and to a lesser extent in other countries there is a general trend towards the running of block loads of a single commodity that need no marshalling at the start, or classification afterwards, this method cannot be adopted in the majority of instances.

While marshalling is a relatively simple mechanical operation, consisting of adding vehicles in ones and twos to the rear end of a train, its classification at the end of a long through run can depend upon geographical circumstances, particularly when freight is arriving for shipment from a large port. Some of the largest and most elaborately equipped classification yards are located a few kilometres in-shore from extensive dock areas. There, arriving trains from many different inland centres, bringing a great variety of consignments, have to be sorted out and classified into trains to go to individual loading points in the docks. Notable examples of this kind of operation were established at Hull and Middlesbrough, in northeastern England, and at Melbourne, Australia. There is also the matter of city distribution of incoming freight at a time when traffic congestion on the highways is becoming critical. From the railway point of view there is a great attraction in concentrating the dispatch and receipt of goods at a few large depots, that will be well equipped with mechanized loading and unloading facilities. But road transport is involved between the actual senders and the consignees, and this inevitably slows down the overall operation. The time cycle has, however, to be considered in relation to the length of run by rail, and in this the shorter runs within the confines of a small country such as Britain cannot be compared even to western Europe, still less to North America.

The lengthy train of mixed traffic, which modern conditions require to be run at speeds at least up to 96 km/h (60 mph), continues to present a field for constant study and evolution in the practice of train handling. In North America formations of 150 cars are common, and these are more than 2.5 km (1.5 miles) long, and weigh anything up to 10,000 tonnes. Pulling power, with modern diesel-electric locomotives, is perhaps the least of the problems facing operators, because two, three or four locomotives may be coupled together electrically as well as mechanically so that they can be controlled by a single man, who may have 12,000–15,000 hp at his disposal. The science of controlling such a train at speed, and especially on long descending gradients, has now become one of the most sophisticated in the entire extent of train operation. The trains are air braked throughout, but the art of braking has advanced immeasurably from the basic principles paten-

The principle of marshalling yard operation is illustrated *below*. The central problem is usually how to split a train of wagons for mixed destinations and reassemble it into an order in which efficient delivery can be effected. Here there are 16 wagons bound for 12 different destinations. The wagons are sorted by two "moves" into the correct order for delivery. It is the job of the "hump master" to see that the moves are carefully worked out to economize on the operation. This task is usually aided today by computer operation.

Truck being slowed in marshalling yards by retarders.

Destinations

Unsorted train

First move

Pull back

Second move

Pull back

ted by George Westinghouse 100 years ago. Numerous refinements have been added to ensure smooth application throughout an enormously long train. The principle of dynamic braking is used to minimize wear of brake shoes and heating during long periods of downhill running. This reverses the action of the engines on the locomotive units, and causes them to be put "on compression" as it were.

Finally, the driver is in radio communication with the guard riding in the caboose at the rear end of the train, and also with the dispatcher at the control centre of the area in which he is running. As it frequently happens that the head end and rear end of an American freight train are completely out of sight of each other for long periods of the journey, radio communication is essential.

Such a freight train may have its formation unchanged for a distance of 1,600 km (1,000 miles) or more, except that "helper" locomotives may have to be used on certain steeply graded sections. When this happens with very long and heavy trains that may require three or four diesel-electric units of 3,000 hp continuously at the head end, the helper units are cut in intermediately, at about the half-way point of the total train. In certain cases the "helper" consists of a "posse" of another three or four locomotives, under radio control from the driver of the lead units. However, if the section of severe grading is relatively short, the "helper" may be manned by local enginemen. The cutting in of the "helper" involves a stop, division of the train, and re-coupling.

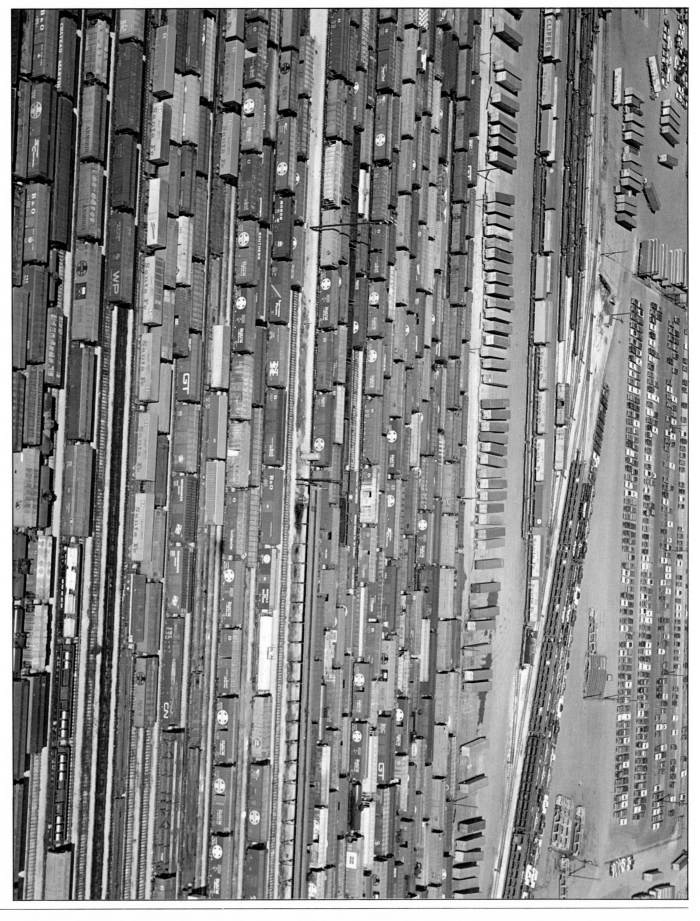

*Above* Chicago yards showing a wide variety of boxcars in the foreground, with piggyback trucks ready for loading in the middle distance, and beyond such trucks loaded up. At the top of the picture cars are seen loaded on to multiple-storey car transporters. This scene gives a good impression of the complexity and scale involved in modern marshalling operations.

*Left* Garratt pulling freight train in East Africa.

# The great marshalling yards

The location of some of the great classification yards of North America shows the philosophy of modern freight train operating on the grand scale. There is Alyth, for example, just to the east of Calgary, on CP Rail. Calgary lies at the intersection of two major routes with the transcontinental main line to Vancouver. The line from the south into Calgary serves a large group of prairie stations, and brings in a vast amount of wheat traffic, while that to the north goes to Edmonton, and mineral bearing regions of north Alberta. There is the great Conway Yard west of Pittsburgh, and Conrail, an enormous concentration area of heavy industrial traffic (see page 80). Out in the west, in addition to Barstow, the Southern Pacific has a very finely equipped modern yard at Colton, near Los Angeles, a concentration and classification point for north, south and east directions, as well as for terminal traffic in Los Angeles itself.

The basic activity in a modern mechanized classification yard is simple. A train from some distant starting point is brought into one of the reception sidings, and then its individual cars have to be sorted and routed into one of about 30 classification sidings, each of which collects traffic for one destination. The sorting is done in one continuous propelling movement over an intervening "hump". It is a continuous flow operation, in which many divergent factors have to be taken into account in order to maintain smooth operations.

The make-up of an arriving train is checked by a photoelectric scanner as it comes in, and this information is transmitted automatically to a main computer, which stores all the information concerning type of car, destination and ownership. This is because in North America there is a great number of individual, privately-owned railroads whose cars are pooled for certain traffics, and which can claim distance rates for usage by other companies. The mechanization in a modern marshalling and classification yard applies to the degree of braking applied to the cars as they roll down from the hump. The cars for different destinations have to be uncoupled by men called "pin-pullers" as they pass towards the crest of the hump, and then rolling down the steep gradient beyond they separate sufficiently for the points to be thrown between successive cars, or groups of cars coupled together, known as cuts.

Once the propelling movement starts from one of the reception sidings, with a locomotive pushing from the rear end, the computer in the main control tower takes charge. It sets the points according to the route required for each cut, and applies braking to the cars according to a bank of information it has collected. The extent to which a cut

Barstow yard looking over control tower, showing the desert conditions in which the yard was constructed. An extensive tree-planting programme will change the landscape completely in a few years' time.

**BARSTOW YARD**

Mojave Desert

to N. East and S. East

to San Francisco

Mojave

San Bernardino

San Fernando

Los Angeles

Pacific Ocean

Trains approach Barstow from three different directions. Those from northern and southern California enter straight into the receiving yard, while those from the east are directed via the hump area and enter at the opposite end.

## Receiving yard

The capacity of the receiving yard allows trains to arrive from all directions without disrupting operations in the yard. All trains enter this yard on arrival from where incoming locomotives move to the diesel service area for necessary attention. The receiving yard contains ten tracks.

## Departure yard

Following the sorting of vehicles in the classification yard, groups are moved to the departure yard to be assembled into trains. The capacity here of nine tracks, which can accommodate about 1,370 vehicles, allows the formation of three trains, one each to northern and southern California and one eastbound. The neighbouring through train inspection yard is for the examination of trains not requiring processing at Barstow.

1 Locomotive washing plant
2 Administrative office building
3 Diesel service building
4 Supervisor's tower
5 Car repair
6 Hump master's tower
7 Mechanical temperature control building
8 Hump conductor's building
9 Caboose service building
10 Mini-hump control building
11 Bowl master's office

Receiving yard
Classification yard
Local yard
Departure yard
Diesel service area
Caboose service area
Wagon repair
Through train inspection yard
Mini-hump
Retarders

View of Barstow yard as seen from knoll in picture, *top left.*

*Left* Barstow yard with hump in the foreground. Sets of retarders can be clearly seen.

## Classification yard

After trains in the receiving yard have been inspected and routes checked with the control office, they are shunted to the crest of the hump for entry to the classification yard. At the hump a total of three on-line computers have al-ready stored information about all stock and, following individual uncoupling, vehicles are guided into any one of 44 tracks by a system of computer controlled switches and braking devices. Four tracks are provided for any re-sorting of stock. The classification yard has a capacity for over 2,000 vehicles.

requires braking will depend upon how much space is available in the classification siding to which it is routed; this the computer "knows" from information constantly collected from the track itself. Then the nature of the route leading into that siding has to be considered; some have more curves on the way than others. The direction and strength of the wind must also be taken into account, because a strong adverse wind can seriously retard the running of a large box car. Lastly there is what is termed the "rollability" of the car – whether it is a good, or a bad, runner. This cannot be determined before it is actually begins to run by gravity down the hump. But apparatus in the track is available to measure this characteristic, calculations being made instantly and fed into the main computer in time for account of the rollability to be taken in applying brake pressure. The brakes, although electronically controlled, apply purely mechanical pressure, by gripping the wheels of a car as it makes its way through the yard.

While the great marshalling yards are nodal points of concentrated activity in freight train handling, no less vital are the centres of overall scrutiny and direction. At the headquarters of the Southern Railway System of the USA, at Atlanta, Georgia, can be seen, on remotely controlled illuminated track diagrams, the whereabouts of every train on this far-flung railway network, extending on its long western and northgoing main lines from New Orleans, Memphis and Cincinnati, around its central complex in Alabama and Georgia to its east coast extensions into Florida, the Carolinas and northward to Washington, DC – an extraordinary panorama of a railway on the move. Each dispatcher in charge of a particular part of this wide-ranging area is able to tell at once the contents and ultimate destination of every freight train under his control. There is, however, one important outcome of this remote supervision. There are few men along the actual lines to scrutinize the passage of trains, and with the freight trains so long it is impossible for either the driver or the guard to see what is happening all along the train. There is the possibility of axle boxes overheating, which if unattended could deteriorate to the point of collapse and derailment of the car. Accordingly an extensive programme of installing "hot-box detectors" has been carried out on American railways. On the extensive Southern Pacific, for example, whose lines extend westward from New Orleans just north of the Mexican border and up the Pacific coast to Portland, Oregon, and includes such busy centres as Los Angeles and San Francisco, there are no fewer than 448 locations fitted with hot-box detectors, which give warning to train crews and train order offices of axle boxes running hotter than at normal conditions.

# The Conrail experiment

The Consolidated Rail Corporation (Conrail) is a private, profit-making corporation established in the USA by the Regional Rail Reorganization Act of 1973, chartered in the Commonwealth of Pennsylvania, and is composed of portions of six bankrupt railroads, namely the Penn Central, the Central of New Jersey, the Lehigh Valley, the Lehigh and Hudson River, the Erie Lackawanna, and the Reading. It began operations as Conrail on 1 April 1976. Of the constituents, Penn Central was by far the largest, and was itself the product of a huge amalgamation in 1968 between the Pennsylvania and the New York Central railways. The New York, New Haven and Hartford was subsequently included in Penn Central. The reasons for the decline and eventual bankruptcy of all these companies was ascribed to the introduction of competitive modes of transport, supported in part by large government financial resources. This led to a heavy fall in railway business, and a decline in railway capital resources.

Now, with access to government investment funds of up to $2,000 million to launch operations and achieve the goal of long-term viability, Conrail is rebuilding on a massive scale. It operates some 27,200 km (17,000 miles) of route, of which Penn Central contributed more than 20,800 km (13,000 miles). A great programme of track improvement is in progress to enable speed of trains to be restored to the high standards achieved in the heyday of all the constituent companies, which include some of the most famous names in American railway history. The system network covers all the states in the northeast corridor, from Washington to Boston, and intensively those of Pennsylvania, Ohio and Indiana, with westward penetrations into Illinois, and northward into Michigan. It operates 4,500 diesel locomotives, and 148 electrics, and runs an average of 1,500 freight trains daily, using more than 151,000 freight cars. There are now eight operating regions, with headquarters in New Haven, New York, Philadelphia, Pittsburgh, Newark (New Jersey), Detroit, Chicago and Indianapolis.

*Above* Lackawanna locomotive, a one-time constituent company of Conrail.

The USA's Consolidated Rail Corporation, or Conrail, began operation on 1 April 1976, with the emblem, *left*, on its rolling stock.

Conrail locomotive.

Conrail train.

# Great Routes

# Through the Alpine fortress 1

The Alpine tunnels are all close together: only the Mont Cenis is not contained on the main map, *right*. It lies between Lyon and Turin (*below*); its northern portal is at Modane.

terrain over 1,000 metres (3,280ft) shown in brown

The Alpine tunnels are the world's most impressive group. However, tunnelling now in progress in Japan will dislodge the Simplon from its position as the world's longest: that between the islands of Honshu and Hokkaido will be 54 km (33.5 miles) long. The diagram, *below*, shows the first Simplon tunnel opened: a second driven parallel to it and opened in 1922 is slightly longer.

| Tunnel | Length | | Opened |
| --- | --- | --- | --- |
| Mont Cenis | 13.590 km | 8.445 mls | open 1871 |
| Grenchenberg | 8.578 km | 5.330 mls | open 1915 |
| Lötschberg | 14.415 km | 8.957 mls | open 1913 |
| Hauenstein | 8.134 km | 5.054 mls | open 1916 |
| Simplon I | 19.803 km | 12.306 mls | open 1906 |
| Gotthard | 14.998 km | 9.320 mls | open 1882 |
| Ricken | 8.603 km | 5.346 mls | open 1910 |
| Albula | 5.865 km | 3.645 mls | open 1906 |
| Arlberg | 10.250 km | 6.369 mls | open 1884 |

*Above* Summit of the Gotthard line. *Below left and right* Early prints of the Gotthard railway: left, the Rohrbach viaduct; right, the bridge and tunnel at Wassen.

The first proposals for a great railway under the Alps were made in 1848, for a connection between the Italian province of Piedmont and the French one of Savoy. But the times were not propitious, with war between Austria and Italy impending. It was not until 13 years later, under the joint efforts of Count Camillo Cavour, of Garibaldi, and of King Victor Emmanuel of Sardinia, that the project of a tunnel from Modane to Bardonecchia under the Mont Cenis pass, was revived. At first the idea was made light of, but when it was appreciated that the promoters were in earnest, much was written of the dangers to be incurred — of the folly of tampering with nature to the extent of driving a tunnel through "the bosom of the mighty fortress", as one English newspaper expressed it. But the Italian engineers persevered and succeeded. It was a task without precedent. In the ordinary way, with tunnel construction as pioneered by George Stephenson and others, it was the practice to sink a number of intermediate shafts to provide both additional access and a surface check on the alignment; but nothing of the kind was possible at the Mont Cenis, where the line passed beneath a mountain 3,500 m (11,500 ft) high.

To secure bearings for the direction of the bores that were to begin at Modane on the French side, and at Bardonecchia on the Italian, it was necessary to use the process known in surveying as indirect triangulation. A geometrical link-up had to be obtained between the lines of entry at the two portals, and this was obtained by taking a succession of bearings up the valley of the Maurienne, high above Modane, over the Mont Cenis pass, and then along the southern side of the pass to Bardonecchia. The survey was conducted with marvellous accuracy, despite the fact that the geometrical link between the two ends was some 64 km (40 miles) long through Alpine mountain country. The Mont Cenis route was constructed as a first class main line, with double track throughout, and the main tunnel is

An early boring machine used in Alpine tunnelling.

13.6 km (8.5 miles) long. The changeover from French to Italian operation of the trains takes place at Modane, so that haulage through the tunnel is entirely Italian. The tunnel is probably unique among the world's great pioneer engineering projects in that the time of construction was very much overestimated. When the work was started in 1857, such was the original nature of the undertaking, and the unknown conditions in those mountains into which the engineers were boring, that it was expected the 13.6 km length would not be completed in less than 25 years. Actually it would seem that the engineers were a little fortunate in not meeting any undue hazards. The final breakthrough, when the parties working from Modane and Bardonecchia met, on Christmas Day 1870, received less notice than it might otherwise have had, because the newspapers at that time were full of dramatic stories of the Prussian siege of Paris, that had followed the catastrophic military defeats suffered by France in the early stages of the Franco-Prussian War of 1870–71. The completion of the Mont Cenis Tunnel, in 1871, provided a through route from Paris to Turin, and thence to Genoa, and it is the route followed by the Rome Express of today. The experience gained by the Italian engineers in carrying out the work on the tunnel was of immense importance when the time came for even longer tunnelling projects through the Alps.

The second great Alpine tunnel was the Gotthard, of

which the spiral alignments leading to it are described on page 19. The Gotthard Tunnel opened an important new international main line from Germany through Switzerland into Italy, leading direct to Milan. It was possible by using the Eastern Railway of France, to Belfort and Basel, to travel from Paris to Milan via the Gotthard Tunnel. But it was a rather roundabout route, and after the war of 1870–71 one could well imagine that French travellers would wish to avoid passing through German territory if possible, and so the great project of the Simplon Tunnel was launched. This was a route of great historic interest. In 1805 Napoleon had ordered the construction of a "diligence" road over the Simplon Pass into Italy, and a great triumphal arch was erected in Milan to celebrate the completion of the work. The tunnel, which was projected in the 1890s, was to be a continuation of the Jura-Simplon Railway, which ran along the north shore of the Lake of Geneva, from Lausanne and then up the Rhône valley to Brig. It would provide a remarkable short cut from the Paris, Lyon and Mediterranean line to northern Italy.

Work began simultaneously at the two ends, near Brig in the Rhône valley, and at Iselle. Unlike the Gotthard the Simplon Tunnel marked the crossing of the international frontier. The gradient was rising on a moderate inclination from each end to a summit point near the middle of the tunnel, and almost exactly below the frontier, which is at the head of the Simplon Pass. It was originally intended that the line would be worked with steam locomotives, and because of the single-line bore of the main tunnel this bore was made very large: 5.9 m (19 ft 6 in) high and of a maximum width of 4.9 m (16 ft 5 in). Every precaution was taken in design to try and ensure there should be no trouble from a concentration of exhaust fumes in a very small space. At first all went well – so well that there were high hopes of the tunnel being completed in far less than the estimated time. Then troubles began to grow. In the workings from the Swiss side the temperature rose to almost unbearable heights, and at a point about 8 km (5 miles) in, it rose to 53°C (127°F). It was found that the only way to keep conditions fit for men to work in was to bring in ice-cold water and spray it on to the rocks. Once these natural hazards were mastered the contractors introduced round-the-clock working in three shifts to speed up the operation, and eventually in February 1905, the breakthrough between the Swiss and Italian workings was effected: but more than a year was to pass before the tunnel was completed and train services began. The actual date of opening to traffic was 30 May 1906, but of course on one track only. So advantageous was the shortened route from France to Italy that very soon the single-line section was proving a bottleneck, and plans were prepared for enlarging the pilot tunnel to full size. The second tunnel was opened for traffic in December 1921.

The fourth of the great main-line Alpine tunnels was the Lötschberg. In view of the forthcoming opening of the first bore of the Simplon the need was expressed for a main north-south line from central Switzerland to link up with the Jura-Simplon line and provide yet another direct connection into Italy. So the Bern-Lötschberg-Simplon Railway was projected, and to reach Brig from Bern and the beautiful shores of the Lake of Thun the line would have to be carried through the heart of the Bernese Oberland. The great tunnel at the summit, just over 14 km (9 miles) long, was to be carried beneath the lofty peaks of the Balmhorn and the Altels, but one of the great initial difficulties was that, unlike the Mont Cenis, the Gotthard and the Simplon, the routes to the tunnel entrances did not lie on any existing highways. The Lonza gorge, leading to the south portal at Goppenstein, is as desolate a ravine as

The northern portal of the Simplon tunnel.

*Above* The construction of the Simplon Tunnel was achieved with much more care than previous tunnels through the Alps. The main tunnel was excavated first by a pilot tunnel (1) which was widened and shored up (2). As this was developed solid brick lining was installed (3) before heightening took place (4). Bricking was completed (5) before the final tunnel emerged with the removal of working shoring (6). To facilitate removal of material a parallel pilot tunnel was bored with crossheads linking the two. These created a continuous flow of air for ventilation, in fact 15 times more air was pumped into the workings than was made available during the construction of the Gotthard. The pilot tunnel was later widened and opened as the second Simplon Tunnel in 1921.

The Alpine tunnels took a long time to build because they passed so far below the surface that it was not practicable to sink shafts into the line of the tunnel to provide extra working faces. The Simplon is 2,100 m (6,890 ft) below the surface at one point. It was initiated in 1898, and completed only in 1906.

SWITZERLAND

Mt. Leone

ITALY

19.803 km (12.305 miles)

12,000 ft
10,000
8,000
6,000
4,000

4,000m
3,500
3,000
2,500
2,000
1,500

# Through the Alpine fortress II

could be imagined, and subject to avalanches. Due to a series of disasters, involving much loss of life (see page 19), the route from the Kandersteg end had to be diverted.

The metre gauge Rhaetian Railway includes some extraordinary spiral and tunnelling locations as it climbs up the Albula valley, making its way on a continuous ascent of 1 in 29 to its summit point in the Albula Tunnel. From there it descends into the Upper Engadine to serve the famous Alpine resorts of St Moritz and Pontresina. Looking down on the railway from the heights above Bergün one sees an extraordinary location that looks more like the efforts of some skilful model railway enthusiast, with little space at his disposal, but anxious to include as many spirals, viaducts and tunnels as he could into the minimum space. Travelling in the smart electric trains of the Rhaetian Railway one loses all sense of direction when negotiating such a stretch, while from the privileged viewpoint of the locomotive cab the succession of curves, high viaducts and tunnels, negotiated at a surprisingly high speed, is simply breathtaking. The stone viaducts are works of art, and adorn rather than disfigure the magnificent scenery, and some idea of the skill in engineering this particular location can be gathered from the gain in vertical height of 416 m (1,365 ft) in a direct distance of 6 km (4 miles). This distance, if mounted directly, would mean a gradient of 1 in 15, but by means of the spirals and reversals of direction the actual gradient is 1 in 29. The speed is maintained at around 48–56 km/h (30–35 mph). The civil engineering and the maintenance of the track in these spectacular locations is of the highest order, and the riding of the coaches so smooth that, even when rounding curves on the edge of near-vertical precipices, there is no sensation of danger – only of wonder.

*Above* Spiral tunnels on the Gotthard line, one of the lines on which these tunnels were pioneered.

Most of the Alpine lines were originally worked by steam, including the Rhaetian Railway, owners of the Albula line and one-time owners of the 1902 0-4-4-0 Mallet type tank engine, *below left*. In only 6 km (4 miles) as the crow flies, the Albula line of the

Rhaetian Railway climbs 416 m (1,365 ft). The gradient has been kept to a manageable 1 in 29 by a series of spiral tunnels. In the diagram, *right*, the mountainside has been cut away to show how the line loops back on itself when climbing to the summit tunnel from the south.

*Below* Two modern electric Swiss trains in a mountain station.

feet 7546  6890  6233  5577  4921

metres 2300  2100  1900  1700  1500

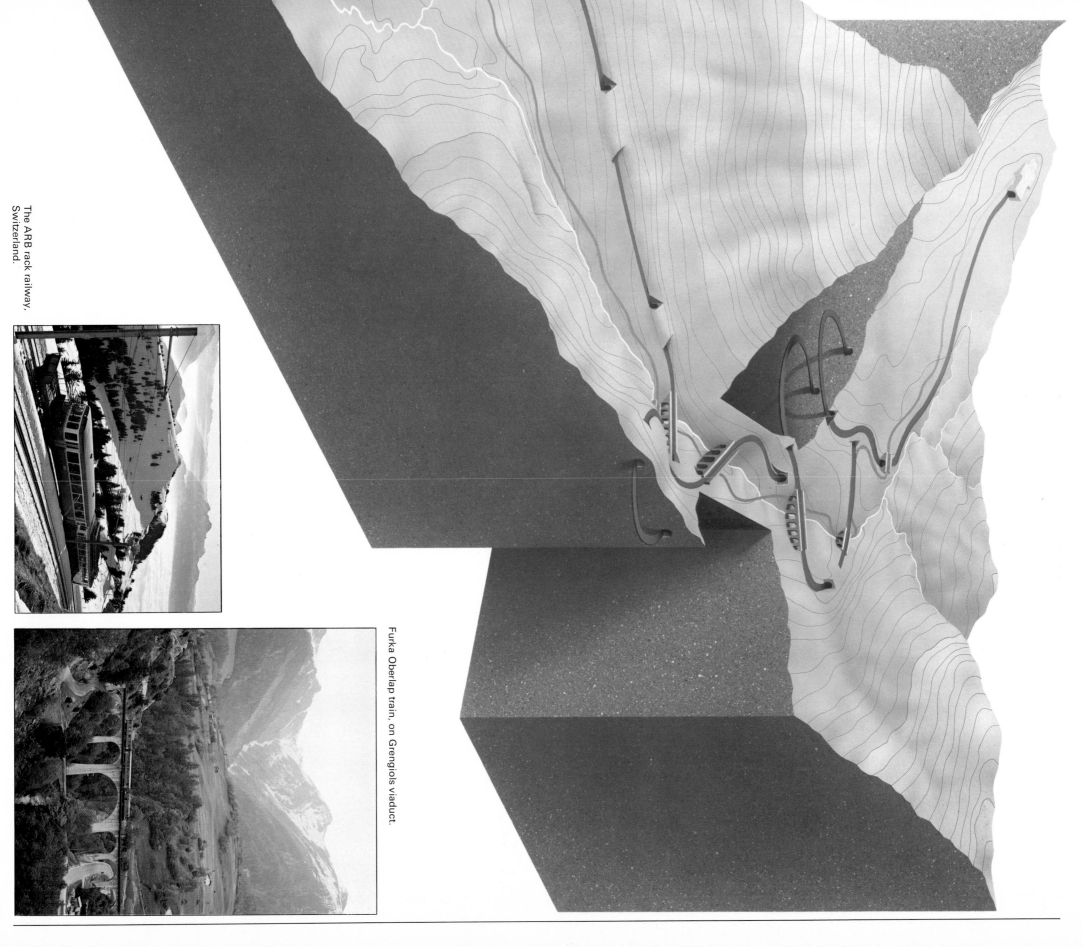

The ARB rack railway, Switzerland.

Furka Oberlap train, on Grengiols viaduct.

# Trans-Europe Expresses

*Above* TEE express leaving Bozen-Brenner tunnel in Italy.

*Left* Göschenen station, north entrance to the Gotthard Tunnel.

*Above* Talgo train, Pancarbo, Spain. *Below* TEE express at San Remo, Italy.

It was in 1957 that the idea was conceived among the original six countries of the European Economic Community, and Switzerland, of a network of fast inter-city trains providing comfortable accommodation for businessmen and other regular travellers. The idea was to combat the loss of railway travel to air services, and to provide out-and-home journeys on the same day, with time for business at the further destination. It has since been extended considerably to include trains of the same standard running into Austria, Denmark and Spain. On some routes, as between Paris and Brussels, Amsterdam and Munich, Paris and Hamburg, there is more than one train in each direction, while in the case of the longer journeys, such as Hanover-Vienna by the Prinz Eugen or Paris-Venice by Le Cisalpin, it is not possible to apply the original out-and-home concept. All the Trans-Europe Expresses (TEE) are named, while some trains that were already well established on their own account have been designated TEE by the standard of their accommodation, speed and service. Such trains are the French Mistral (Paris-Nice); the Rheingold (Netherlands-Germany-Switzerland); and the Étoile du Nord (Amsterdam-Paris). All TEE trains are first class only, and require a special supplement, according to the distance travelled. On some trains it is necessary to specify at the time of booking the type of meal required, because this determines the section of the train where the passenger's reserved seat would be allocated.

## Six types of TEE train

The first are operated jointly by the French and Belgian railways, and consist of six to twelve car trains, according to traffic requirements, hauled by electric locomotives. The passenger accommodation is in compartments and open saloons, and meals are served at passengers' own seats. When booking seats it is necessary to state whether meals are required. The Étoile du Nord is made up of Pullman-type stock. The load is usually increased considerably, by extra coaches, at Brussels, for the non-stop run to Paris. The second type of TEE train is that of the German Federal Railways, and is known as the Rheingold type. The accommodation varies according to route, from three to nine cars, in compartments and open saloons, and meals are served in a separate 42-seat restaurant car. Some trains in this category are locomotive hauled, as with the Rheingold itself, while others, like the Parsifal, between Paris and Hamburg, via Cologne, are unit trains with power units at each end. The third category of TEE train includes, among others, the French 200 km/h (125 mph) flyers Aquitaine, L'Étendard and Le Capitole. The accommodation ranges from seven to nine cars, with separate 42-seat restaurant cars. The Cisalpin, running through to Venice, includes some Swiss coaches in its formation. The trains in the third group are electrically hauled except for L'Arbalete, from Paris to Zürich, which takes the eastern region line through France, via Troyes, and is diesel hauled as far as Basel.

The fourth group of TEE trains includes only the "heavyweights" of the PLM route in France, the Mistral and the Rhodanien. Both are specified as providing 470 seats in 14 cars; meals are served in the open saloon-type coaches, or in a separate restaurant. Furthermore, the Paris-Nice section of the Mistral includes a bookstall, bar and hairdressing saloon. The Mistral, with a nine-hour run between Paris and Nice, is an afternoon train in each direction, but the Rhodanien, leaving Marseille at 07.10 hrs, provides nearly four hours in Paris (13.44 to 17.37 hrs), with the return train arriving in Marseille just after midnight. These trains with their great weight provide some of the most interesting and severe locomotive duties to be found anywhere in the world at the present time. The Rhodanien runs the 507 km (317 miles) between Paris and Lyon non-stop, in each direction, in 223 min southbound and 226 min northbound, at respective average speeds of 136.5 and 134.7 km/h (85.3 and 84.2 mph). The Mistral calls additionally at Dijon, and does the 312 km (195 miles) from Paris (Lyon) in 139 min southbound, and 140 min northbound. The former entails an average speed of 134 km/h (84 mph). Taking into account the slow running in the suburbs of Paris, both the Mistral and the Rhodanien must run at 160 km/h (100 mph) for most of the way, and on the long southward climb into the

Côte d'Or mountains to the summit at Blaisy-Bas tunnel, south of Dijon, the speed is not usually much below 152 km/h (95 mph).

The fifth group of TEE trains includes those operated by the Swiss Federal Railways, which are five-car unit train sets, electrically worked, and have seating for 168 passengers, in open saloons, with a separate restaurant car. One of these is the Gottardo, between Basel and Genoa, running non-stop over the highly picturesque Gotthard line between Zürich and Lugano. This train arrives in Genoa with just enough turn round time for the same train set to take up the return working. But a businessman can leave Zürich at 08.47 hrs, reach Milan at 13.35 hrs, and have more than four hours in this latter city before returning at 18.00 hrs, to reach Zürich at 20.57 hrs. The other TEE trains in the fifth group run between Brussels and Zürich via Luxembourg, Strasbourg and Basel. During the winter months the Iris leaves Brussels at 07.01 hrs and reaches Zürich at 13.59 hrs. The return times are 15.42 hrs and an arrival at 22.39 hrs. The complementary service is that of the Edelweiss, leaving Zürich at 06.59 hrs, and departing from Brussels on the return run at 16.11 hrs.

The sixth group is that operated by the Italian State Railways, and includes some very interesting trains, like the Settebello, described on pages 118–119. These are electrically operated, and have accommodation varying between four and eight cars, according to service. There are two other trains on the Milan-Rome line in addition to the Settebello, the Ambrosiano and the Vesuvio, which latter runs through to Naples. Then there is the Lemano, working between Milan and Geneva, and named for its long run beside Lac Leman (Lake of Geneva), and the Ligurian Sea. This latter runs between Milan and Avignon, via Genoa, the Ligurian Riviera, the Côte d'Azur and Marseille. This is a long run, of more than 7 hr, but it is

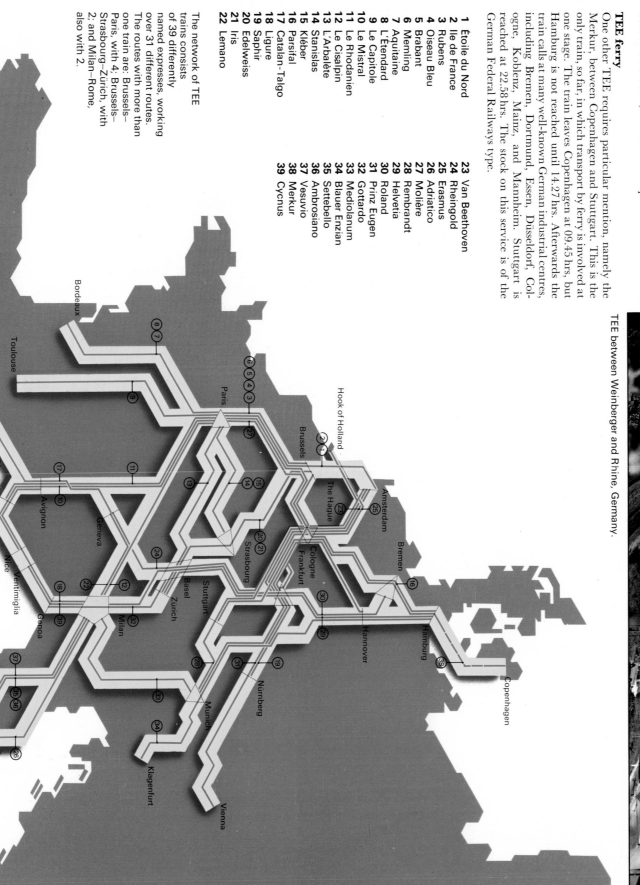

TEE between Weinberger and Rhine, Germany.

interesting as providing connection, at Avignon, with another TEE, the Catalan-Talgo, which runs between Geneva and Barcelona. This latter is unique among the TEE trains, because it is made up of the special Talgo type of coach, each of which seats only 17 passengers in an open saloon. There are nine of these cars, and meals are served in a separate 48-seat restaurant. On this service the coach wheel sets are adjusted at Cerbère from the French gauge to the Spanish, in each direction. The full journey is a long one, taking 9½ hr, travelling via Lyon, Avignon and Narbonne, and, after crossing the frontier between Cerbère and Port Bou, via Gerona in Spain.

## TEE ferry

One other TEE requires particular mention, namely the Merkur, between Copenhagen and Stuttgart. This is the only train, so far, in which transport by ferry is involved at one stage. The train leaves Copenhagen at 09.45 hrs, but Hamburg is not reached until 14.27 hrs. Afterwards the train calls at many well-known German industrial centres, including Bremen, Dortmund, Essen, Düsseldorf, Cologne, Koblenz, Mainz, and Mannheim. Stuttgart is reached at 22.58 hrs. The stock on this service is of the German Federal Railways type.

1 Étoile du Nord
2 Ile de France
3 Rubens
4 Oiseau Bleu
5 Brabant
6 Memling
7 Aquitaine
8 L'Étendard
9 Le Capitole
10 Le Mistral
11 Le Rhodanien
12 Le Cisalpin
13 L'Arbalète
14 Stanislas
15 Kléber
16 Parsifal
17 Catalan-Talgo
18 Ligure
19 Saphir
20 Edelweiss
21 Iris
22 Lemano

23 Van Beethoven
24 Rheingold
25 Erasmus
26 Adriatico
27 Molière
28 Rembrandt
29 Helvetia
30 Roland
31 Prinz Eugen
32 Gottardo
33 Mediolanum
34 Blauer Enzian
35 Settebello
36 Ambrosiano
37 Vesuvio
38 Merkur
39 Cycnus

The network of TEE trains consists of 39 differently named expresses, working over 31 different routes. The routes with more than one train are: Brussels–Paris, with 4; Brussels–Strasbourg–Zürich, with 2; and Milan–Rome, also with 2.

# The great British route: London to Glasgow

Known as the West Coast main line, the 642.4 km (401.5 mile) section from London (Euston) to Glasgow is one of the most historic in Great Britain. It includes major lengths of two great pioneer railways, the London and Birmingham, built by Robert Stephenson, and the Grand Junction, built by Joseph Locke. North of Lancaster it includes two of the earliest fast running main lines built through mountain country, the Lancaster and Carlisle, passing through the eastern flanks of the English Lakeland mountains, and then the Caledonian, continuing the line to Glasgow. Both these great routes were engineered by Joseph Locke. An important cut-off link in England was the Trent Valley line, from Rugby to Stafford, on which through trains to the north bypassed the complicated area around Birmingham. Always a very busy main line, it was until January 1923 worked by two great railways in partnership, the London and North Western, in England, and the Caledonian north of Carlisle. From 1923 they were amalgamated into the London Midland and Scottish Railway, and then became separated again at the time of nationalization of the British Railways in 1948, into the London Midland and the Scottish Regions of the new organization.

The heritage was a diverse one. When the London and Birmingham Railway was built the capacity of steam locomotives was very limited. Robert Stephenson, as a designer and manufacturer, was well aware of this and in

sperity of the NNWR was continually enhanced and the company set towards insuring the future by allocating large proportions of the profits towards improvements on the line, such as new signalling, marshalling yards and improved junction layouts.

It has never been a purely Anglo-Scottish route. In fact, the very intensity of the present-day traffic and the justification for the great modernization works carried out on it in recent years lie in the number of important centres that are served from its main stem. Over the most southerly 131 km (82 miles), between London and Rugby, there are separate services to Birmingham and Wolverhampton, to Liverpool, to Manchester, to North Wales, and over the Irish Mail route to Holyhead, to Blackpool and the Fylde coast, and to west Cumbria – all these in addition to the Anglo-Scottish services, which again are quite separate. The section between Euston and Rugby, where the Birmingham trains diverge, is without question the most intensively used section of railway in the world. When the great modernization plan for British Railways was launched in 1955, it was not surprising that this line was chosen for conversion to electric traction, together with the northward continuation to Liverpool and Manchester, and the main line network through Birmingham and Wolverhampton. Experience elsewhere in the world had shown that electrification of railways always seemed to attract new business, what is sometimes called "the sparks effect", and the modernization plan as it was developed provided for considerably more elaborate service than previously, and a great increase in scheduled speed. Whereas in steam and diesel days the hallmark of a fast express was a start-to-stop average speed of 96–105 km/h (60–65 mph), the new services were planned to raise that speed to 130 km/h (80 mph).

With many more trains, and higher speeds, the track and all the equipment had obviously to be strongly upgraded. The line itself was virtually rebuilt, putting in new rails, continuously welded, with the latest type of

reinforced concrete cross-sleepers, and extra deep granite ballasting. The system of electrification chosen was 25,000 volts, alternating current, at the commercial frequency of 50 cycles per second, with overhead line current collection. The standard of speed on the open line for express passenger was set at 160 km/h (100 mph), although when the line was first brought into service in 1966 there were many places, junctions, curves and such like, where reductions were necessary. Some of these restrictions have now been removed by the completion of realignment schemes. Colour light multiple-aspect signalling was installed throughout.

The task of carrying out the work of modernization was immense, because it all had to be done while operating what was even then one of the busiest railways in the world. Numerous temporary speed restrictions had to be enforced while track was renewed. The actual work of relaying was done mostly at weekends, but during the preparation for such work, and during the consolidation afterwards, long stretches of line at a time had to be covered at 50 km/h (30 mph) or less. Late running was frequent, and at a time when train times were at their best scarcely competitive with a fast car, let alone with internal airlines, there was an acute danger that traffic might be lost, and once lost difficult to regain. To travellers by train there was ample evidence that a great amount of work was in progress, with installation of standards for carrying

*Far left* Night electric Scot, British Rail.
*Above* Inter-city express departs from London, Euston.

The electrification of the London (Euston) line through to Glasgow, largely carried out in the 1960s, marked a considerable step forward in the history of Britain's railways. Stages in electrification meant a progressive reduction of time to make the route competitive with the air shuttle between the two cities. Further improvement will come with the introduction of the Advanced Passenger Train.

(Map labels: London, Rugby, Birmingham, Stafford, Crewe, Manchester, Liverpool, Preston, Carlisle, Glasgow)

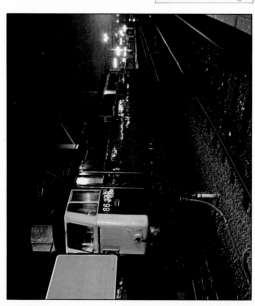

planning the line he decided that the steepest gradient should be 1 in 330. Although the country in the south of England did not involve crossing any mountain ranges, there were chalk escarpments on the north side of the Chiltern Hills, a northeastern extension of the Cotswold limestone at Blisworth and the Kilsby Ridge. To avoid steep gradients, Stephenson had to excavate, by hand, some tremendous cuttings and the tunnel under the Kilsby Ridge was one of the most troublesome works on the line. But the result was a magnificent route over which heavy loads could be operated with relatively small locomotives. Indeed, the rapid increase in the volume of traffic became an embarrassment, and before the nineteenth century was out two additional 96 km (60 mile) running lines had to be laid. Most of this Trent Valley line is quadruple tracked, as is the line north of Stafford as far as Weaver Junction, 280 km (175 miles) north of London.

The London and North Western, and the Caledonian Railways were regarded as the premier lines of England and Scotland, respectively. They had the largest annual revenues, and their pre-eminence was shown indirectly on their coats of arms. The LNWR adopted 'Britannia' herself, while the Caledonian took the Royal Arms of Scotland. The West Coast main line was also the principal artery of mail traffic between London and the North, as well as to Ireland via Holyhead, and it was known as the Royal Mail Route. Trains carrying travelling post offices from many parts of Great Britain fed into the postal trains of the West Coast main line at Tamworth, Crewe, Preston and Carlisle. Both companies prided themselves on their punctuality of running. The nineteenth-century chairman of the LNWR, Sir Richard Moon, always said that the publication of a timetable was the promise of an English gentleman and should be honoured as such. The prooverhead wires and the rebuilding of stations. Then stage by stage the electrification was completed: Manchester to Crewe first, then southwards to Nuneaton, and a phenomenal change came over the train running in the almost uncanny acceleration from rest, and in the smoothness of travel at high speed. The management of the London Midland Region was, however, anxious that the improved service on the electrified line should be reflected in the important connecting services that must remain for some time diesel operated, and an intricate pattern of cross-country connections was devised, centred upon Birmingham, whereby trains from the southwest of England, and South Wales, connected by cross-platform interchange with trains to the northwest and Scotland. No longer were long waits for connections to be tolerated, or missed connections through late running. New Street station, Birmingham, was to be the nodal point of the entire service, with the direct Liverpool, Manchester and Scottish trains using the Trent Valley line, and bypassing Birmingham so timed that on the critical London–Rugby section their running fitted in with London–Birmingham trains involved in the New Street connectional pattern.

The continuation of the electrified system northwards to

Carlisle and Glasgow was a much discussed, and some-what delayed, project. Although the through train services from London to the Scottish cities were joined north of Preston by those from Liverpool and Manchester, there was not the same density of passenger traffic as on the line south of Crewe, and there was at first some difficulty in establishing financial justification for the capital outlay. But with electric traction there was the possibility of spectacular acceleration of service on the mountain gradients of the north country. Between Carnforth, on Morecambe Bay, and Shap Summit, for example, the line rises 270 m (885 ft) in 50 km (31.5 miles), and with heavy trains in pre-electrification days one could not expect to cover that distance in much less than 35 min. But the powerful electric locomotives were able to climb a 1 in 75 gradient at 145 km/h (90 mph) with a 12-coach train, and it has been possible to schedule a point-to-point time of 22 min up that long climb, an average speed of 137 km/h (85 mph). The curves in places preclude maximum speeds, but today the 145 km (90 miles) between Preston and Carlisle are regularly run in less than 65 min, start to stop.

The acceleration is the same in Scotland where the formidable Beattock Bank has to be climbed – 16 km

(10 miles) at an inclination of 1 in 75. As a result of electrification, passenger train speeds north of Preston are 160 km/h (100 mph) wherever the track permits, except on the steepest gradients. But no less important is the manner in which the very heavy night freight trains are operated. The basic speed for these is 120 km/h (75 mph), and with the maximum tonnage freightliners, conveying 60 con-tainers on 20 flat wagons (three on each), a pair of electric locomotives are used in order to maintain the high speed required uphill, which is little below 120 km/h (75 mph), on a 1 in 100 gradient.

With electric locomotives of 5,000 hp and trains of 12 modern air-conditioned coaches, the time over the 642 km (401.5 miles) between London and Glasgow is 5 hr, an average of 130 km/h (80 mph) including one stop, or a few minutes longer on trains that make more than one intermediate stop. It is planned to introduce the Advanced Passenger Train on to this route, which through its tilting feature will allow the curves as at present engineered to be traversed at considerably higher speed. With the APT sets in operation it is expected that the overall time between London (Euston) and Glasgow will be reduced to 4 hr, an average from start to stop of 160 km/h (100 mph),

Erecting the overhead wiring, slung from the catenary masts. Performed from the flat roofs of special coaches.

Running the test train to check proper circuitry.

The opening of the line for high-speed running using electric motive power. When the line first opened between Crewe and London there was an immediate saving of 30% on the original journey time.

Pouring cement into the holes from a special cement train, equipped with a number of mixers.

Raising catenary masts for bolting on to the concrete base.

Erecting new four-aspect coloured light signalling.

*Left to right:*
Raising bridges to make room for overhead wires.

Digging a new track base.

Digging holes for the erection of metal masts to hold the catenary system.

The process of electrif-ication used on the London to Glasgow route.

# Rail versus air: a real contest

By air
By rail

**New York – Washington**
2 hrs 40 mins *air*
4 hrs 6 mins *rail*

**Tokyo – Osaka**
2 hrs *air*
3 hrs 10 mins *rail*

**Hamburg – Zurich**
3 hrs 20 mins *air*
9 hrs 24 mins *rail*

**Hamburg – Munich**
3 hrs 6 mins *air*
7 hrs 35 mins *rail*

**New York – Chicago**
4 hrs 10 mins *air*
18 hrs *rail*

**Paris – Lyons**
3 hrs 30 mins *air*
3 hrs 45 mins *rail*
1 hr 45 mins in 1982

**London – Glasgow**
3 hrs 10 mins *air*
5 hrs *rail*

Centre-to-centre journey times are increased by air travel because of the time spent travelling to the airport; this can make rail travel very competitive, though there is a limit as to how far such speed-ups will be possible.

*Above* Munich station, a modern inter-city train – clean, sleek, fast and exciting.

Modern electric inter-city train on Euston-Glasgow line.

In the early 1960s there was much talk in the advanced countries of the world that railways had become obsolete, except for crowded and unattractive commuter areas, where they would continue to compete with the increasingly congested road approaches to large cities. The experience of the great long-distance railways in the USA in losing practically all their high-class passenger business to airlines seemed a pointer to what could happen elsewhere. In Europe railways had taken a terrible beating in the Second World War and recovery at first was not rapid; and when the modernization plan for British Railways was first launched, there were some influential people who did not believe that any appreciable acceleration of service was either necessary or desirable: all that was needed was to get rid of steam traction. Fortunately, wiser councils prevailed, and as in France, and to a slightly lesser degree in West Germany and Italy, the cue has been taken from the astonishing success of the *Shinkansen* lines in Japan. In Britain, as in France, the target for inter-city overall speed is being pressed to well above 130 km/h (80 mph). In both countries there are intermediate stages of lengthy inter-city journeys from one intermediate station to another, booked at start-to-stop average speeds of more than 160 km/h (100 mph), within overall averages, including intermediate stops, of around 145 km/h (90 mph).

This tremendous upsurge in passenger train speed, coupled with punctuality of service, smoothness of running, and reliability in all but the most extreme of winter weather conditions, is definitely reversing the trend of travel habits in countries having the journey times at present prevailing in Europe. It is, however, not likely that any appreciable change will be seen in countries such as the USA, in which the distances are so great that air travel holds an advantage that not even the most dramatic of railway accelerations can outweigh. But in Britain, with the regular journey time between London and Liverpool, and between London and Manchester, down to no more than 2.5 hr, that between London and Birmingham at 1.5 hr, and between London and Bristol less than 1.5 hr, the advantage is passing to the railways. The service is from city centre to city centre, avoiding all the delay and frustration of travel to the airports, inevitable delays at crowded air terminals, and, with the dependence of air travel upon good weather conditions, the risk of cancellation or prolonged delay.

Fog and other conditions of bad visibility – hazards to air traffic – are no longer hindrances to the running of high-speed railway services. Colour light signals them-

selves have a far greater range than the oil lamps of the previously-used semaphores, but today most high-speed main lines in Europe have some form of cab signalling to supplement the wayside signals, and on lines such as that from London to Bristol, or the electrified line from Euston to the North, the continued incidence of audible signals in the cab as every colour light signal is passed gives the necessary confidence to run at full speed. On the Japanese *Shinkansen* lines there are no wayside signals at all, and the visual indications in the cab, derived from an inductive link-up with electric currents flowing in the track circuits, display to the driver the speed at which he must run. If conditions on the line ahead require a reduction of speed, this is immediately shown on the display panel in front of the driver, and if within a short time he has not taken appropriate action the train brakes are applied. Such equipment serves to show that even while the speed of passenger trains has increased to such an extent as to give

them a distinct advantage when competing with air travel over relatively short distances, that increase in speed has not been achieved at the expense of the safety that is such a cherished attribute of rail travel the world over. Neither does the present level of passenger train speed represent the foreseeable limit. The Advanced Passenger Train will set newer limits, and the French are now building the new TGV line between Paris and Lyon, which will be the fastest railway in the world.

It would appear therefore that in the battle for supremacy as a means of efficient transport, the railway networks of the world – with their intrinsic advantages – are still very much a force to be reckoned with.

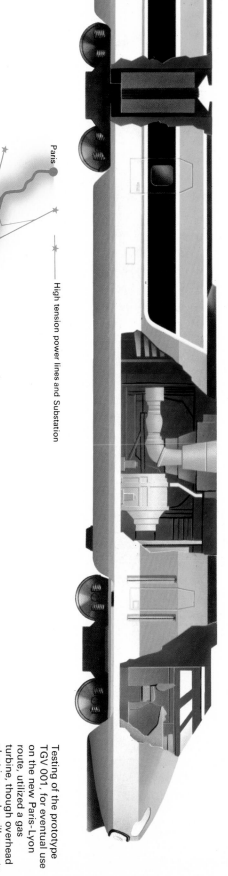

Testing of the prototype TGV 001, for eventual use on the new Paris–Lyon route, utilized a gas turbine, though overhead electric supply will operate.

The French National Railways have pressed the aim of high-speed services with a great deal of success on lines to the southwest, over the routes of the former Paris–Orleans–Midi Railway, now covering the 580km (360 miles) between Paris and Bordeaux non-stop in 3 hr 50 min, an average speed of 151 km/h (94 mph). The 'rapides'' on this route run at 200 km/h (125 mph) on favourable stretches of line, but it is not on this route that the most urgent need for development presented itself. It was the southeastern route from Paris to Dijon and Lyon that was becoming saturated, and which by its nature could not accommodate speeds of more than 160 km/h (100 mph). The decision was taken to build an entirely new line on which speeds of 300 km/h (185 mph) could be run. Like the British HST sets, and the Japanese *Shinkansen* trains, the new French *très grande vitesse* (TGV) sets will be entirely self-contained electric formations, and it is the intention that all day services leaving Paris from the Gare de Lyon will eventually be of this type. Although travelling TGV trains will travel at the new level of high speed while on the new line, and beyond it they will run at the maximum now permitted on the existing routes.

This arrangement will make possible some striking accelerations that will make it difficult for the airlines to compete. For example, the present fastest time from Paris to Lyon, 507 km (317 miles) is 3 hr 44 min, an average of 137 km/h (85 mph). By the TGV route the time will be the level 2 hr. Continuing beyond Lyon along the existing route to the south, the present and future times to Avignon are 5 hr 37 min and 3 hr 49 min, and to Marseille 6 hr 33 min and 4 hr 43 min. This latter, over a distance of 856 km (535 miles) from Paris represents an average speed of 180 km/h (113 mph), even though 349 km (218 miles) is over an ordinary, and not a TGV line. The new line now being built runs through very hilly country to the west of Dijon, but in order that TGV trains can reach Dijon and continue from there to the Swiss frontier at Vallorbe, and on to Lausanne, connection with the existing main line is made at Saint-Florentin. Similarly, connection is again made at Saint-Florentin. Similarly, connection is again with the existing line at Macon for passage on to the line to Geneva and Turin via the Mont Cenis Tunnel. Again the service accelerations forecast are impressive, reducing the time from Paris to Lausanne from 4 hr 37 min to 3 hr 29 min, and to Geneva from 5 hr 30 min to 3 hr 19 min.

The new Paris–Lyon line, which will open in 1982, is being built to cater for a high passenger traffic demand. It will link urban areas which make up 40% of the French population, and also provide a high-speed connection for international travellers. The new line conforms to very high standards consistent with speeds of 300 km/h (186 mph) by the TGV series of motive power. This will reduce journey time over the route from the 3 hr 44 min today, to just 2 hours.

This latter saving of more than two hours on a journey of international importance will be of great advantage to a large number of rail users.

The new line does not actually enter Paris, but begins at a junction with the existing line at Courbs la Ville. South of that station progress will then be so swift that passengers will see little of the intervening country, and its place among the great railway routes of the world will be based solely on statistical performance, rather than on any accompanying appreciation of the passing scene. This latter is of course very much the case with air travel, and it is with the air that the TGV trains will compete. Like the *Shinkansen* lines in Japan, this new French line will carry only passenger trains; but their removal from the existing line will leave that splendidly equipped railway relatively free to carry the ever-increasing freight traffic. This is due to development of the port of Fos between Marseille and the Rhône delta.

One important feature of the TGV sets now under construction is that their electrical equipment will require to accommodate different systems of electric power supply. The existing PLM line into Paris, and south of Lyon, is operated on 1,500 volts dc, but the new line will have the present French standard system of 25,000 volts ac, at 50 cycles. Furthermore, on the TGV sets that work to Lausanne, provision will be made to operate on the Swiss system at 16,000 volts ac at $16\frac{2}{3}$ cycles per second. The equipment is so designed to facilitate changing from one to another at the changeover points without stopping. Although from a sightseeing point of view there will be complete uniformity in the appearance and speed of all trains using the new lines, it will nevertheless be regarded as an epoch-marking step forward in the history of rail transport in the twentieth century.

*Right* Construction in progress on the new Paris–Lyon route cutting through open country with the minimum of disturbance.

# Across Asia : the eastern goal

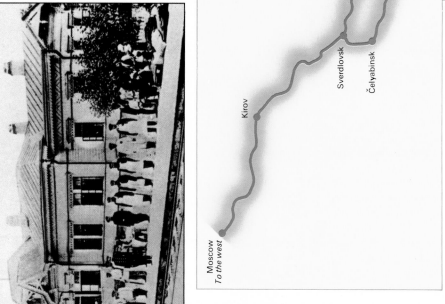

It has been said that the Trans-Siberian Railway is the backbone of the USSR. It is the longest continuous railway in the world, for the distance from Moscow to Vladivostok is nearly 10,000 km (6,000 miles). The Russians began their eastern progress in the sixteenth century, and the first Russian troops to reach the Pacific were a regiment of Cossacks in 1639. The absorption of Siberia into the Russian Empire continued during the following 200 years and it was in 1858, during the worldwide railway mania, that the first proposals were made for a Trans-Siberian Railway to the Pacific. The Russian government turned a deaf ear to these proposals, for the Crimean War had drained the Russian exchequer and it was not until 1875 that the Ministry of Communications dared to put forward an official plan, and even then it was not approved. But the seed had been sown, and a succession of official and semi-official plans were put forward during the following years. In the late 1880s a survey and estimates were made, and in 1891 the government gave its official approval and, later in the same year, Crown Prince Nicholas cut the first sod at Vladivostok during his Far Eastern tour.

By that time the Russian railways had reached across the Siberian border to Čel'abinsk and construction began at both ends. But the Russian Finance Minister was still daunted by the estimated cost of the line at a period when a succession of bad harvests had caused financial stringency and it was not until Sergius Witte, a professional rail-wayman, became Finance Minister that progress on a large scale began, partly with loans from French and other sources. A Trans-Siberian Committee was formed, with Prince Nicholas in the chair and a membership that included almost every important figure in government circles, and the whole vast undertaking was put on a business footing.

The projected line passed through Omsk, Novosibirsk and Krasnojarsk, to Irkutsk, near Lake Baykal. Thus far the project was fairly straightforward, as the line would be comparatively level, passing through the fertile strip

bounded on the north by tundra and on the south by arid country. From Irkutsk, however, engineering difficulties began, for the country was mountainous from Lake Baykal eastwards. After consideration the Committee decided that it would save time and money to cross the lake by train – ferry rather than to circumvent it by rail. From the eastern shore of Lake Baykal the line would pass through Ulan-Ude and Čita.

The engineers had put in a pessimistic report about the section of the railway circumventing the Chinese province of Manchuria. The country north of the Amur river (the frontier) was very rough and much earthwork would be

*Top* An early view of Obi, one of the stations on the Trans-Siberian Railway, showing a wood-burning locomotive fitted with a spark-arresting chimney.

*Right* The dramatic sight of huge Russian stock hauling a train across the frozen wastes traversed by the Trans-Siberian Railway.

needed, which would consume time and money. The Committee decided that it would be much better if some arrangement would be made with the Imperial Chinese government which would allow the railway to be built through the comparatively flat land of Manchuria, as this would be both shorter and cheaper. The coronation of the Tsar Nicholas II in 1895 gave the Russians an opportunity of meeting high Chinese officials, and invitations were sent. They were pleased when the Imperial Chinese government selected the Marquis Li Hung-chang as their envoy, for not only was he the most capable man of his time, but he was a believer in railway construction. Furthermore, he was known to be apprehensive of a war with Japan and thus inclined to seek other friends. An agreement resulted to create the Chinese Eastern Railway, a joint Sino-Russian company stretching across Manchuria and thus permitting the completion of the Trans-Siberian Railway. The agreement went further and permitted the Russians, jointly with the Chinese, to construct a branch of the Trans-Siberian line southwards about 800 km (500 miles) to Talien (Lüda) and Port Arthur at the southernmost tip of Manchuria. These were both ice-free ports, and thus preferable to Vladivostok.

The Russians lost no time in forming the company and in pushing ahead with construction. They had, however, difficulties with the "Hung Hudze", wild and aggressive tribes that looted construction camps and wire from the tracks. The railway police, almost wholly Russian in personnel, were reinforced to keep order, and the Russians became dominant in northern Manchuria. The lack of hard roads was another difficulty faced by the engineers, who finally decided to build a supply line of low quality along the selected route, and to build the permanent line alongside it. This saved time and money.

In 1903 the Chinese Eastern Railway was complete, not only the west to east line, but also the branch to Port Arthur, and as the connecting lines on both frontiers had already been built, through running from St Petersburg (Leningrad) to Vladivostok was possible, except for the line round Baikal, completed in 1904.

The quality of the line was, however, low, due to the original orders of the Committee. The line had been laid with light rails which allowed an axle load of only 13 tonnes, and the sleepers were untreated, while ballast was very thin due to shortage of stone on several sections of the route. The Chinese Eastern line also gave much trouble. Nevertheless the line was completed and traffic beginning to flow, hindered only by numerous derailments. A big programme of improvements, the cost of which would be met partly out of revenue, was put in hand and lasted for many years, although the advent of the Russo-Japanese War held up development. The railway was in no fit state to cope with large-scale military traffic, and its limitations were an important, if not the prime, cause of the Russian defeat. The peace treaty included the cession to the Japanese of two-thirds of the southward Trans-Siberian line and the loss of Talien and Port Arthur.

The Committee had already decided that it was necessary to circumvent Manchuria and the Chinese Eastern Railway, and construction began. It was difficult and was not completed until 1916 when it was at once used to its full capacity in carrying war material from Japan and the United States to help Russia's war effort in the First World War. By that time, however, the quality of the whole Trans-Siberian Railway had been much improved and it withstood the traffic satisfactorily.

The line was vital in the civil war that followed the Russian Revolution, but after a pause the programme of improvements continued and has, in fact, never ceased. The Russians sold their share of the Chinese Eastern Railway to the Japanese in 1935, but have pushed on with railway construction in their own territories. The line from Moscow to Irkutsk has now been doubled and electrified, while the remainder is now worked almost wholly by diesel power. The quality of the passenger accommodation is now on a par with the Wagons-Lit company trains of the 1900s, which were regarded as equal to anything in the world at that time.

View from Trans-Siberian Railway.

The Trans-Siberian railway from Moscow to Vladivostok was built at a cost of $250,702,000. The construction of a more northerly line, from Lake Baykal to the River Amur, has recently been announced with completion due in the 1980s. Basically seen as a strategic plan, the new 2,880 km (1,800 mile) route will have the added advantage of opening up eastern Siberia for settlement and trade.

# Across Asia: the great dream

## The Trans-Asian Railway

It was not until recently that the name "Trans-Asian Railway" came into prominence, the reason being that although the railways in Turkey, Iran, Pakistan, India, Bangladesh, Burma and Thailand were all developing and extending over the years, it was a comparatively short time ago that governments and railway authorities gave attention to the possible advantages of linking them up. In recent years the United Nations Committee for Asia and the Pacific (ESCAP) became interested, and now holds biennial meetings to review progress. ESCAP's researches indicate that although it is unlikely that long-distance through traffic will be large, short-distance traffic on sections of the Trans-Asian Railway will often be considerable, and they cite the example of Turkey and Iran where there has been a big increase of international traffic since the railways were linked up in 1971. ESCAP also estimates that the costs of freight traffic overland will be competitive with those of seaborne traffic.

The Trans-Asian Railway starts at Haydarpasa, Istanbul's eastern terminus across the Bosporus. The railway from Europe to Istanbul was completed in the 1880s and train ferries now take railway rolling stock across the Bosporus, until such time as the planned railway tunnel under the straits is built. From Haydarpasa the line climbs to Eskişehir and then runs eastwards across rolling country to Ankara, the capital. From there it runs through Kayseri and Malatya to Tatvan on the shore of Lake Van. Train ferries carry trains across the lake, and so to the Iranian frontier at Qotûr. In Iran the line skirts Lake Urmia to Tabrîz and continues on to Tehrân, through hilly and windswept country. From Tehrân the line runs south to Qom Junction and from thence southeastwards for some 800 km (500 miles) to Kermân, the present railhead. From Kermân the line has been surveyed to a junction with the isolated section of the Iranian State Railway running from Zâhedân to Mîrjaveh on the Pakistan border, a distance of less than 500 km (300 miles). At Mîrjaveh the gauge of the railway will change from standard gauge to the Pakistan and India gauge of 1,676 mm (5 ft 6 in). This means that all passengers and freight must be transhipped; though later it is intended to reduce the amount of transhipment by changing the gauge of through vehicles, as is done between France and Spain. The branch line of the Pakistan Railway which runs to Mîrjaveh will be rebuilt to main line standards to take the anticipated through traffic. Trans-Asian trains will use this line, crossing the Indus at Rohri and from there they will continue at speed on the electrified main line to Lahore.

From Lahore the line runs to the Indian border and from there to Delhi, and so down the Ganges valley to the neighbourhood of Calcutta.

Once the gap between Kermân and Zâhedân is filled, there will be a through rail route from Europe to Calcutta, and the economic forecasts are favourable. The remainder of the Trans-Asian route, however, is not as yet finally settled. It will diverge from the line to Calcutta some

Train crossing Turkey on an early part of the route.

300 km (186 miles) north of the city. All railways in Burma, Malaysia, Thailand, Cambodia (Khmer) and Vietnam are built to metre gauge and there must, therefore, be a transfer point from 1,676 mm (5 ft 6 in) gauge to metre gauge for all traffic somewhere in eastern India or in Bangladesh. Where this transfer point is situated will depend on where the Brahmaputra River is bridged. If this is done at Bâhâdurâbâd, as seems most probable, the change of gauge is likely to be made at Katihâr, where a transfer point already exists.

The Trans-Asian Railway will then cross into Bangladesh and run through the lush delta country to Chittagong. Its forward route is not yet settled. The government of Burma has already given its approval in principle to the plan of a railway across Burma but has not yet indicated what route it prefers the railway to follow. One alternative would be for the line to run south from Chittagong through Cox's Bâzâr and on towards Sittwe before turning east, penetrating the Arakan mountains and crossing the Irrawaddy to Myingyan. From there it could run on existing lines to Thazi Junction and on to Taunggyi before turning south on new construction to cross the Salween River to Thailand. Once across the frontier, in very mountainous country, it could join the Thailand State Railway at Chiang Mai. This is one alternative, but there are several others, all equally difficult from the engineering viewpoint, and depending also on political decisions. The only point that seems to have been decided is that the line built in 1943–44 will not be followed.

Once on the Thailand State Railways, the Trans-Asian Railway will descend to the plains and pass through Bangkok. From there it will run in an easterly direction to the frontier of Cambodia at Aran Pradet (Paôy Pêt), and from there to Phnum Pênh, the capital. This is the present railhead, but a line has been surveyed from Phnum Pênh to Ho Chi Minh City (Sai-gon). The Vietnam Railways system runs from Ho Chi Minh City to Hanoi along the coast, and then turns inland to Pingxiang which is the frontier town of China. At Pingxiang there already exists a transhipment point where all traffic must transfer from metre gauge to Chinese standard gauge.

## Chinese railways

The Chinese railways have, in recent years, come to appear more obviously Chinese. This might seem surprising, because until less than 50 years ago there were no Chinese standards and specifications, and each railway adopted the methods and designs of the country that financed the railway's construction. As a consequence, British, French, American, Japanese, Russian, and even Dutch and Belgian, designs could be seen at work, which lent the railways a colourful variety unmatched elsewhere. Now that Chinese standards and specifications are used, they are not uninfluenced by the good railway ideas of other nations. The net result, however, is indubitably Chinese.

There are just eight rail entrances to China. As China is an enormous country, covering one-eighth of the habitable area of the world, this may seem very few, but China has

Development of the Trans-Asian Railway, Istanbul to Peking, is now controlled by a United Nations committee. As shown, the majority of the route is already in existence, although with a variety of gauges, and only a few stretches remain to be built, of which Zâhedân-Kermân is scheduled for completion by 1980. Burmese plans have yet to be announced, however, and the project is hindered by war in Indo-China. It is likely to be many years before operation of such a route will be effected.

never encouraged intercourse with other nations, and of the eight existing entrances, only two are in common use, these being the railway between Hong Kong and Canton, and the entrance from eastern Europe which is a line leaving the Trans-Siberian Railway at Ulan-Ude, crossing the Gobi Desert, and reaching Jining in China where the bogie wheels of Russian 1,524 mm (5ft) gauge are changed for others of the Chinese standard gauge. Of the remaining entrances, two are from North Korea, two from Vietnam, and two others from the Trans-Siberian Railway in Manchuria, the last four all requiring a change of gauge.

The Chinese railways are well maintained, well run, and profitable. The standard gauge track is solid and well ballasted. Bridges are being strengthened and loading gauges give ample room. A relic of British influence is that on many railways high platforms are in use, though passenger cars always have end gangways and steps, with a deck that is used at high platforms. Carriages have an eastern European general appearance, and the wagon stock, though based on British and Japanese designs, has a generally American appearance. Motive power is at present mainly steam, though electric traction is used on lines with heavy traffic and heavy grades. In districts where water is short and fuel has to be transported long distances, diesel locomotives are being built to handle passenger traffic.

The principal lines run a distance of 2,260 km (1,400 miles), from Canton in the south, to Peking in the north, via Wuhan, where the Yangtse is crossed on a magnificent road and rail bridge. The route is mainly through hilly and attractive farmland, though after crossing the Yellow River on another remarkable bridge, the hills disappear, and the line crosses the great North China Plain, finally arriving at Peking.

A second main route is that from Peking, through Tientsin and Tsinan in Shantung, to Nanking on the Yangtse, crossing even a finer and larger bridge en route.

Steam train in front of Agra fort, India.

From Nanking the line runs southeast through rice fields to the outlying factories of Shanghai, one of the largest cities in the world. From Shanghai it runs south to Hangchow, onwards in a southwesterly direction through lush farmland becoming slowly more hilly, until it joins the Canton-Wuhan line at Chuchou.

Perhaps the most remarkable of the Chinese railways is

First train across the Yangtse bridge, China.

that that runs east and west across China, with interconnections with the two main routes already described. After crossing the fertile land of Honan, this enters loess country, and the scenery becomes spectacular, especially when running on a shelf above the Yellow River. Sian, an ancient capital of China, is passed and we reach Lanchow,

a rapidly developing city. The line then runs over 1,000 km (620 miles) westwards to Tumen, with its oil wells, and on to Urumchi, and finally to Kelamayi, another oil city.

Two separate lines now unite China proper with Manchuria, both reaching Shenyang (Mukden). This is at the centre of a highly industrialized district with the great Fushun open-cast coalmine and the great Anyang steel-works a short distance to the south. From Shenyang railways run south to Lüda (Talien), southeast to Korea, northeast to Hailung, and north to Changchun and Haerbin, an industrial city on the former Chinese Eastern Railway, which has its junctions with the Trans-Siberian Railway to east and west.

There are many other lines in China, but those already mentioned are the most important. The most spectacular one of all, however, is the line running northwest from Peking through the Nankow Pass, under the Great Wall, to Kalgan and from there westwards to Baotou and Lanchow. As can be seen from the foregoing account, China's railways are on a par with any others in Asia and are expanding faster than any in the world.

Quetta
Lahore
Amritsar
Delhi
Allahabad
Patna
Calcutta
Sukkur
PAKISTAN|INDIA
INDIA|BANGLADESH
Dacca
BANGLADESH|BURMA
Chittagong
Mandalay
Taunggyi
BURMA|THAILAND
Chiang Mai
Bangkok
THAILAND|CAMBODIA
Phnum Pénh
CAMBODIA|VIETNAM
Sai-gon
Ha-noi
VIETNAM|CHINA
Nanning
Canton
Hengyang
Wuhan
Zhengzhou
Peking
Shanghai

# Australia: crossing the arid continent

Nullarbor Plain, 320 km (200 miles) east of Kalgoorlie, taken from rear observation platform.

When the proposal was first put forward of integrating the individual Australian colonies into a unified federation, Western Australia stood apart. She was alone, separated from the rest by the virtually unknown desert lands of the Nullarbor Plain, and saw no advantage to herself in being united. Yet it was felt that without her, federation could not be a success, and as an inducement for her to join the federal government, it was offered that a railway would be constructed eastward from Kalgoorlie to join the nearest point of the South Australian system, which was then at Port Augusta. On the strength of this, and of other inducements, Western Australia agreed to join, and the Commonwealth of Australia was inaugurated on New Year's Day 1901. Between Kalgoorlie and Port Augusta, however, lay more than 1,600 km (1,000 miles) of virtually unexplored territory, and with no more than a few handfuls of Aboriginal tribes scattered over the land, it is not surprising that it took some time to launch the actual constructional work on the railway.

## Lines across the desert

The prospectors went out on camels. The expeditions took some preliminary organizing, because there would be no chance of living off the land. It was so absolutely devoid of physical features and human habitation that any survey party would have to go out furnished for a stay in a waterless desert. One thing the early surveyors did find, however, is that the line could be made literally straight, and practically level for hundreds of kilometres. Many years passed before estimates could be placed before the federal government, to get the expenditure approved, and it was not until 14 September 1912 that the first sod was cut, with great ceremony, by the Governor-General of Australia. The building of the line was like nothing that had gone before: no great mountain ranges to cross, no primeval jungles to cut through, no hostile natives, no attacks by wild animals. The working parties had to be completely self-contained. In the 1,682 km (1,051 miles) between Kalgoorlie and Port Augusta there was not a single running stream, and the provision of water supplies for the constructional gangs was the greatest problem of all. Water had to be divined, wells sunk, and reservoirs constructed, and out in the open, with not a tree for hundreds of kilometres, the midday heat was intense. Track laying began in 1913, and four years later the first through train steamed out of Kalgoorlie.

It was not a through train in the ordinary sense because

the "Trans", as it is still called today, was laid to the 1,435 mm (4 ft 8½ in) standard gauge, and at both ends the gauge was 1,067 mm (3 ft 6 in). Why the difference? At the time the "Trans" was authorized, the problem of different gauges in Australia was highly controversial. Only New South Wales had the standard gauge. But the federal government had set its sights on ultimate standardization, and the standard gauge seemed the logical one to use, rather than the 1,600 mm (5 ft 3 in) of South Australia and Victoria, or the restrictive 1,067 mm of Western Australia and parts of South Australia. The decision was a far-sighted one, because in recent years commercial interests justified the construction of a standard gauge line from Kalgoorlie through Western Australia to the Indian Ocean, and the final link up with the standard gauge of New South Wales came in 1970.

When the Trans-Australian section of the Commonwealth Railways was built, in 1913–17, a vital consideration was the means of servicing steam locomotives. The line had to be entirely self-contained. At each end it was flanked by narrow gauge lines over which its locomotives could not run. Along its vast length of 1,682 km (1,051 miles) the "stations" were spaced not because of any need to serve local communities, because these did not exist, but to suit the operating requirements of the line. They were sited to suit the coaling and watering requirements of locomotives, and for their changing and re-manning on the way. Three major intermediate depots were set up, so as to equalize roughly the run from Port Augusta to Kalgoorlie; these depots were at Tarcoola, Cook, and Rawlinna, and gave successive distances of 412, 409, 485 and 376 km (257, 256, 303 and 235 miles). At each of these engines were changed, but the crews changed more frequently. All along the line little townships were built to house and provide for the needs of men working on the line. When first opened the journey time for the whole distance was 37.5 hr, giving an average speed of 45 km/h (28 mph). There were three passenger trains a week in each direction, and long before the introduction of regular air mail services an excellent connection was provided from the fortnightly mail steamer from England. Landing at Fremantle, and travelling over the 1,067 mm (3 ft 6 in) gauge line to Kalgoorlie, passengers could then change to the "Trans", and eventually reach the eastern cities of Australia. By this means the passenger was able to save 48 hours on the journey from London to Melbourne, and 3 days if proceeding to Sydney.

Nowadays, with powerful modern diesel-electric locomotives, there is no need for any changing of engines between Port Augusta and Kalgoorlie, but the crews change at Tarcoola, Cook, and Rawlinna. They work successive stages on a four-day roster from their home station. Thus a Kalgoorlie crew would work to Rawlinna the first day, lodge and then go on to Cook next day. On the third day they work back to Rawlinna, lodge again, and make the final run home on the fourth day. Similar workings are organized from Port Augusta. It is an extraordinary experience to ride in the driver's cab over the 475 km (297 mile) straight section of the "Trans". When the line was first built the sleepers were laid on the surface of the ground with very little ballasting; but now the line is heavily ballasted, and speeds up to 113 km/h (70 mph) are permitted on some sections. But it is the feeling of absolute nothingness that holds one enthralled. There are some areas of low bluish scrub, but nothing else on the horizon all round. The effect is extraordinary again when one approaches one of the passing stations. First there are a few specks on the far horizon, which become gradually revealed as low buildings, and one realizes that they are being sighted over the curve of the earth, as in the first sight of islands or approaching ships at sea.

## The Indian-Pacific

It was in 1970 that the through train service across Australia was inaugurated, the "Indian-Pacific", named

The Australian continent is linked from east to west by rail, a distance of 3,938 km (2,461 miles). Through running trains were made possible by the construction of standard gauge lines between Broken Hill and Port Pirie, and Kalgoorlie and Perth, which had previously been available only to narrow gauge traffic.

Today a coast-to-coast passenger service is run, first started in 1970, providing four trains in each direction each week.

from the oceans at each end of the 3,938 km (2,461 mile) journey. It travels over 1,166 km (729 miles) of New South Wales tracks, 347 km (217 miles) on the South Australian before reaching the "Trans" at Port Pirie. The section of 91 km (57 miles) from this latter important junction to Port Augusta was changed to standard gauge many years ago.

The Indian-Pacific now runs four days a week, leaving Sydney on Mondays, Wednesdays, Thursdays and Saturdays at 15.15 hrs. The arrival in Perth is at 07.00 hrs on the fourth day, after two changes in time. The run over the "Trans" section takes from 16.45 hrs on one evening at Port Pirie to 20.30 hrs on the next evening at Kalgoorlie. However, because of the change from Central to Western time at Cook, the actual journey time is 28.75 hr, at an average speed of 62 km/h (38.5 mph). The intermediate stops are Port Augusta, Pimba (serving Woomera), Tarcoola, Cook, and Rawlinna. The fastest intermediate running is across the Nullarbor "straight", which begins 117 km (73 miles) east of Cook. From the latter station the 485 km (303 miles) to Rawlinna, 358 (224) of them on the long straight, are covered in 7 hr, at an average speed of 70 km/h (44 mph). This, of course, includes stops as required at some intermediate passing stations. Passenger rolling stock on the Indian-Pacific is of the highest standard in Australia — and compares favourably with TEE and other prestige passenger stock. The stainless steel carriages are completely air conditioned and there are many on-board amenities.

Perth–Merredin/Kalgoorlie standard gauge Prospector at Midland Junction.

Tarcoola

Pimba

Port Augusta

Port Pirie

Peterborough

Jamestown

Mannahill

Cockburn

Broken Hill

Menindee

Ivanhoe

Roto

Condobolin

Parkes

Molong

Orange

Lithgow

Katoomba

Penrith

Sydney

# New Zealand: southernmost route

Between 1863 and 1870 a number of short lines were built, mostly projected by the various provincial governments. These had several different gauges, but in 1870 the central government passed an Act that required all future railways in the colony to be built to the 1,067 mm (3 ft 6 in) gauge. Today the principal main line in the North Island runs from Wellington to Auckland, and there are important branches terminating at New Plymouth on the west coast and Gisborne on the east. In the South Island the principal main line runs south from Christchurch to Dunedin, and Invercargill in the far south. There is an important northward connection from Christchurch to Picton, on the Cook Strait, while the east-west line, passing through the Southern Alps in the Otira Tunnel, connects to the industrial and mining centres of Greymouth and Westport. In a mountainous country the railways of New Zealand include many spectacular feats of engineering, dating from earlier years when the cost of deep tunnelling could not be justified. The Otira Tunnel was not com-

menced until 1908, but partly because of delays through New Zealand's participation in the First World War, it was not completed until 1923. It has a total length of 8.4 km (5.3 miles).

An early highlight of New Zealand railways construction in the North Island was the Rimutaka Incline on which the line ascended 300 m (1,000 ft) in 23 km (14 miles), and then descended 265 m (869 ft) in less than 5 km (3 miles). A centre rack rail was employed, with special brake vans with brakes gripping the centre rail when descending, while tank locomotives with horizontal grip wheels were used to haul the trains up – often four locomotives to one train. Now the mountain range is pierced by the Rimutaki Tunnel, which is 8.75 km (5.47 miles) long, the longest in the British Commonwealth and opened in November 1955. Modern machinery and expertise enabled it to be built in a fraction of the time taken for the Otira. The secondary line to Napier and Gisborne, running for much of its northern part along the east coast of North Island, includes the highest viaduct in New Zealand, the Mohaka; at its maximum it is 97 m (318 ft) high, and consists of a series of latticed steel towers, tapering sharply in width towards their bases.

Since the early days, now that traffic has increased, and with it the weight of locomotives and coaching stock, some considerable improvements have been made to the alignment in places to permit faster running; but one of the most spectacular locations on the North Island main line remains. Travelling south from Auckland, and entering the central mountain massif, the line comes to Raurimu, and ahead is the task of climbing 213 m (700 ft) in the next 5.6 km (3.5 miles), in the direct line. Such a gradient as 1 in 26 would have been quite impracticable for the moderate powered steam locomotives originally employed; but the track was laid out in the form of an ascending spiral. It

includes a complete circle, two horseshoe bends, and two short tunnels, and so artificially increases the distance between Raurimu and National Park to 11 km (7 miles), with an average gradient of 1 in 52. Once up at Park the traveller can behold at relatively close range one of several active volcanoes.

The division of New Zealand into two halves by the Cook Strait has inevitably been a point of transport difficulty; and although there are of course air services that facilitate the rapid transit of such passengers who are in a hurry, there has always been the need to transfer railway goods wagons and road vehicles. In 1962 there was introduced a 4,226 tonne Rail-Road ferry between Wellington and Picton, working on the roll-on, roll-off principle, and this and two similar ships have certainly revolutionized inter-island transport. Except in the approaches to the Otira Tunnel, the railways in the South Island do not include such spectacular engineering as in the North Island; but this is amply compensated for by the great historic interest of some parts of the system, and the survival of steam traction. The very first railway in New Zealand was built between the port of Lyttelton and Christchurch, a distance of 6.8 km (4.25 miles). Lyttleton is backed by a range of hills, and the original proposal was to go directly through by a tunnel 2 km (1.25 miles) long; but this promised to be too expensive. Today part of the route of this pioneer line, at Ferrymead, is operated by a steam preservation group.

The journey south from Christchurch by a diesel train called the Southerner has the particular fascination of

leading further south than anywhere else in the world by train. The journey of 589 km (368 miles) from Christchurch to Invercargill takes just 10 hr, and from the latter town the rails continue, but without any regular passenger service, to Bluff, the furthest south. The main line south, after keeping beside or near to the east coast for the first 448 km (280 miles), to Balclutha, then swings inland and westward before turning south again at Gore. This station is the junction for Lumsden, whence one can travel during the summer season by one of the most fascinating, but alas most remote, steam trains in the world. A branch line runs from Lumsden into the mountains to Kingston, lying at the foot of the most beautiful Lake Wakatipu, and here one meets the Kingston Flyer – a train with a pedigree extending back nearly 100 years.

In the 1880s the branch line service between Gore, Lumsden and Kingston was run by three gorgeous little 2-4-0 tender engines built by Rogers, in the USA. They were highly decorated with a wealth of polished brass and copperwork, and their drivers used to run the branch trains in such dashing style that they were nicknamed the "Kingston Flyers". In 1971 the idea was born of running New Zealand's only vintage steam trains over the same route, and two of the celebrated Ab class Pacific engines were saved from the scrap heap and restored to first-class working order to run the modern Kingston Flyer. One cannot expect "speed" as it is known today on the railways of the world, because it now takes 1.5 hr to cover the 61 km (38 miles) between Lumsden and Kingston.

The total length of the New Zealand Railways covers

*Above left* 2-6-2 at Ferrymead Museum.

*Above* 4-8-4 near Arthur's Pass on final run, now in Ferrymead Museum, Christchurch.

Two Ea locos about to be uncoupled at Arthur's Pass. Three together can haul a 500 tonne train up a 1 in 33 incline in Otira Tunnel at 32 km/h (20 mph).

The Auckland-Wellington line and that from Christchurch to Invercargill, constitute the north and south trunk routes, respectively. In the daytime the Silver Fern, a luxury railcar, runs on the northern route, followed at night by the Northerner. In the South Island the route is served by the Southerner, with distinctive blue stock, which provides a daily service. The other "named" train in New Zealand is the Endeavour which runs in daytime between Wellington and Napier. All these lines are single track but are used by an increasing amount by passenger traffic.

Steam on the Dashwood Pass.

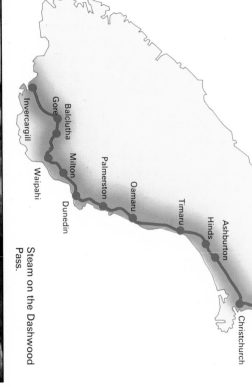

about 4,800 km (3,000 miles), and about 75 per cent of the revenue comes from freight traffic. Passenger business, though very efficiently operated, mostly in handsomely styled diesel railcars, is quite small, not amounting to more than about 5 per cent of the total earnings. The remaining 20 per cent of the revenue comes from various ancillary services, including the Wellington-Picton train ferry.

Operationally the New Zealand Railways, so far as general equipment is concerned, are among the most complete and up to date in the world. They were one of the pioneers, outside the USA, of Centralized Traffic Control (CTC), which has now been applied to most of the main lines. Today further cut-off lines are in course of construction, involving long tunnels. The passenger services on most routes run during the daytime, but on the busiest route and the longest through run, that between Auckland and Wellington, there are both day and night services. The distance is 680 km (425 miles) and the daytime Silver Fern does the journey in about 13 hr, with five intermediate stops. This is a railcar type of train with buffet included. The really show train of the service is the Silver Star, leaving the two cities at 20.00 hrs, and including full dining and sleeping cars. The journey time is 12.5 hr in each direction.

# Japan's Shinkansen 1

*Above* Local railcar set.

*Left* C61 class 4-6-4 at Miyazaki on Kyūshū.

*Below Shinkansen* and motorway: direct routes.

The first railway in Japan, built along the old Tokaido Trail in 1872, had no pretensions towards a speedway. On the recommendation of British engineers, it was built to the 1,067 mm (3 ft 6 in) gauge, as in South Africa, New Zealand and much of Australia; and to minimize the cost of construction it took a meandering course near to the east coast, skirting obstacles and including sections of steep gradients. At first this did not matter. As a nation, the Japanese of the nineteenth century had a complete inability – indeed a reluctance – to hurry, and the trains were very slow. They became little faster as the line was extended southwards to the furthest extent of the main island of Honshū. How, in a mere 50 years, the Japanese changed from this pastoral, easygoing existence, first to defeat Tsarist Russia in a major war, and then to advance to become one of the leading industrial and military powers of the world, is one of the phenomena of history. In the process, the Tokaido line of the Imperial Japanese Railways, though enlarged to double track throughout, and with the addition of several cut-off lines to ease gradients and reduce overall distance, became completely saturated. In the late 1930s, although its 552 km (345 miles) of route between Tōkyō and Osaka represented only 3 per cent of the total Japanese railways, it was carrying 25 per cent of the total passenger and freight traffic. This was perhaps not surprising since 40 per cent of the total population of the Japanese islands, and 70 per cent of the industrial output, was concentrated in the narrow belt of land between the central mountain range and the sea, and served by what can be called the Old Tokaido line.

A scheme was then worked out for an entirely new line, that would enable the time between Tōkyō and Osaka to be cut to 4.5 hr. This was a startling proposal because such a time would involve an average speed of 120 km/h (75 mph) – infinitely faster running than anything that

had previously been made in Japan. But the country's precipitate entry into the Second World War, and the tremendous damage to her railways and industries that ensued before her surrender, necessarily caused suspension of the great plan. When it was revived after the war it took an even more ambitious form. With the speeds that were proposed it was considered that the 1,067 mm gauge would be inadequate, and this led to the conception of a new, or *Shinkansen* line, quite separate from the existing 1,067 mm gauge network, on the standard gauge. Moreover, having taken this decision the Japanese National Railways determined to build a line of such straightness and massive construction that the standard passenger train speed on it would be 200 km/h (125 mph). By comparison with what had been achieved previously in Japan, this was a staggering proposition. In August 1957 the government decided to set up an investigation committee. A year later an aerial survey of the route was made, in March 1959 funds for construction of the line were included in the national

Royal engine at Miyazaki.

Kagoshima
Nagasaki
Tosu
Hakata/Fukuoka
Hiroshima
Okayama
Kyōto
Osaka
Nagoya
Toyama
Niigata
Numata
Fukushima
Sendai
Morioka
Aomori
Seikan Tunnel
Sapporo
Tōkyō
Narita (Airport)

budget, and in a matter of weeks these were approved.

The incredible speed with which the line was built was fully in keeping with the fast service that was promised. No more than one week after the project had been approved by Parliament, a ceremonial first "ground breaking" was performed, and in the astonishing time of five years and five months, full commercial service between Tōkyō and Osaka began. In view of the work involved this time does indeed take some believing. To permit of uninterrupted high speed there was, outside the city area of Tōkyō, no curve with a radius of less than 2.4 km (1.5 miles). There were no level crossings and in that densely populated strip of country the line was carried for the most part on viaducts, high above the towns, and at all places where there might have been intersections of any kind. Lengthy viaducts were built to take the line on the level across river valleys, and where there were mountains blocking the direct line of the railway, there was no thought but to tunnel straight through. In view of the high speeds to be attained and the intense utilization of the tracks forecast, very great care was taken in forming the embankments to secure an adequate degree of compactness in the piled-up earth. The tremendous amount of work put into this feature of the construction was vitally necessary seeing that a high-speed passenger service was to be inaugurated at once. On older railways in Great Britain and elsewhere it was usually the practice to run at moderate or even slow speeds at first, while all the earthworks were fully consolidating; but the time-schedule permitted no such settling in period on the New Tokaido line. In crossing urban areas the line is carried on elevated track structures with rail level about 6.4 m (21 ft) above ground, consisting of concrete rigid frames. These required a much narrower right-of-way at ground level than if conventional embankments had been built.

There were some very long bridges on the new line, mostly crossing the estuaries of rivers and the adjoining marshland. One of these gives a magnificent view of the sacred Mount Fuji, and has from the outset been a favourite place for publicity photographs of the new trains at speed. Great care has been taken in the design of these bridges, many of which are in localities of natural beauty. The frequency of trains, both in these areas and where the line crosses urban complexes, has led to the need to minimize noise. High parapet walls have been built on many viaduct sections. There are no fewer than 66 tunnels between Tōkyō and Osaka, and by this more direct alignment the length of the line was reduced from the 552 km (345 miles) of the Old Tokaido line to 515 km (322 miles) long, and in all of them the aerodynamic effect of two trains passing at speed, which would be more than 400 km/h (250 mph), had to be taken into account. The standard distance between the nearest rails of opposing tracks in Great Britain is 1.8 m (6 ft), but in the tunnels of the New Tokaido line this distance has been made 2.7 m (9 ft). This is the standard "distance between" on the new line as far south as Osaka, but south of that city, and on subsequent extensions where speeds of 257 km/h (160 mph) are provided for, this width has been increased to 2.9 m (9 ft 6 in).

Traffic operation on the New Tokaido line matches the basic conception and the magnificent civil engineering. From 06.00 hrs till 21.00 hrs one of the *Hikari*, or "Lightning" trains leaves Tōkyō approximately every 15 min for Osaka, covering the 515 km (322 miles) in 3 hr 10 min inclusive of brief stops at Nagoya and Kyōto. This is an average speed of 160 km/h (100 mph) and the volume of traffic can be imagined from these trains each consisting of 16 cars, and providing seating for about 1,400 passengers.

The loading averages about 1,000 passengers per train, taking an average over the entire day, and over all 365 days in the year. At midday most of the trains are completely full, and taking the averages over the year one can indeed wonder why 55,000 people want to travel from Tōkyō to Osaka every day, while another 55,000 are travelling in the reverse direction. As a scenic ride the *Shinkansen* is a rather disappointing journey. The windows of the air conditioned coaches are placed rather high up in comparison to those of modern British or Continental European trains, and one gets the impression of a landscape sweeping past, and of built-up areas passing swiftly below. It is only when crossing the broad river valleys, where there are glimpses of distant mountain ranges, that the lookout is appealing. Then again, so much of the line is in tunnel. This is not so marked on the original section as it is on the newest stretches south of Osaka. On the Sanyō *Shinkansen*, south of Okayama, through Hiroshima to the very south end of the island of Honshū, where the island itself is narrowing, nearly 55 per cent of the line is in tunnel – nearly 225 km (140 miles) of it. It is hardly the kind of journey one would choose for sightseeing, though it is certainly excellent for getting quickly to one's destination. Today the 1,030 km (640 miles) from Tōkyō to Shimonoseki take 6.75 hr.

The new section, south of Osaka, to Shimonoseki, is 509 km (318 miles) long, and the *Hikari* trains cover the distance in 3.5 hr. But the fastest trains running south of Osaka do not stop at Shimonoseki, but continue by means of the tunnel under the Kanmon Strait to the island of Kyūshū. There the *Shinkansen* line terminates at Hakata, which is reached in 6 hr 56 min from Tōkyō. The Kanmon Strait is quite narrow, between relatively high ground on both sides, and the 1,067 mm (3 ft 6 in) gauge line tunnelled beneath on a location that involved sharp curves

The first stretch of the *Shinkansen* network between Tōkyō and Osaka was opened in 1966 and was later extended to Hakata. Extensions to this basic network were started, but financial problems led to considerable disruption of work and surveys. Thus the Seikan undersea water tunnel between Hokkaidō and the mainland was commenced and work continued while the lines leading to it were actually stopped. It was not until 1977 that the future of the tunnel in the *Shinkansen* network was ensured.

# Japan's Shinkansen 11

To Tokyo

From Tokyo

*Hikari* :05 *Kodama* :15 :20 :25 :30 :35 :40 :45 :50 :55 :59
:10 *Hikari* *Kodama*

06:00
07:00
08:00
09:00
10:00
11:00
12:00
13:00
14:00
15:00
16:00
17:00
18:00
19:00
20:00
21:00
22:00
23:00
24:00

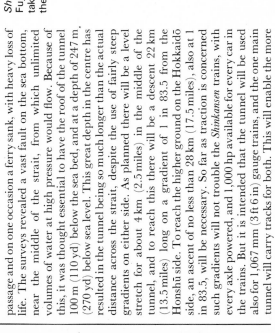

at each end and steep gradients. The *Shinkansen* line, on which high speeds are required throughout, needed a much longer and deeper tunnel, and the effect of this is seen in the timings operated by the faster of the new trains, which do not stop at Shimonoseki, and which cover the 213 km (133 miles) from Hiroshima to Kokura in 74 min — an average of 172 km/h (108 mph) start-to-stop. The accompanying map shows the routes proposed for further extensions of the *Shinkansen* network, north of Tōkyō. None of these have yet progressed far, but a major project, which will benefit the existing 1,067 mm (3 ft 6 in) system in the north of Honshū, as well as the projected *Shinkansen* extension, is the great undersea tunnel between Honshū and the northernmost island of Hokkaidō.

The Seikan Tunnel, as it is to be named, will be the longest undersea tunnel in the world, longer indeed than the tunnel under the English Channel was planned to be. Although the Seikan will have an overall length of 54 km (33.5 miles), only 23 km (14.5 miles) will be actually under the sea. It was originally planned for completion in 1979, but unexpected and serious difficulties have arisen in the construction, despite the most exhaustive preliminary surveys. There was every reason for embarking on this daring project. At present communication between the two islands is by train ferry, and the crossing from Aomori to Hakodate takes four hours. It can be a very stormy

*Right*, the passage of *Shinkansen* trains in both directions as observed from a point approximately 150 km (95 miles) from Tōkyō, close to Mount Fuji, over an 18-hour period. Though all trains, which are 16 car sets, average almost 160 km/h (100 mph) the *Hikari* (Lightning) stop less at intermediate stations than the Kodama (Echo). The high traffic density handled on the network is one of the greatest of any system in the world, and calls for highly developed systems.

*Shinkansen* passing Mount Fuji in the position taken by the observer in the opposite diagram.

passage and on one occasion a ferry sank, with heavy loss of life. The surveys revealed a vast fault on the sea bottom, near the middle of the strait, from which unlimited volumes of water at high pressure would flow. Because of this, it was thought essential to have the roof of the tunnel 100 m (110 yd) below the sea bed, and at a depth of 247 m. (270 yd) below sea level. This great depth in the centre has resulted in the tunnel being so much longer than the actual distance across the strait, despite the use of fairly steep gradients on either side. As planned there will be a level stretch for about 4 km (2.5 miles) in the middle of the tunnel, and to reach this there will be a descent 22 km (13.5 miles) long on a gradient of 1 in 83.5 from the Honshū side. To reach the higher ground on the Hokkaidō side, an ascent of no less than 28 km (17.5 miles), also at 1 in 83.5, will be necessary. So far as traction is concerned such gradients will not trouble the *Shinkansen* trains, with every axle powered, and 1,000 hp available for every car in the trains. But it is intended that the tunnel will be used also for 1,067 mm (3 ft 6 in) gauge trains, and the one main tunnel will carry tracks for both. This will enable the more local trains from either side to benefit from the tunnel and make the use of the train ferry unnecessary.

The method of constructing the tunnel is interesting, in view of the exceptional depth below the sea. Along the line of the main tunnel what is termed the "bottom drift" method has been used. A pilot tunnel is driven first, to a distance of about 0.5 km (0.33 mile) ahead of the main working to investigate rock conditions. Then the main tunnel is excavated to its full size in two stages, first the upper half and then the lower. The concrete for the arch is put in, before the lower section, and then lastly the side walls are built in. In the course of the work many additional pilot tunnels have been driven to test rock conditions on either side. The completion of this great work will be awaited with the utmost interest, but at present authorization of *Shinkansen* extensions north of Tōkyō has not yet been forthcoming. It is likely, however, that these lines will differ from the Tokaido and Sanyō *Shinkansens* in that they will carry a mixed traffic instead of being exclusively passenger. It was the original intention that the Tokaido *Shinkansen* should be mixed, carrying freight traffic at night; but such was its success as a mass-carrier of passengers that a great number of additional trains had to be run beyond those originally planned, up to the present maximum of four *Hikari* per hour, and the night time was needed for track maintenance. There was no chance to do anything in the brief intervals between trains in the daytime.

Today, 90 *Shinkansen* trains a day leave Tōkyō for the south. The pattern has changed a little from that in operation before the extension beyond Okayama was open. A typical set of departures are 12.00, 12.12, 12.16, 12.24, 12.36, 12.40, and 13.00 hrs. The 12.16 and 12.40 hrs are "Kodama" and "all stations" to Osaka, which, however, means only three more stops than the *Hikari* at the other departure times. Already, however, the line is becoming saturated, and the Japanese National Railways are considering the construction of yet another line to cater for the exceptional section Tōkyō-Nagoya-Kyōto-Osaka. Because of its construction features as the pioneer, the running speeds on the present line cannot be increased above the present 210 km/h (130 mph). The "crunch" is expected to come after 1980, and the concept at present is that another entirely new line might be constructed, but this time not using a conventional railway at all, but the principle of magnetic leviation. It is the basis of the experiment made both in Great Britain and France with the so-called "hover trains". In Japan experiments have been in hand for some time with a car propelled by a

"linear motor", and although there is still much to be done the prospects are enthralling. The Japanese set new standards with the building of the Tokaido *Shinkansen* line, when they reduced the Tōkyō-Osaka time from the 6 hr 40 min of the 1,067 mm (3 ft 6 in) gauge limited express trains to 3 hr 10 min; but with magnetic leviation, and cars propelled by linear motors, the target time is only one hour. It is thought that a new line operated in this manner would take the ultra-prestige traffic, leaving the original Tokaido *Shinkansen* to cope with the many who would be content with a 3 hr 10 min run between the two cities.

*Above* The Seikan Tunnel under construction on a 1 in 80 slope. The tunnel, started in the late 1960s, was continued in the face of economic difficulties. For some time it was doubtful whether *Shin-*

*kansen* trains would ever be able to use the tunnel, but the situation was resolved favourably. When it opens the Seikan Tunnel will be the longest in the world.
*Right* Monorail, Tōkyō.
*Below Shinkansen* train.

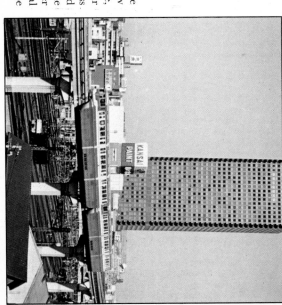

# Crossing North America 1

## Routes in the USA

At the zenith of steam operation in the USA, busiest among the great trunk routes were the rivals operating between New York and Chicago. The New York Central, with its "water level" route, had the advantage of no gradients, but the Pennsylvania had the shorter distance. The physical characteristics balanced each other, however, and both were maintaining a 16-hour service between the two cities, by the two world-famous trains, The Twentieth Century Limited by the NYC, and The Broadway Limited, with average speeds of 96 and 90 km/h (60 and 56.25 mph) over 1,536 and 1,440 km (960 and 900 miles), respectively. The Pennsylvania Railroad had much the hardest route, because it cut through the very heart of the Allegheny mountains. From Harrisburg the quadruple tracked main line makes a picturesque course up the valley of the Juniata River to Altoona, where the great workshops of the Pennsylvania Railroad were situated, and then by means of the great "Horseshoe Bend" it climbs to its summit in the mountains in the Gallitzin Tunnel. Then comes an equally severe and picturesque descent to Pittsburgh. The New York Central, on the other

hand, went due north at first, beside the Hudson River, and then at Albany turned west to run near to the south shore of Lake Erie – mostly level, but hard going with loads of more than 1,000 tonnes requiring to be hauled continuously at around 130 km/h (80 mph).

Westward from Chicago, the Atchison Topeka and Santa Fe Railway provides a truly great route to the west coast. The main line of the Santa Fe from Chicago to Los Angeles is 3,577 km (2,223 miles) long. It runs through seven states, three time zones, crosses three great mountain ranges, and today witnesses daily some of the fastest passenger and freight operation in the USA. At the peak of the steam era, during the Second World War, when an efficient service of very heavy trains to the west coast was a national necessity, only two locomotives were needed for the entire journey. A 4-6-4 was used over the relatively level eastern section of 1,595 km (990 miles) from Chicago to La Junta, Colorado, and there it was changed for a 4-8-4, which took the trains over the 1,982 km (1,232 miles) on to Los Angeles, through the mountain ranges of New Mexico, Arizona and California. The mountains are stark, rugged, and near-desert in places, and show magni-

*Below* Once the mountains in the east had been crossed and the Mississippi reached, the railway builders in North America turned their minds to the great leap to the west coast. Vast sums of money were involved, even by 19th-century standards; thousands of men struggled in frightening conditions and thousands more argued about the relative desirability of such schemes. The transcontinental routes which emerged, forged two nations and certainly as far as the United States was concerned provided the impetus to further expansion and development.

*Above* US narrow gauge in Colorado. Silverton train, Rio Grande.

1 & 2 Canadian National Railway
3 Canadian Pacific Railway
4 Great Northern Railway
5 Northern Pacific Railway
6 Chicago, Milwaukee, St Paul and Pacific Railroad
7 Union Pacific Railroad

8 Denver and Rio Grande Western Railroad/Western Pacific Railroad
10 Atchinson, Topeka and Santa Fe Railroad
11 Southern Pacific Lines
12 Central Pacific (Southern Pacific)

ficient colouring under the blistering heat of cloudless skies. The full journey takes more than two whole days, and there is much night travelling. The great train of steam days was the Chief, supplemented by the diesel-hauled Super Chief; Today's successor, under the Amtrak organization, is the Southwest Limited.

For sheer spectacular country and superb train operation, however, the Denver and Río Grande Western, between Denver and Salt Lake City, can scarcely be surpassed. The present main route, used by the three-weekly Rio Grande Zephyr, and daily by a dozen or more enormous freight trains in each direction, is a composite one. The original main line took a rather circuitous route, running due south at first from Denver to Pueblo, then turning west to cut through the Colorado Rockies in the breathtaking Royal Gorge, and from there over the Tennessee Pass, with its fearsome gradients. The distance from Denver to Salt Lake City by this route was 1,192 km (745 miles). By 1934 the magnificent line of the Denver and Salt Lake Railroad had been connected to the original Rio Grande by the "Dotsero Cut-off" line, and the end-to-end distance was reduced to 912 km (570 miles). Although running west to cut through the scenery of the Royal Gorge, the shorter route via the Moffat Tunnel is itself magnificent, and also inspiring to the student of railway engineering, climbing from the plains of Denver for 61 km (38 miles) on a continuous gradient of 1 in 50, and passing through 30 tunnels hewn from solid rock in a distance of 23 km (14 miles), even before reaching the great Moffat Tunnel under the main range of the Rockies. Beyond this summit, in canyon and near desert country, the line crosses the states of Colorado and Utah, eventually breasting Soldier Summit in the Wasatch mountains of Utah, before descending to Salt Lake City.

The Southern Pacific, the manifold activities of which extend from New Orleans almost to Seattle, in the Pacific northwest, carries a great train called the Coast Starlight between Los Angeles and Seattle, passing through Oakland (San Francisco) intermediately. Like most of the American railways of today, the Southern Pacific is a mighty freight operator, with originating traffic in two distinct areas, namely in the cities of Texas and the Gulf of Mexico, and in California. These two areas are connected by the long main line running from Los Angeles near to the Mexican border, and then there are the two great prongs by which the Southern Pacific takes its traffic to hand over to the Union Pacific at Ogden, Utah, for its run to Chicago, and northward to link up with the Burlington at Portland, Oregon. In the steam era the Southern Pacific was distinguished by its cab-in-front articulated locomotives of gigantic proportions, for the freight trains, and by its gaily painted 4-8-4s on the north to south passenger trains. The Coast Starlight of today is a night train only between Eugene and Oakland (San Francisco); for the rest of the long journey in both directions it runs in daylight, and even on the northbound run, in high summer it is light enough, soon after daybreak, to see the scenic gem of the whole route, the exquisite Mount Shasta, shortly after passing Dunsmuir. The southern part of the same journey

includes much fine coastal scenery, both north and south of Santa Barbara, and except where the curves demand caution the modern diesels wheel their heavy trains along at 113 km/h (70 mph).

The eastward "prong" of the Southern Pacific today is the route of the one-time Central Pacific, climbing over the Sierra Nevada range, and heading for the historic end-to-end meeting point with the Union Pacific, at Promontory, Utah, where in 1869 the last spike of the first transcontinental railway across America was driven. Then the line was carried round to the north of the Great Lake on a considerable detour, but now, with the aid of a bridge, the line is carried across the lake, and the place where the "last spike" ceremony took place is now no more than a tourist attraction, with the two restored locomotives standing rather forlorn and facing each other out in the desert.

The Union Pacific, on to whose metals eastbound trains pass at Ogden, is another great railway. It cuts through rugged country in the mountains of Utah and Colorado, and then makes fast time across the plains of Nebraska to reach the west bank of the Missouri River at Omaha, to make connection with the third partner in the chain of communication between Chicago and San Francisco – the Chicago and North Western. Until the recession following the Second World War, the passenger trains to and from the west travelled on the direct line from North Platte to Cheyenne, but now the San Francisco Zephyr, the only through passenger train between Chicago and San Francisco, under the auspices of Amtrak, travels via Fort Morgan and Denver, going from there due north to regain the former route at Cheyenne. Ogden, Utah, is in many ways the grand junction of the Union Pacific. For while the running further west on the transcontinental line is taken up by the Southern Pacific, the "UP" had main lines running southwest to Los Angeles, north to Butte, Montana, and northwest to Portland, and today its distinctively coloured diesel locomotives are a familiar sight.

Another great route to the west is that now followed by Amtrak's Empire Builder – through between Chicago and Seattle. This is a most interesting journey because it uses parts of three different railways. From the scenic point of view the eastbound run is the more rewarding, leaving Seattle just before noon. The name of the train, which Amtrak inherited from the Great Northern, is in memory of the great nineteenth-century tycoon, J. J. Hill who was once a member of the famous syndicate of four who organized the formation of the Canadian Pacific Railway Company. But he disagreed with the others so violently over the route to be followed, which he wanted south of Lake Superior, and so through American territory, that he left the syndicate, and enterprised his own all-American line to the west coast – the Great Northern. Through his vigorous and successful prospecting of railways in all directions Hill became known as "the Empire Builder".

The train of today, however, takes the former Northern Pacific line out of Seattle (now part of the Burlington Northern system), and from East Auburn where it turns

Logo of the Grand Trunk Western Company.

Preserved American steam. Note the powerful headlamp, the warning bell, and rather small cow-catcher.

# Crossing North America 1

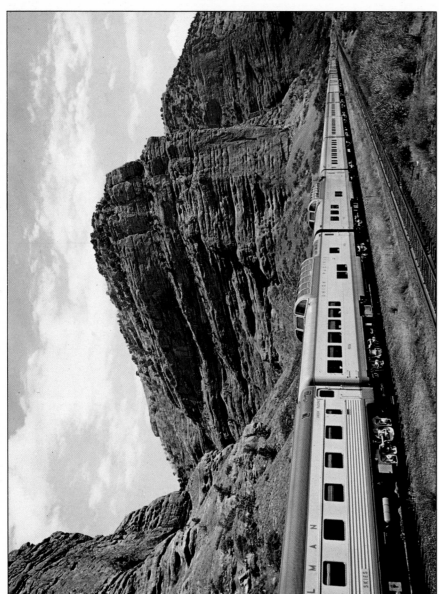

City of Los Angeles in Echo Canyon, Utah.

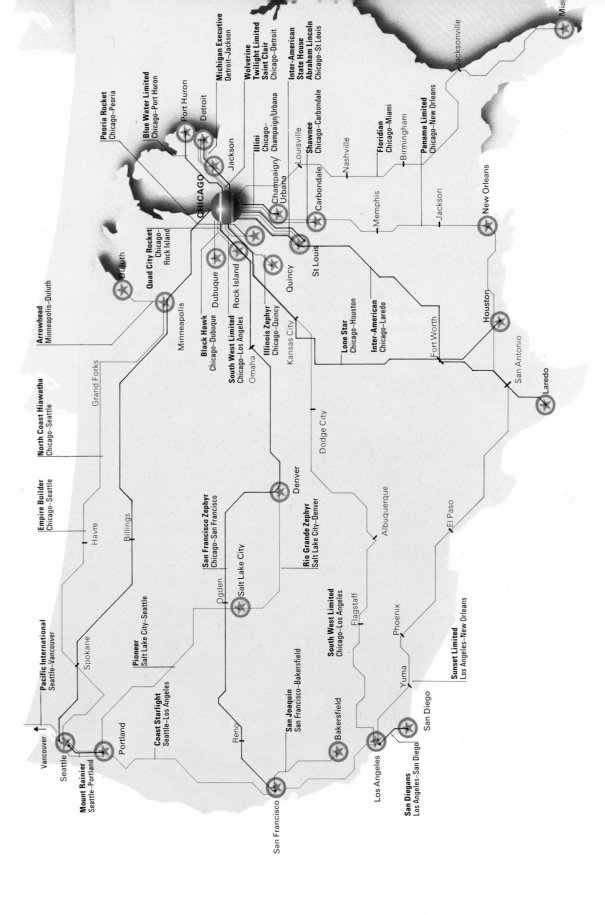

away from tidewater, the long ascent through the Cascade Range begins. There follows over an hour of delightful travelling, through densely wooded mountain country, as the train climbs to nearly 900 m (3,000 ft) and there are many glimpses of the great Mount Rainier. By nightfall Spokane is reached, a general junction, and there the train passes on to the former Great Northern line. It is just daylight again when the train runs beside the Glacier National Park, and then comes the fast day-long run across the prairies of Montana and North Dakota. Yet another night in the train, with breakfast soon after leaving Minneapolis. The line is now that of the Chicago, Milwaukee, St Paul and Pacific – the "Milwaukee Road" – over which the steam hauled Hiawathas of prewar days used to speed at 160 km/h (100 mph). The line at first makes a delightful course beside the upper reaches of the Mississippi River, leaves the great river at La Crosse and passes eastwards to reach the shores of Lake Michigan at Milwaukee. From there, almost within sight of the lake for the rest of the journey, it arrives at Chicago.

## Routes across Canada

Canada has been wittily described as a country 5,000 km (3,000 miles) long and two railroads wide. It is nothing more than plain truth that the building of the Canadian Pacific Railway helped enormously in welding the far-scattered provinces of Canada into a single, strong and united nation; and the route by which it went through the great mountain ranges of British Columbia befits, in every respect, its role in what has been so aptly called the "National Dream". It was the section between Calgary and the canyons of the Fraser River, by which van Horne defied earlier councils, that had "decided" the route must go much further north through the Yellowhead Pass. In the wellnigh incredible adventures that the pioneers had in finding any sort of a route at all through that maelstrom of mountain peaks, densely forested slopes, and swift flowing rivers, in the magnificent engineering embodied in building the line, and in the never ceasing challenge its curves, gradients and tunnels make to the locomotive men of today; it must remain a route without parallel on the world's railways. It is no mere mountain track built to open up a virgin land, but a major artery, nevertheless so terribly graded that on one stretch, the Beaver Hill, it needs 13 3,000 hp diesel locomotives to lift every one of the 10,000 tonne coal trains — four every day — that run from the Crow's Nest Pass to Vancouver, for export to Japan. This great operation, which is only one of many services, takes place in the shadow of some of the grandest mountain scenery to be enjoyed from a train anywhere in the world.

Although the Canadian Pacific was first through to the west coast, the Yellowhead Pass did not have to wait so very long for its railway. Two rivals to the Canadian Pacific struck out west-north-west from Winnipeg, both heading for Edmonton, Alberta. The Canadian Northern and the Grand Trunk Pacific strove to open up different parts of the intervening country, but they were never very far apart, and when both were merged into the Canadian National system, and when Saskatoon was chosen for the through transcontinental services. That great pioneer engineer Sandford Fleming had good reason to recommend this route on the score of gradients, because west of Edmonton the approach to the great range of the Rockies is relatively gentle. There is much beautiful scenery as the line draws near to Jasper and passes through its nature park. There is, it is true, some stiff climbing in the final approach to the Yellowhead Pass; but on the westbound Super Continental train it is night, and the

passenger is only conscious of difficult country when riding high up in one of the dome cars, watching the way the locomotive headlight swings from one side to another when rounding the many curves. From Edmonton to the Yellowhead Pass the present main line is a synthesis of the best locations of the previous two rivals, sometimes Grand Trunk Pacific, sometimes Canadian Northern, making up a splendid fast running main line.

Beyond the Yellowhead the routes diverge. The Super Continental train turns south and downhill into the valley of the Thompson River, coming in the early morning to Kamloops. Then follows an amazing run down the canyons where the Canadian Pacific is on one side and the Canadian National on the other, never out of sight of each other until reaching tidewater, and never more dramatically than when they execute a scissors movement — each crossing from one side to the other, as the viaduct of one strides over the viaduct of the other, at Cisco.

The Fraser River, into which the Thompson River debouches at Lytton, provides travellers by both the Canadian Pacific and the Canadian National routes to Vancouver, with some grand spectacles, quite apart from the "scissors" location at Cisco. But even these are perhaps less astonishing than the first sight of the Fraser River from the Cariboo Dayliner of the British Columbia Railway, when descending from Williams Lake to Lillooet, on the southbound run from Prince George to North Vancouver. This is a route of astonishing scenic variety, ranging from an almost pastoral Scottish-strath quality between Prince George and Williams Lake, and finishing alongside Howe Sound, in fiord-like scenery, from Squamish into Vancouver. This last section now has the compelling attraction of a vintage steam run, regularly scheduled, and worked by one of the magnificent Royal Hudson 4-6-4 locomotives.

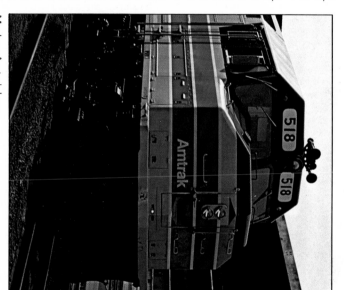

Modern Amtrak loco in Union station, Los Angeles.

Broadly speaking the Amtrak network of named trains is based on three major centres, Chicago, New York and Washington, DC, though there is some overlap involved in this distinction. Shown here are only the named trains. Other services do exist, particularly in the northeast. Though many of these trains bear romantic and colourful names, Amtrak do not utilize a system of name boards and associated paraphernalia which would enhance their image for the enthusiast. Because of a worsening financial situation, Amtrak has been forced to reduce service availability.

# The Andes: highest in the world 1

Diesel locomotive of ENAFER, Peru.

*Below* The network of the Central Railway of Peru, the most important railway in South America for engineering scale. Much of it was built by Henry Meiggs, and it was his most staggering achievement.
The line from Huancayo to Huancavelica includes 103 tunnels and 76 bridges.

[Map labels: La Oroya, Carhuamayo, Cerro de Pasco, Goyllarisquizga, Mina Rangra, Huaythayo, PERU, Matucana, Cocachacra, Chaclay, Lima]

*Above* Cuzco-Machu Picchu line, Peru.

The trans-Andine railways include seven major routes. Two connect Chile and Argentina, three give the landlocked country of Bolivia access to the Pacific Ocean, one links Lima with the mountain valleys and mineral region of central Peru, and the most northerly connects Guayaquil and Quito in Ecuador. These railways were built, mainly between 1870 and 1914, to a variety of gauges: standard gauge in Peru, 762 mm (2 ft 6 in) and metre gauge in Chile and Bolivia, and 1,067 mm (3 ft 6 in) in Ecuador. At the time they were built they helped to bring some political unity to the scattered and diverse populations of the countries they served, but their main function was economic and their main interest freight traffic. They were, and still are, vitally important to the mining industries of Peru, Chile and Bolivia. Passenger traffic has never been more than a troublesome obligation.

Crossing the Andes meant building the highest railways in the world. The Peruvian Central Railway reaches 4,829 m (15,845 ft), the now-closed Collahuasi branch of the Antofagasta (Chili) and Bolivia Railway 4,826 m (15,835 ft), and the Río Mulatos-Potosi line in Bolivia 4,787 m (15,705 ft). The Andes rise steeply from the Pacific coast of South America. They consist of a number of mountain ranges and plateaux dissected by deep, narrow valleys. Railway construction presented civil engineers with serious problems, for they had, in a confined space and short distance, to build railways over passes which exceeded Mont Blanc in altitude. The solutions they adopted were tight curves, zigzags, and, in two cases, rack sections. Operating the lines created further difficulties: steep gradients, the lack of local sources of fuel, heavy wear and tear on motive power and rolling stock, and frequent landslips and washouts. Only the southernmost route, from Los Andes in Chile to Mendoza in Argentina, encountered the hazards of heavy snowfalls and avalanches. Despite road and air competition in the last 20 years, all the seven lines remain in operation, though with varying degrees of efficiency and reliability. They offer the traveller some of the most exciting railway scenery on any line in the world.

## The Central Railway of Peru

The Peruvian Central is perhaps the most impressive of the seven routes. The engineering of the route involved immense problems. From Lima to Chosica the gradients are gentle and the route is straightforward. East of Chosica, though, the deep Rimac valley, the only feasible route to central Peru, narrows to a maximum width of perhaps 200 m (656 ft). Within its limits the engineers had to find a way of climbing from 854 m (2,802 ft) above sea level at Chosica to 4,783 m (15,693 ft) at Ticlio, a distance of no more than 76 km (47 miles) by the modern direct road which runs along the bottom of the valley. The twists and turns which the railway needs to gain height have made the rail distance far greater: 117 km (73 miles). To keep the ruling gradient down to 1 in 23, the single-track railway has to use the whole width of the valley, crossing frequently from one side to the other; and even this would be impossible without the use of the famous zigzags to gain height. Between Chosica and Ticlio there are six double and one single zigzags, 66 tunnels and 59 bridges to cross the Rimac and the deep side valleys which open into it.

Contrary to the general belief it was not the famous American entrepreneur Henry Meiggs who surveyed and laid out the route, but a former Peruvian government engineer, Ernesto Malinowski. Meiggs's task was to convince the sceptics of the practicability of the route and to contract and organize the necessary labour and materials. Construction of the line, which began in 1870, presented many problems. Thousands of workers died of a mysterious disease at Verrugas, and by 1877, when Meiggs died, Peru was bankrupt and the rails extended only as far as Chicla, 129 km (80 miles) from Lima and 3,723 m (12,215 ft) above sea level. Meiggs had, however, laid out the roadbed as far as the summit at Ticlio, 29 km (18 miles) further on, and the Peruvian Corporation, which took the railways on lease from the Peruvian government in 1890, therefore had a comparatively straightforward task in completing the line to the proposed

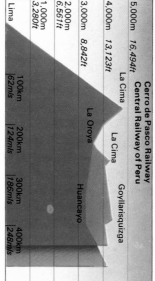

**Cerro de Pasco Railway**
**Central Railway of Peru**

| | 100km 62mls | 200km 124mls | 300km 186mls | 400km 248mls |
|---|---|---|---|---|
| 5,000m 16,494ft | La Cima | | | |
| 4,000m 13,123ft | | La Cima | La Oroya | |
| 3,000m 8,842ft | | La Oroya | | Goyllarisquizga |
| 2,000m 6,561ft | | | Huancayo | |
| 1,000m 3,280ft | Lima | | | |

After the first 40 km (25 miles) the line climbs steeply, reaching the Galera Tunnel at 4,832 m (15,848ft). The highest summit is at La Cima, 4,818 m (15,806 ft). The line is notable for its zigzags.

*Above* Cuzco-Santa Anna train, passing through mountain gorge, Peru.

terminus at La Oroya, 209 km (130 miles) from Lima and 3,712 m (12,179 ft) above sea level. Later extensions took the tracks on to Cerro de Pasco (1904), Huancayo (1908), and a metre gauge line was constructed from the latter point to Huancavelica in 1926.

For many years the Central Railway's commercial returns were disappointing, and as late as the 1890s the management was still considering ways to drive off the competition of 800 miles which took advantage of the graded route between La Oroya and Lima. Only in 1897, when a rise in prices made it economic to mine copper in Cerro de Pasco, Morococha and Casapalca, did the Central Railway begin to give an adequate return on the capital invested in it, and the large quantities of mineral traffic gave it about 30 years of commercial success, ended by the world depression of the 1930s. The problems faced by the Central Railway were common to most high-altitude railways. The costs of operating it forced it to charge some of the highest freight tariffs in the world. The large number of bridges and tunnels made engineering maintenance expensive. Seasonal rains, between January and April, caused landslides which at best closed the railway for a few days each year, and at worst left behind a huge repair bill. Floods in 1925

caused £70,000 of damage and interrupted traffic for 82 days. Steam locomotives had to be strong enough to withstand the rough conditions and powerful enough to haul heavy freight trains up the continuous gradient. British locomotives invariably proved too weak for these demands, but the management's record in adapting to these problems was extraordinarily good. They made several attempts to save on the heavy fuel bill. In 1909 converted their locomotives to burn oil, and later considered plans to electrify part of the line. The mechanical department developed the powerful Andes class of 2-8-0 locomotives, which could negotiate the tight bends and steep gradients with a payload of 180 tonnes of freight. They also constructed special wagons which could be used to haul oil up the hill and minerals down, thus cutting down on expensive haulage of empty rolling stock. After 1930 the railway's financial problems worsened. The Central Highway, which ran parallel to its tracks, was completed in 1935 and attracted much of the more valuable traffic. The government proved reluctant to allow the railway to raise tariffs or to protect it from this competition. In the 1960s, however, foreign loans financed a modernization plan. By 1967 Alco diesels had replaced steam locomotives. The expense, though, led the railway

into even more financial difficulties, and the government nationalized the line in 1972.

The chief interest of the Central Railway has always been freight, and it remains essential to the mining industry. Fortunately, however, the ordinary traveller too can still depart from Desamparados station in Lima at 07.00 hrs on any day of the week to enjoy the nine-hour journey to Huancayo. Except for those unfortunate travellers who suffer from altitude sickness and have to be given oxygen by the green-coated attendants, all will marvel at the ingenuity of the men who built this railway and at the ability of those who have operated it since, amidst some of the most rugged landscapes on earth.

## Southern Peru and Bolivia

Three railways serve the *altiplano*, a grassy plain 3,900 m (12,800 ft) above sea level, which extends for about 300 km (200 miles) from north to south in southern Peru and Bolivia. The Southern Railway of Peru, a standard gauge line, was largely built by Meiggs between 1869 and 1875. It runs from Mollendo through Arequipa, the second city of Peru, to the town of Juliaca on the *altiplano*. There it divides. A short, level 46 km (29 mile) line runs around the shores of Lake Titicaca to the port of Puno. A 338 km (211 mile) line runs north to Cuzco, the ancient Inca capital, crossing a summit of 4,314 m (14,154 ft) at La Raya. A steamer service across Lake Titicaca gives the Southern Railway access to Bolivia, where in 1906 it completed a short metre gauge line from Guaqui, the Bolivian port, to the capital city of La Paz.

Although the Southern Railway climbs, at Crucero Alto, to 4,471 m (14,668 ft), it presented no serious engineering problems. The average construction cost of the 523 km (325 miles) between Mollendo and Puno was less than half that of the Central Railway's Callao-Chicla

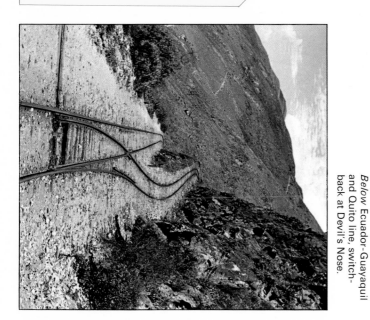

*Below* Ecuador-Guayaquil and Quito line, switchback at Devil's Nose.

# The Andes: highest in the world II

section. The line is single track throughout. Passenger trains have succumbed, on the Mollendo-Arequipa section, to road competition, but east of Arequipa, on the mountain section, passenger traffic has increased in the past few years and extra trains have been put on to cope with the demands of a growing tourist trade. Like all the Andean railways, passengers have never provided the Southern Railway with more than a small fraction of its receipts. The freight traffic for Bolivia has always been important, making the navigation of Lake Titicaca an integral part of the railway's operations. There were steamers here in the 1860s, before the railway. The *Yavari* and *Yapurá*, which were carried up from the coast by mule and assembled on the lake, can still be seen at Puno. Later the Peruvian Corporation added three more steamers on the Puno-Guaqui run, and in 1971 introduced a train ferry service across the lake to the Matilde mine in Bolivia.

The 458 km (284 mile) railway between Arica and La Paz was completed in 1913. It was built by the Chilean government to fulfil the terms of the 1904 peace treaty between Chile and Bolivia. Construction was extremely lengthy and difficult, and until the firm of Sir John Jackson took over the contract it seemed unlikely that it would be completed. It includes a 42 km (26 mile) rack section of the Abt two-bar type between Central and Puquios. There were no commercial reasons for the construction of another route between Bolivia and the Pacific, and the railway made an operating loss until 1922. The problems were manifold. All up trains had to be broken into three to traverse the rack section, and government control of both the Chilean and Bolivian sections brought inefficient management. This dated back to the opening of the line when the official party, consisting of leading figures from both countries, arrived at La Paz to find that their baggage had been left behind at Arica. The port, moreover, was little more than an open roadstead, and gained an unhealthy but deserved reputation for pilfering and delays. Except for the times when, for political reasons, the Bolivian government has encouraged traffic to use this route, the line has been an economic failure, although its strategic importance to both countries is considerable.

The Antofagasta (Chili) and Bolivia Railway, usually known as the FCAB, lies further south and it is the longest of the lines serving Bolivia. The FCAB started life in the 1870s as a 762 mm (2ft 6in) gauge line running inland from Antofagasta to the nitrate *pampas*. After the Pacific War (1879–1883), Chilean capitalists extended it inland to the Bolivian town of Uyuni, which it reached in 1889. In the same year British interests bought out the Chileans, and built the railway on to the mining centre of Oruro on the *altiplano*, 930 km (680 mile) from Antofagasta. The line has always been the most profitable of all the Andean railways. There were few engineering problems to raise costs and the management could rely on three major sources of traffic: nitrates and copper from the Chilean section and tin from Bolivia. In 1908 the FCAB took over the recently constructed metre gauge line between Oruro and Viacha, changed its own line to metre gauge as far south as Uyuni, and began the construction of branches to the important cities of Potosí and Cochabamba. Both railways involved a climb to over 4,100 m (13,450 ft) in the eastern chain of the Andes, and their construction posed far more serious problems than anything found on the main line. The Cochabamba branch was not completed

The Southern Railway of Peru, the Antofagasta, and the Arica-La Paz lines, cannot match the splendour of the Central Peru, yet their scale is still impressive. The Southern approaches Bolivia by way of ferry across Lake Titicaca; Arica requires rack working to reach the heights; and the Antofagasta has seen better days as the Bolivian political instability prevents through traffic. Yet it is said by travellers that the approach to La Paz must rate as one of the railway wonders of the world.

*Below* Although no longer properly operating through Bolivia, many parts of this system are utilized in Chile and Bolivia. The main summit reaches 4,084 m (13,396 ft) but an old branch to Punto Altobut reached 4,826 m (15,835 ft).

The Southern Railway of Peru does not require the zigzags of the Central yet reaches 4,472 m (14,668 ft) 357 km (223 miles) from the coast. At Puno passengers must take to ship in order to cross Lake Titicaca; the railway company maintains five for this purpose and the voyage takes 12 hours.

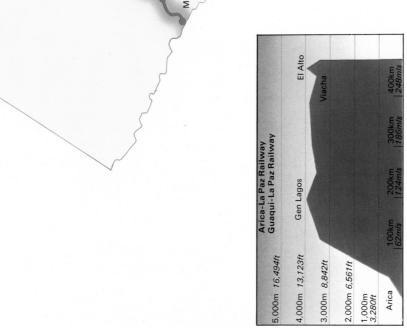

### Arica-La Paz Railway / Guaqui-La Paz Railway

| | |
|---|---|
| 5,000m 16,494ft | El Alto |
| 4,000m 13,123ft | Gen Lagos · Viacha |
| 3,000m 8,842ft | |
| 2,000m 6,561ft | |
| 1,000m 3,280ft | Arica |

100km 62mls · 200km 124mls · 300km 186mls · 400km 248mls

The Arica-La Paz line never achieved the importance of its neighbours even though at 471 km (293 miles) it is easily the shortest route between the capital and the coast. This was because the port facilities at Arica were poor, but also because 42 km (26 miles) of the climb are operated by rack on a 1 in 6 gradient.

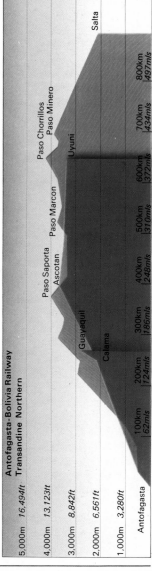

### Antofagasta-Bolivia Railway / Transandine Northern

Paso Chorrillos · Paso Minero · Paso Marcon · Paso Saporta · Ascotan · Uyuni · Guayaquil · Calama · Salta

| | |
|---|---|
| 5,000m 16,494ft | |
| 4,000m 13,123ft | |
| 3,000m 8,842ft | |
| 2,000m 6,561ft | |
| 1,000m 3,280ft | Antofagasta |

100km 62mls · 200km 124mls · 300km 186mls · 400km 248mls · 500km 310mls · 600km 372mls · 700km 434mls · 800km 497mls

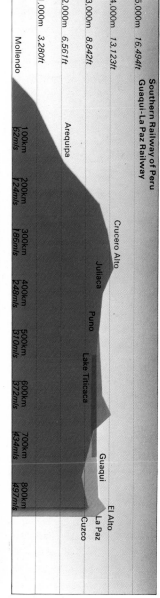

**Southern Railway of Peru
Guaqui–La Paz Railway**

5,000m 16,494ft
4,000m 13,123ft
3,000m 8,842ft
2,000m 6,561ft
1,000m 3,280ft

Mollendo · Arequipa · Crucero Alto · Juliaca · Puno · Lake Titicaca · Guaqui · El Alto · La Paz · Cuzco

100km 62mls · 200km 124mls · 300km 186mls · 400km 248mls · 500km 310mls · 600km 372mls · 700km 434mls · 800km 497mls

San Antonio · Cerrillos · Salta · Uyuni · Rio Mulatos · Challapato · Potosi · Oruro · Challapata · Tomas Barron

Freight train hauled by steam locomotive running through mining countryside in Bolivia near San Juan.

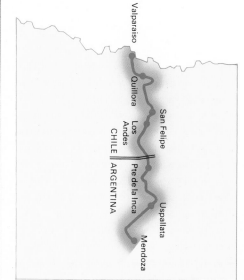

**Argentine Transandine Railway**

5,000m 16,494ft
4,000m 13,123ft
3,000m 8,842ft
2,000m 6,561ft
1,000m 3,280ft

Valparaiso · Los Andes Valparaiso · Cumbre Tunnel · Mendoza

100km 62mls · 200km 124mls · 300km 186mls

San Felipe · Quilota · Los Andes · Pte de la Inca · Uspallata · Mendoza

CHILE || ARGENTINA

*Top and above* Part of the trans-Andine railway is the line between Valparaiso in Chile and Mendoza in Argentina. It is not a remarkable line though it reaches its summit at the Cumbre Tunnel 3,187 m (10,452 ft). Rack working is necessary on both sides of the summit.

until 1924, and cost almost £17,000 for each kilometre.

Each of the three routes serving Bolivia had disadvantages. On the Peruvian line freight had to be transhipped twice to cross the lake. On the Arica line the rack section caused delays and expense. And until 1928, when the FCAB in a carefully planned operation changed the gauge of its Chilean section, all freight on that route had to be transhipped at Uyuni. None of the ports, until the construction of Matarani in southern Peru in 1948, had adequate warehousing or harbour facilities. The major engineering problem, though, with the exception of the difficult section of the Arica route, was not the crossing of the Andes, but the descent into the city of La Paz, which lies in a ravine 700m (2,300ft) below the *altiplano*. The Peruvian Corporation's Guaqui–La Paz line, completed in 1906, had to use gradients of 1 in 14 and electric traction to descend into the city. The FCAB completed its own line in 1917 but frequent landslips and washouts caused it to relocate the line in 1924 with a ruling grade of 1 in 33. The modernization of these routes since the 1950s has had varying degrees of success. The Southern Railway introduced Alco diesels and new rolling stock, including lightweight coaches, after 1958, and the line has been completely operated by diesels since the mid-sixties. Currently financial problems, following nationalization in 1972, are impeding the purchase of spare parts, and services are frequently interrupted by breakdowns. The Bolivian railways faced similar problems after nationalization in 1964. Despite attempts to undertake the comprehensive dieselization of the railways in the late 1960s, frequent breakdowns and slow repairs meant that steam locomotives were still common in parts of the FCAB in the mid-1970s. The Chilean section of the FCAB escaped nationalization in the early 1970s, and is now the only railway in South America still under British control.

**The Argentine–Chile links**

Two routes, both of them uneconomic, connect the

Chilean and Argentine railway systems. The younger, a metre gauge line between Antofagasta and Salta, was not completed until 1948. The dream of connecting the Atlantic and Pacific by rail, though, had been held since the mid-nineteenth century, and the first rail connection was completed in 1910 after over 20 years of construction. This metre gauge line runs from Los Andes, between Valparaiso and Santiago, to Mendoza in western Argentina, a distance of 254 km (159 miles). It is not high in comparison with the other trans-Andine railways, rising only to 3,186 m (10,453 ft) in the Cumbre tunnel, but it includes six rack sections on the Chilean side and seven on the Argentine, using the Abt three-bar system. Moreover, it is far enough south to suffer quite severely from snow and avalanches, unlike the other trans-Andine routes. Landslips and washouts have always been common. One, in 1934, destroyed part of the Argentine section, interrupting through rail traffic for ten years. The railway has never justified the hopes of those who promoted it a century ago.

**The Guayaquil and Quito Railway**

The G & Q (misleadingly nicknamed the "Good and Quick") connects the two major towns of Ecuador: Guayaquil on the coast and Quito in the mountains. Work began in 1871, but it was not until 1908 that the contractors completed this rather rare 1,067 mm (3 ft 6 in) gauge railway. It extends for 463 km (288 miles) and climbs to 3,609 m (11,841 ft). Curves are tight, and the maximum grade of 1 in 18 is quite staggering for a steam-operated adhesion railway. Like the Central Railway of Peru, the Guayaquil and Quito uses zigzags to gain height in a confined space. It has never been a commercial success, and the resulting lack of money for spares and replacements has given it a dreadful reputation for chaotic administration, breakdowns and derailments. Its locomotives and other equipment are often virtually antique. The fact that it continues to operate is perhaps more amazing than the fact that it was ever built.

# Mountain climbing: rack and pinion

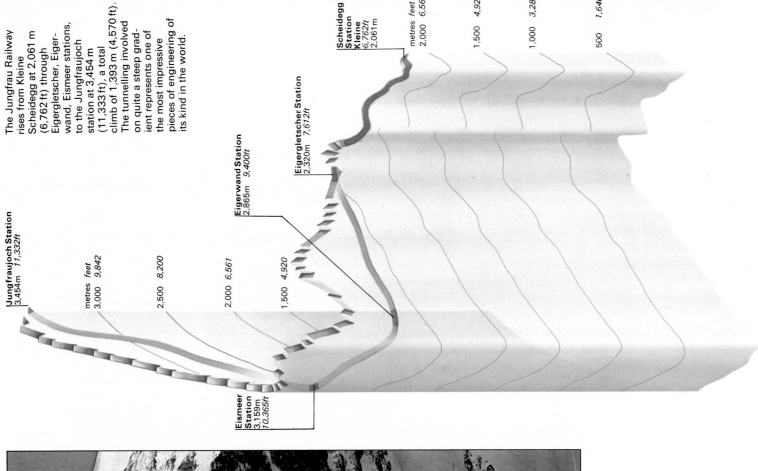

The Jungfrau Railway rises from Kleine Scheidegg at 2,061 m (6,762 ft) through Eigergletscher, Eigerwand, Eismeer stations, to the Jungfraujoch station at 3,454 m (11,333 ft), a total climb of 1,393 m (4,570 ft). The tunnelling involved on quite a steep gradient represents one of the most impressive pieces of engineering of its kind in the world.

Jungfraujoch Station
3,454m  11,332ft

metres  feet
3,000  9,842

2,500  8,200

2,000  6,561

1,500  4,920

Eismeer Station
3,159m
10,365ft

Eigerwand Station
2,865m  9,400ft

Eigergletscher Station
2,320m  7,612ft

Scheidegg Station Kleine
6,762ft
2,061m

metres  feet
2,000  6,561

1,500  4,920

1,000  3,280

500  1,640

The north face of the Eiger, showing the position of the Eigerwand station windows, high up on the north wall.

The breathtaking panorama to be enjoyed from the summit of a high mountain is normally not one to be attained without a great deal of physical effort of a skilled and specialized kind; but daring and highly ingenious railway engineering has enabled some of the most famous peaks in Europe to be ascended by train. The very first mountain railway in the world, however, was constructed in the USA in 1869 when Silvester Marsh, using a ladder type of rack between the rails, with circular rungs engaging with a vertical pinion under the locomotive, built a cogwheel railway to the summit of Mount Washington, the highest point in the White Mountains of New Hampshire, 1,918 m (6,293 ft) above sea level. This pioneer line is still worked entirely by steam. In 1871 the first mountain railway in Europe was opened, to the summit of the Rigi, overlooking the Lake of Lucerne. The engineer was Niklaus Riggenbach, and while using the same general principle as the rack pioneered by Marsh, he used a greatly improved form of rung in the ladder, which ensured a better locking effect on the locomotive pinion wheel. Nevertheless, the maximum inclination permitted was 1 in 5. In the meantime another inventor, Edouard Locher, had designed a remarkable form of rack rail. It is provided with two parallel sets of horizontal teeth and each axle of the electric motor coaches has double horizontal pinion wheels. These engage and grip the central rack on both sides, and with this arrangement it was safe to have gradients up to a maximum steepness of 1 in 2.

In 1889, the sensational rack railway up Mount Pilatus was built, again overlooking the Lake of Lucerne. It climbs from a station on the lakeside to a height of 1,629 m (5,344 ft) in no more than 4 km (2.5 miles), making an average gradient of 1 in 2.75 throughout. It was steam operated at first. The seating in the present electric motor coaches is in step formation, so that the passengers are sitting roughly level on each step as the ascent is made. At

times the outlook from the car is breathtaking, but nowhere more so than when the stark, precipitous face of the Eselwand is rounded, and the track is carried on a ledge blasted out of a solid, almost vertical, rock wall with a dizzy drop below on the left-hand side. Near the summit the line is taken through a tunnel hewn out of the rock to emerge on a plateau between mountain tops at the summit, and to find the hospitality of two hotels waiting at an altitude of 2,066 m (6,778 ft) above sea level.

In sheer altitude, however, the Pilatus railway is far surpassed by that of the Jungfrau, in the Bernese Oberland, which mounts to a ridge between the great mountains Jungfrau and Mönch at a height of no less than 3,454 m (11,333 ft) above sea level. At that great height a deficiency of oxygen in the air may cause faintness when a passenger steps out of the train at the summit. As a piece of mountain tunnel engineering, the Jungfrau Railway is magnificent, but because so much of it is in tunnel the ride

is not as interesting or as thrilling as that up the Pilatus. The approach ride, throughout from Interlaken, is one of great natural beauty, with superb mountain scenery; but the Jungfrau Railway proper begins at Kleine Scheidegg, and it is then 9.2 km (5.75 miles) to the summit station of Jungfraujoch. That run takes 65 min, and for no less than 50 min the train is continuously in tunnel. For mountain grandeur, however, apart from sheer sensation, the Gornegrat Railway, from Zermatt, easily takes first place, because the ascent is made in full view of that most majestic and striking of Alpine peaks, the Matterhorn. From the engineering viewpoint the Gornegrat Railway is notable as being the first in Switzerland to be operated by electricity from the outset. It was opened in 1898, 14 years before the completion of the Jungfrau line. The ruling gradient is 1 in 5, and the passenger is lifted 1,485 m (4,872 ft) in 9.2 km (5.75 miles). The ascent from Zermatt is made in 43 min, inclusive of stops.

# Great
# Expresses

# The Orient Express: the glory that faded

Few trains have been surrounded by a greater aura of mystery and romance than the Orient Express, yet few outside the most erudite of railway scholars knew its routes and their ramifications. Unlike many other great trains of the world, the Orient Express has varied and greatly diversified since it was first put on in 1883. Then its purpose was to provide a through service between Paris and Constantinople, but at that time it was not possible to travel the entire distance by train. The through carriages from Paris could go only as far as Giurgevo, a town on the Danube in Romania where that river formed the frontier with Bulgaria. Passengers crossed the Danube by ferry, and continued by train across Bulgaria to the Black Sea port of Varna, thence by steamer to Constantinople. From the winter of 1889 however the line through Turkey was completed, and the Orient Express, running once a week only beyond Vienna, took the main line of the Hungarian State Railway, southwards from Budapest, and travelled

via Zaribrod, and on to the Baron Hirsch Railway in Turkey. The distance by this route from Paris to Constantinople was 2,970 km (1,857 miles). Travellers left Paris by the Eastern Railway of France on Wednesday night at 19.30 hrs and arrived at Constantinople at 17.35 hrs on the Saturday evening, an overall average speed of 43 km/h (27 mph). No fewer than ten railway companies and six countries were involved.

There were at first many peculiarities in its operation. It was organized by the International Sleeping Car Company, and substantial supplements over the ordinary first class fare were charged. These varied over different parts of the route, and for this the car company was sometimes blamed. Actually the Sleeping Car Company received no more than a fraction of the supplement. The railway companies "cashed in" on the luxury traffic and charged what they liked, according to whether there were any competitive services.

After the introduction of the through service to Constantinople via Belgrade, a connecting train ran twice weekly from Vienna to Bucharest. It is this service that today still carries the famous name Orient Express. It leaves Paris nightly at 23.35 hrs and arrives at Bucharest at 11.45 hrs on the third morning. The journey time today is 36 hr 10 min, giving an overall average speed of 68 km/h (42.5 mph) over 2,448 km (1,530 miles). While there are through carriages between Paris and Bucharest the sleeping car service is not continuous.

## The Direct Orient

When the Simplon Tunnel was opened in 1906 a rival to the original Orient Express was put on, using the Paris, Lyon and Mediterranean route in France and travelling through Switzerland, Italy, Austria and into Serbia. It was

named the Simplon Orient Express, and more recently the Direct Orient, and it is this through service, between Paris and Constantinople (Istanbul) that was withdrawn in May 1977. It was a service that was twice interrupted, during the First and Second World Wars, and now it has disappeared again. The Simplon Express runs from Paris to Belgrade, and if a traveller wishes to continue to Istanbul it means an overnight stay in Belgrade and taking the Marmara Express next morning. Before the withdrawal of the Direct Orient Express in May 1977, departure from Paris (Gare de Lyon) was at 23.53 hrs and arrival at Istanbul at 08.25 hrs on the fourth morning, a total of 56½ hr for 3,024 km (1,890 miles), or 53.6 km/h (33.5 mph) overall. There was a time, after the end of the Second World War, when the service was yet again interrupted, during the civil war that broke out in Greece. Then it was necessary to detrain at the Bulgarian frontier station of Svilengrad, take a motor truck through the Grecian province of Thrace, and climb into another train at Uzunköprü. When the service was restored in 1949, and it was possible once more to travel in a through carriage from Paris to Istanbul, the journey through Thrace was considered somewhat hazardous. One intrepid traveller has described how five empty wagons were propelled ahead of the locomotive, to explode any mines that might have been placed on the tracks. Immediately behind the locomotive came four Turkish postal vans, followed by the dining car and two through carriages. Following these came some very old coaches carrying soldiers "at the ready"; and finally a truck carrying an armoured car mounted with a field gun – also at the ready. Travelling in this way through Thrace, the speed was no more than 32 km/h (20 mph).

In more recent times, when normal operation had been

The route of the Orient Express varied over the years and it used many types of train. The main routes shown on the map, *below*, are:
1 1900 Paris–Vienna.
2 1900 Paris–Constantinople. 3 1932 London–Bucharest. 4 1932 Simplon Orient Express. 5 1932 Arlberg Orient Express.

6 1932 Ostende–Vienna.
7 1932 London–Bucharest/Istanbul. 8 1977 Paris–Bucharest. The great romantic era of the Orient Express was in the interwar period, when it was possible to cross the Bosporus at Constantinople and travel on to Baghdād and Tehrān.

1884: dining car of the Orient Express.

*Above* Postcard showing French express engine on the Orient Express, c.1900. *Right* The Direct Orient in Yugoslavia, pulled by two 05 4-6-2's. *Below* Scenes from the EMI motion picture *Murder on the Orient Express*, taken from the Agatha Christie novel.

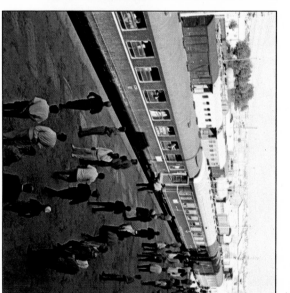

*Above* North Iraq, the Istanbul-Baghdad train, linking direct with the Orient Express.

restored, the romance and unique character of the service begins – for a traveller from the west – when the train passes from Italy into Yugoslavia at Sežana, not far beyond Trieste. There was a time, when steam still reigned supreme, when there was no mistaking the change, because instead of the silent Italian electric locomotive could be heard, just after midnight, the pounding beat of massive steam power climbing the gradients, and then a clanking of rods as it ran downhill. Now, however, more and more of the Yugoslav railway network is being electrified, and with good reason. The Direct Orient Express was one of a procession that came into Belgrade in the early morning, beginning at 05.27 and including arrivals at 05.37, 05.57, 06.19, 06.40, 06.59, at 08.03 the Direct Orient, 08.33, 08.43, and so on. Some of the large stations in Paris would find it hard to equal such an intense early morning procession. East of Belgrade too the line into Bulgaria and its capital city of Sofia has provided a major operating problem. Until recently it was single tracked, and although the passenger trains are not so numerous as on the line west of Belgrade, it is used not only by traffic into Bulgaria, and thence to Istanbul, but as far as Niš by trains running south into Greece and ultimately to Athens. Today the connections at one time provided from Paris by the Direct Orient Express are continued from Belgrade by the Athens Express.

East of Belgrade, the Direct Orient Express used to make slow progress. Stops used to be frequent, to cross trains travelling westward, and many of these would be of caravan length. At one time the Direct Orient Express carried its Athens and Istanbul sections – the present Athens and Marmara expresses – combined as far as Niš but the loads became too great. The pastoral scene, as the train rolls placidly through the eastern part of Yugoslavia, is fascinating, but the traveller thinking of sustenance will be disappointed, because the restaurant car service, once such a special feature of the International Sleeping Car Company's train, is now largely non-existent. The Direct Orient Express used to have a dining car on the Turkish part of the journey, but now the would-be diner has to wait until the length of Bulgaria has been traversed, entirely in darkness, and until 02.00 next morning when the Turkish dining car is put on at Kapikule. When organized by the Sleeping Car Company, it purchased its supplies from each of the countries passed through, since it was not permitted to convey food across international frontiers. The train does not exactly hurry across Bulgaria. It takes 2 hr 18 min to cover the 72 km (45 miles) from Dimitrovgrad to Sofia, and another 4¾ hr for the 312 km (195 miles) on to Svilengrad. But it is unimaginable that many business people, or men of affairs, have ever taken this train for its romantic associations.

**Between the wars**

The Orient Express proper, to Bucharest, and the Direct Orient, to Istanbul, were at their heights of prestige and popularity in the years between the two world wars. Stories of mystery and intrigue have been written around the journeys of the "King's Messengers" from the British Foreign Office who travelled alone in reserved compartments with their diplomatic bags. One of these distinguished servants of the country in his reminiscences has written: "Romantic writers tell us of beautiful spies and glamorous young secret agents who haunt the international trains for the purpose of extracting information from couriers, but the Greyhound knows his business far too well to mix dalliance with duty. A king's Messenger I knew – a noted Lothario – was scandalised at the suggestion that he might have commerce with the sirens of the Orient Express – 'besides', he added naively, 'I have never seen them'."

The Direct Orient Express, or the Marmara Express of today, reaches the Turkish frontier in the early hours of the morning. It is however at Edirne that the traditional atmosphere of the Orient first strikes the traveller. On the station, in English, French, German and Italian, is a large board carrying the words 'Welcome to Turkey'; and if it is sufficiently light the first minarets may be glimpsed from the train. Locomotives and rolling stock carry the crescent and star in large embossed characters on their sides. Then begins the final run towards Istanbul which takes only 6.5 hr and brings the Marmara Express in at about 08.30 hrs in the morning. The terminus is at Sirkeci, on the banks of the Bosporus, beside the junction with the Golden Horn, and from this station ferries cross the waterway to the Haydarpasa station, where one takes the train for Ankara and the rest of Turkey.

# The Irish Mail: over a century of service

Communication between London and Dublin was a vital feature of transportation within the British Isles long before the coming of railways, or indeed that of stage coaches. When the British railway network began to develop rapidly in the 1840s there was controversy as to where the principal packet station for the Irish traffic should be located. Robert Stephenson was engineer for the projected Chester and Holyhead Railway, while his great friend and professional rival, I. K. Brunel, proposed a broad gauge line from Worcester through the heart of central Wales to Porth Dinllaen, on the Lleyd peninsula, near to the present village of Nevin, near Pwllheli. Stephenson's route was preferred, and the line was ready for the inauguration of the Irish Mail train service on 1 August 1848. It can be claimed as the first named train in the world, although it did not carry its title on the carriage roof boards until 1927. In 1848 one could not travel the entire way from London to Holyhead by train, because Stephenson's greatest work on the Chester and Holyhead — the great Britannia tubular bridge over the Menai Strait — was not finished. Passengers, luggage and mails had to be detrained at Bangor, travel by coach across the strait by Telford's beautiful suspension bridge, and join another train to Llanfair, for the journey across Anglesey. The Britannia Bridge was completed in 1850, and from that time the Irish Mail was carried throughout from Euston to Holyhead by train. One picturesque tradition of earlier days remained and was continued for nearly 90 years. Each evening the "King's Time" was sent from London to Dublin by a watch sent from the General Post Office in St Martin's le Grand, conveyed by the Irish Mail train, thence by the packet steamer to Kingstown (now Dún Laoghaire) and finally by train to Dublin.

Until 1850 the sea portion of the journey had been

carried out by Admiralty packets, but in that year the contract, lasting for ten years, was awarded to the City of Dublin Steam Packet Company. The magnificent inner harbour at Holyhead had not then been built, and they sailed from the Admiralty pier. The City of Dublin company retained the contract for 70 years, and this brought a complication. The Admiralty pier would not take the weight of the express locomotives working the train from Chester, and engines had to be changed at the junction where the line to the pier left the main line into the inner harbour station. The principal service was at night, leaving Euston at 20.45 hrs, but there was also a day mail, leaving at 08.30 hrs and carrying a travelling post office

and all the facilities of its senior partner that ran at night. In later years the day mail carried restaurant cars, while the night mail had sleeping cars. The times of both trains were arranged to suit the convenience of the Post Office, and the mail contracts stipulated the speeds that had to be run, both on land and sea. The contract of 1860 required an overall speed of 68 km/h (42 mph) between Euston and Holyhead, and the total journey time between London and Dublin became 11½ hr. This was a remarkable achievement for that period, because it included the intermediate stops necessary. These were certainly cut to the minimum, and it was, in fact, to permit of non-stop running between Chester and Holyhead that the first

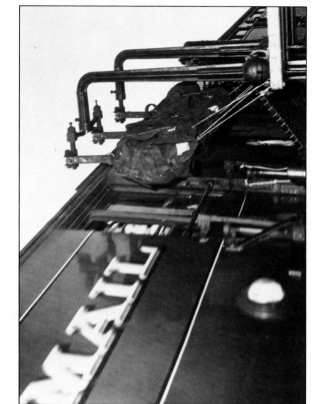

*Top* In London and North Western days: the down day mail (08.30 hrs from Euston) leaving the Britannia tubular bridge, hauled by a Precursor 4-4-0.
*Right* Mail pick-up at speed using traditional system, now phased out.

The route of the Irish Mail once followed the coach road built by Thomas Telford: communication between London and Dublin has long been of paramount importance, and at first the trains ran to a schedule set by the Post Office.

London (Euston)
*dep 21·10*

Rugby
133km (83mls)
*dep 22.21*

Crewe
254km (158mls)
*dep 00·07*

Chester
318km (198mls)
*dep 00.47*

Holyhead
424km (263mls)
*arr 02.28*
*ferry dep 03·15*

*ferry crossing*

Dun Laoghaire
524km (326mls)
*arr 06.45 dep 07·05*

Dublin
535km (332mls)
*arr 07.30*

*Left* The day mail in the last years of steam leaving the Conway tubular bridge, hauled by a Britannia Pacific locomotive.

Although the arrival time of the Irish Mail service in Dublin is a convenient 07.30 hrs, it must not be forgotten that passengers have to change from train to ship at Holyhead at 02.00 hrs, and have to be ready to leave the ship again at Dun Laoghaire at 06.45 hrs.

water troughs anywhere in the world were laid down near Aber, east of Bangor. As the train passed over the troughs, the fireman would lower a scoop, through which sufficient water was forced into the tender.

To meet Post Office requirements the outward-bound night mail arrived at Holyhead around 02.00 hrs – a grisly hour for passengers to change from train to the steamer, out on the end of the Admiralty pier! As traffic between England and Ireland increased, the London and North Western Railway, with its own steamers, put on two additional express services between London and Dublin, the day express leaving Euston at 13.20 hrs and the night at 21.50 hrs. These connected with steamers sailing from the inner harbour at Holyhead, and were much more convenient for passengers. After the First World War, when, because of political troubles, traffic to Ireland was much reduced, the ordinary day and night mail trains provided the only service. At the same time the London and North Western Railway secured the mail contract for the sea passage, and the packets thereafter sailed from the inner harbour at Holyhead. When the London and North Western became part of the London Midland and Scottish Railway, in 1923, the coach and engine livery became crimson lake, and in 1927 the carriage roof boards were added. By the time the famous train celebrated its centenary, in 1948, it was being worked by the nationalized British Railways.

*Above* The Irish Mail waiting to depart from London, Euston.

THE IRISH MAIL

In the days of steam haulage, this headboard adorned the front of the Irish Mail's locomotive, usually at the top of the smokebox.

117

# The Settebello: speed and luxury

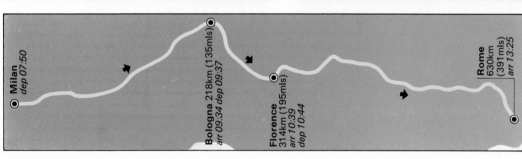

07:50
Milan
dep 07:50

Bologna 218km (135mls)
arr 09:34 dep 09:37

Florence 314km (195mls)
arr 10:39
dep 10:44

Rome 630km (391mls)
arr 13:25

13:25

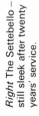

*Right* The Settebello – still sleek after twenty years service.

A free translation of the Italian name for this fast luxury train of today is "the lucky seven", and travellers by it are indeed lucky in comparison with their forebears who had to travel on the so-called *Rapidos* of Italy, in pre-Fascist days. Certainly the passenger has to pay a substantial supplement over the ordinary first class fare for the privilege of travelling on any train now designated as a Trans-Europe Express (TEE): but by and large it is worth it. In pre-Fascist days even the main line express trains and famous international services such as the Rome Express were haphazard, to put it mildly, in their operation. But Mussolini said, among a great many other rhetorical utterances, that Italian trains must run to time – full stop! And railway operation was certainly improved to an almost unbelievable extent. The Settebello provides a high speed luxury service between Milan and Rome, but in light of the previous reference to the Rome Express, it should be explained that the latter old-established and famous express does not use at any time the route of the Settebello. The Rome Express, leaving Paris just before midnight, comes into Italy through the Mont Cenis tunnel, calls at Turin, and then takes the historic line of I. K. Brunel down to the Mediterranean at Genoa. It then takes the coastal route to Rome, through Pisa, where to be sure someone on the platform will try and sell the unwary traveller a model of the leaning tower.

The Settebello, leaving Milan now at 07.50 hrs does follow the same route as another famous international express train, the Italia, which brings through sleeping cars from Calais, Hamburg and Brussels to Rome. This train does not go into the huge central station at Milan, which is a terminus. Coming in from the north, from the Gotthard line, it takes the avoiding spur, and stops at the Lambrate station of Milan. But it joins the main line to the southeast close on the heels of the Settebello, only 7 min later in fact; but being a much heavier train the time interval between gradually lengthens until it is nearly three-quarters of an hour behind, on arrival in Rome. This does not mean, however, that the Italia is a laggard. The days are long past when Italian trains were composed of rather primitive wooden coaches with bare boards in the third class, and red plush on the seats in the first.

## Self-contained and high speed

The Settebello itself, introduced in 1953, was something of a pace-setter, not only in speed. The Italian Railways were one of the first to realise that if traffic was to be saved from passing to internal airlines, and the private motor car driven in the Italian style – flat out, with horn blaring most of the time – the railways had to provide something more than comfortable compartment coaches and trains that ran at 120–130 km/h (75–80 mph) between stops. Something very much faster was needed to entice the busy executive, and the more opulent tourist. Great progress had been made after the end of the Second World War with electrifying the principal main lines in Italy, and improving the quality and maintenance standards on the track, and the conception was formed of a unit train with power units at both ends that would avoid the use of separate locomotives, and avoid locomotive changing at a station like Florence, which is a terminus, and where through trains changed their direction of running. So the Settebello was designed as a self-contained 7-car unit train.

The new train set a standard of speed and luxurious travelling accommodation previously unknown in Italy and rivalling anything else on European rails and, indeed, anything throughout the world, at that time. The high supplement charged for this service, as already mentioned, is virtually double the ordinary first class fare, but the passenger is offered a service which is comparable to that of a five-star hotel. Each coach consists of five spacious compartments containing comfortable armchairs and couches. There are tables and lockers for hand luggage. The toilet facilities include showers and special 'ladies' rooms. All the coaches are completely soundproofed and there is an extremely efficient system of air conditioning. The three middle coaches of the train contain a restaurant, bar and kitchen; a baggage room where passengers' luggage is stored at the beginning of the journey; and also an office where a traveller can make a telephone call to anywhere in Italy. The interior decor is elegant and restful.

It is a style of high-speed express passenger train that has

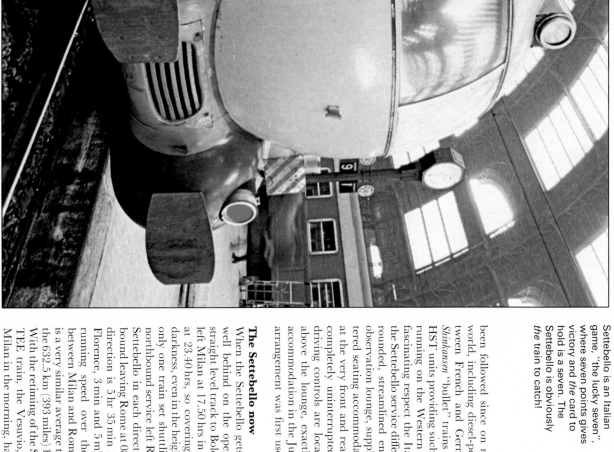

# IL SETTEBELLO

Settebello is an Italian game, "the lucky seven", where seven points gives victory and *the* card to hold is a seven. The Settebello is obviously *the* train to catch!

been followed since on railways in several parts of the world, including diesel-powered TEE trains running between French and German cities, for the spectacular *Shinkansen* "bullet" trains in Japan, and quite recently the HST units providing such an intense service of high speed running on the Western Region of British Rail. In one fascinating respect the Italian ETR-300 trains operating the Settebello service differ from all their successors. In the rounded, streamlined ends of the 7-car set there is an observation lounge, supplementary to the ordinary registered seating accommodation, where passengers can ride at the very front and rear ends of the train, and enjoy a completely uninterrupted view of the line ahead. The driving controls are located in an upper 'flight deck', above the lounge, exactly in the style of the first class accommodation in the Jumbo jet airliner, except that the arrangement was first used on the Settebello.

## The Settebello now

When the Settebello gets going it leaves everything else well behind on the opening run from Milan over the straight level track to Bologna. In its earlier days the train left Milan at 17.50 hrs in the evening, and reached Rome at 23.40 hrs, so covering a large part of the journey in darkness, even in the height of the summer. Then there was only one train set shuttling back and forth, because the northbound service left Rome at 10.50 hrs. Now there is a Settebello in each direction in the mornings, the northbound leaving Rome at 08.05 hrs. The overall time in each direction is 5 hr 35 min including stops at Bologna and Florence, 3 min and 5 min respectively, and the average running speed over the complete 630 km (390 miles) between Milan and Rome is 113.9 km/h (71.2 mph). This is a very similar average to that of the *Flying Scotsman*, over the 632.5 km (393 miles) between London and Edinburgh. With the retiming of the Settebello, and use of another fast TEE train, the Vesuvio, it is possible to leave Rome or Milan in the morning, have a full afternoon in either city,

catch the respective Vesuvio and be back in one's home city before midnight. The Vesuvio is not quite so fast as the Settebello, taking 5 hr 50 min in each direction.

On its present timing the Settebello naturally does its fastest running over the 218 km (135 miles) between Milan and Bologna, the timings being 104 min southbound and 102 min northbound. The latter represents a start-to-stop average speed of 130 km/h (80 mph). The central section of 96 km (60 miles) between Bologna and Florence is the slowest, being allowed 62 min. This is not so much an indication of severe gradients in the ascent to the great Apennine Tunnel, as the restriction on speed necessary over the many curves leading up to the piercing of the mountain range. This is indeed a thrilling stretch over which to ride in the forward observation lounge, with the track swinging first to one side and then to the other, magnificent views over the countryside as the train gathers height, and the passage through the tunnel itself 18.4 km (11.5 miles) long. Until recently an observer riding at the head end of the train through the tunnel would have been surprised to see what looked like a station midway between the two ends. There was indeed a regularly manned signal box there that controlled the entrance and exit from two long sidings. These were made to provide refuges for slow-running freight trains, and the signalman down there, at Precedenze, as the box was called, surely had one of the strangest jobs on the world's railways, hundreds of metres below the crest of the mountain, and about 8 km (5 miles) from daylight at the nearest end.

The southern end of the journey provides some further splendid sightseeing. The line from Florence to Rome makes a winding course through mountainous country; but there is more opportunity for fast running here, and the 326 km (203 miles) are covered in 161 min. This is nothing to what is intended when the new "Direttissima" is complete. The track distance between the two cities will be reduced to 251 km (157 miles), and the average speed is hoped to be about 160 km/h (100 mph).

# The Aquitaine: pioneer of electric traction

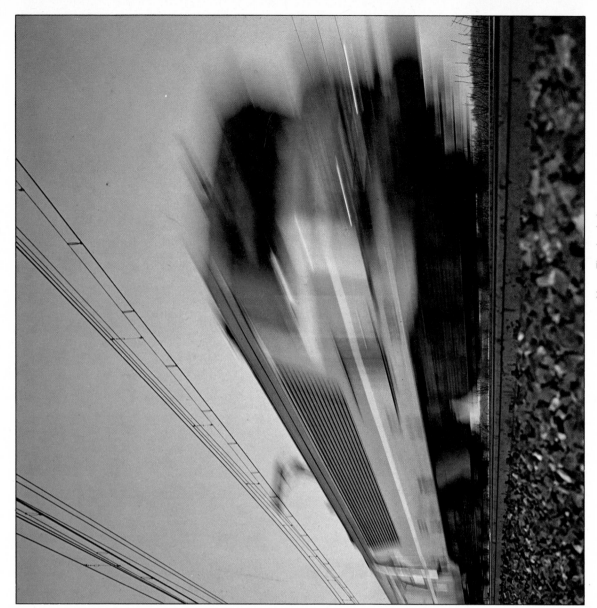

The main line between Paris and Bordeaux has from the middle of the nineteenth century been one of the most enterprising of French express routes. The Basque coast was already a favoured holiday region, and at the same time the route formed an important stage on the international line from Paris to Madrid and Lisbon, even though there was, as now, a change of rail gauge at the Spanish frontier. At that time the Paris-Orléans was the owning company as far south as Bordeaux. There one entered into the territory of the Midi Railway. The name "Aquitaine" for one of the fastest trains on this line, and indeed one of the fastest in all Europe, has been no more than recently bestowed; but the present magnificently appointed 200 km/h (125 mph) electric train is one of the manifestations of a great heritage of express passenger train operation. Although the traction is now all electric, in the years until the advent of electric traction, the Paris-Orléans Railway was the scene of one of the greatest steam locomotives the world has ever seen.

## The Orléans company

To take the story back nearly 100 years, the Orléans company had a deluxe train from Paris to Bordeaux that was the fastest long-distance express on the Continent of Europe. But there was a big difference in the overall time. Leaving Paris at 18.58 hrs it was not due at Bordeaux until 03.30 hrs the next morning, whereas the Aquitaine leaves at 17.53 hrs and after a non-stop run arrives at 21.43 hrs. The respective average speeds are 68 and 150.9 km/h (42.5 and 94.3 mph) – a startling example of the advancement of railway service on this route in 90 years. The train of 1888 stopped at Les Aubrais (Orléans), St-Pierre-des-Corps (Tours), Poitiers, Angoulême, and Coutras. The stopping times were 4 min at each place except Coutras. At Bordeaux it was taken over by the Midi for the rest of the journey to Biarritz. On the Orléans it was hauled by the strikingly picturesque 2–4–2 locomotives designed by M. Forguenot.

Early in the twentieth century the Orléans company purchased some very fine compound Atlantic engines of Alfred de Glehn's design, and these engines provided the power for acceleration of service with heavier trains, and in 1907 the company was the first in Europe to introduce locomotives of the Pacific type. At the same time most of the carriages on the trains from Paris to the towns and cities of Aquitaine were four-wheelers, though relatively large, with a long wheel base. The compartments inside were comfortable with tasteful décor, though with rather feeble oil lighting. Between stops the Atlantics and Pacifics used to wheel their long trains at speeds up to 113 km/h (70 mph) along the tracks. Then 120 km/h (74.5 mph) was the maximum speed permitted by law anywhere in France, and it was a limit that was strictly observed. The Orléans Railway was affected less than most of the French railways during the First World War, and in the mid-1920s the company embarked upon a programme of electrification that was intended to include the entire lengths of its two main lines, to Bordeaux and to its junction with the Midi Railway at Montauban, near to Toulouse. The system of traction chosen was the French standard of 1,500 volts direct current from an overhead line, and in December 1926 the first section was brought into oper-

ation, from Paris to Vierzon. This latter station was at the beginning of the hilly section of the Toulouse line. This diverged from the Bordeaux line at the junction of Les Aubrais (Orléans) and it meant that trains for Bordeaux and the south changed from electric to steam traction at Les Aubrais. Those responsible for steam locomotive workings on the Orléans realized that with the powerful new electric locomotives at work and the acceleration of service that they made possible, unfavourable comparisons could well be made between the standards of train running north and south of Les Aubrais. At that time the very latest of the steam passenger locomotives in service were nearly 20 years old. Furthermore, the large Pacific engines had not come up to expectations, and when it came to maximum output were not a great deal better than the much smaller Atlantics. So a most thoroughgoing research was commenced to try and pinpoint their deficiencies.

## Chapelon and the Tours works

The work was entrusted to a young engineer named André Chapelon, and by 1929 one of the old Pacifics had been extensively rebuilt, to his recommendations, at the Tours works of the company. In tests out on the line it was shown that the capacity of the engine had been increased by no less than 50 per cent. More engines of the type were rebuilt and it could soon be said that little if any difference could be discerned in the quality of the train running north and south of Les Aubrais. Steam, nevertheless, was fighting a rearguard action on the Orléans, because the policy of the company was to extend electrification southwards, thereby displacing more steam locomotives. And when the amalgamation with the Midi Railway came, in 1934, steam traction was caught in a "pincer movement", because the main line of the Midi was electrified south of Bordeaux. But what had been done by the men of the

*The sleek and shiny headboard carried by today's Aquitaine symbolizes the SNCF's modern approach to rail transport.*

*Above* The Aquitaine at speed, an SNCF publicity photograph.

**17:53**

The Aquitaine is scheduled to run from Paris to Bordeaux non-stop, at an average speed of 150.8km/h (94.3 mph). This heavyweight train covers the distance in a very fast time of 3 hr 50 min.

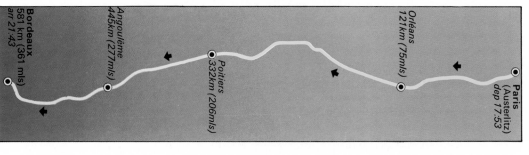

Paris (Austerlitz) dep 17.53

Orléans 121km (75mls)

Poitiers 332km (206mls)

Angoulême 445km (277mls)

Bordeaux 581 km (361 mls) arr 21.43

**21:43**

*Right* The Étendard, sister train of the Aquitaine, with the Capitole alongside.

Bordeaux is one of the largest French ports, and straddles major routes to Spain and Africa. It is also a tourist attraction: especially the twelfth-century church of Ste Croix.

Publicity photo of buffet car on the Aquitaine.

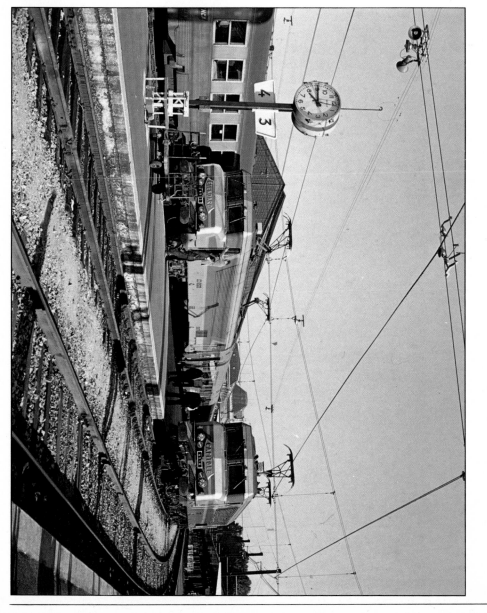

Orléans, at the Tours works, echoed round the railway world, and was the pattern for many improvements in steam locomotive design in far distant lands such as the USA and Russia, as well as elsewhere in France and in Great Britain.

## The Aquitaine's "Flyers"

After the Second World War the rest of the former Orléans main lines were electrified, now under national ownership, and a great drive began towards the attainment of higher speeds. New electric locomotives were introduced and some thrilling high-speed trials conducted south of Bordeaux on which the record maximum speed of 329.6 km/h (206 mph) was attained on two successive trips. With the experience of these runs, and use of the same types of locomotive in general service on several different routes elsewhere in France, the present magnificent 8,000 hp electric locomotive was produced that has made practicable the very fast schedule worked by the Aquitaine, and other express trains on the Paris-Bordeaux route. Over a considerable proportion of the line continuous running at 200 km/h (125 mph) is now permitted, and a remarkable high-speed train service is now provided. Until the autumn of 1976 it was considered very good going to cover the 580 km (360 miles) from Paris to Bordeaux in exactly 4 hr, that is an average speed of 145 km/h (90 mph); but in September of that year some further accelerations were made.

Although there are many fast trains on this route the two outstanding "flyers" are the Étendard and the Aquitaine. Southbound the Étendard leaves Paris at 07.51 hrs and reaches Bordeaux in 4 hr 5 min with three intermediate stops – St-Pierre-des-Corps, Poitiers, and Angoulême. The successive start-to-stop average speeds are 150, 162.5, 140 and 123.5 km/h (93.8, 101.6, 87.5 and 77.2 mph). The Aquitaine, leaving at 17.53 hrs, goes down non-stop in 3 hr 50 min, an average of 150.8 km/h (94.3 mph). In the opposite direction the Aquitaine, leaving Bordeaux at 08.00 hrs, reaches Paris in 3 hr 59 min with stops at Angoulême and Poitiers, while the Étendard comes up non-stop in 3 hr 50 min arriving in Paris at 21.40 hrs. These trains are no lightweights. In some countries, notably West Germany, the fastest trains that are locomotive-hauled rather than of fixed-unit formation like the Settebello, and certain of the TEE services for which the West German

Federal Railways provide the rolling stock, are restricted to limited formations; but the French have always specialized in the haulage of gargantuan loads, and a train like the Sud Express, which leaves Paris just after the Étendard has departed in the morning, may have a total load of up to 16 or 17 cars.

The Aquitaine and the Étendard, which are scheduled to run at 200 km/h (125 mph), are actually limited, though the limit is not a low one. They take a maximum of ten of the huge "Grand Confort" cars, which loaded with passengers and luggage weigh about 550 tonnes. It is not that the great CC 6500 class electric locomotives cannot take any more, at the very high speeds scheduled: it is that in so doing they would take too much electric current out of the overhead line. In this respect the Orléans line is paying the penalty of being a pioneer in electric traction in France. When this line was electrified in the mid-1920s, and had the wires extended farther south in the 1930s, there was no thought that such demands for power would be made as the haulage of a 550-tonne train at 200 km/h (125 mph). The sub-stations supplying the overhead power line were spaced at distances thought to be more than adequate for the heaviest demands foreseen at that time. That they are able to meet the needs of today is a tribute to the foresight of those who planned the electrification: but there is a limit.

## Future acceleration

The accelerations of September 1977 do not represent the limit of point-to-point speed on this enterprising route, without exceeding the maximum speed of 200 km/h (125 mph) and with it the maximum demand for power. On the very first day of the new timetable the Aquitaine had to make an emergency stop, called for by signals, on the first stage, and reached Angoulême 6½ min late. No time was regained on the next stage, on which the 113 km (70 miles) to Poitiers have to be run in 45 min start-to-stop – an average of 149.6 km/h (93.5 mph). But on the final run up from Poitiers to Paris, 330 km (206 miles), allowed 135 min, not only was all the lost time regained, but the effect of four slight checks was absorbed, and an arrival in Paris made 2 min early. Allowing for the effect of those checks the net time from Poitiers was only 123.75 min – an average of 160 km/h (100 mph), and 11.5 min better than

# The Chief: America in style

The Atchison Topeka and Santa Fe is one of the largest railways in the USA, with a route length of more than 20,800 km (13,000 miles). Over its lengthy main line of 3,562 km (2,226 miles), from Chicago to Los Angeles, there used to run some of the most famous trains on the North American continent, such as the Fast Mail and the California Limited; but the queen of them all, and one of the world's greatest trains, was the Chief. In the days before and during the Second World War it was always popular with the very élite of travellers. Consequently heavy, it frequently had to be run in two sections. At the zenith of steam days on the Santa Fe, however, it ran in two sections only from Chicago to the West Coast – a Hudson type 4-6-4 over the more level eastern section of 1,595 km (991 miles) from Chicago to La Junta, Colorado, and then one of the mighty 4-8-4s of the 3765 or 3776 classes, onwards to Los Angeles.

The normal load of the Chief was 14 cars leading from the locomotive as follows: two mail storage vans, travelling post office, a combination baggage and dormitory lounge car, four sleeping cars, dining car, three sleeping cars, and an observation lounge car bringing up the rear. The journey time from Chicago to Los Angeles was nearly two days, and the accommodation and service *en route* were up to the finest American standards. In days before air travel became the premier way of travel for wealthy patrons and men of affairs, the standards set by the Atchinson Topeka and Santa Fe were second to none on the railways of the world.

## Seven states and fourteen crews

No fewer than seven states were passed on the journey to the west: in succession Illinois, Missouri, Kansas, Colorado, New Mexico, Arizona and California. Given such a cavalcade it was fortunate that some of the finest scenery was passed through in daylight. On the eastern end, with the Hudson-class locomotive, five separate engine crews were involved. Then from La Junta, with a 4-8-4 on the head end, nine different crews in succession were put on to work the train, making a total of 14 different crews on the entire two-day journey. Crews were changed at Fort Madison, Kansas City, Newton, Dodge City, La Junta, Raton, Las Vegas, Albuquerque, Gallup, Winslow, Seligman, Needles, and finally at Barstow before the train

finally ended its journey at Los Angeles. Because of its accessibility, the fuel used throughout from Chicago to Los Angeles was oil, and the locomotives were serviced twice on the route.

From La Junta westwards the route crosses one mountain range after another, in majestic and often breathtaking scenery. First comes the Sangre de Cristo range, and the gradient up to the Ratou Tunnel, 1 in 28, is so severe that even the huge 4-8-4 locomotives had to take a "helper". Then comes fast downhill running and then another hard climb, from Las Vegas, New Mexico, to the crest of the Glorieta Range. Next, downhill into the Apache Canyon, along the old Santa Fe trail. It is "give and take" hard slogging for the locomotive all the way from La Junta until the summit of the Cajon Pass is reached in the early morning of the third day out from the start in Chicago. As an enthusiastic American observer once wrote: "Often it seems they are doing the impossible, as they smash at long sustained grades at high speed, tip over high mountain passes, drift down, to attack a gleaming tangent at one hundred miles an hour". Tangent

is the American railroader's term for a straight track. At Albuquerque, after 553 km (344 miles) of hard going, the locomotive was detached from the train briefly, and went to a bay in the neighbouring roundhouse for servicing. Then she came back with the fourth crew of the journey in charge, and on a gradual ascending grade climbed to the top of the Continental Divide at an altitude of 2,209 m (7,248 ft). The ensuing descent towards Gallup, New Mexico, is one of the finest racing stretches of the whole route, and it was a regular thing for these enormous engines to cover 214 km (133 miles) here in two hours. Then to Winslow, Arizona, where the locomotive was serviced again, during a twenty-minute stop. It would be dark here in the summer by the time the train left again, and so it continued through the night and into California. In doing this type of work, with continuous hard steaming, nothing but the most intense and immaculate servicing by dedicated staff ensured the reliability demanded of the Santa Fe.

The diesel-hauled Super Chief was running by 1939. But although it was faster it never supplanted the Chief in

*Left* A memorable advertisement for the Chief.

The Chief crossed 7 states in its journey from Los Angeles to Chicago, and 14 crew changes were involved. The growth of the city of Los Angeles and its port was largely linked with the coming of the railroads: today it is America's third greatest city.

**Flagstaff**
2,705km (1,681mls)
*dep 12:51*

**San Bernardino**
3,483km (2,164mls)
*dep 21:28*

**Los Angeles**
3,577km (2,223mls)
*arr 23:15*

*Above* Santa Fe's first California Limited, fore-runner of the Chief, running into Los Angeles in the 1880s.

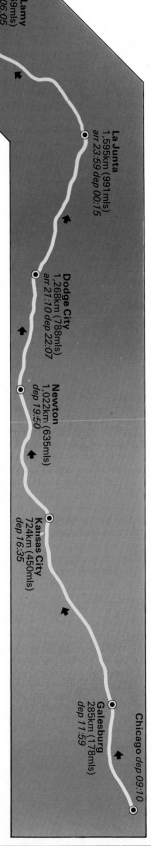

In the postwar era the Chief was diesel hauled, and all Santa Fe diesels carried the device, *above*, emblazoned on their front; it has since been changed.

*Below* The Chief in stock which is the most familiar to this route.

**Albuquerque**
2,148km (1,335mls)
*dep 07:30*

**Lamy**
2,042km (1,269mls)
*dep 06:05*

**La Junta**
1,595km (991mls)
*arr 23:59 dep 00:15*

**Dodge City**
1,268km (788mls)
*arr 21:10 dep 22:07*

**Newton**
1,022km (635mls)
*dep 19:50*

**Kansas City**
724km (450mls)
*dep 16:35*

**Galesburg**
285km (178mls)
*dep 11:59*

**Chicago** *dep 09:10*

**09:10**

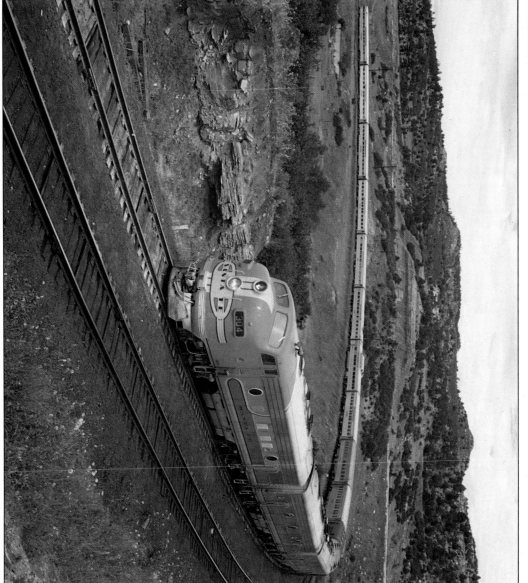

popularity, until the great recession in American railway passenger travel began in the 1950s and the cream of the business passed to the airlines. Nevertheless, among older travellers the Chief of the Santa Fe is remembered with affection.

**Super Chief and Southwest Limited**

Today, under the auspices of Amtrak, its place has been taken by the Southwest Limited. With the aid of a trio of 3,000 hp diesel-electric locomotives, it runs from La Junta to Los Angeles, and the time is five and a half hours faster than with steam. Two of those three locomotives work right through from Chicago; the third couples on at La Junta to help in the heavy-grade work over the western mountain ranges. There is much running at 137 to 145 km/h (85 to 90 mph) on the straight and level stretches. Diesel- or steam-hauled it is a run that could scarcely be paralleled anywhere else in the world, both for its sustained interest for the railway historian and enthusiast, and for the variety and grandeur of its ever-changing scenery.

*Above* The Southwest Limited, the modern Amtrak equivalent of the Chief, arrives at Los Angeles.

Chicago, a terminal point of the Chief, is the second city of the USA and claims to be the world's largest railroad traffic centre. The Super Chief began running in 1939 but the Chief retained its popularity until the 1950s.

# The Blue Train: pride of South Africa

Cape Town is the chief port of South Africa and the southern terminus of the South African railway network. The Blue Train originally ran as a link with the ships to Britain, and had therefore to match the luxury available on board.

**Cape Town** 1,608km (999mls) arr 12:00

**Worcester** 1,433km (890mls) dep 08:52

---

If one were asked to nominate a train in which the accommodation was the most luxurious ever offered to the travelling public, the Blue Train of the South African Railways would easily come first. The name would immediately remind English travellers of something much nearer home, because for some time before the South African Railways adopted the title the Paris, Lyon and Mediterranean had been running the *Train Bleu*, a nightly sleeping car express from Paris to the much favoured resorts on the Côte d'Azur. In South Africa the need for a luxury train from the Cape to the cities of the Transvaal came as part of the rehabilitation programme at the conclusion of the Boer War. In 1903 the new service between Cape Town and Pretoria was put on, and even in those days the coaching stock was the height of luxury, and ran in connection with the arrivals of the Union Castle mail steamers from England. Each train ran two days a week in each direction, leaving Cape Town at 10.45 hrs and reaching Johannesburg at 16.30 hrs on the following afternoon. At the time of its introduction it was operated jointly by the Cape Government Railway as far north as Kimberley, and there the Central South African Railway (CSAR) took over for the rest of the journey. Practically all the equipment of the CSAR was new, and supplied from Great Britain.

## After the Union

When the Union of South Africa was formed in 1910, and the previously independently worked railways of the Cape of Good Hope, and of Natal, amalgamated with the CSAR to form the South African Railways, the name of the luxury express running between Cape Town and Pretoria was initiated as the Union Limited. Although it remained first class only, and required supplementary fares, there was an "all classes" express train running from Cape Town to the north on the five days that the Union Limited did not run, taking 39 hr to reach Johannesburg, with many more intermediate stops, against the 29½ hr of the de luxe train. The Union Limited, despite its exclusive nature, became a most popular train requiring many more coaches. The locomotives grew in size from the smart Pacifics of the CSAR to giant 4-8-2s in the 1930s. Although the track gauge is no more than 1,067 mm (3ft 6in), physical conditions have enabled the locomotives to be built considerably wider and taller than those on the standard gauge railways of Great Britain. Speeds are not high by present-day standards, and with steam traction the maximum permitted is 88.5 km/h (55 mph).

In April 1939 the name was changed to the Blue Train, this coinciding with the introduction of some magnificent new rolling stock, which, unlike all other passenger coaching stock on the South African Railways, was painted blue. The new carriages had clerestory roofs, and the upper panels were painted cream. The steam locomotives of the South African Railways had always been black, but black or not, the engines of the Union Limited, and later of the Blue Train, were always immaculately turned out. As to the modern coaching stock, the compartments are more like Royal saloons, or de luxe apartments on board ship, than the interior of trains available to the general public. They are upholstered in blue leather, and on the seats there are loose cushions. The compartments have writing tables, attractive headed notepaper, and available throughout the journey there is an excellent valet service. The dining car is sumptuously appointed, and at the rear end there is an observation car. The South African Railways sets store upon the public relations rendered by the travelling staff, and all those allocated to the Blue Train are specially selected. The train is now electrically hauled between Pretoria and Kimberley, and again between Beaufort West and Cape Town, by locomotives specially painted blue, in contrast to the standard russet colour of non-steam units on the SAR. Until fairly recently the central part of the journey was steam hauled, but now specially painted diesel-electric locomotives operate this section. The train now leaves Cape Town at 12 noon, and reaches Johannesburg in 24.5 hr, an excellent overall average speed of 63 km/h (39 mph). Pretoria is reached at 14.00 hrs. On the southbound run departure from Pretoria is at 10.00 hrs, arriving at Cape Town at 12 noon. The stops after Johannesburg are Klerksdorp, Kimberley, De Aar Junction, Beaufort West and Worcester.

## Anniversary celebrations

In April 1969 the 30th anniversary of the Blue Train was celebrated in most spectacular fashion. At the suggestion of the Historical Transport Association of Johannesburg, a special anniversary run was organized, steam hauled throughout in both directions. In the ordinary way great pride is taken in the appearance and turnout of the main line steam locomotives of the South African Railways, and on this occasion a trophy was awarded to the crew of the best prepared engine. The staging points for engine changing on this special occasion were the same as the normal passenger stops, except that in Cape Province engines were changed at Touwsrivier. Six locomotives were involved in each direction of running and the competition between crews for the trophy produced some truly sensational efforts. The wheels, motion, and all the running gear were alike cleaned to watchmaker's standards, but the climax was attained when one of the huge 4-8-4s of Class 25 backed down on the train at Kimberley at nine o'clock at night and the great crowd assembled on the platform saw the interior of the engine cab, with not only all the paintwork of that usually dirty place immaculately clean, but every metal part burnished till that interior looked like a jeweller's shop. At every place crowds were out in force to greet the train – even in the dead of night. That fantastic once-in-a-way steam-hauled Blue Train will live in the memory of all who saw her. Meanwhile the regular luxury train continues on its silent and effortless way.

The modern Blue Train.

**Beaufort West**
1,064km (661mls)
arr 02:14
dep 02:39

**De Aar**
801km (498mls)
arr 22:16 dep 22:21

**Kimberley**
563km (350mls)
arr 18:46 dep 19:11

The modern Trans Natal near Durban, a great rival of the Blue Train.

**Klerksdorp**
256km (159mls)
dep 14:39

When the Blue Train was first electrified, it carried a bilingual headboard, *left*.

BLUE · BLOU
TREIN · TRAIN

Locos of the 25 class which once used to pull the Blue Train, but which were superseded by diesel and electric stock, and by a more modern "clean" image.

**Pretoria**
dep 10:00

**Johannesburg**
70km (43mls)
arr 11:10
dep 11:30

10:00

Before the rise of air travel finished the ocean liner, the Blue Train was an important link between the administrative capital, Pretoria, and the outside world, via the port at Cape Town. Pretoria is characterized by the Voortrekker Monument, to Dutch pioneers who first colonized the high veldt.

# The Canadian: transcontinental connection

The Canadian of Canadian Pacific Rail is indeed a train with a pedigree. Its antecedents take the history of travel in Canada back to the very dawn of transcontinental communication, and that is to the inception of the Dominion itself. The integration of the far-flung centres of early colonization into a unified community that was so soon to grow into a great nation depended entirely upon the provision of a line of railway that would connect British Columbia and Vancouver Island with the prairies, the cities of the St Lawrence basin, and with the maritime provinces. And when the great pioneers had found their way, and built their line through the colossal barriers of the Rockies and the Selkirk ranges, and the last spike had been driven at Craigellachie on 7 November 1885, this extraordinary route had to be operated, 4,680 km (2,908 miles) of it, between Montreal and Vancouver.

## Crack express

Across the length of the Canadian Pacific Railway the crack transcontinental express of the early 1900s, the Imperial Limited, made its stately way. It was not a fast train, and in the mountain passes of British Columbia, where some of the gradients were as steep as 1 in 25, it needed one locomotive to every two cars in the train. Very soon the burden of working this fearful incline, with a gradient of 1 in 22 for 6.5 km (4 miles), had become a bottleneck and in 1909 the tremendous task was undertaken of easing it by boring two spiral tunnels in the Swiss fashion, and reducing the gradient to 1 in 45. It was still, however, a single-track railway, and even though very much larger locomotives were introduced the weight of trains went on increasing, and by the beginning of the 1930s the need for three giants in tandem was not unusual. The atmosphere in those single-track tunnels in the cab of the third of three hard-worked steam locomotives took some withstanding! By that time the crack transcontinental train was known as the Dominion, and the Canadian Pacific, in 1931, were running another, called the Canadian, not on this same route, which was then the fastest in the world. On the Montreal-Toronto run it covered the 200 km (124 miles) from Montreal West to Smith's Falls in 109 min. There was then fierce competition for the intercity traffic between the Canadian Pacific and the Canadian National Railways, which ended soon afterwards with a pooling agreement.

Vancouver Island, a natural west coast harbour, was the goal of the first Canadian transcontinental line to be built (the Canadian Pacific's) and was reached in 1887. A through travellet will have been in 4 time zones when he arrives after breakfast on the fourth day.

In the meantime the Dominion continued as the principal transcontinental train until 1955, when in the floodtide of postwar development a second train, consisting of splendid new stainless steel coaching stock, was put on. This train was named the Canadian and supplanted the Dominion as the premier service. Both continued, however, for another ten years on the Montreal/Toronto to Vancouver service; but after that declining traffic led to the withdrawal of the Dominion. Today the Canadian, diesel-hauled, leaves Montreal at 11.15 hrs. The Toronto section, which does not have so far to go, leaves at 15.30 hrs, and the two are combined at Sudbury, Ontario, leaving there at 22.25 hrs. It is a most luxurious train. The cars are of seven varieties. Marshalled next to the locomotive is a baggage dormitory car, which includes living quarters for the dining and buffet car crews and for stewards. For while the locomotive crews are changed at each divisional point, the train crews are changed only once on the long journey, at Winnipeg. Then, in order going rearwards from the locomotive come the de luxe coaches, providing seating for 60 passengers, followed by the scenic dome coach. This includes a buffet and snack lounge and the skyline coffee shop. The dining cars come next, and then there are the sleeping cars. Finally at the

rear end of the train is the dome observation lounge, which includes a high elevated dome portion, and a lower level stern-walk lounge buffet – a most satisfying car in which to ride. Except for the baggage car, and the 60-seater open saloons, all cars on the Canadian are named, some with the prefix "Chateau" and others with the suffix "Manor". They are named after men famous in Canadian history, such as *Chateau Montcalm, Chateau Cadillac, Wolfe Manor* and *Dufferin Manor*.

## The Canadian's magnificent route

The route of the Canadian across the country varies in its scenic and historical interest; but apart from the tremendous scenery in the Rockies one of the most beautiful stretches – especially if the weather is fine – comes soon after breakfast time on the second day out from Montreal, when the train is making its way along the northern shores of Lake Superior. It was a terrible section to build, cutting a ledge in towering walls of rock rising sheer from the waters of the lake; working in a land where the best way of getting forward the necessary supplies was to bring them across the lake by water, or by sledge during the winter months when the lake is always completely frozen over. Today the passenger can enjoy the ride, as the train rounds

one bay after another, passes through tunnels in the solid rock, and it is not necessary to be in one of the domes to see the front and rear of the long train at the same time. At Thunder Bay, reached about lunch time, the first change of watches takes place, from Eastern to Central time. Winnipeg on the threshold of the prairies is not reached until late in the evening of the second day.

The richest of the prairie regions are passed in the night, and at Swift Current watches are put back a second time, when entering the region of Mountain Time. There are some long runs across the western prairies on the third day, in daylight from Swift Current to Medicine Hat, 236 km (147.5 miles), and then on into the province of Alberta and its capital city of Calgary. By that time the long, fascinating snow-capped range of the Rocky Mountains is already in sight. The train stops for half an hour at Calgary and for the payment of one dollar passengers may break their journey with a "lift" to the top of the Husky Tower, part of the station complex, a Calgarian equivalent of the Post Office Tower in London, for a marvellous view of the city and the surrounding country. So back to the train, and with the shadows closing in a dive into the mountains in earnest, and the third night on the journey. Vancouver is reached about breakfast time on the fourth day.

Kamloops
4,235km (2,632mls)
arr 00.45

3,801km (2,362mls)

Vancouver
4,680km (2,908mls)
arr 08.25

Lake Louise
3,801km (2,362mls) arr 15.55

Banff
3,745km (2,327mls)
arr 15.00 dep 15.10

Calgary
3,650km (2,268mls)
arr 12.20 dep 12.55

Medicine Hat
3,300km (2,051mls)
arr 09.02

Moose Jaw
2,905km (1,805mls)
arr 04.00

Regina
2,835km (1,762mls)
arr 02.55

The claim of the crest of the Canadian Pacific to "span the world", derives from the corporation's other interests in shipping and air travel.

*Above* Stopping point for the Canadian in the Prairies, here pulled by only two power units – see the doubling opposite.

*Above left* The Canadian crossing typical lands in the Rockies.

*Right* The Canadian at a halt in the Rockies, British Columbia. *Far right* The Canadian in the new livery, VIA being an amalgam of Canadian National and Canadian Pacific Railways.

**Winnipeg**
2,250km (1,398mls)
arr 20:15 dep 20:45

**Thunder Bay**
1,590km (988mls)
arr 12:55

**Franz**
1,105km (687mls)
arr 04:39

**Chapleau**
875km (606mls)
arr 02:50

**Sudbury**
700km (435mls)
arr 21:15 dep 22:25

**Montreal (Windsor)**
dep 11:15

**Ottawa (Union)**
175km (109mls)
arr 13:25 dep 13:35

11:15

The French-speaking city of Montreal is the world's largest inland port, due to the St Lawrence Seaway. It is the headquarters both of the Canadian Pacific, the operators of the Canadian, and also of the other major carrier, Canadian National.

# The Rajdhani Express: India's fastest

Decorative Indian steam.

New Delhi, occupying an almost central position in the Indian subcontinent, has been the capital of India since 1931.

**New Delhi** *dep 17:00*

*Mathura 141 km (88mls)*

*Sawai Madhopur 358km (222mls)*

*Kota 469km (291mls)*

*Ratlām 732km (455mls) dep 02·28*

*Vadodara Junction 993km (617mls) dep 06·07*

*Surat 1,122km (697mls)*

**Bombay** 1,384km (860mls) arr 10·55

Bombay has been called The "Gateway to India" because of its fine harbour: it is second only to Calcutta as India's leading port. Today its population is approaching six millions.

Diesel electric unit hauls Rajdhani Express.

The traditional steam competitor of the Rajdhani Express.

In Imperial days there were several famous express trains crossing the Indian subcontinent, such as the Frontier Mail and the Imperial Indian Mail, from Bombay to Calcutta; but since independence the railway requirements of India have changed considerably, and one of the most important considerations has been to give improved and accelerated service without incurring heavy capital investment, or recurring capital charges. The outcome of much research work in the fine establishment of the Indian Railways at Lucknow has been the introduction of two Rajdhani Expresses, one running between New Delhi and Calcutta, the other from New Delhi to Bombay. One Rajdhani runs between New Delhi and Howrah, the great terminus on the right bank of the Ganges opposite to Calcutta. This fine train, which runs twice a week in each direction, covers the 1,450 km (900 miles) in just over 16 hours, an average speed of 88.5 km/h (55 mph). It stops only at Kānpur and Mughalserai, and is classed as a deluxe train, conveying both first and second class passengers. A small supplement is charged for the speed of transit. Until recently a speed of 96 km/h (60 mph) was the maximum permissible with passenger trains on the broad gauge 1,676 mm (5 ft 6 in) lines in India; but the research establishment at Lucknow is now working to make possible speeds of 160 km/h (100 mph) and the Rajdhani Express

already runs at speeds of up to 120 km/h (75 mph) over long stretches of its journey. Eventually, overall journey times will be reduced considerably.

The design of the coaching stock is interesting. The train runs through the night, leaving New Delhi at 18.15 hrs on the eastbound run, and Calcutta (Howrah) at 17.10 hrs westbound. The coaches are fully air-conditioned throughout in the sitting and sleeping accommodation. The "chair" cars each have 73 seats, and taking advantage of the wide gauge, these are arranged three on one side and two on the other side of the gangway. The price of a seat in one of the "chair" cars includes the cost of evening tea, dinner, early morning tea and breakfast, and meals are served airline style in boxes to every seat. The sleeper coaches for travel, in which the fare is three times that in a "chair" car, each have three four-berth compartments, and three coupés with extra wide windows and sunk-in upper berths. There is an air conditioned pantry car on the train, in which food prepared at base establishments is stored, hot or cold, until it is served at the appropriate meal times.

The other Rajdhani service between New Delhi and Bombay is a journey of 1,384 km (860 miles), the route lying through Kota and Vadodara Junction (Baroda). This is also a night service. The southbound train leaves at 17.00 hrs and reaches Bombay at 10.55 hrs, with stops at Ratlām and Baroda. The overall average is nevertheless the very good one of 77 km/h (48 mph) for this long run. The corresponding northbound train leaves Bombay at 15.30 hrs. Like the Rajdhani trains to and from Calcutta, the Bombay trains run twice weekly in each direction. On the Calcutta route the trains are hauled by electric locomotives.

Atlas

Mi.
150

100

50

Km.
150

100

50

NORTH SEA

Mi.
150
100
50
0

Km.
150
100
50
0

# Northern Europe

# Spain and Portugal

# Western and Central USSR

144

Mi.
600

400

200

0

Km.
600

400

200

# Eastern and Central USSR

Mi.
600
400
200
0

Km
600
400
200
0

SEA OF JAPAN

PACIFIC OCEAN

SEA OF OKHOTSK
OCHOTSKOJE MORE

VOSTOČNO-SIBIRSKOJE MORE
EAST SIBERIAN SEA

Bering Sea

CHINA
MANCHURIA

REPUBLICS

STANOVOJ CHREBET

CHREBET DŽUGDŽUR

CHOTE-ALIN'

KURIL'SKIJE OSTROVA
KURIL ISLANDS

POLUOSTROV
KAMČATKA

SREDINNYJ CHREBET

KORAKSKOJE NAGORJE

PENŽINSKIJ CHREBET

ANADYRSKOJE
PLOSKOGORJE

JUKAGIRSKOJE
PLOSKOGORJE

KOLYMSKAJA NIZMENNOST

Arctic Circle

SAINT LAWRENCE ISLAND

NUNIVAK ISLAND

Habomai, Shikotan, Kunashiri, and
Etorofu, occupied by the U.S.S.R.
since 1945, are claimed by Japan
pending a final peace treaty.

147

# Southeast Asia

India and Pakistan

154

# Western North Africa

# Eastern North Africa

158

# Southern Africa

The United Nations declared an end to the mandate
of South Africa over Namibia in October, 1966.
Administration of the territory by South Africa
is not recognized by the United Nations.

*Tropic of Capricorn*

**Mi.**
600

**Km.**
600    400    200    0

160

Canada

162

United States

164

# Northern South America

CARIBBEAN SEA

PACIFIC OCEAN

VENEZUELA

COLOMBIA

ECUADOR

PERU

BOLIVIA

BRAZIL

CHILE

PANAMA

COSTA RICA

NICARAGUA

NETHERLANDS ANTILLES

LESSER ANTILLES

TRINIDAD

GRENADA

WINDWARD ISLANDS

Bogotá

Lima

La Paz

Caracas

Quito

SELVAS

DESIERTO DE ATACAMA

CORDILLERA OCCIDENTAL

CORDILLERA CENTRAL

CORDILLERA ORIENTAL

LLANOS DE MOXOS

SIERRA PARIMA

LA GRAN SABANA

Amazon

Orinoco

Negro

Madeira

Mi.
600
400
200
0

Km.
600
400
200
0

Copyright © by Rand McNally & Co.
Map prepared by Esselte Map Service AB Stockholm.
A-64H05264

Southern South America

# Legend

## Legend to Maps

### Transportation
- Railway
- Primary Road
- Secondary Road
- Minor Road, Trail
- ✈ Airport
- Navigable Canal
- Ferry

### Inhabited Localities

1:3,000,000
- ° 0–10,000
- ○ 10,000–25,000
- ⊙ 25,000–100,000
- ▣ 100,000–250,000
- ■ 250,000–1,000,000
- ■ >1,000,000

1:6,000,000

1:12,000,000
- · 0–50,000
- ⊙ 50,000–100,000
- ⊙ 100,000–250,000
- ■ 250,000–1,000,000
- ■ >1,000,000

Urban Area (area of a continuous industrial, commercial, and residential development)

### Capitals of Political Units
- **BUDAPEST** Independent Nation
- Luanda Dependency (Colony, protectorate, etc.)
- Villarica State, Province, etc.
- White Plains County, Oblast, etc.

### Political Boundaries

International (First-order political unit)
- Demarcated, Undemarcated, and Administrative
- Disputed de jure
- Indefinite or Undefined

Internal
- State, Province, etc. (Second-order political unit)
- County, Oblast, etc. (Third-order political unit)

### Miscellaneous Cultural Features
- ▲ Point of Interest (Battlefield, cave, historical site, etc.)
- ⌘ Church, Monastery
- ∴ Ruins
- ⊤ Castle

### Hydrographic Features

- Intermittent Stream
- The Everglades Swamp
- Rapids, Falls
- Glacier
- SEWARD GLACIER
- Reef
- Intermittent Lake, Reservoir
- Tuz Gölü Salt Lake
- Dry Lake Bed

### Topographic Features
- Mt. Kenya △ 5199 Elevation Above Sea Level
- 76 ▽ Elevation Below Sea Level
- Mount Cook △ 3764 Highest Elevation in Country
- 133 Lowest Elevation in Country
- Khyber Pass 1067 Mountain Pass

Elevations and depths are given in meters

Highest Elevation and Lowest Elevation of a continent are underlined

---

# Country Comparisons

The figures listed below cover all countries in the world with a railway system. Direct comparison is made between major railway statistics and the basic area and population data for the country concerned. Figures usually relate to the state system, but where this does not exist, or where the level of private ownership is significant, this position is reflected. Metric values are given, *with imperial equivalents in italic*. Information is based on United Nations and Rand McNally sources, supplemented by other available material.

Information is set out under country headings, as follows:

Capital
- **A** Area – km² *miles²*
- **B** Population
- **C** Route length (km *miles*) per 10,000 km² *10,000 miles²*
- **D** Route length (km *miles*) per 10,000 population
- **E** Net tonne km *miles* per capita
- **F** Passenger km *miles* per capita

Information not available marked n/a

## A

**Albania**
Tiranë
- A 28,748 *11,100*
- B 2,520,000
- C 101.6 *164*
- D 1.2 *0.7*
- E n/a
- F n/a

**Algeria**
Algiers
- A 2,381,741 *919,595*
- B 17,045,000
- C 16.6 *26.6*
- D 2.3 *1.4*
- E 11.2 *7*
- F 62.1 *38.8*

**Angola**
Luanda
- A 1,246,700 *481,353*
- B 6,090,000
- C 18 *29.1*
- D 3.7 *2.3*
- E 732.3 *457.7*
- F 68.6 *42.9*

**Argentina**
Buenos Aires
- A 2,776,889 *1,072,162*
- B 25,550,000
- C 144.1 *233.3*
- D 15.7 *9.8*
- E 418 *261.3*
- F 563.1 *352*

**Australia**
Canberra
- A 7,686,849 *2,967,909*
- B 13,645,000
- C 55.9 *90.5*
- D 31.5 *19.7*
- E 2,183.7 *1,364.8*
- F n/a

**Austria**
Vienna
- A 83,849 *32,374*
- B 7,745,000
- C 695.2 *1,125.3*
- D 7.5 *4.7*
- E 1,360.4 *850.2*
- F 863 *539.4*

## B

**Bangladesh**
Dacca
- A 142,775 *55,126*
- B 77,650,000
- C 200.2 *324*
- D 0.4 *0.2*
- E 5.3 *1*
- F 26.7 *16.7*

**Belgium**
Brussels
- A 30,513 *11,781*
- B 9,865,000
- C 1,353.8 *2,911.9*
- D 284.9 *178.1*
- E 672.7 *420.4*
- F 832 *520*

**Benin**
Porto Novo
- A 112,622 *43,484*
- B 3,180,000
- C 51.4 *82.6*
- D 1.8 *1.1*
- E 39.8 *24.8*
- F 30.4 *19*

**Bolivia**
Sucre and La Paz
- A 1,098,581 *424,164*
- B 5,715,000
- C 32.6 *52.8*
- D 6.3 *3.9*
- E 63.9 *39.9*
- F 47.2 *34.9*

**Brazil**
Brasília
- A 8,511,965 *3,286,487*
- B 108,640,000
- C 75.8 *122.6*
- D 5.9 *3.7*
- E 393 *245.6*
- F 97.6 *61*

**Bulgaria**
Sofia
- A 110,912 *42,823*
- B 8,765,000
- C 386.8 *626.1*
- D 4.9 *3.1*
- E 1,945.5 *1,215.9*
- F 855.7 *534.8*

**Burma**
Rangoon
- A 678,033 *261,790*
- B 31,415,000
- C 45.7 *74*
- D 1 *0.6*
- E 13.4 *8.4*
- F 90.6 *56.6*

## C

**Cambodia**
Phnum Pénh
- A 181,035 *69,898*
- B 8,215,000
- C 35.8 *58*
- D 0.8 *0.5*
- E 1.2 *0.7*
- F 6.6 *4.1*

**Cameroon**
Yaoundé
- A 475,442 *183,569*
- B 6,450,000
- C 24.7 *39.6*
- D 1.8 *1.1*
- E 827.9 *517.4*
- F 40.9 *25.6*

**Canada**
Ottawa
- A 9,976,139 *3,851,809*
- B 22,975,000
- C 70.9 *114.8*
- D 30.8 *19.3*
- E 8,583.9 *5,365*
- F 127.5 *79.7*

**Chile**
Santiago
- A 756,945 *292,258*
- B 10,685,000
- C 120.2 *194.6*
- D 8.5 *5.3*
- E 180.8 *113*
- F 196.5 *122.8*

**China**[1]
Peking
- A 9,561,000 *3,691,500*
- B 845,300,000
- C 57.5 *93.1*
- D 0.7 *0.4*
- E 356.1 *222.6*
- F n/a

**Colombia**
Bogotá
- A 1,138,914 *439,737*
- B 21,960,000
- C 30.2 *48.6*
- D 1.6 *1*
- E 56.8 *35.5*
- F 23.3 *14.5*

**Congo**
Brazzaville
- A 342,000 *132,000*
- B 1,360,000
- C 23.2 *37.6*
- D 5.8 *3.7*
- E 373.2 *233.3*
- F 180.9 *113.1*

**Costa Rica**
San José
- A 50,900 *19,650*
- B 1,990,000
- C n/a
- D n/a
- E n/a
- F n/a

**Cuba**
Havana
- A 114,524 *44,218*
- B 9,340,000
- C 441.2 *714.2*
- D 5.4 *3.4*
- E 173.1 *108.2*
- F 101.3 *63.3*

**Czechoslovakia**
Prague
- A 127,876 *49,373*
- B 14,875,000
- C 1,042.4 *1,677.6*
- D 9.5 *6*
- E 4,755.6 *2,972.3*
- F 1,241.5 *776*

## D

**Denmark**
Copenhagen
- A 43,069 *16,629*
- B 5,100,000
- C 577.1 *933.9*
- D 4.9 *3*
- E 416.5 *260.3*
- F 637.6 *398.5*

**Dominican Republic**
Santo Domingo
- A 48,734 *18,816*
- B 4,760,000
- C 57.5[1] *92.5*[1]
- D 0.6[1] *0.4*[1]
- E n/a
- F n/a

## E

**Ecuador**
Quito
- A 283,561 *109,483*
- B 6,615,000
- C 39.5 *63.6*
- D 1.7 *1.1*
- E 7 *4.4*
- F 9.2 *5.7*

**Egypt**[2]
Cairo
- A 1,002,000 *386,900*
- B 38,045,000
- C 45 *72.9*
- D 1.2 *0.7*
- E 67.3 *42.1*
- F 190.8 *119.2*

**Eire** — Dublin
A 70,285 27,137
B 3,165,000
C 311.4 504.1
D 1.0 0.6
E 179.1 111.9
F 253 158.1

**El Salvador** — San Salvador
A 21,393 8,260
B 4,152,000
C 289.8 466.1
D 1.5 0.9
E n/a
F n/a

**Ethiopia** — Addis Ababā
A 1,221,900 471,778
B 28,265,000
C 6.4 10.3
D 0.3 0.2
E 8.6 5.4
F 3.8 2.4

## F

**Finland** — Helsinki
A 337,032 130,129
B 4,710,000
C 176.7 286.1
D 12.6 7.9
E 1,388.5 867.8
F 665 415.6

**France** — Paris
A 543,998 210,039
B 52,930,000
C 639.7 1,035.5
D 6.6 4.1
E 1,294.3 808.9
F 966.7 604.2

## G

**Germany, East** — East Berlin
A 108,178 41,768
B 17,365,000
C 1,329.7 2,152.4
D 8.3 5.2
E 2,983.2 1,864.5
F 1,286.7 804.2

**Germany, West** — Bonn
A 248,533 95,959
B 62,650,000
C 1,157.6 1,873.9
D 4.6 2.9
E 945.1 590.7
F 612.2 382.6

**Ghana** — Accra
A 238,537 92,100
B 9,990,000
C 40 64.3
D 1.0 0.6
E 30.5 19.1
F 52.1 32.5

**Greece** — Athens
A 131,944 50,944
B 9,010,000
C 194.2 314.5
D 2.8 1.8
E 103.4 64.6
F 172.3 107.7

**Guatemala** — Guatemala
A 108,889 42,042
B 5,920,000
C 83.9 135.9
D 0.5 0.3
E 17.9 11.2
F n/a

**Guinea** — Conakry
A 245,857 94,926
B 4,460,000
C 38.2 61.8
D 2.1 1.3
E n/a
F n/a

## H

**Honduras** — Tegucigalpa
A 112,088 43,277
B 3,150,000
C 46.6[1] 75.4[1]
D 1.7[1] 1[1]
E 133.3 83.3
F 92.8 58

**Hong Kong** — Hong Kong
A 1,034 399
B 4,385,000
C 324 526.3
D 0.1 0.05
E 10.6 6.6
F 57.2 35.7

**Hungary** — Budapest
A 93,032 35,920
B 10,510,000
C 867.9 1,404.8
D 7.7 4.8
E 2,145.4 1,340.9
F 1,271.9 795

## I

**India** — New Delhi
A 3,183,643 1,229,210
B 604,000,000
C 189.4 306.6
D 1.0 0.6
E 236.9 148.1
F 223.1 139.4

**Indonesia** — Djakarta
A 1,950,963 753,271
B 133,840,000
C 35.7 57.8
D 0.5 0.3
E 76.7 47.9
F 31.4 19.7

**Iran** — Tehrān
A 1,648,000 636,300
B 33,365,000
C 28 45.3
D 1.4 0.9
E 160.2 100.1
F 67.9 42.5

**Iraq** — Baghdād
A 434,924 167,925
B 11,300,000
C 58.1 94.1
D 2.2 1.4
E 151.1 94.4
F 56 35

**Israel[2]** — Jerusalem
A 20,770 8,019
B 3,480,000
C 287.9 466.4
D 1.7 1.1
E 296.9 185.6
F 699.5 437.2

**Italy** — Rome
A 301,250 116,313
B 56,060,000
C 531.6 860.5
D 2.9 1.8
E n/a
F n/a

**Ivory Coast[3]** — Abidjan
A 322,463 124,504
B 6,795,000
C 19.7 31.7
D 2.9 1.8
E 276.8 173
F 405.2 253.3

## J

**Jamaica** — Kingston
A 10,962 4,232
B 2,035,000
C 404.7 655.7
D 1.2 0.7
E 12.1 7.5
F 0.6 0.3

**Japan** — Tōkyō
A 372,197 143,706
B 111,680,000
C 721.8 1,168.4
D 2.4 1.5
E 428.5 267.8
F 2,875.1 1,797

**Jordan[2]** — 'Ammān
A 97,740 37,738
B 3,430,000
C 51.2 82.1
D 1.5 0.9
E 8.2 5.1
F n/a

## K

**Kenya[4]** — Nairobi
A 582,644 224,960
B 13,550,000
C 33.4 53.8
D 1.5 0.9
E 120.9 75.6
F 40.2 25.1

**Korea, North[5]** — Pyŏngyang
A 120,538 46,540
B 16,035,000
C 317.3 513.8
D 2.4 1.5
E n/a
F n/a

**Korea, South[5]** — Seoul
A 98,477 38,022
B 34,290,000
C 259.8 420.4
D 0.7 0.5
E 959.3 599.6
F 51.7 32.3

## L

**Lebanon** — Beirut
A 10,230 3,950
B 3,485,000
C 404.7 655.7
D 2.8 1.8
E 533.2 333.2
F 68.8 43

**Liberia** — Monrovia
A 111,369 43,000
B 1,730,000
C 44.3 71.6
D 2.8 1.8
E 2,303[6] 1,439.3[6]
F n/a

**Luxembourg** — Luxembourg
A 2,586 998
B 335,000
C 1,048 1,693.4
D 8.1 5
E 1,869.9 1,168.7
F 877.6 548.5

## M

**Madagaskar** — Tananarive
A 587,041 226,658
B 9,025,000
C 15 24.7
D 1.0 0.6
E 31.8 19.9
F 27.5 17.2

**Malawi** — Lilongwe
A 118,484 45,747
B 5,070,000
C 47.8 77
D 1.1 0.7
E 43 26.9
F 12.1 7.5

**Malaysia** — Kuala Lumpur
A 332,633 128,430
B 12,180,000
C 54.1 87.6
D 1.5 0.9
E 109.6 176.2
F n/a

**Mali** — Bamako
A 1,239,710 478,655
B 5,810,000
C 5.2 8.3
D 1.1 0.7
E 28.7 17.9
F 17.2 10.8

**Mauritania** — Nouakchott
A 1,030,700 397,950
B 1,340,000
C 6.3 10.2
D 4.9 3
E 5,080.6 3,175.4
F n/a

**Mexico** — Mexico City
A 1,972,546 761,604
B 61,040,000
C 87.5 141.7
D 2.8 1.8
E 176.1 110.1
F 49.1 30.7

**Mongolia** — Ulan Bator
A 1,565,000 604,200
B 1,460,000
C 9.1 14.7
D 9.8 6.1
E 1,583.6 989.7
F 142.5 89

**Morocco** — Rabat
A 446,550 172,415
B 17,785,000
C 45.4 73.1
D 1.1 0.7
E 232.8 145.5
F 22.4 14

**Mozambique[7]** — Maputo
A 783,763 303,771
B 9,380,000
C 49 79.1
D 4.1 2.6
E 232.8 145.5
F 49.1 30.7

## N

**Namibia** — Windhoek
A 823,168 317,827
B 870,000
C 1.0 1.7
D 4.5 7.2
E 0.05 0.03
F n/a

**Nepal** — Kāthmāndu
A 140,797 54,362
B 12,705,000
C 4.5 7.2
D 1.5 0.9
E 0.8 4.5
F n/a

**Netherlands** — Amsterdam
A 40,844 15,770
B 13,695,000
C 691.7 1,119.8
D 2.1 1.3
E 19.4 12.1
F 605.5 378.4

**New Zealand**
Wellington
A 268,675 103,736
B 3,120,000
C 178.5 289
D 15.4 9.6
E 1,266.7 791.7
F 2,045.8 1,278.6

**Nicaragua**
Managua
A 130,000 50,200
B 2,185,000
C 24.5 39.2
D 1.5 0.9
E 76.9 48.1
F 153.8 96.1

**Nigeria**
Lagos
A 923,768 356,669
B 75,080,000
C 38.1 67.7
D 0.5 0.3
E 18 11.2
F 13.6 8.5

**Norway**
Oslo
A 323,878 125,050
B 4,040,000
C 130.9 212
D 10.5 6.6
E 343.1 214.4
F 246.5 154.1

**P**

**Pakistan**
Islāmābād
A 895,496 345,753
B 72,000,000
C 98.4 159.2
D 1.2 0.8
E 120.7 75.4
F 178.7 111.7

**Panama**
Panamá
A 75,651 29,209
B 1,485,000
C 58.3 90
D 3 1.8
E n/a
F n/a

**Paraguay**
Asunción
A 406,752 157,048
B 2,755,000
C 12.2 19.6
D 1.8 1.1
E 11.8 7.4
F 97.9 61.2

**Peru**
Lima
A 1,285,216 496,224
B 16,080,000
C 16.8 27.2
D 1.3 0.8
E 45.7 28.6
F 16.8 10.5

**Philippines**
Manila
A 300,000 115,831
B 43,300,000
C 39.2 63.5
D 0.3 0.2
E 1.5 0.9
F 22.2 13.9

**Poland**
Warsaw
A 312,677 120,725
B 34,175,000
C 760.1 1,230.4
D 7 4.3
E 3,829.1 2,393.2
F 1,252.5 782.8

**Portugal**
Lisbon
A 92,082 35,553
B 9,110,000
C 387.3 627.4
D 3.9 2.4
E 93.9 58.7
F 59.3 37

**R**

**Romania**
Bucharest
A 237,500 91,699
B 21,220,000
C 460.7 745.7
D 5.2 3.2
E 3,053.7 1,908.6
F 1,055.8 659.9

**S**

**Saudi Arabia**
Riyadh
A 2,149,690 830,000
B 9,105,000
C 2.8 4.6
D 0.7 0.4
E 172.2 107.7
F 0.007 0.005

**Senegal**
Dakar
A 196,722 75,955
B 4,480,000
C 52.5 84.5
D 2.3 1.4
E 65.2 40.8
F 50.7 31.7

**South Africa**[8]
Cape Town and Pretoria
A 1,222,161 471,879
B 25,815,000
C 109.6 176.2
D 8.4 5.2
E 2,552.6 1,595.3
F n/a

**Spain**
Madrid
A 504,750 194,885
B 35,765,000
C 282.4 483
D 4 2.6
E 301 188.1
F 466.4 291.5

**Sri Lanka**
Colombo
A 65,610 25,332
B 14,250,000
C 233.8 378.4
D 1.1 0.7
E 20.8 13
F 203.8 127.4

**Sudan**
Khartoum
A 2,505,813 967,500
B 14,790,000
C 19.1 30.9
D 3.2 2
E 146 91.3
F n/a

**Surinam**
Paramaribo
A 163,265 63,037
B 430,000
C 5.3 8.4
D 2 1.2
E n/a
F n/a

**Swaziland**
Mbabane
A 17,366 6,705
B 500,000
C 126.1 214.3
D 4.4 2.7
E 1,058.8 661.7
F n/a

**Sweden**
Stockholm
A 449,750 173,649
B 8,190,000
C 256.7 415.6
D 14.1 8.8
E 1,887.2 1,179.5
F 654.9 409.3

**Switzerland**[9]
Bern
A 41,288 15,941
B 6,410,000
C 708.9 1,147.4
D 4.5 2.9
E 881.7 551.1
F 1,267.4 792.1

**Syria**[2]
Damascus
A 185,180 71,498
B 7,460,000
C 100.2 162.1
D 2.5 1.6
E 21 13.2
F 13.5 8.5

**T**

**Taiwan**
T'aipei
A 35,961 13,885
B 16,305,000
C 280.2 453.5
D 0.6 0.4
E 165.6 103.5
F 515.9 322.4

**Tanzania**[4,10]
Dar es Salaam
A 945,087 364,900
B 15,330,000
C 33.4 53.8
D 1.5 0.9
E 120.9 75.6
F 40.2 25.1

**Thailand**
Bangkok
A 514,000 198,500
B 42,860,000
C 73.2 118.5
D 0.9 0.5
E 58.4 36.5
F 131.3 82.1

**Togo**
Lomé
A 56,000 21,600
B 2,240,000
C 78.9 127.3
D 2 1.2
E 2,396.4 1,497.8
F 34.6 18.7

**Tunisia**
Tunis
A 164,150 63,379
B 5,905,000
C 127.3 206
D 3.5 2.2
E 216.2 135.1
F 108.5 67.8

**Turkey**
Ankara
A 780,576 301,382
B 39,675,000
C 66.3 107.3
D 1.3 0.8
E 171.5 107.2
F 119.2 74.5

**U**

**Uganda**[4]
Kampala
A 235,886 91,076
B 11,705,000
C 33.4 53.8
D 1.5 0.9
E 120.9 75.6
F 40.2 25.1

**United Kingdom**
London
A 244,013 94,214
B 57,605,000
C 752.8 1,278.6
D 3.2 2
E 384.5[11] 204.3[11]
F 692.8[11] 433[11]

**Upper Volta**[3]
Ouagadougou
A 274,200 105,800
B 6,115,000
C 19.7 31.7
D 0.9 0.6
E 34.3 21.5
F 73.3 45.8

**Uruguay**
Montevideo
A 177,508 68,536
B 2,780,000
C 169.5 272.3
D 10.8 6.7
E 86 53.7
F 127 79.4

**USA**[12]
Washington, DC
A 9,519,617 3,675,545
B 214,580,000
C 335.2 542.5
D 14.9 9.3
E 5,135 3,209.4
F 73.2 45.8

**USSR**
Moscow
A 22,274,900 8,600,350
B 255,520,000
C 62.1 100.5
D 5.4 3.4
E 12,914.8 8,071.8
F 1,223.1 764.4

**V**

**Venezuela**
Caracas
A 912,050 352,144
B 12,185,000
C 1.9 3.1
D 0.14 0.09
E 1.2 0.8
F 3.4 2.2

**Vietnam**[1,13]
Ha-noi
A 332,559 128,402
B 46,430,000
C 66.2 107.1
D 4,738.3 2,961.4
E 0.04 0.03
F 3.7 2.3

**Y**

**Yugoslavia**
Belgrade
A 255,804 98,766
B 21,465,000
C 406.5 658
D 4.8 3
E 978.9 611.8
F 460.1 287.6

**Z**

**Zaire**
Kinshasa
A 2,345,409 905,567
B 25,205,000
C 22.4 36.2
D 2.1 1.3
E 119.7 74.8
F 17.7 11.1

**Zambia**[10]
Lusaka
A 752,614 290,586
B 4,960,000
C 13.8 22.3
D 2.1 1.3
E 183.3 114.6
F n/a

**Zimbabwe**
Salisbury
A 390,580 150,804
B 6,405,000
C 86.2 139.5
D 5.3 3.3
E 992.7 620.4
F n/a

**Notes**

1 Estimated figures
2 Figures do not reflect changes in 1967
3 Upper Volta and Ivory Coast railway data combined
4 Kenya, Tanzania and Uganda railway data combined (East African Railways)
5 Demilitarized zone, 1,252 km² (487 miles²), not included
6 Standard gauge only
7 Figures are pre-independence
8 South Africa and South West Africa railway data combined
9 State system only
10 Tazara line excluded
11 Excluding Northern Ireland
12 Class I railways only
13 South Vietnam only

# Railway
# Systems

# Europe: Scandinavia

Mining and quarrying
Iron and steel production
Manufacturing centre
Chemical processing
Port
Rail depot/construction

All figures include 182 km state-owned 891 mm gauge line, and 300 km of a privately owned passenger-carrying line. Privately owned freight-only lines omitted from all totals.

*Above left* A modern Swedish electric loco. *Above right* The East Södermanland narrow gauge railway. *Left* Near Ragunda in winter at −30°C.

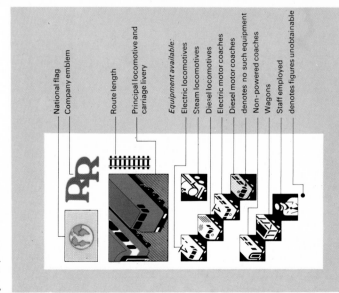

Railways were a European invention and, with the exception of Albania, a comprehensive system has been developed in every country. The extent of the commitment to railways has been shown twice this century, by the rapid and thorough repair of the damage inflicted in the course of the two world wars. From an early date, most governments took control of the railways, and attempts were made to unify gauges and to create a truly continental network that transcended national boundaries. Today, gauge-changing facilities are necessary only at the borders of Finland, USSR and Spain. This unification made possible the introduction, at the end of the last century, of international trains, the Orient Express being the most famous. Although the luxuriousness of such trains is now but a memory, their decline in speed has been compensated for by dramatic increases in speed.

1 Belgium p 182
2 Ireland p 180
3 Netherlands p 183
4 Denmark p 179
5 Sweden p 178
6 USSR p 192
7 East Germany p 185
8 United Kingdom p 180
9 West Germany p 184
10 Norway p 179
11 Finland p 179
12 Poland p 185
13 Czechoslovakia p 187
14 Luxembourg p 182
15 Spain p 188
16 Austria p 186
17 Switzerland p 186
18 Romania p 191
19 Italy p 190
20 Greece p 191
21 Portugal p 188
22 France p 189
23 Hungary p 187
24 Yugoslavia p 190
25 Albania p 190
26 Bulgaria p 191

## SWEDEN *Statens Järnvägar (SJ)*

The Swedish railway system began in 1849 with a narrow gauge line 8 km (5 miles) long between Fryksta and Klarälven, using horse-drawn trains; but the main line network and the state-owned system dates from 1856. Today the Swedish State Railways (*Statens Järnvägar*) operates more than 90 per cent of the total traffic, and has a route length of approximately 11,379 km (7,067 miles). More than half of this is electrified. There are several railways in Sweden that are still privately owned, notably the Grängesberg-Oxelösund, which has a main line 296 km (185 miles) long. This is an east-west route threading its way from the coast at Oxelösund through the picturesque lake country to the west of Stockholm. It is entirely electrified, though its experiments with a non-condensing steam turbine locomotive in 1932 led to the building of similar, but much larger, locomotives in Great Britain and the USA. From Stockholm, headquarters of the state system, main lines run westward to Charlottenberg, on the Norwegian frontier, and southwards to Gothenburg and Malmö, and it is over these two latter routes that fast express trains are operated. Northwards from Stockholm the main line runs through Uppsala, to the junction of Ange, where there is a large mechanized marshalling yard for dealing with the traffic coming eastward from Trondheim in Norway. The main line continues to Boden, where it intersects the important northwest-to-southeast ore-carrying line of the Riksgransen Railway that comes across the Arctic Circle, from Narvik, via the Norwegian State Railways, to the port of Luleå on the Gulf of Bothnia. Except where the Swedish railways approach the mountainous Norwegian frontier, more than a third of the lines are carried over generally level track. Another 20 per cent is on gradients no steeper than 1 in 200. The rail gauge is the standard European, carried on sleepers of impregnated wood. This gauge permits the operation of several important international train services. There is a train ferry between Helsingborg and Helsingör in Denmark, and a through sleeping car express runs between Stockholm and Hamburg, via Copenhagen.

On pages 178–208, a DATA PANEL appears for all countries owning a railway system. Those omitted have either closed all their railways, or have yet to open one, or have their line worked by someone else. The data panels summarize the principal railway assets of each country. In some cases, such information is unobtainable, or the most recent available statistics may not reflect the contemporary situation.

National flag
Company emblem
Route length
Principal locomotive and carriage livery
*Equipment available:*
Electric locomotives
Steam locomotives
Diesel locomotives
Electric motor coaches
Diesel motor coaches
Non-powered coaches
Wagons
Staff employed
denotes no such equipment
denotes figures unobtainable

## NORWAY *Norges Statsbaner (NSB)*

The Norwegian railways, of which the first section was opened in 1854, have the particular fascination of being operated for the most part in exceedingly rugged country, subject to great extremes of climate. In striking contrast to Sweden, less than 6 per cent of the total length of about 4,241 km (2,634 miles) is on gradients of less than 1 in 100. More than three-quarters of the total is on truly mountain gradients of 1 in 40 to 1 in 67. Until the Second World War the very severe Dombas line, forming the main route from Oslo to Trondheim, was worked by some of the most powerful steam locomotives in Europe. The principal main lines are electrified, but the line from Trondheim northwards across the Arctic Circle to Boden is diesel-worked. This line was opened as recently as 1962. In the far north, the line from Narvik to the Swedish frontier is completely isolated from the rest of the Norwegian State Railways system, but forms part of the important iron ore route into northern Sweden. The fastest trains in Norway are those following the southern coast line from Oslo, south to Kristiansand and then northwest to Stavanger. This runs on easier gradients than the great mountain routes from Oslo to Bergen and Oslo to Trondheim, and the Stavanger Express covers the 592 km (370 miles) from Oslo in 8 hr, inclusive of 10 stops. The special Sorlands Express, which serves Kristiansand only, makes the run of 352 km (220 miles) in 4½ hr, non-stop from Oslo, an average speed of almost 80 km/h (50 mph). The Norwegian railways must be one of the very few, anywhere in the world, to be completely equipped with a system of colour light signalling.

*Below* Electric header at Flamsdalen, Norway.

The 39 km of line to the northern town of Narvik is divorced from the rest of the network and worked as a part of the Swedish system.

Norway

iiii 4,241 km (2,651 mls)

*not including 29 electric multiple-unit sets.

158 170 94 50
911 8,929 18,052

## DENMARK *Danske Statsbaner (DSB)*

The geographical structure of Denmark, with some of its most important and populous areas on islands, naturally presented special problems when it came to building up an efficient railway network. The first section was that from Copenhagen to Roskilde, opened in 1847. It involved the construction of larger bridges to provide communication between the islands. In certain cases the distances were too great for bridges, and train and car ferry services evolved. No fewer than four of the train ferries involve international co-operation: Rødby-Fehmarn with the Federal Railway of West Germany; Gedser-Warnemünde with the State Railway of East Germany; and Copenhagen-Malmö and Helsingør-Helsingborg with the Swedish railways. It is only in the Copenhagen suburban area that electric traction is used in Denmark. The principal main line services are worked either by diesel-electric locomotives or diesel-railcars. The internal fast trains are the Intercity (IC) regular interval services, and the "Lyntog", or lightning diesel trains, which are high-speed diesel railcar sets, having a limited accommodation. There are a few steam locomotives still in service.

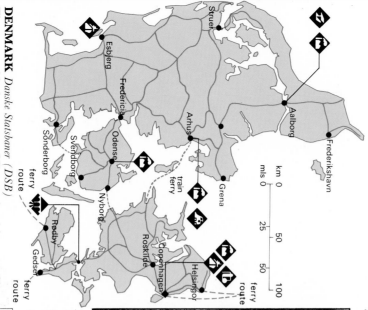

Denmark

**DSB**

iiii 2,485 km (1,553 mls)

*multiple-unit sets: there are also 251 diesel railcars.

1,067
9,713
335 283 22*
10

All the figures include 486 km of privately owned passenger-carrying lines. The state system has no steam engines.

Finland

iiii 6,010 km (3,732 mls)

*stored as a strategic reserve; last regularly used 30 Sep. 1975.

22,004
1,173
27
369 80 250*
199
29,070

Finnish lines are built to Russia's gauge of 1,524 mm, necessitating transfer facilities at Tornio where the Swedish system is met.

## FINLAND *Valtionrautatiet (VR)*

From their inception in 1862, the Finnish State Railways, because of the long eastern frontier, have been oriented towards those of Russia rather than those of the rest of Europe. The rail gauge is 1,524 mm (5 ft), although at Tornio, in the far north, there are exchange facilities with the standard gauge Swedish system. Each day from Helsinki there is a through express with sleeping cars, one for Leningrad and one for Moscow, the departure times being arranged to provide arrivals in the Russian cities at around 09.00 hrs. Finland is subject to extremes of climate, and the railways are efficiently operated in the depths of the sub-Arctic winters. Although there is a general transition to diesel traction, the Finland Railway still operates a number of modern steam locomotives, and upwards of 150 more steam locomotives are held in reserve. There are ferry services across the Baltic between Helsinki and Lübeck and between Naantali and Stockholm.

# United Kingdom and Ireland

BR Class 40 hauling Glasgow-Leeds express near Bingley.

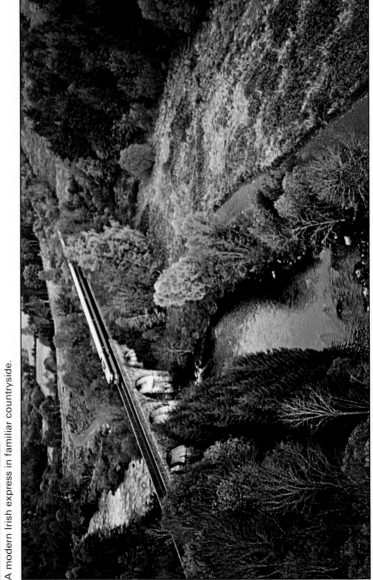

A modern Irish express in familiar countryside.

**IRELAND** *Coras Iompair Eireann (CIE)*

The railways in this now politically divided land originated in the same way as those of Great Britain, and were subject to the surveillance of the Board of Trade at Westminster. In a rural and not prosperous country there was, however, not the same opportunity for intense railway development. Trunk routes were enterprised from Dublin to Cork, to Wicklow and Wexford, and to Belfast; and this latter, the Great Northern, had the distinction of becoming an international main line, operating in both Eire and Northern Ireland after the partition in 1922. The cross-country connections were also important, serving Waterford and Limerick, while in the north the Belfast and Northern Counties (to Londonderry) was a busy and prosperous concern, later taken over by the English Midland Railway.

Because of the need to provide transport in the rural areas where a full-scale main line railway would not pay, in a series of "Light Railway Acts" Parliament authorized the construction of many narrow gauge lines. These lines later became of much interest to the seekers after the unusual in railway practice, from the picturesque steam locomotives used to the happy, leisurely ways of doing business. In 1925 the railways of Eire were grouped. The Great Northern, because of its international character, remained untouched; but all other lines were merged into a new Great Southern system, still under private ownership. In 1945 it was nationalized as Coras Iompair Eireann, and in 1958 took over also that portion of the former Great Northern Railway situated in Eire.

The data panel figures refer only to Republic of Ireland. N. Ireland, although a province of the United Kingdom, has a system independent of British Rail and built to the Irish broad gauge of 1,600 mm. A freight service from Londonderry to the Republic is worked by CIE locos. Stock totals for Northern Ireland Railways – the system's title – are not in the data panels either for Ireland or for the UK. The latest available figures for NIR are: 6 diesel locos, 87 diesel-powered coaches, 67 other coaching units, 31 wagons and 1,229 staff to work a system of 357 route-km.

## Ireland

CIE

2,189 km (1,368 mls)

229
57
485
6,519
9,123

Legend:
- Mining and quarrying
- Iron and steel production
- Manufacturing centre
- Oil refining
- Chemical processing
- Port
- Rail depot/construction
- Tourist centre

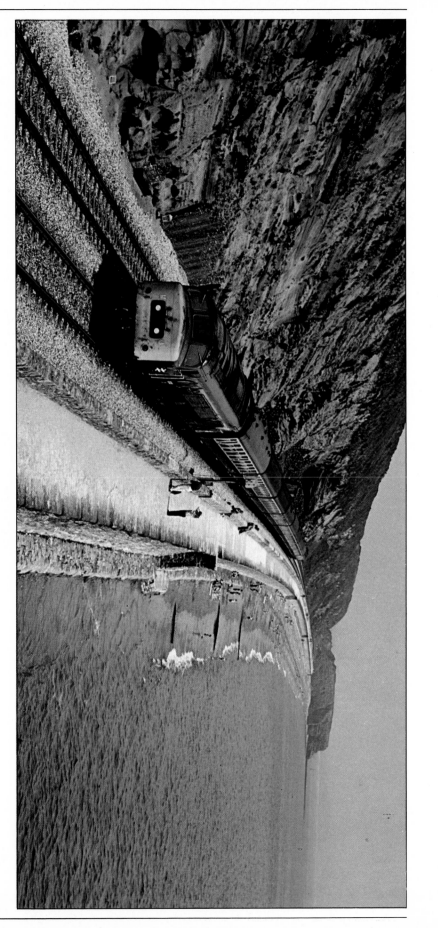

# UNITED KINGDOM *British Rail*

The intricate railway network of Great Britain originated in a series of privately enterprised, and quite unconnected, local projects. Although there were men of vision like George Stephenson who looked forward to a time when the whole country would be provided with railways, there was no overall planning, and no attempt at co-ordination by the governments of the day. Parliament exercised control only to the extent that the fixed equipment and rolling stock had to satisfy the examination of inspecting officers appointed by the Board of Trade. From the success of the pioneer enterprises like the Stockton and Darlington, the Liverpool and Manchester, and the Newcastle and Carlisle, the earliest trunk lines were projected, including the London and Birmingham, the North Midland (Derby to Leeds) and the Great Western (London to Bristol), and from these the nationwide network developed. Success led to an immense proliferation of new schemes, some quite spurious and with no solid financial backing. There were many proposals for amalgamation, but while Parliament looked favourably upon mergers, lengthwise as it were, like that of the London and Birmingham with northern companies that brought the line from London to Lancaster and Carlisle under a single management, any amalgamation of competitive routes was vetoed, because it was felt that the existence of competitive facilities would be in the interest of the travelling public.

By the 1880s there were three independent routes from London to Scotland, each providing a lavish train service to Edinburgh from London, and two out of the three serving Glasgow. There were three competitive routes from London to Manchester, and five different ways of travelling from England and Wales to Ireland. There was competition between London and Plymouth, London and Portsmouth, and London and the Kentish resorts and packet stations. But the network as it grew up could be criticized for the way in which attention became focused upon London. While cross-country routes existed, the train services operated were for the most part slow and unattractive. The exception was between Liverpool and Manchester, where two rivals to the original line of 1830 were built, and a swarm of fast express trains ran throughout the day on all three routes. With no competition other than that of canals, freight traffic became heavy, and it was handled in relatively small four-wheeled wagons at slow speed. Small consignments could be sent from one end of the country to the other. Remote country stations all had their freight sidings, at which goods of all descriptions could be brought for dispatch, or collected, by private conveyances.

The early years of the twentieth century in Great Britain saw the heights of railway pre-eminence as carriers of all kinds; but already there were signs of dissatisfaction, particularly with the goods service. Nevertheless, despite the steeply rising cost of coal – the almost exclusive form of locomotive fuel – and rising costs of other services, the private railways were prosperous throughout Britain. At the outbreak of the First World War in 1914 there were 16 trunk systems, with tracks extending from the Channel ports to Wick and Thurso, from East Anglia to Penzance, together with a number of active and prosperous companies with localized activities, such as the great coal carriers in the valleys of South Wales, the Furness, and the Hull and Barnsley. During the war all the British railways were brought under government control, and in 1921 legislation was imposed upon them by Parliament, forming the whole network into four group companies. The ownership was still entirely private, but the company amalgamations, and the composition of each group, was laid down by Act of Parliament. The era of the "Big Four" – Great Western, Southern, London Midland and Scottish, London and North Eastern – began on 1 January 1923.

The "grouped" companies carried on through a period of extreme financial difficulty, and increasingly severe competition from road hauliers. Legislation governing the fixing of rates and fares remained unchanged from the days of unchallenged railway pre-eminence in transport and handicapped the "grouped" railways in their fight for traffic. Fortunately the managements saw to it that maintenance of track and rolling stock was kept at the highest level, and the railways, once again under government control, were able to render a great national service in the Second World War. Less than three years after its conclusion, as from 1 January 1948, the British railways were nationalized. Since that time a considerable reduction in total mileage has been made, by elimination of one-time competitive routes and closing of unremunerative branch lines. The last British Rail steam train ran in 1967 and the first High Speed Train was introduced in 1976.

*Above* British Rail train hauled by Peak class diesel electric High Speed Train (HST), holder of the world record.

*Below* The British Rail diesel on the wall at Dawlish.

## United Kingdom

🚂 18.190 Km (11.298 mls)

47.153 Km (29.287 mls)*

22.902

248.682

196.635

352

3.508

3"**

*included in carriages total.
**narrow-gauge.

UK totals refer only to British Rail and exclude several major networks, eg National Coal Board lines and the London Underground.

# Belgium and Luxembourg

**BELGIUM** *Société Nationale des Chemins de Fer Belges (SNCB)*

Belgium was the first country in the world to have a railway system that from the outset was almost entirely state owned. The principle of state ownership was accepted by an Act of Parliament passed as long ago as 1834, and the railway network in the country was planned as a co-ordinated network. It grew to be one of the busiest and most intense to be found anywhere, reckoned on the basis of route distance per square kilometre of territory served. Belgium has a high proportion of intensely industrialized areas, comparable to the English Black Country, and frequent service of fast passenger trains coupled with ample freight facilities became necessary at an early stage of development.

But while the demands of Belgium itself have always been heavy, the geographical situation of the country makes it an important connecting link in many international train services. Historically Belgium has been called the "cockpit" of Europe; from the railway point of view it does form a general crossroads. While the original network was planned to have all the main lines radiating from Brussels, not all the international trains of today pass through the capital. The crack trains from Paris to the Rhineland take a route to the south, passing through Charleroi, Namur and Liège to enter West Germany at Aachen, and there is a busy electrified main line diverging eastwards from the principal north to south line at

Mechelen, and passing through Louvain and Landen to reach Liège.

It was not until comparatively recent times that through international trains like those from the Dutch cities to Paris, or those from Ostend to West Germany, or the Luxembourg line, could pass through Brussels without reversal of direction at some point. Today there is an underground main line through the heart of the city connecting the Nord and Midi stations, and a prestige train like the Étoile du Nord Pullman from Amsterdam to Paris, passes beneath the city centre. It is the same with the sleeping car express that leaves Ostend about 21.00 hrs, and carries through sections for Swiss resorts, and for Milan.

Because of its geographical position at a railway crossroads in western Europe, and the intensity of the internal traffic of the country, which developed well before the end of the nineteenth century, the technical equipment of the Belgian railways rapidly became some of the most sophisticated outside Great Britain. Comprehensive signalling was installed at large centres such as Antwerp, Gent and Liège, in addition to those around Brussels, and these units incorporate full interlocking. Steam traction has now been entirely dispensed with, and roughly one third of the total route covered is electrified. The system used differs from those of all the neighbouring countries, as they do from each other; but modern methods of changeover at the international frontiers are swift and efficient, and in some cases performed without the train stopping, thus speeding up services considerably.

Belgium retains 221 km of secondary railways, a feature which has largely disappeared in Europe. A reason for its survival is that most is electrified.

### Belgium

🚆 4,003 km (2,486 mls)

232, 911, 629, 98, 5

2,535, 47,345, 58,718

all totals excepting staff include the metre-gauge SNCV.

*Above* New Belgian EMU.
*Right* Brussels Midi Station.

**LUXEMBOURG** *Société Nationale des Chemins de Fer Luxembourgeois (CFL)*

One of the most important international routes is that running southeast from Brussels, and making its way through very mountainous country to enter Luxembourg at Arlon. Until 1946 there were several privately owned railways in the Grand Duchy, but in April of that year all the railways were taken over by a new company – the Luxembourg National Railways. The capital was split between the Belgian and French governments, 51 per cent each, and the Belgian and French governments 24.5 per cent each. The system consists of a north to south line, and an east-west system intersecting the former at Luxembourg city. Much of the latter is electrified, but most of the international north to south route is worked by diesel locomotives. The total route length in the Grand Duchy is only about 264 km (165 miles), half of which is electrified. Luxembourg city is itself a most important railway centre, at the meeting-point of five international routes. The southwest is part of the Luxembourg-Lorraine iron mining region and is well served by the Grand Duchy's railways, which are concentrated in the south.

### Luxembourg

**CFL**

271 km (169 mls)

19, 56, 6, 12, 77

3,419, 4,323

Luxembourg's position is important astride European routes and the French and Belgian governments each appoint five members to the Board, and each subscribes 24.5% of the company's capital.

# Netherlands

**NETHERLANDS** *N.V. Nederlandse Spoorwegen (NS)*

In the Netherlands railways were built, and are maintained today, in physical conditions that are not paralleled anywhere in the world. Except on the eastern frontiers the countryside is flat, and intersected by an elaborate system of inland waterways; but the ground is soft and spongy, and anything but ideal for sustaining the weight and pounding effect of heavy, fast, railway traffic. The existence of a frequent and efficient service is a tribute to the excellence of the civil engineers' maintenance of the track and of the formation beneath it. Until January 1938 there were a number of independent railways in Holland, one owned by the state and the rest private; but in that year full amalgamation took place, and the consolidated organization took the title of Netherlands Railways.

Although the tasks of the original companies lay, to quite a large extent, in providing international services, the growth of industry and commerce in Holland has led to the development of a different pattern of activity today. In the nineteenth century the close connection between the royal houses of Great Britain and Imperial Germany invested the mail service between England and Germany with great importance, while the prevailing fashion for wealthy English families to patronize the spas of south Germany sustained another prestige service, as with the Anglo-German mails through Holland. The steam locomotives on most of the Dutch railways were almost without exception built in Great Britain.

The growth of railways in Holland in the nineteenth century was in many ways similar to that in Britain. Companies were promoted and lines built in direct competition with one another, and there was during this early period no attempt by the state to coerce, or squeeze, the private companies out of the picture. One could, for example, travel from Rotterdam to Amsterdam either by the Holland Railway, via Delft and The Hague, or by the Dutch Rhenish Railway via Utrecht. There were rivals, each with their own packet stations for the cross-channel business from England. The State Railway ran to Flushing, whence there were sailings at first to Queenborough in the Isle of Sheppey and later to Folkestone, and against this the Dutch Rhenish Railway worked in connection with the steamers from the Hook of Holland to Harwich. Both these rivals were deeply concerned in the Anglo-German traffic; yet small as Holland is, the State Railway did not carry this traffic right across the country to the German frontier. At Boxtel they handed over to yet another private railway, the North Brabant German, which although entirely Dutch owned, ran for a considerable distance into Germany, to reach Wesel. The Dutch Rhenish as its name suggests, went as far as the Rhine, to Arnhem. Another interesting private line was the Netherlands Central, which ran from Utrecht northeastwards through Amersfoort to Zwolle. The central station at Utrecht at times had the colourful glamour of some great English junction, because there one could see the bright green locomotives of the State Railway, the Indian-reds of the Rhenish, the dark green of the Holland Railway, and the bright yellow of the Netherlands Central. It is interesting that the first major amalgamation of railways in Holland did not concern the state system, but was between two of the private concerns, the Holland Railway and the Dutch Rhenish. Travellers with experience of railways in many parts of the world were quick to notice one significant difference between the largely private railways of Holland and the nationally owned railways of Belgium: in the nineteenth century the Dutch were much more efficient.

## High density, high speed

Today the network of passenger train service in Holland is provided by a system of fast, closely integrated electric multiple-unit trains, so timed that if a through train is not provided between the towns or cities that a passenger wishes to visit, there are connections at intermediate points where the change of trains involves a wait of no more than a few minutes. Obviously in the operation of such a dense service of trains, the establishment of punctuality is essential, and this is ensured by a high standard of punctual operation of service, coupled with a comprehensive system of traffic regulation, coupled with the automatic operation of the major junctions. The apparatus is programmed to operate in accordance with the planned time-

table, and it is only in the event of irregularities or late running that the men in the control centres have to intervene.

Not all the Dutch railway network is electrified. Routes on which the traffic density is less are worked by diesel multiple-unit sets trains. There are a number of international express trains that originate in Holland, such as the Rheingold with sections from both Amsterdam and the Hook of Holland running south through the Rhineland to Switzerland, and other trains for north and northwest Germany. These are hauled by electric locomotives, of the same type that are used for the freight trains. Amid all this modern operation, however, the enthusiast should break his journey at Utrecht, to visit the magnificent Transport Museum, where the origins and development of railways in the Netherlands can be studied from pictures, maps, models and full size preserved examples of locomotives and rolling stock.

*Above* Rotterdam station.

*Right* Amsterdam station.

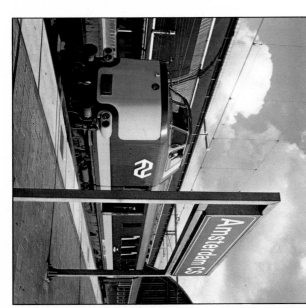

The route total includes 11 km of line scheduled for 1977 (Den Haag-Zoetermeer). A 55 km line is being built for 1982 completion: Amsterdam-Leiden via Schipol Airport.

**Netherlands**

◇ Oil refining
◇ Mining and quarrying
◇ Iron and steel production
◇ Manufacturing centre
◇ Chemical processing
◇ Port
◇ Rail depot/construction

2,825 km (1,754 mls)

*multiple-unit sets: there are also 30 diesel railcars.

# West Germany

Krupp stock running up Rhine valley.

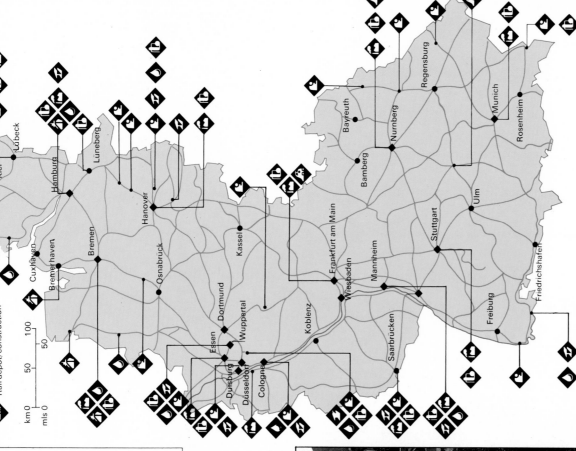

*Below* TEE train running alongside the Rhine.

## Map legend

- Mining and quarrying
- Iron and steel production
- Manufacturing centre
- Oil refining
- Chemical processing
- Grain processing
- Port
- Rail depot/construction

km 0   50   100
mls 0   50   100

**West Germany** DB

28,564 km (17,741 mls)

2,629
3,097
1,076
17,726
287,365
396,000

The data panel's figures are for the state system only. In addition there are at least 180 private railways with another 4,600 km.

## WEST GERMANY *Deutsche Bundesbahn (DB)*

The railways of Germany, like those of Great Britain, began as a large number of independent, unconnected private enterprises. They developed at a time when Germany itself did not yet exist as a single co-ordinated state. The first was in Bavaria in 1835, from Nürnberg to Fürth. Gradually, however, the various lines were taken over by the states in which they ran, and many of them came under the control of Prussia. Their origins could be discerned from the names of the "Administrations" they carried, such as "Magdeburg", "Right Rhine", "Breslau" and "Hannover". After the war with France in 1870–1, Bismarck tried to amalgamate all the railways of Germany under one imperial control. He failed because the southern states, like Saxony, Bavaria and Baden-Württemberg, stood out strongly against such a merger. The annexation of most of the French provinces of Alsace and Lorraine after the war included the French railway of that name. It was thoroughly Germanized, being renamed Imperial Elsass-Lothringen, controlled directly by Prussia. Its track layout changed from the French practice of running on the left-hand track to the German right-hand running. At the new frontier point between Nancy and Strasbourg, special junctions were laid in to facilitate the transfer. When the provinces were restored to France after the First World War, the junction layout was not altered, and it remains unchanged today. They retained their own state-controlled railways until after the end of the First World War. Nevertheless the railways of Germany tended to be focused upon the imperial capital, Berlin, as those of Great Britain were upon London. The great complexity and proliferation of routes in the Ruhr and the Rhineland corresponded in some respect to the situation in Britain at that time, especially in Lancashire, Yorkshire and the North Midlands.

### One administration

In 1920 the state railways were brought into a single administration, the *Deutsche Reichsbahn*, and under this organization great improvements were made in technology and in the services offered, both nationally and internationally. Up till that time German railways in general had not been renowned either for convenience of timetabling or for the speed of passenger trains; but under the *Reichsbahn* organization they gradually stepped into the very front rank of speed, particularly with the diesel railcar trains of the 1930s. Much of the system suffered severe damage during the Second World War, and before any appreciable steps had been taken towards reconstruction the partition of the former "Reich" into two separate and ideologically contrasting states of West and East Germany, in 1945, immediately changed the significance of the railways. The *Deutsche Bundesbahn*, operating in West Germany, was faced with providing service in a state that was very largely cut off from the former imperial capital, and the traffic pattern became very largely one of "north and south", with main routes towards Berlin confined to those from Hamburg, Hannover, Bebra, and Nürnberg.

A great deal of rethinking was necessary to adapt the railway organization to this new pattern. In addition to the main route up the valley of the Rhine, a popular tourist route, the line running roughly parallel to the frontier with East Germany, from Nürnberg northwards through Würzburg, Bebra, Göttingen to Hannover and Hamburg, became of great importance. There developed also a much closer liaison with the railways in the countries of the West, with freely-used exchange points with the Dutch, Belgian and French railways, and operation of an increasing number of international express train services. In imperial days Germany had sought to reduce to a minimum railway connections with France and Belgium. Her purpose had been to secure a preponderance of traffic from England to east and south European business and holiday centres. But now, all that is changed. Frankfurt is the headquarters of the *Deutsche Bundesbahn*, and the very picturesque valley of the Rhine, with its lofty heights, vineyards, and many a medieval castle, provides an intensely-used artery of railway traffic. There are double-tracked main lines on both banks, and frequent connections by bridges from one bank to the other. It is a fascinating run by train, but the volume of both passenger and freight traffic can perhaps be appreciated most by taking a trip on one of the many pleasure steamers cruising on the river. From such an unusual railway-spotting vantage point, the enthusiast receives a dramatic impression of the *Deutsche Bundesbahn* in action.

Route length is about half West Germany's, omitting 352 km of narrow-gauge lines. 10% of routes are electrified and steam will survive into the 1980s.

*not including narrow-gauge lines.

## East Germany

*Deutsche Reichsbahn (DR)*

14,215 km (8,884 mls)*

### EAST GERMANY *Deutsche Reichsbahn (DR)*

The state railway of East Germany retains much of the radial layout of earlier days, with Berlin as the focal point. It has, however, only about half the route length as the system of West Germany. Its services are co-ordinated more with those of Poland and Czechoslovakia than with the West. Apart from the connections mentioned in the section dealing with West Germany, the radiating main lines from Berlin are those going east to Warsaw and beyond to the frontier with the U.S.S.R., southeast to Prague, and south to the West German frontier and onwards to Munich. Additionally, there are two routes going north from Berlin, which diverge at Neustrelitz. They lead to the train ferry ports of Warnemünde and Sassnitz, respectively, and over them through train services are operated to Copenhagen and to Stockholm.

An ex-*Deutsche Reichsbahn* 2-10-0 *Kriegslok* waits to leave Opole, Poland, for Nysa.

While the modernization of motive power has progressed rapidly in West Germany, and there are no longer any steam locomotives remaining in regular service, less than 1,600 km (1,000 miles) of the East German system are electrified as yet, and many steam locomotives remain. The international set-up in Berlin has to some extent simplified the railway terminal arrangements, which at one time included many stations belonging to the former independent companies. Today only a single route, known as the *Stadtbahn*, passes from West into East Berlin. Arriving in the International zone from the west, the stations reached are first Charlottenburg and then Zoo; after passing into East Berlin there is first Friedrichstrasse, and then Ost, prior to reaching the complicated set of junctions by which *Reichsbahn* trains can proceed to the Baltic ferry ports, Warsaw, Leipzig and Dresden.

### POLAND *Polskie Koleje Państwowe (PKP)*

The Polish State Railways has one of the most complicated histories imaginable. Firstly, when railways were first constructed in eastern Europe, Poland, as an independent country, did not exist at all. The territory was divided up between Germany and Russia, and remained so until 1919. The first railways — which were initiated as long ago as 1835, though not actually brought into service until several years later — were sponsored by those countries to suit their own needs. As a result those in what could be termed the German and Austrian sectors were built on the European standard gauge, and those in the Russian sector on the 1,524 mm (5 ft) gauge. The Austrians built a line to connect Warsaw with Vienna, while the Russians enterprised a line north from Warsaw to join up with the Grand Russian Railway. This provided a through route to St Petersburg (Leningrad). By 1862 Warsaw was connected by rail to St Petersburg, to Vienna, and with the Prussian railway system, and therefore with systems throughout western Europe.

During the First World War the Russian part of Poland was overrun by German and Austrian forces, and after the war the lines in these territories were converted to the standard gauge. The establishment of the new independent state of Poland — including the highly strategic "Polish Corridor" to the Baltic at Danzig, cutting East Prussia from the rest of Germany — brought railway, as well as political, problems. This was particularly true in the working of through trains from the west to Königsberg (Chojna). In the meantime the Polish State Railways were extensively modernized, only to suffer appalling destruction during the Second World War. One of the most important improvements had been to equip all the freight rolling stock with continuous automatic air brakes, and to install much colour light signalling. Both advances were contained in contracts placed in Great Britain — all unhappily to have little lasting effect. A total of 46 per cent of all tunnels and bridges, 600 steam locomotives, and 60,000 carriages were destroyed. Today, although there are still some 4,000 steam locomotives at work in Poland, rapid progress is being made towards electrification, and by reason of its geographical position the Polish State Railways has a great significance for transit traffic travelling westwards from other countries of eastern Europe, and equally for traffic from western Europe.

All totals exclude narrow-gauge lines. Like most Eastern European countries, figures for Poland are unavailable or, at best, incomplete. Rolling stock totals are for 1974, except the diesel loco figure which represents locos bought during the 5 Year Plan which ended in 1975.

*excludes locos built pre-1971
**multiple-unit sets

## Poland

*Polskie Koleje Państwowe*

PKP

23,421 km (14,547 mls)

8,283
198,524
310 · 361,200
1,270
4,156
2*
23**

*excludes locos built pre-1971
**multiple-unit sets

# Switzerland and Austria

## SWITZERLAND *Schweizerische Bundesbahnen (SBB)*

The railways of Switzerland, most of which are nationalized, can be divided into two distinct geographical groups. There is the close, intensely-used network in the broad valleys linking up Zürich, Basel, Lucerne, Lausanne, and Bern with a series of fast inter-city electric trains; and then there are the great mountain routes. The mountain routes are famed for some of the most spectacular railway engineering in the world, with many examples of spiral track locations, viaducts of breathtaking height, and some of the longest tunnels ever driven beneath mountain ranges. But in the mountain routes, too, there are strong subdivisions. There are those like the Gotthard, the Lötschberg and the Simplon, that are teeming arteries of heavy north-south international traffic, and others built on the metre gauge to provide access to some of the more remote resorts. It was soon after the establishment of the Swiss Confederation in 1848 that the government invited Robert Stephenson to submit proposals for a national railway system. At that time only one railway had been built, connecting Zürich with Basel. Stephenson proposed a main line from Zürich through fairly level country to Lausanne and Geneva, and it is this extremely busy line that forms the internal backbone of Switzerland's railway operation today.

### Crossing the Alps

It was when railway connections with the neighbouring states came to be made that the Alpine ranges had to be crossed. The Gotthard route was the first, heading south from the twin central "springboards" of Zürich and Lucerne, beneath the historic mountain pass into the Italian-speaking canton of the Ticino, and from there through Como to Milan. To obtain an acceptable gradient for steam locomotives – even though this had to be 1 in 37 – the technique of spiral tunnelling in the mountain sides was adopted for the first time ever. The great Gotthard Tunnel was opened in 1882. The approach to the Simplon Tunnel, opened in 1906, does not involve such dramatic engineering because the former Jura-Simplon Railway followed the valley of the Rhône from the head of the Lake of Geneva, near Montreux. The Gotthard and the Jura-Simplon lines are now part of the Swiss Federal Railways. But at Brig, at the eastern entrance to the Simplon Tunnel, the line into Italy is joined by the greatest of the private railways of Switzerland, the Bern-Lötschberg-Simplon. This mammoth enterprise has tunnelled under the mighty ranges of the Bernese Oberland and provided some truly spectacular sights for the traveller on the ascent to the Lötschberg Tunnel from Spiez on the lake of Thun, and perhaps even more awe-inspiring views on the descent into the Rhône valley.

Finally, there is the magnificently-engineered metre gauge Rhaetian Railway, leading from Chur to the famous Alpine resorts of Pontresina and St Moritz in the Upper Engadine. The Albula Line, as it is otherwise known, is also spectacular in the sharpness of its curves, and for the speed and smoothness with which they are negotiated, often on the edge of towering precipices.

## AUSTRIA *Österreichische Bundesbahnen (ÖBB)*

The city of Vienna, once a great imperial capital, was the focal point of a remarkable system of railways, and it is surprising to recall not only that at one time there were seven trunk routes radiating from the city, but that these belonged to five different companies. Competing for the traffic to Prague and southeast Germany were the Austrian North Western and the Imperial Royal Austrian State – which were state-owned – and the Austro-Hungarian State, which despite its name was privately owned. To the west, the Imperial Royal had the field to itself; but to the northeast of Vienna, the Kaiser Ferdinand's Northern (state-owned) provided the main link to Warsaw. The Southern, which was privately owned, ran to the shores of the Adriatic at Trieste, which was then in Austrian territory. After the general break-up of the Austro-Hungarian Empire at the end of the First World War, the republic of Austria was left with the one-time Imperial Royal line to Salzburg and the west, and the interesting Southern line, leading over the famous Semmering Pass on to the province of Styria. The construction of this line by the celebrated Karl Ghega was one of the epics of early railway building. In the 1840s, with no modern aids such as aerial surveys to act as a guide, the surveying had to be done entirely from ground level, and on the northern approach to the pass the land is just a wild confusion of crags, ravines and steep slopes. There is no ordered geographical pattern, and to make things worse for the pioneers the slopes were all thickly wooded. How Ghega managed to contrive a line on a steadily ascending gradient of 1 in 40 is a marvel; and when he had done it no one believed that any locomotive would ever be able to climb that gradient. But it was done, and for 100 years steam worked all the traffic.

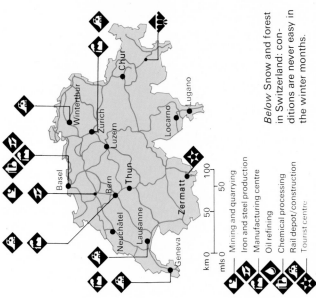

*Below* Snow and forest in Switzerland: conditions are never easy in the winter months.

The figures for Austria, *below*, exclude privately owned lines even though 646 route-km carry passengers. The state system's remaining steam locos are all narrow-gauge (ÖBB has 454 route-km of narrow gauge lines).

Austrian class 52 2-10-0 at Hieflau.

Map legend:
- Mining and quarrying
- Iron and steel production
- Manufacturing centre
- Oil refining
- Chemical processing
- Rail depot/construction
- Tourist centre

**Austria**

5,418 km (3,365 mls)

54
85
25
519
71,274
618
35,987
4,110

*not including multiple-unit sets: 95 electric, 16 diesel

**Switzerland**

*left,* has the highest track length per head of population in the world, though this is not apparent from the data panel figures, which are for the state system only. 45%, another 2,165 km, of Swiss railways are privately owned. Two of these are: the Bern-Lötschberg-Simplon Railway, which conveys international trains through its 14 km Lötschberg Tunnel; and the Rhaetian Railway, a metre-gauge system with 363 route-km covering the canton of the Grisons.

2,913 km (1,809 mls)

1,074
254
194
3,635
11,565
37,780

*not including 93 electro-diesel (dual system) locos

## CZECHOSLOVAKIA *Czechoslovenské Státní Dráhy (ČSD)*

When the state of Czechoslovakia was set up under the provisions of the Treaty of Versailles after the First World War, the rationalizing of the railway system was a matter of some urgency and difficulty. The provinces of Bohemia, Moravia and Silesia had formerly belonged to Austria, with railways focused upon Vienna and Prague; while the province of Slovakia had belonged to Hungary, with its railways directed towards Budapest. From 1924, therefore, the policy of the ČSD had to make provision for better west-to-east communication within the new country. No less than 160 km (100 miles) of new main line was constructed in the later 1920s. About 240 km (150 miles) of previously single-tracked secondary line was converted to double track, and brought up to full main line standards. In the Second World War the ČSD was severely damaged, and after the war it was necessary to repair many tunnels and bridges, while more than 1,920 km (1,200 miles) of line had to be renewed. Many new lines have been built subsequently, and conversion to electric traction is proceeding steadily, including the principal west-east line throughout the country. Out of a total of some 12,800 km (8,000 miles) of route about 2,400 km (1,500 miles) are electrified. At the same time many steam locomotives remain in use, including some of the most advanced modern design. The main lines from the west, entering the country at Cheb, from West Germany, and Děčín from East Germany, join up at Prague and continue east through Přerov. Here the line from Vienna to Warsaw intersects, and proceeds eastwards through Žilina to the frontier station with Soviet Russia at Čierna. From Prague southwards to Vienna the main line today is that of the former Imperial Royal Austrian State Railway, entering the present Austria at Gmünd.

*Double header pulling mixed freight through dramatic scenery in Czechoslovakia.*

The rolling stock figures are for 1968. By the end of the 1970-75 Plan, 25% of the system should be electrified. 1,200 new locos were bought and only 5% of traffic remained steam-hauled.

### Czechoslovakia ČSD

136,150  
10,835  
715  
1,077  
88  
991  
2,307  
208,533  
13,186 km (8,190 mls)

*excludes 1,200 locos diesel and electric, bought 1970-1975

*Right* Familiar route concentration in Czechoslovakia – road, rail and river.

## HUNGARY *Magyar Államvasutak (MÁV)*

In imperial days there were three separate railways operating in Hungary, roughly one-third of the system being state-owned. The privately-owned lines were the Austro-Hungarian State (despite its name) and the Austrian Southern. Budapest was very much the centre of all railway activities. The Hungarian State, and the Austro-Hungarian State, were in direct competition for the traffic between Budapest and Vienna, one on each side of the River Danube. But today, although both routes still exist, the northerly one — the former Austro-Hungarian — is no longer competitive; it forms the most easterly section of the main line between Budapest and Prague. From Budapest the Hungarian State had three routes striking out to the north and east, but one of the most important was that running south to Belgrade. Until the First World War the River Danube marked the frontier between Hungary and Serbia, as it was then known. The third railway entering Budapest was the Austrian Southern, from the southwest. This made a junction with the line over the Semmering Pass from Vienna, and provided a through route from Budapest to Trieste. Because of the changing of state boundaries after the First World War, the extent of the Hungarian State Railways has been reduced from the original route length of 9,120 km (5,700 miles), an amalgam of the three separate railways, to 7,483 km (4,647 miles) today. Since the end of the Second World War, considerable progress has been made with electrification, and the circular railway in Budapest, 19 km (12 miles) long, is also electrified. Although the railways of Hungary use the European standard gauge, the loading gauge is much taller. Hungarian steam locomotives are often built to the maximum possible heights, and like those of Austria they seem immense compared with those of western Europe. But, as everywhere else, steam traction is gradually being superseded, though many locomotives still remain in service. The now withdrawn Orient Express originally turned south from Budapest to serve Belgrade and eventually Constantinople.

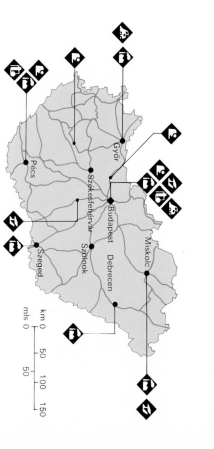

### Hungary

290  
126,346  
7,550 km (4,689 mls)

Almost no figures are available for Hungary. About 16% of the system is electrified. The route length includes 35 km built to the Russian gauge of 1,524 mm, and 329 km of 760 mm gauge. Two classes of narrow gauge diesel loco exist.

# Portugal and Spain

**PORTUGAL** *Companhia dos Caminhos de Ferro Portugueses (CP)*

The first railway in Portugal was opened in 1856 between Lisbon and Carregado, and the national network, amounting eventually to 3,520 km (2,200 miles) of route, was built up under private enterprise. The principal main line, within the country, connected Lisbon with Oporto, and had a connection running northward into Spain and continuing to Coruña. Important west-east international routes provide connections from Lisbon to Madrid, Barcelona and Seville, while a more northerly line reaching the Spanish frontier at Vilar Formoso, is used by trains providing the international service between Lisbon and Paris. These routes are laid to the Portuguese broad gauge standard of 1,665 mm (5 ft 5¼ in). Until 1926 the lines at present worked were roughly half private and half state-owned, and then the government handed over, by lease, its own lines to the private company. In 1947, however, the whole concern was brought directly under the Ministry of Communications though remaining company worked, and in 1951 the government granted the company a 50-year concession to work the lines previously leased.

## Narrow gauge steam

A feature of Portuguese railways of great interest to enthusiasts and photographers is the system of narrow gauge feeder lines in the north. There is a series of branches extending northward into the frontier regions from the Oporto–Barca d'Alva broad gauge main line, and on these the metre gauge trains are worked by historically interesting and immaculately maintained steam locomotives. On the broad gauge lines steam traction finally ended in March 1977. In the Lisbon suburban area, and on the main line northwards towards Oporto, electrification is in progress, using the same system – 25,000 volts alternating current at 50 cycles – as standardized in Great Britain and France, while on other routes extensive use is now being made of diesel electric traction, locomotives on long distance and international trains, and railcars for local branch line work. On the narrow gauge lines steam locomotives are still used for some of the work, though diesel railcars, diesel locomotives and some petrol-driven railcars, have been introduced.

Braga, Portugal, two shunting engines.

**SPAIN** *Red Nacional de los Ferrocarriles Españoles (RENFE)*

Railway operation in Spain began in 1848 under rather curious circumstances. Before this 29 km (18 mile) length of line between Barcelona and Mataro had been built, a Royal decree of 1845 had insisted on extensive state intervention, and among other things demanded the adoption of a wider gauge than the European standard of 1,435 mm (4 ft 8½ in). It is thought that this was influenced by the work of I. K. Brunel, in England; and while Spain had the same gauge – or nearly the same – as Portugal, 1,674 mm against 1,665 mm, there developed a major confrontation at the French frontier, that still remains today. From that beginning Spanish railway construction, dependent upon foreign capital and the need for foreign advisers, progressed slowly. Major companies incorporated later were the Northern, in 1858, to build a line from Madrid to Irun; the Madrid, Zaragoza and Alicante in 1857, and the Andalusian Railway. All suffered in due course from lack of staple traffics, the difficulties of operating in mountainous country; and the imposition of low rates for both goods and passenger business. Unable to

renew their assets the general situation went into decline. In 1924 a convention in Madrid, signed by the state and the companies, provided for the supply of state capital for railway restoration, and to authorize the establishment of more realistic rates. This latter condition was not however fulfilled, and despite the infusion of state capital the railways were in poor shape when there came the tragedy of the Civil War in 1936.

## The Civil War and after

The destruction was widespread and severe. More than a thousand locomotives – over half the total stock – were destroyed, and many bridges, tunnels and lengths of track damaged. After the war the government took control of the railways, and in 1943 purchased the whole of the stock of the previous private companies, and an autonomous corporation, nominally independent of the government, was set up to operate the railways. This was named *Red Nacional de los Ferrocarriles Españoles*. Under this unified management great progress has been made in rebuilding and re-equipping the Spanish railways. Many sections were electrified; others were changed from steam to diesel traction, and one of the most important developments has been the construction of the new direct line from Madrid to Burgos via Aranda, avoiding the long westward detour via Avila, Medina del Campo and Valladolid and saving a total of 120 km (75 miles) on the journey between Madrid and the French frontier.

Figures for CP's multiple-unit sets have proved impossible to discover. The route length includes 759 km of metre gauge. Portugal's last steam engines are all narrow gauge: the last broad gauge steamers ran in 1977.

RENFE owns only broad (1,676 mm) gauge lines; another government agency FEVE operates (without owning) 1,757 km of narrow gauge lines. All totals include these lines, but exclude other privately owned railways.

Spain

14,254 km (9,413 mls)

403   795   55'   364'   80,108   2,563   37,736

* not including multiple-unit sets · 349 electric, 59 diesel

Portugal

3,841 km (2,386 mls)

47   232   157'   54   638   8,019   • 24,267

* not including at least 17 electric multiple-unit sets

Mining and quarrying
Iron and steel production
Manufacturing centre
Oil refining
Chemical processing
Port
Rail depot/construction
Tourist centre

Port Bou
Barcelona
Lerida
Zaragoza
Pamplona
Bilbao
San Sebastian
Burgos
Santander
Palencia
Valladolid
Salamanca
Madrid
Valencia
Albacete
Alicante
Cartagena
Granada
Cordoba
Sevilla
Málaga
Algeciras
Cadiz
Huelva
Badajoz
Caceres
Faro
Lisbon
Setubal
Coimbra
Porto
Orense
El Ferrol
La Coruña

km 0   50   100   150
mls 0   50

# FRANCE *Société Nationale des Chemins de fer Français (SNCF)*

Railways in France began, as in Great Britain, with local mineral lines using horses for traction, but at a very early stage in the development the government, seeing what was happening with unbridled competition in other states, divided the whole country into a number of clearly defined geographical regions, and gave the pioneer railway companies concessions to build only within those limits. In this way it was hoped that wasteful competition and unnecessary proliferation of routes would be avoided. The individual companies, of which there were originally seven, held concessions to terminate in the 1930s, and during the intervening period the dividends paid to their shareholders were guaranteed by the government. Five out of the original seven continued in this manner until nationalization in 1937, but the Western was seriously affected by the establishment of the French State Railways, in 1878, which brought competition into Western territory, and so contravened the original conception. The Paris-Orléans Railway was also affected, though not to such a serious extent. The other four original railways remained in almost exclusive possession of their allotted territories. These companies were the Northern, Eastern, Paris, Lyons and Mediterranean, the Southern (Midi) and the Alsace-Lorraine.

## Nineteenth-century complacency

The monopolies these companies held tended to generate policies lacking in enterprise, and train services in the nineteenth century were relatively poor. The exception was the Paris-Orléans, which did become affected by competition. At both Bordeaux and Toulouse it handed over traffic for the south to the Midi, which also received similar traffic from the PLM. The Midi was encouraged to favour the Orléans traffic for the better service from the north provided by that company. Before the general amalgamations of 1937–8, the Paris-Orléans and the Midi had themselves amalgamated, in 1934. Competition between the state-owned system, the Etat, and the Western Railway led to the absorption of the latter in 1908. Of the original companies the Alsace-Lorraine was profoundly affected by the Franco-Prussian War of 1870–1, after which most of the territory in which it operated was annexed by Germany. For a period of 48 years until 1919 it was controlled and operated by Prussia, and its equipment changed to correspond with standard German practice.

## Era of speed and efficiency

The *Société Nationale des Chemins de fer Français* was set up in January 1938; but long before this act of nationalization all of the individual French railways had thrown off their nineteenth-century complacency and were between them providing some of the fastest and most efficient train services in the whole of Europe. From the experience of invasion, in 1870 and again in 1914, there was reluctance to electrify any of the lines leading to the eastern frontier, and development in this respect had come first on the Paris-Orléans and on the Midi railways, in the 1920s. In the Second World War the greatest destruction took place not at the time of the general overrunning of the country by Nazi forces in 1940, but just prior to the re-entry of Allied forces in 1944, when systematic strategic bombing to hinder the movement of troops led to the almost complete disruption of the entire railway network and much destruction of stock.

Since the war recovery has been remarkable. The lines to the eastern frontier have been electrified, and fast services inaugurated, but the highest speeds so far are run on the former Paris-Orléans lines up to a maximum of 200 km/h (125 mph) with heavy luxury express trains. The greatest development, however, is now in course of construction, namely the new high-speed line between Paris and Lyon, on which speeds up to 300 km/h (185 mph) will be run, by special TGV (*très grande vitesse*) electric trains. The new line is being built roughly parallel to the former PLM main line, though passing somewhat to the west of Dijon. It is planned that when the new route comes into operation in the early 1980s the journey time between Paris and Lyon, now 3 hr 44 min, will be reduced to 2 hr. Thus, since the end of the war, France has become a world leader in railway innovation.

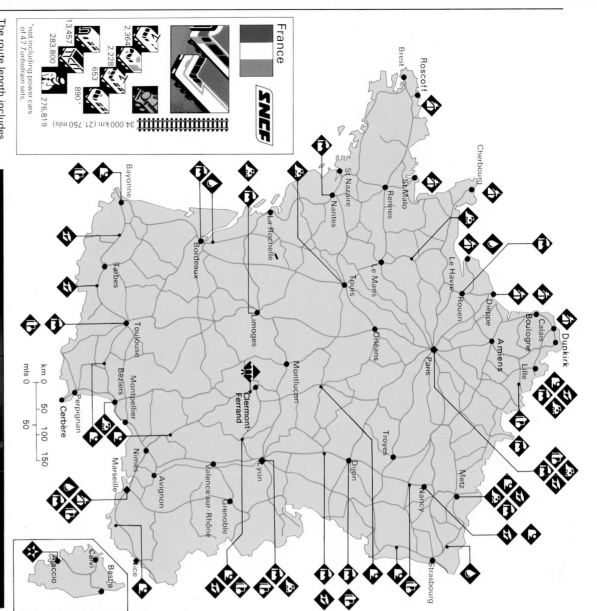

France
SNCF

34,000 km (21,750 mls)

13,457
283,800
276,819
2,364
2,228
653
890

*not including power cars of 47 Turbotrain sets

The route length includes the new 13.4 km line to Roissy Airport but shows only SNCF lines. Excluded are the remains of a once-extensive network of secondary lines – about 975 km metre gauge, and 1,125 km standard, still exist. The wagon total includes private stock.

*Right* A night train departs, Paris. *Below left* Font Romeau, La Tour de Carol system. *Below right* Steam French style.

# Italy, Yugoslavia, Albania

**ITALY** *Ferrovie dello Stato-Italia (FS)*

Although the first railway in Italy was built in 1839, and various other projects followed, there was no co-ordination, because at that time Italy had not been unified as a single country. Lombardy was then occupied by Austria. The Dukedom of Tuscany and the Papal States were then independent. After the union of 1861 plans were drawn up for a national network, and from the various independent and unconnected lines five companies were set up: the Upper Italian, operating in Lombardy and Piedmont; the Roman, taking over lines in Tuscany and the Papal States; the Southern, working east of the Apennine mountains; the Royal Sardinian, in Calabria; and the Victor Emmanuel Railway in Sicily. In 1885 a further grouping took place into three private companies, and finally between 1905 and 1907 all came under the control of the state.

Italy was one of the first countries to introduce main line electric traction, on the line between Genoa and the French frontier at Ventimiglia, and on the heavily graded Giovi Incline, but the system adopted did not prove adaptable to heavy modern traffic, and the lines were re-equipped. During the Fascist era notable strides were made towards the improvement of the national network. The piecemeal nature of the original build-up, at a time when reliance had to be placed on foreign capital, resulted in many important routes being sharply curved, and

constructed so as to minimize initial costs. While the main lines eastward from Milan to Venice, and from Milan through Bologna to Rimini and Ancona, were straight and capable of use by fast trains, the important route from Bologna to Florence and Rome was extremely sinuous and heavily graded. In the Fascist era a new direct line was built from Bologna to Florence, involving a great new tunnel through the Apennine range 19 km (12 miles) long, and opened in 1934. Another great project was the building of a new high-speed direct line between Rome and Naples, running near to the coast for much of the way, and avoiding use of the old inland route that was so unsuitable for fast running.

These improvements left the old line between Florence and Rome as the only remaining section of the route between Milan and Naples in the old style. In mountainous country it was perhaps the most difficult of all to operate. Eventually the decision was taken to build a new direct line regardless of the natural obstacles. It has involved some tremendous engineering works in great viaducts and long tunnels, in fact nearly one third of the entire distance of 257 km (160 miles) from Florence to Rome is in tunnel. The end-to-end average speed of the fastest trains is planned to be no less than 177 km/h (110 mph), with a maximum of about 250 km/h (155 mph). This high-speed line will take much of the traffic burden off the old route.

**YUGOSLAVIA** *Jugoslovenske Železnice (JŽ)*

The state of Yugoslavia, created after the end of the First World War, inherited a mixed collection of railways. There had been groups of lines in Croatia and Slovenia, the lines of the former Serbian State Railways, and metre gauge lines, and some even narrower in Bosnia, Herzogovina and Dalmatia. The first aim of the Yugoslav government was to establish the northwest to southeast link from Ljubljana through Belgrade to Caribrod (now Dimitrovgrad), as an international main line. Today Belgrade is a focus point of main routes from Austria and Italy in the west, Hungary in the north, and Greece and Turkey in the east. While it is no longer possible to travel through in one carriage from Paris to Istanbul, the Simplon Express from Paris to Belgrade connects there with the Marmara Express, and also the Athens Express. The Republic of Yugoslavia is divided into six socialist republics, and in 1954 the railways introduced workers' self-government, and so the Community of Yugoslav Railways lost the title of State. There are five Railway Transport Enterprises, or regional headquarters, in Belgrade, Zagreb, Ljubljana, Sarajevo and Skopje. The co-ordinating authority is in Belgrade.

Albania's first railway was opened in 1947, and the system is still expanding: at present a link is being built to Bar (Yugoslavia). Steam locos are 2-8-2 Polish tanks, while CKD (the Czech manufacturer) has recently supplied three classes of diesels.

292 km (182 mls) *

* excluding 12 km narrow-gauge mineral line.

**Albania**

11,856 km (7,410 mls)

The route length figure is from 1973 and includes 1,045 km of narrow gauge, some having been closed subsequently. By 1985 it is hoped that 35% of the system will be electrified. The last steam locomotive is due to be phased out in 1980.

* not including multiple-unit sets · 27 electric, 266 diesel

**Yugoslavia**

556
321    794    524
3,396    52,350    131,809

**Italy**

**FS**

16,014 km (10,009 mls)

933
479*    969
1,815    1,207
164,979    · 59,693

* not including 23 electric multiple-unit sets

The figures exclude 4,240 km privately owned (26% of Italy's total route). FS still has some steam: mostly only on standby.

Mining and quarrying
Iron and steel production
Manufacturing centre
Oil refining
Chemical processing
Port
Rail depot/construction
Tourist centre

Sardinia's first railway opened in 1864, a mule-powered mineral line. By 1883, 435 km of standard gauge lines were built, which today link with the mainland by ferry. Italy's first narrow gauge line was built here, and its 950 mm gauge became a standard throughout Italy. About 1,050 km were opened, the last as late as 1932.

**ROMANIA** *Caile Ferate Romane (CFR)*

The first railway in Romania, built in 1869, was the result of a concession granted to two Englishmen, John Barkley and John Staniforth, and connected Bucharest with the Danubian port of Giurgiu, 72 km (45 miles) distant. But building and operating railways by private enterprise did not last long and in 1888 all railways in Romania became state owned. Although the rail gauge is the European standard, there is a short length of mixed gauge, with three rails, to provide access for the Russian standard gauge of 1,524 mm (5 ft 0 in). The total route length on standard gauge is 10,100 km (6,300 miles). The principal route into Romania from the west enters the country from Budapest at Apiscopia Bihor, and links up with a more southerly route at Teius. Bucharest, the former eastern terminus of the Orient Express, is a major railway centre, lines running north to cross the Russian border at Ungeny, and east to the Black Sea port of Constanza.

Romania

237,522

<ins>⛏</ins>10,941 km (6,838 mls)

Few figures are available for Romania, *above*, or Bulgaria, *below*. Both retain some steam locos, though both are electrifying. The route totals include narrow gauge lines.

**BULGARIA** *Bulgarski Durzhavni Zeleznitsi (BDŽ)*

For a relatively small country railway construction in Bulgaria began on quite a large scale, with a main line 225 km (139 miles) long from the Danubian port of Ruschuk to Varna on the Black Sea, in 1866. A still greater milestone was however the completion of the international main line across the country from Dragoman on the present Yugoslav frontier, through Sofia to Svilengrad, and providing the all-rail route of the Orient Express to Constantinople. King Boris of Bulgaria was a keen railway enthusiast and frequently drove the steam locomotives of fast trains. Today more than half the total route of 4,300 km (2,700 miles) is electrified, and the rest is operated by diesel traction and steam locomotives.

Steam train waiting in a Bulgarian station.

Bulgaria

<ins>⛏</ins>4,290 km (2,681 mls)

BDZ

The route total, *below*, includes 2 narrow gauges. The rolling stock figures are for those in service by end 1975. Mid-1976, OSE had 74 steam locos, of all 3 gauges, officially in stock; most were stored.

**GREECE** *Organismos Siderodromon Ellados (ΣΕ)*

It is remarkable in view of its ancient civilization that Greece should have been one of the most backward of European countries to adopt modern means of communication in the form of railways, and still more remarkable perhaps that the country was not connected to the rest of Europe by rail until 1916. One of the first railways in Greece was indeed directed away rather than towards Europe, and came from a concession granted to a company called the Piraeus, Athens and Peloponnesus to build a line across the isthmus of Corinth and into the Peloponnesus. It was built on the metre gauge, and by the turn of the century had a total route length of about 800 km (500 miles). It passed through Athens to reach the port of Piraeus.

The standard gauge main line from Piraeus and Athens to the north was opened in sections between 1904 and 1909 to Papapouli. At that time its limit was the Turco-Greek frontier; but at the Treaty of Bucharest, following the Balkan war of 1913, the frontiers were redrawn, and that of Greece was pushed northward to border those of Serbia and Bulgaria. This brought the Thessaly Railway into Greek territory, and in 1916 the link was made between Papapouli and Platy. This enabled through carriage services to be established between Athens and other European cities. In 1962 all railways in Greece were amalgamated under the title of Hellenic Railways, and in 1971 these railways were set up as a state-owned company with the title of Hellenic Railways Organisation Ltd.

Greece

ΣΕ

<ins>⛏</ins>2,572 km (1,597 mls)

574
10,170
•12,901
188
105
5

Steam heading freight in typical Greek scene.

km 0  50  100  150
mls 0  50  100

km 0  50  100  150
mls 0  50  100

km 0  50  100  150  200
mls 0  50  100

# USSR

## USSR *Soviet Railways (SZD)*

The railways of Soviet Russia represent the largest single railway system in the world. They extend from the Polish frontier to Vladivostok, a distance of some 10,000 km (6,300 miles), and from the White Sea in the north to Turkestan. The first public railway was opened in 1836 with British locomotives from both Stephenson and Hackworth, and from a modest beginning great expansion followed the completion of the main line between Moscow and Leningrad (then St Petersburg) in 1851. By 1913 the railway network consisted of no fewer than 25 state lines and 13 private lines; but although then the largest system in Europe there was little co-ordination between individual companies and strategically the lines were built with emphasis towards the southern frontiers, towards Afghanistan and India rather than towards the west.

### After the revolution

The almost legendary Trans-Siberian line was still under construction at the turn of the century, though communication between Moscow and Vladivostok had been established by shipping passengers and goods by ferry across Lake Baikal, until the line was completed, blasted out of the solid rock along the shores of the lake. The absence of good railways in the European provinces of Russia was in part responsible for the collapse of the military position in the First World War. After the Revolution of 1917 the railways were nationalized and great efforts made towards reconstruction. It was realised that efficient communication was the first essential of the new state, and by the 1930s the railway system had been so modernized that from being a serious liability it had been advanced to become one of the greatest assets to the national economy. Although a great deal of damage was done to the lines in the war zones in 1941-4, reconstruction and development continued and today the route length is more than 136,969 km (85,073 miles), of which more than 32,000 km (20,000 miles) is electrified, including the Trans-Siberian line as far east as Chita. In non-electrified areas there is a general move to replace steam locomotives by diesel, and a new high-speed line has been inaugurated between Moscow and Leningrad on which speeds of 200 km/h (125 mph) are projected.

Russian steam heading Trans-Siberian, with familiar decoration.

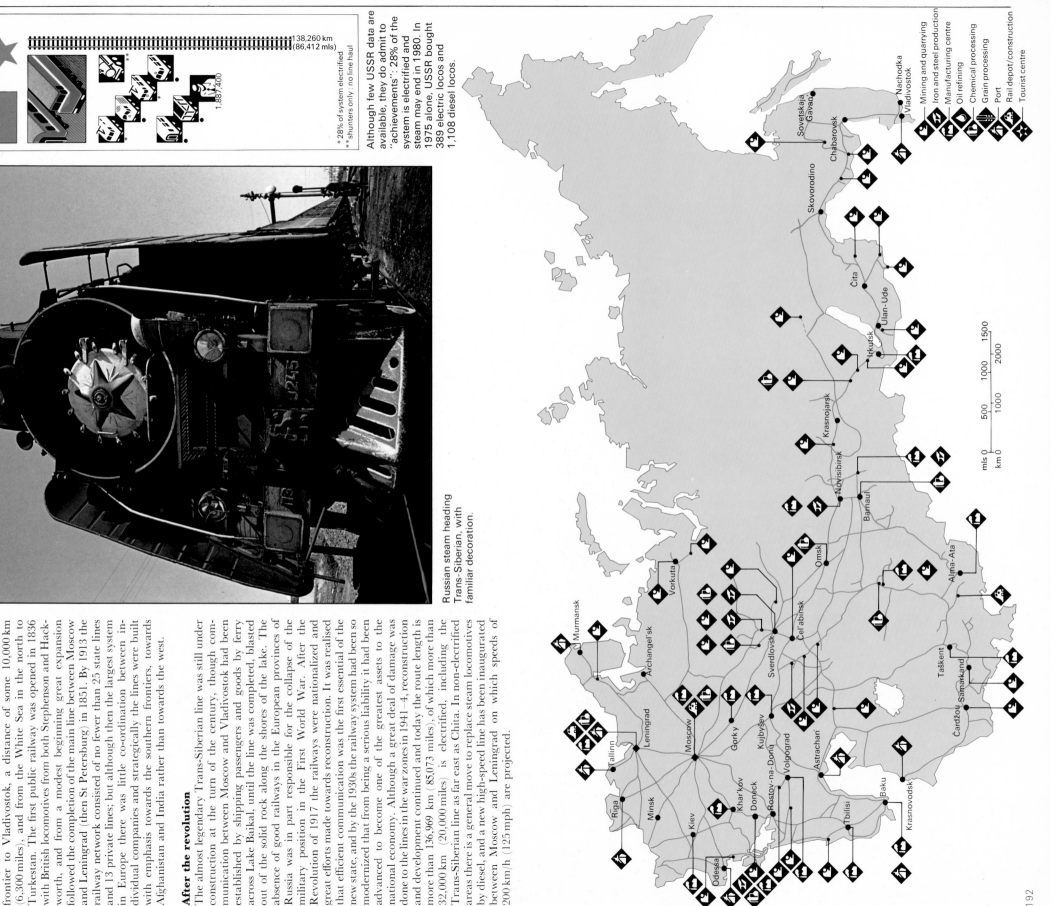

USSR

138,260 km
(86,412 mls)

1,887,400

* 28% of system electrified
** shunters only : no line haul

Although few USSR data are available, they do admit to "achievements": 28% of the system is electrified and steam may end in 1980. In 1975 alone, USSR bought 389 electric locos and 1,108 diesel locos.

Mining and quarrying
Iron and steel production
Manufacturing centre
Oil refining
Chemical processing
Grain processing
Port
Rail depot/construction
Tourist centre

# Asia: Turkey and Middle East I

Asia has some of the oldest, and some of the most modern, trains in the world. It is thought that China is still building steam locos, and India yet has 8,000. On the other hand, the Japanese opened their *Shinkansen* line in 1964: over a major trunk route, trains are run at a frequency usually associated with commuter lines at speeds up to 210 km/h (130 mph). Asia is a varied mixture of rich and poor, of countries which were once colonies and those which were left to develop their own rail system in the national, rather than the colonizing power's, interest. As a result, Asia's lines are a multiplicity of gauges, some countries own systems much more comprehensive than others, and the completion of a serious proposal (see page 94), is many years away from realization.

1 Turkey p193
2 Syria p193
3 Iran p194
4 Pakistan p195
5 India p194
6 Bangladesh p194
7 Burma p194
8 China p195
9 South Korea p195
10 North Korea p195
11 Japan p196
12 Lebanon p193
13 Iraq p194

14 Jordan p193
15 Thailand p196
16 Indonesia p196
17 Vietnam p195
18 Israel p193
19 Saudi Arabia p194
20 Sri Lanka p194
21 Malaysia p196
22 Cambodia p196
23 Hong Kong p195
24 Philippines p195
25 Taiwan p195

## TURKEY  Turkish State Railways (TCDD)

The old Ottoman Empire straddled the Bosporus, and the Turkish railway system consisted of little more than the route of the Orient Express in Europe, and about 4,000 km (2,500 miles) of route in Asia Minor, independent, unconnected and serving local areas. After the Balkan War of 1913, however, Turkey was left with no more than a foothold in Europe, while her association with the Central Powers in the First World War, and involvement in their collapse, left the country and its railways in very poor shape. While under strong German influence a railway had been built, through Asia Minor to connect Constantinople with Baghdad, completed in 1918, the starting-point of the modern railway system of Turkey was the proclamation of the republic in October 1923, and the move of the capital city from Constantinople to Ankara – then little more than a remote settlement. A well balanced system of railways being essential to build up the economy of the country, plans were prepared for a fully integrated network in Asia Minor. In 1927 the "General Management of the Railways and Harbours of the Republic of Turkey" (TCDD) was set up and since then the railway length has virtually doubled. Ankara was placed on the principal main line from Istanbul to the Iraqi and Soviet frontiers, although the route of the Taurus Express, from Istanbul to Baghdad, is that of the German-sponsored line built earlier. In mountainous country the Turkish railways of today follow the winding river valleys and cross high mountain passes.

### Israel

Israel's lines are now all standard gauge, though the first (1890) was metre and the second, 1,050 mm (Haifa-Dera'a, Syria: now closed, it included 80 km below sea level). Middle East politics have isolated Israel: before 1948, trains ran to Egypt, Lebanon and Jordan via Dera'a. The system is expanding.

A 2-10-0 near Siringo in Turkey.

### Jordan

Jordan's first train ran in 1904, as part of the Turkish-inspired Pilgrim's Railway (Damascus-Medina). The line was damaged in 1918, and fell derelict south of Ma'an. Part was refurbished in connection with the new Aqaba line (opened 1975). Steam locos and passenger trains are only found north of Amman.

### Lebanon

Lebanon was carved out of the Turkish empire with no regard to the existing rail system. Running inland from Beirut (and with 32 km of rack rail) is part of the 1,050 mm Damascus line. Others are standard gauge, but the junction of the system in Syria. All lines were closed by the civil war and have not yet reopened.

### Syria

The diesel loco figure is old, unreliable: recently, standard gauge steam has ended and the route-km has doubled (expansion in the north). Syria has two systems: 1,050 mm linking Damascus with Lebanon and Jordan; in the north, a standard gauge system links Hims/Aleppo with Lebanon and Turkey, soon reaching Damascus.

* narrow gauge
** see accompanying caption

Israel — 647 km (401 mls)
114  2,168  57  1,860

Jordan — J.R.C. — 500 km (310 mls)
6  330  666  15  15  2

Lebanon — 414 km (259 mls) — Figures for 1974
15  881  1,487  6  32

Syria — 1,855 km (1,159 mls)
233  1,694  20*  13  45**

### Turkey

5,128 km (3,185 mls)
18  1,175  19,291  192  767  30*  27*  63,502

* multiple-unit sets: excludes 25 diesel railcars

The route figure includes 47.5 km of line scheduled to open in 1977. Rolling stock totals are 1974 and rather out of date: 300 more diesels should be delivered before 1978.

# Middle East II and India

**INDIA** *Indian Government Railways*

The railways of India as a basic national network were planned by the Marquis of Dalhousie when Governor-General in the early 1850s. The plan was to develop trade routes connecting the seaports of Calcutta, Bombay and Madras, and to provide good communication from the ports to the North-West Frontier, where the greatest military danger was thought to lie. From 1853 when the first railway was constructed from Bombay the main line network was built on the 1,676 mm (5ft 6in) gauge recommended by Dalhousie; but later, when many more lines were found necessary and the cost of construction was high, the government agreed to the establishment of a system of feeder lines on the metre gauge. Railway building in India and what is now Pakistan involved some tremendous feats of civil engineering, in crossing the range of the Western Ghats, eastward from Bombay, in crossing the great rivers Indus and Ganges, and in carrying strategic lines of communication into the mountain ranges of the North-West Frontier.

In imperial days the railways of India were household names in transport and engineering circles: Great Indian Peninsula; Bombay, Baroda and Central India; Madras and Southern Mahratta; East Indian; Bengal Nagpur; Eastern Bengal; and above all "His Exalted Highness the Nizam's Guaranteed State Railway". Some of the railways were state-owned, others were operated by private companies holding concessions and certain financial guarantees. When the concessions ended they were brought under government control. After the granting of independence to India and Pakistan the railways were nationalized, and the railways of India are operated in nine territorial zones: Great Northern, Western, Central, Southern, Eastern, North Eastern, South Eastern, North-East Frontier and South Central. Since independence great strides have been made towards the provision of all rolling stock and technical services by indigenous manufacture and technology.

Indian railways, *left*, have 4 different gauges. The broad gauge (1,676 mm) is used for 30,274 route-km and the metre gauge for 25,551 km. Two narrower gauges of 762 mm and 610 mm account for 4,476 route-km (7½% of the total). The wagons figure therefore need increasing by the same percentage.

Mining and quarrying
Iron and steel production
Manufacturing centre
Oil refining
Chemical processing
Grain processing
Port
Rail depot/construction

Railway construction began in Iraq, *below right*, in 1902, part of the Berlin-Baghdad project, seen as a standard gauge through route. After the British invasion of 1914, Basra-Baghdad was built with surplus metre gauge equipment from India, and Iraq has a similar length now of both gauges.

*Below:* Saudi Arabia's first railway now lies derelict, damaged by Lawrence of Arabia in 1918. Trains got to Tabūk from Jordan in 1906, and reached Medina in 1908. The line now working opened in 1951, built by ARAMCO as one of the conditions of their oil exploration licence.

**Bangladesh**

The Bangladesh Railway originated as an integral part of the Bengal-Assam Railway, which was arbitrarily divided at the Partition of India and Pakistan in 1947. Further, administrative, upheaval came in 1973 in the wake of the civil war which created a separate Bangladesh. The system is built to both Indian gauges: about a third is broad (1,676 mm) gauge, the rest metre.

2,858 km (1,786 mls)

337 — 4 — 178 — 1,204 — 18,882

**Sri Lanka**

Sri Lanka's first railway opened in 1865 to the Indian 1,676 mm gauge. This will soon be the only gauge, if the 762 mm Kelani Valley Railway closes. KVR totals are included in the panel.

1,496 km (0,929 mls)

40 — 74 — 135 — 932 — 4,094 — 6,226

totals include 139 km narrow gauge route scheduled for closure

**Burma**

Burmese Railways, *left*, own the longest double-track metre-gauge line anywhere (the 220 km north from Rangoon). The first line opened in 1877: all were built by the government of India, from which Burma separated in 1937. Few recent figures are available. A 1975 estimate gives 200 steam, and more than 50 diesels at Rangoon depot alone. The remaining steam locos include Garratts for the 1 in 25 grade of the Lashio line.

3,127 km (1,942 mls)

129* — 23** — 29,233 — 166* — 9,636 — 1,326

*multiple unit sets
**in 1968 (latest available)

**Iran**

Iran, *below*, acquired its first line in 1916, built by the Russians from their frontier to Tabriz. It was 1,524 mm gauge (5 ft) until 1958. The Trans-Iranian railway (Persian Gulf-Caspian Sea) was opened throughout only in 1938. The link to Turkey was completed in 1971. A 10-to-25 Year Development Plan, drawn so it can be proceeded with as fast or slowly as required, calls for another 9,500 km to be built – twice as much as the country owns now. One line planned is a link to Pakistan Railways, whose system extends over their border to Zāhedān (where gauge-changing facilities will be needed). A section of this line, from Zarand to Kermān, opened in 1977. The plan also proposes extensive electrification. The first line being done is the original one to the Russian frontier, but no details are yet available of the progress made.

4,617 km (2,885 mls)

4* — 348 — 429 — 29,639 — 12,898

*Turbotrain sets

**India**

60,301 km (37,688 mls)

696 — 1,694 — 1,215 — 32,269 — 508,000*

* excluding those of gauges narrower than one metre

**Iraq**

2,529 km (1,580 mls)

19 — 4 — 163 — 240 — 3,280 — 1,377

**Saudi Arabia**

612 km (380 mls)

26 — 4 — 25 — 1,144 — 1,521

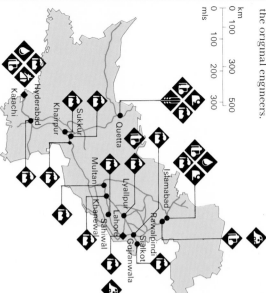

## PAKISTAN *Pakistan Railways* (*PR*)

The first line in Pakistan was the 173 km (108 mile) Scinde Railway between Karachi and Kotri, opened in 1861. It was promoted because of the hazardous navigation along the lower Indus. By 1865, a route had been completed via Amritsar to Delhi, the capital of British India, but it still included a 912 km (570 mile) river voyage. Thus began the North Western Railway, which became the largest railway company on the Indian subcontinent. Divided by the 1947 Partition of India, the major portion became what is now Pakistan Railways. The countryside presents extraordinary challenges. One line crosses the Sind desert, another climbs above the snowline. The Quetta route climbs 1,524 m (5,000 ft) in 80 km (50 miles). Above all, the railway is plagued by the capricious flooding of the River Indus, despite much magnificent bridge building by the original engineers.

Like India, Pakistan's railways were built to 4 gauges, but 88 per cent is 1,676 mm gauge. The line from Lahore to Khanewal is electrified, but no electric loco figures are available (and the steam total may refer to before this line was energized).

### Pakistan

* at least 300 route-km have recently been electrified

2,815   39,710   39   469   615   29   71   •134,887

8,808 km (5,505 mls)

### Vietnam

About 2,210 km of metre gauge lines were opened in Vietnam, the first in 1885. However, the system suffered extensively in years of warfare and at present it is planned to rebuild only 1,680 km. Through services between Hanoi and Saigon only restarted in January 1977.

'106   '660   47   7   •2,750

2,210 km (1,381 mls)

* stock figures only available for what was S Vietnam.

### Philippines

Most of the Philippines' lines are on Luzon, the main island, where the first railway was opened in 1892 by the English Manila Railroad Co. Ownership was acquired by the government in 1917. The totals include the 116 km Phividec Railway on another island, Panay.

80   238   1,900   81

1,176 km (735 mls)

## CHINA *Chinese Republic Railways*

It is only 100 years since a railway line opened in China, but the possibilities of development were soon exploited by foreign investors and building accelerated, particularly after the war with Japan in 1894. From 1908 all foreign contracts had to give complete administrative control to the government, and the formation of the republic led to a degree of consolidation of the railways with the establishment of central control in 1915.

At the time of the Japanese invasion of Manchuria in 1931, total route length reached 14,436 km (9,022 miles), but in the period following over 6,000 km (3,728 miles) was ceded to the Japanese. This led to a divided development of the area with the war with Japan attempting to build new lines to compensate for their losses to the Japanese in the northeast. The two systems were reunited following the Japanese surrender in 1945.

Postwar development until 1960 after the establishment of the People's Republic in 1949. It was in this period that the link between Peking and Ulan-Ude in Russia via Ulan-baatar was completed, thus cutting 2,400 km off the old Trans-Siberian route to Europe via Haerbin.

Since the split with the USSR the Chinese have forged ahead with railway expansion, tackling difficult terrain with great determination, and a doubling of the present route length is envisaged in the next few years. The whole network is extremely well maintained, the main source of power still being based on steam; but diesel and electric traction are increasing in importance.

Figures for China's railways are virtually non-existent. It is thought that steam locos are still being built, though dieselization has begun and at least 675 km are electrified.

### China

* at least 626 km electrified

200,000   200,000

55,000 km (34,375 mls) at least

CHINA map cities: Yumen, Kunming, Chengdu, Lanzhou, Guyang, Nanning, Canton, Macau, Hengyang, Wuhan, Nanchang, Taiyuan, Sian, Luoyang, Zhengzhou, Peking, Tientsin, Tsingtao, Yantai, Yingk'ou, Yuda, Shenyang, Fushun, Changchun, Luoyang, Haerbin, Taipei, Fuchou, Shanghai, Nanjing, Hangzhou

### South Korea

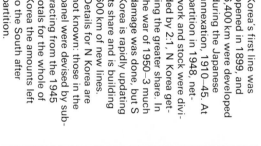

90   1,785   16,208   171   436   128   68   •39,776

2,558 km (1,598 mls)

* recent figures for N Korea not available – see caption, right

### North Korea

Korea's first line was opened in 1899, and 6,400 km were developed during the Japanese annexation, 1910–45. At partition in 1948, network and stock were divided by 2:1, N Korea getting the greater share. In the war of 1950–3 much damage was done, but S Korea is rapidly updating its share and is building 600 km of new lines. Details for N Korea are not known: those in the panel were devised by subtracting from the 1945 totals for the whole of Korea the amounts left to the South after partition.

500   1,280   9,154

3,825 km (2,391 mls)

### Hong Kong

Hong Kong's railway opened in 1910, the British section of the Kowloon-Canton line. The rest is now part of China's system, though wagons still cross the frontier. Hong Kong is building a separate mass transit line.

96   104   10

33.5 km (21 mls)

### Taiwan

Taiwan's first train ran in 1891. Recently its 1,067 mm gauge was adopted for all lines, the 176km East Line built to 762mm gauge in 1939, currently being converted. The electric locos were bought for the West Line electrification scheme going live in 1977. An 82 km link line joining these two will open in 1978. The totals exclude 2,838 km of government-owned plantation lines.

94   1,160   7,172   161   13   141   63   23,678

1,007 km (630 mls)

* multiple units sets

# Far East 11

## Indonesia

🚆 6,972 km (4,357 mls)

202 · 10 · 70,795
311 · 2,423 · 22,279
11

Indonesia's railways are built to 3 gauges. The widest is now 1,067 mm: during the last war the Japanese narrowed the standard gauge lines. The first 26 km line opened in 1864. Java has since acquired a comprehensive network but Sumatra only 3 isolated systems. In recent years Indonesia has become famous among enthusiasts for its steam locos.

## Malaysia

🚆 1,807 km (1,126 mls)

84 · 45* · 14,509
154 · 6,714 · 417*

* excluding 6 diesel multiple-unit sets

Railways in Malaya began in 1885. By 1918 the 787 km West Coast line from Thailand to Singapore was complete except for the Johore Strait causeway. The East Coast line was completed in 1931, providing another route to Thailand. The totals include the Sabah State Railway, built 1896–1905 by the British North Borneo Co. (Sabah was N Borneo until 1963).

## Kampuchea

🚆 649 km (406 mls)

24 · 4 · 680
13 · 4

Figures are not available from the present Cambodian regime, and it is not known whether the system is working: it was badly damaged in the war. The line to Kompong Som was wrecked only four months after its 1969 opening.

## Thailand

🚆 3,855 km (2,394 mls)

71 · 45* · 33,976
243 · 9,691 · 1,008

* 2-car multiple-unit sets

Thailand's first line was begun in 1891, to standard gauge. But metre gauge was used for the south line, begun 1898, to link with Malaya. Burma also chose this gauge and it was decided to convert the first gauge, finishing in 1930.

## Japan

🚆 29,085 km (18,065 mls)

8** · 502,000
2,171 · 2,150 · 28,659 · 125,844
8,599

* includes trailer cars
** no steam on state system

The Japan figures include 146 privately-owned lines (hence the steam locos). The rolling stock totals are for the end of 1974.

## JAPAN *Japanese National Railways (JNR)*

There could not be a greater contrast between the leisurely, almost primitive beginnings of the Japanese railway system in 1872 and the tremendous volume of passenger traffic carried at equally tremendous speed on the *Shinkansen* high-speed lines of today. With British advisers and mechanical engineers, the first lines were constructed on a meandering 1,067 mm gauge (3 ft 6 in) track along the coast from Tōkyō to Yokohama. The first railways suited the temperament of the people of those days, in being quite unable to hurry. Eventually a narrow gauge system was extended across the country, built by both the government and private enterprise. The mountainous nature of the country called for some heavy engineering works and confirmed the original choice of a narrow gauge. When the government nationalized the 17 major private railway companies in 1906, it made itself the owner of 6,407 km (4,004 miles) of route. From an early reliance upon foreigners, the Japanese railways had quickly become self-sufficient, and a high standard of engineering was established.

A major consideration in any railway building was to take every possible precaution against the effect of earthquakes, but in spite of this much of the system, particularly the lines around Tōkyō and Yokohama, suffered terribly in the catastrophic earthquake of September 1923. Accompanied by a tidal wave and fires, it destroyed much of those two great cities. However, reconstruction was rapid, and by the early 1930s the traffic on busier parts of the system was approaching saturation point.

Plans were then made for the building of a new high-speed line, using the European standard gauge, to provide for through traffic on the most congested line (that between Tōkyō, Nagoya, Kyoto and Osaka). It was not to be a mere duplication of the existing line, but entirely new and virtually straight in order to permit of far higher speeds. The limit on existing lines was then 100 km/h (62 mph).

Development of this plan was interrupted by the Second World War, in the later stages of which the Japanese railways were severely damaged by aerial attack. Such setbacks delayed the opening of the first of the new high-speed, or *Shinkansen*, lines until 1964. Its engineering is spectacular, carrying the tracks straight through or across any obstacle, and permitting speeds of 210 km/h (130 mph) continuously. It has set the pattern not only for extensions in Japan, but also for new lines in Italy, France and West Germany. The *Shinkansen* was originally intended to be a general-purpose railway, but its popularity has proved so great that it is used exclusively for passenger traffic. Indeed, despite the fact that 90 *Shinkansen* trains leave Tōkyō every day for the south, the commuter services are badly oversaturated and the building of new high-speed lines is under way.

The unmistakable *Shinkansen* trains of Japan.

1 Guinea p198
2 Upper Volta p198
3 Morocco p198
4 Algeria p198
5 Tunisia p198
6 Zaire p199
7 Uganda see EAR p200
8 Kenya see EAR p200
9 Tanzania see EAR p200
10 Senegal p198
11 Mauritania p198
12 Mali p198
13 Sudan p197
14 Egypt p197
15 Ethiopia p197
16 Togo p199
17 Ivory Coast p198
18 Benin p199
19 Cameroon p199
20 Liberia p198
21 Ghana p199
22 Nigeria p199
23 Congo p199
24 Zambia p200
25 Botswana p201
26 Malawi p200
27 Malagasy Republic p200
28 Angola p199
29 S. W. Africa p201
30 South Africa p201
31 Zimbabwe p201
32 Mozambique p201

The development of the African rail network up to the present time can be divided into two distinct phases. The first was as an aid to colonial exploitation and expansion by several European powers, notably Britain and France. The colonial experience left Africa with a series of lines running inland from the coast: only in southern Africa were lines joined up into the semblance of a network.

The second phase began at independence. Railways were seen as a means of binding together countries which in some cases were little more than loose amalgamations of tribal areas. Separate lines were linked to form a national railway system, branch lines were built and attempts have been made to extend the railway into parts of the country not previously served.

A third, future, stage is the creation of a pan-African rail network. This can be said to have begun with the vision of Cecil Rhodes, who foresaw a line running the length of the continent, from the Cape to Cairo. Rhodes' legacy is the fact that most of the railways in southern Africa were built to the same 1,067 mm (3 ft 6 in) gauge (3 ft 6 in), and several countries are now linked together. In the 1920s, a through service operated from Cape Town to Bukama, at the upper limit of navigation on the River Congo. Southern African politics at present preclude such services, but in theory it would be possible for trains from Cape Town to travel to Kindu (Zaire); to Lobito, Angola's main port; and to Dar-es-Salaam, the capital of Tanzania.

The 1,860 km (1,162 mile) line from Zambia to Dar-es-Salaam was a major undertaking, only completed in 1975. Gabon, which emerged from the colonial era without any railways, is now building a line of 695 km (434 miles). The first section should open in 1978. Thus in Africa at least, railways are still regarded as a vital part of a nation's infrastructure.

**EGYPT** *Egyptian Republic Railways*

Although much of Egypt appears to be far from the railway, most of the population is confined to the delta and Nile valley. These inhabited areas are as well served by rail as many densely populated areas of Europe.

As early as 1834, a railway was mooted from Alexandria to Suez as a means of expediting the Indian mails. Work on such a line began in 1851 with Robert Stephenson as engineer: Cairo was reached in 1856 and Suez in 1858 (though the stretch across the desert was made unnecessary by the opening of the Suez Canal, and was dismantled 20 years later). Stephenson's appointment was no doubt responsible for the standard gauge being used on the Egyptian railways.

The system developed in two separate groups, the comprehensive network in the delta, and the Upper Egypt (or Nile valley) railway. The two were not linked at Cairo until 1898. South of Luxor, the Upper Egypt line was 1,067 mm (3 ft 6 in) gauge (standardized in 1926). At Shellal steamers waited to convey passengers to Sudan, and this line's completion in 1898 was seen as a link in Rhodes' envisaged Cape to Cairo route.

The two world wars internationalized the system further. By 1918, Egyptian stock could be seen in Jerusalem. During the Second World War, the north coast line reached 'Tobruk (Libya); and Egypt was linked with Europe when the Lebanese coastal railway was completed. Political turmoil in the Middle East since the end of the Second World War has prevented any through services from being developed.

**SUDAN** *Sudan Railways*

The first railway in Sudan opened in 1875, as a means of circumnavigating a cataract on the Nile. Running south from Wādī Halfā', it eventually extended 270km (168 miles) to Kerma. It was essentially a military railway, used by the government of Egypt (first Turkish, then British) to intervene in Sudan. Rendered unnecessary by later developments, it was closed in 1905. It was built to the same 1,067 mm (3 ft 6 in) gauge as lines then under construction in the Cape, and these two decisions undoubtedly influenced the choice of gauge for many African railways and may have sparked the idea of a Cape to Cairo line. The first of the present lines is also of military origin, built by General Kitchener across the Nubian desert to Khartoum during his campaign against the Mahdist revolt (1897–9). Kitchener was certainly aware that his line might form a part of the Cape to Cairo route and insisted upon equipment of 1,067 mm (3 ft 6 in) gauge for it.

The next quarter century saw the north effectively opened up. Trains reached the Red Sea in 1905, Al-Ubayyid in 1912 and Kassalā in 1924. The south had to be more patient: the branch south from Sennar opened in 1954, and the first trains did not reach Wāw until late in 1961. Even now the system is regarded as incomplete, as at present the provincial capital of Jūbā has only the railways-operated White Nile steamer service. Since cotton and cottonseed are the principal cash crops of Sudan, accounting for 60 per cent of the country's export earnings, the Gezira Light Railway, serving the cotton fields, is of great importance.

## Egypt

4,510 km (2,819 mls)

1,416
18,088
624
50
454
23

The steam locos all belong to the Basse Egypt Railway, a metre-gauge system of 253 route-km based at Mansura. Serving the delta is (or was) the 750 mm Egyptian Delta Light Railway, once 950 route-km but being replaced by buses. EDLR totals are therefore not included in the data panel.

## Ethiopia

* metre gauge

1,087 Km (679 mls)**

* 950 mm gauge
** including 100 km in Djibouti

Due to the civil war, few trains are now running in Ethiopia. The 950 mm gauge Northern Railway closed in 1976; mid-1977, the southern line was cut between Dire Dawa and Djibouti.

## Sudan

4,780 km (2,987 mls)

832
6,942
41,099
230
100*
6

* only about half are active

The staff figure includes those operating the river steamers over routes totalling 3,480 km. All totals exclude the 600 mm Gezira Light Railway: more than 800 km of track used only when picking cotton.

Mining and quarrying
Iron and steel production
Manufacturing centre
Oil refining
Chemical processing
Grain processing
Port
Rail depot/construction

km 0   100   200   300   600
mls 0   100   200   300

# West Africa

## ALGERIA *Société Nationale des Chemins de Fer Algériens (SNCFA)*

The first line in Algeria in 1862 and from 1863 was worked by the French Paris, Lyons and Mediterranean Railway. The PLM acquired other lines in Algeria, including some leased from the French Colonial Department. Two other major railway companies were established: the Algerian State Railway extending from Tunisia to Algiers, with a sub-centre at Oran including the 1,055 mm (3 ft 5⅜ in) gauge line south to Colomb-Béchar in the desert; and the Algerian Western Railway, worked by the PLM from 1922. In 1933 a joint administration was set up, the *CF Algériens*, but with what was now the French state railway still involved as major partner. In 1939 came financial autonomy and the present name was adopted. The line along the coast is standard. Bulk traffic transport on Algeria's railways is assuming increasing importance due to the extensive exploitation of mineral deposits. Most lines running inland are narrow gauge. Exceptions are the Touggourt branch, standardized in 1957 when oil was discovered, and the line to Djebel Onk, built to exploit phosphate deposits (part is Algeria's only electric line).

Algeria totals include all items ordered during the 5 Year Plan which ended with 1977. There are two major gauges, standard and 1,055 mm, as well as 120 km of metre gauge. 600 mm gauge military lines were the first in Morocco. Totalling 1,888 km, in 1915 they opened to the public. All have been converted to standard gauge, the first by 1923. The first electric line was energized in 1927. An Algerian line extended into what is now Tunisia in 1876. Thus the lines NW of Tunis are standard gauge. In 1897 a metre gauge line was built to exploit the phosphates at Gafsa. Today three-quarters of the system is metre gauge.

### Tunisia

2,089 km (1,306 mls)

### Morocco

2,029 km (1,261 mls)

\* 41% of the system electrified

### Algeria

3,942 km (2,450 mls)

**Map legend**
- Mining and quarrying
- Iron and steel production
- Manufacturing centre
- Oil refining
- Chemical processing
- Port
- Rail depot/construction
- Tourist centre
- Grain processing

Map labels: Tunis, Bizerta, Sousse, TUNISIA, Sfax, Djebel Onk, Constantine, Bejaia, Algiers, ALGERIA, Oran, Tanger, Meknès, Rabat, Casablanca, MOROCCO, Marrakech, Safi

Scale: km 0 100 250 500 / mls 0 300 250 200

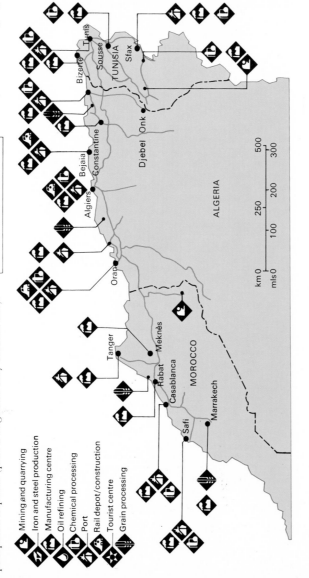
Dakar–Bamako train, Senegal.

### Ivory Coast and Upper Volta

1,173 km (730 mls) RAN

The metre gauge Ivory Coast Railway (sometimes called the CF Abidjan-Niger) runs inland from Abidjan to the capital of Upper Volta. Despite serving 2 countries, it is one administrative unit. The first stretch opened in 1904, but trains did not enter Upper Volta until 1934, and Ouagadougou until 1954. The line has been fully diesel since 1956.

### Liberia

493 km (308 mls) no standard livery

There are 3 railways in Liberia, all engaged with the mining of iron ore. All run inland from a suitable port, and the only 2 which meet (at the same port, Monrovia) are of different gauges. The first was opened in 1951, to 1,067 mm gauge. The 2 later lines, 348 km, are standard gauge, the southernmost being built for trains of 14,000 tonnes capacity.

### Guinea

939 km (587 mls)

A metre gauge line was begun in 1900. By 1914 it had reached Kankan. Construction was due to begin in 1975 on the 1,200 km standard gauge Trans-Guinea Railway, replacing some of this metre gauge. Progress made so far is unknown, and only metre gauge totals are included in the data panel (so excluding the 134 km CF de Boké, opened in 1973 with 15 diesel locos).

### Mali

642 km (399 mls) CFM no standard livery

Until the dissolution of the Federation of Mali in 1960, the lines in Senegal and Mali were part of one company, known since 1933 as the Dakar-Niger line. It was built in 4 stages by the French colonial administration to facilitate penetration of the Senegal River valley. The first line linked the mouth of the navigable Senegal River with Dakar's deep-water harbour. This

### Senegal

1,033 km (642 mls)

line, Senegal's first, opened in 1885. The next stage linked the upper limit of the Senegal navigation (at Kayes) with the Niger at Koulikoro. Begun in 1881 but not completed until 1904, this was Mali's first line. In 1924 a link between the 2 lines was opened. Since then, several branches have opened in Senegal, but there has been no railway building.

### Mauritania
650 km (404 mls)

Mauritania's railway was opened in 1963, to ship out iron ore discovered at Fdérik. Passengers are also carried. The line is standard gauge, with an odd L-shaped route caused by the need to avoid the Spanish Sahara: this added an extra 80 route-km. At Choum, where the line turns north, is a tunnel almost 2 km long. Shifting sand constantly threatens to bury 80 km of the line.

# Central Africa 1

## Ghana

Railway equipment first arrived in Ghana in 1873 when the British governor Garnet Wolseley decided it might help him to win an Ashanti war. But he managed without, and it was not until gold was discovered that a railway was considered. Construction began from Sekondi in 1898, reaching Tarkwa in 1901 after great hardships. The line got to Kumasi in 1903. Another from the capital Accra inland was begun in 1909. It finally reached Kumasi in 1923, completing a circuitous route of 583 km. A more direct route from Sekondi to Accra, via Achiasi, was completed in 1956.

↑1953 Km (592 mls)

* in store

## Nigeria

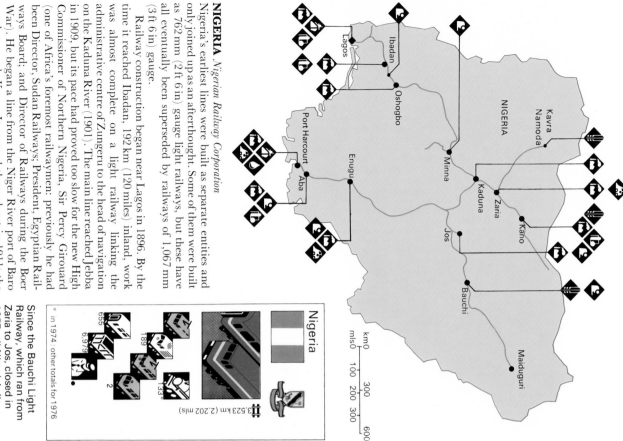

miles 0   100   200   300
km 0   300   600

**NIGERIA.** *Nigerian Railway Corporation*

Nigeria's earliest lines were built as separate entities and only joined up as an afterthought. Some of them were built as 762 mm (2 ft 6 in) gauge light railways, but these have all eventually been superseded by railways of 1,067 mm (3 ft 6 in) gauge.

Railway construction began near Lagos in 1896. By the time it reached Ibadan, 192 km (120 miles) inland, work was almost complete on a light railway linking the administrative centre of Zungeru to the head of navigation on the Kaduna River (1901). The main line reached Jebba in 1909, but its pace had proved too slow for the new High Commissioner of Northern Nigeria, Sir Percy Girouard (one of Africa's foremost railwaymen; previously he had been Director, Sudan Railways; President, Egyptian Railways Board; and Director of Railways during the Boer War). He began a line from the Niger River port of Baro north towards Kano. It opened throughout in 1911; the original line did not meet it until 1912. Work on the Eastern Railway began in 1913. It reached its initial objective – the coal near Enugu – in 1916, but did not join up with the other lines until 1926.

The last line built was the Maiduguri Extension, completed in 1964. However, an ambitious scheme contained in the Third National Development Plan (1975–80) envisages most or all of the 1,067 mm (3 ft 6 in) gauge lines being replaced by standard gauge lines. Work was scheduled to begin in 1977.

Since the Bauchi Light Railway, which ran from Zaria to Jos, closed in 1957, all Nigeria's lines have been of the 1,067 mm gauge. However, work was due to begin in 1977 on the scheme to convert the entire network to standard gauge.

iiii 3,523 km (2,202 mls)

* in 1974 – other totals for 1976

## Togo

↑442 Km (275 mls)

no standard livery

## Benin

↑579 Km (359 mls)

no standard livery

Benin and Togo have similar systems opened at about the same time (*circa* 1905). Both are metre gauge; both are fully dieselized with equipment resembling that in so many other former French colonies (though Togo was German until 1914).

## Cameroon

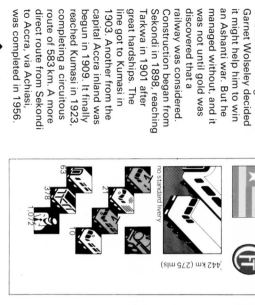

↑1,173 km (727 mls)

Cameroon's metre gauge system was begun in 1906 by the German colonial administration. After the 1914–18 War, the French extended it to Yaoundé. Since independence it has been extended another 633 km, reaching Ngaoundéré in 1974.

**ZAIRE AND CONGO** *Chemin de Fer Congo-Océan (CFCO)*

*Société Nationale des Chemins de Fer Zaïrois (SNCZ)*

Railways in Zaire and Congo make better sense if considered with the rivers which still form an integral part of the area's transport system. Zaire's first line opened in 1898 round the rapids which keep ocean-going ships below Matadi. It linked Matadi with Kinshasa, terminus of river services up the Congo, and Kasai. Congo's main railway is a similar line on the other side of the river, completed in 1934. Transport up the Congo was improved by lines round two other obstacles: from Kisangani to Ubundu, and from Kindu to Kongolo. Thence the river is navigable to Bukama. Rails reached Bukama from southern Africa in 1919, and these connections were seen as part of the Cape to Cairo route. The Congo River lines were built by a company formed in 1902 to build the missing link from the Congo to the Nile. Today such a route is partly supplied by the 600 mm (1 ft 11⅝ in) gauge Vicicongo line running west from Aketi.

## Congo

↑795 Km (497 mls)

no standard livery

## Zaire

iiii 5,245 km (3,278 mls)

## Angola

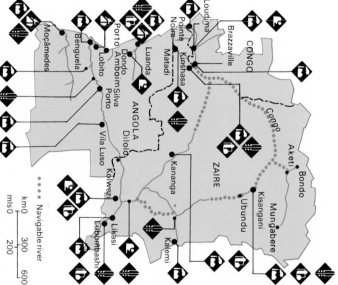

miles 0   300   600
km 0   200

···· Navigable river

**Angola** has 4 unconnected railways, each running inland from a port. Only the line from Porto Amboim is not 1,067 mm gauge, though the Luanda State Railways were regauged in the 1960s. The most important line is the Benguela, begun in 1903: it meets the Zaire system at Dilolo. But the still-smouldering civil war has stopped through traffic.

iↄ 1,244 Km (1,402 mls)

199

CENTRAL AFRICA 1

# Central Africa 11

Malagasy

883 km (559 mls)

no standard livery

15
54
86    975

Malawi's first line opened in 1908 and the system is still expanding. Since 1970 it has linked 2 separate Mozambique lines, and data panel totals do not include the 112 km Salima-Lilongwe line due to open before 1978. Malawi Railways operates the Lake Nyasa steamer service.

Malagasy's first line was opened in 1903 by the French colonial adminis-tration. The development of the northern system of lines was completed in 1923. In 1934 an isolated line opened, running inland from the port of Manakara. A 253 km line to link this to the others has been begun.

Malawi

566 km (352 mls)

2
30
23    649    3,597

## EAST AFRICAN RAILWAYS

In 1948, Tanganyika Railways and the Kenya and Uganda Railways amalgamated to form East African Railways. While the union was effective under British influence, differences between the governments arising since independence caused such difficulties that EAR has again separated into its two constituent parts.

Unusually for former British possessions in Africa, EAR operates on the metre gauge. In Tanzania's case this is because most of the lines were built by the Germans, whose colony it was until the First World War. The Kenya and Uganda Railway seems to have been built to this gauge owing to a series of misunderstandings because no one in Britain wanted it built, seeing it as a mad imperialist venture on which the expenditure of public money was unjustified. Finally, grudgingly, it was built to metre gauge because cheap second-hand equipment would be available from India.

The first line in the area was the 600 mm (1 ft 11½ in) gauge, 96 km (60 miles), Central African Railway. It was later taken up and relaid as a tramway in Mombasa. The first of the present lines was started from Tanga in 1891, but it was only 40 km (25 miles) from the coast in 1896 when building began at Mombasa. In 1901 Lake Victoria was reached, in 1914 Lake Tanganyika. Kampala's first train arrived in 1931, and Pakwach's in 1964. All these lines were built originally to aid the area's agricultural development.

### Kenya, Uganda and Tanzania EAR

5,895 km (3,663 mls)

235
192
536    17,000    43,539

Totals exclude Tazara Railway: see separate panel

The East African unified rail system is at present being dismembered, after 28 years, because of dis-agreements between owning governments. Normal services between Tanzania and Kenya ceased in 1974, and Lake Victoria wagon ferries stopped early in 1976. No figures for the individual countries are available yet.

Zambia Railways formed in 1967 when the Rhodesia Railways Unitary System split. Before, the lines were part of Rhodesia Rail-ways administered from Bulawayo. The dividing point was the centre of the Victoria Falls bridge. The first line opened in Zambia in July 1905, though the bridge was not opened until September: it was built with equipment swung across the gorge on a cableway. Before 1910, the rails were at Zaire's border. One of the line's main functions is to transport the copperbelt's production, though when opened it was seen as part of the Cape to Cairo route.

### Zambia ZR

1,044 km (0,648 mls)

3
98
86    2,980    7,800

Totals exclude Tazara Railway: see separate panel

### Tazara Railway

1,857 km (1,161 mls)

102
100    2,100

## TAZARA RAILWAY *Tanzania Zambia Railway Authority*

The Tazara Railway links Zambia Railways with Dar-es-Salaam, 970 km (600 miles) lying in Tanzania and 890 km (550 miles) in Zambia. It is run as a single entity and has therefore been kept separate from the other totals for these countries. Built with generous technical and financial assistance from China, its successful completion has with-out doubt earned China enormous prestige in Africa. China provided 25,000 men, one-third of the workforce, and an interest-free loan of £167 million with generous repayment terms. It is the largest railway construction project completed since the Second World War. The line is built to Zambia's 1,067 mm (3 ft 6 in) gauge and was completed in 1975. Over one million tonnes of freight was carried by the line in its first year of operation.

For Tanzania, the line will develop the neglected southwest, enabling vast coal and iron ore deposits to be exploited. Zambia sees the line as an essential link to that part of Africa with which she feels sympathetic. Before the Tazara line was opened, all her routes led south, and events have conspired to make her wish it had been built much earlier: Rhodesia's unilateral declaration of inde-pendence in 1965 closed the Victoria Falls route, and the Angolan civil war has seriously disrupted Benguela Rail-way traffic since 1975.

One 16 km (10 mile) section between Mlimba and Makambako in Tanzania contains 30 per cent of all earthworks, bridges and tunnels on the line, including Irangi No. 3 tunnel, which attains a length of almost 2.5 km (1.5 miles).

KENYA

Thika

Mombasa

Moshi

Arusha

Dar es Salaam

Eldoret

Nakuru

Nairobi

Kisumu

Tororo

Jinja

Kampala

UGANDA

Arua

Lake Victoria

Mwanza

Shinyanga

Mpwapwa

TANZANIA

Kigoma

ZAMBIA

Lusaka

Kitwe

Mazabuka

Livingstone

km 0    50    100    150    200    300
mls 0    100    200    300

Mining and quarrying
Iron and steel production
Manufacturing centre
Oil refining
Chemical processing
Grain processing
Port
Rail depot/construction

# Southern Africa

**SOUTH AFRICA** *South African Railways (SAR)*

The closely knit, efficient network of the South African Railways began as a series of individual and unconnected enterprises at a time when the whole land south of the Zambesi River was entirely pastoral and, being slowly colonized by Europeans whose aims extended no further than farming. Short lines were pioneered inland from Cape Town and Port Elizabeth, Mountain ranges inland, and the experiences of those who had taken part in the Great Trek, had suggested that there was little to be gained by carrying the rails further inland, until, in 1869, there came the sensational discovery of diamonds in great numbers at Kimberley. Even then, railway construction did not proceed rapidly. For one thing there was the question of gauge to be settled. The Cape Town and Wellington Railway had set out on the standard gauge, but when it came to carrying the line northward to the diamond 'diggings', and the severe terrain of the Hex River Pass had to be dealt with, the government's consulting engineer, William G. Brounger, recommended 1,067 mm (3 ft 6 in) as the standard for Cape Province. It was then that the race to connect up Kimberley with Cape Town began in earnest, while a rival line driving inland from Port Elizabeth had the same objective. Railways were the only alternative to the primitive carts used by the pioneer trekkers. Something more reliable had to be used in conveying the precious diamonds to ports from which they could be shipped to Europe.

## The gold race

An even more dramatic change came over the whole South African scene in 1886, when gold was discovered on the Witwatersrand. By a strange twist of irony this discovery, that transformed the entire economic and financial structure of South Africa, was made at the very place where the peace-loving pastoral farmers of the south had ended their trek in search of a place where they could settle and till the land. From that resting place rose Johannesburg. At the very start there was a railway race, not between trains, but between two rival organizations seeking to be first in connecting the gold fields with the sea. One was the British, under the dashing leadership of Cecil Rhodes, pressing ahead with the extension of the Cape Government Railway northward from Kimberley. The other was the Dutch coming westward from Lourenço Marques (now Maputo) in Portuguese East Africa. Due to Rhodes's tenacity and diplomacy, the first train from the south steamed into Johannesburg in September 1892, nearly three years ahead of the Dutch. In the British colony of Natal, also, railways were being pushed inland from Durban, and these came prominently into the picture as military targets during the Boer War. After the end of the war much was done to consolidate railway working in the four states that were eventually brought together in the Union of South Africa in 1910. In the period between the end of the war and the Union, the Cape Government and the Natal Government Railways had carried on as previously, while the lines in the two former Boer republics had operated under the name of the Central South African Railways. The three organizations were amalgamated to form the South African Railways shortly after the establishment of the Union.

Since 1910 the system has developed into one of the greatest in the world, operating entirely on the 1,067 mm (3 ft 6 in) gauge. In recent years great progress has been made with electrification at both ends of the system. The busy suburban area of Cape Town, and the main line as far north as Wellington, is so equipped, while the intense network around Johannesburg is a natural place for its advantages to be exploited to the full. At the same time extensive use is still being made of steam. The South African Railways, with the co-operation of British firms, developed the steam locomotive to its highest degree on the 1,067 mm (3 ft 6 in) gauge, and it is still being maintained to high standards. Except on the Blue Train, most motive power is steam in the central part of the system south of Kimberley and north of Beaufort West. The system now includes, however, the railways in the former German colony of South West Africa (now Namibia), where near-desert conditions and absence of water have favoured the introduction of diesel-electric locomotives on the line running north from De Aar Junction to Windhoek.

4-8-2 moving coal trucks at Wankie Colliery, Rhodesia.

### South Africa

8,600
175,636
1,511
924
1,097
227,820
2,030

22,426 km (13,918 mls)

figures include 2,338 route-km in Namibia, operated by SAR

### Zimbabwe (Rhodesia)

631
16,658
85
189
21,430

3,367 km (2,104 mls)*

* excluding 642 route-km in Botswana, operated by Rhodesia

Rhodesia's first line opened to Bulawayo, 1897. In 1899 Umtali-Salisbury opened, and when the two were joined in 1902, 3,256 km of continuous railway existed from Cape Town to Beira. The system was to continue north from Gwelo to Lake Tanganyika, but it was diverted to the Wankie coalfield and so crossed into what is now Zambia at Victoria Falls. Until 1967, the Zambian lines were run from Bulawayo as part of Rhodesia Railways. RR has operated the Botswana line since 1966.

### Mozambique

**CFM**

8,039
184
79
35

3,843 km (2,402 mls)

There are 6 lines in Mozambique, linking ports with the hinterland. Since 1970, 2 of the major ones are linked via Malawi, and plans exist to join them to the southern Maputo system. The first line was begun in 1892 by a contractor under pressure from Cecil Rhodes to open a line from Rhodesia to the sea quickly. Beira-Umtali was complete by 1898 and widened to 1,067 mm in 1900. Today only the line from João Belo is not this gauge. Mozambique also runs the 224 km Swaziland railway, opened in 1964.

km 0
mls 0
100
200
200
400

NAMIBIA
Walvis Bay
Swakopmund
Windhoek
Tsumeb
Cape Town
Worcester
Oudtshoorn
Mossel Bay
SOUTH AFRICA
Queenstown
Port Elizabeth
East London
Kimberley
Bloemfontein
Pietermaritzburg
Durban
BOTSWANA
ZIMBABWE (RHODESIA)
Bulawayo
Gwelo
Que Que
Salisbury
Vila Pery
Benoni
Pretoria
Johannesburg
SWAZILAND
Maputo
Beira
Vila Cabral
Entre Rios
Nampula
MOZAMBIQUE
Moçambique

# Canada and United States

## CANADA

Railway development in Canada began along the line of the St Lawrence River, with the Grand Trunk, authorized in 1852 and incorporating some earlier projects. It knew no international frontiers. When its first line was completed it ran from Sarnia through Toronto and Montreal to Portland, in the American state of Maine, and by this provided a means of communication with Europe during the winter months when the St Lawrence estuary was frozen over. At its western end it came to penetrate into the USA. It was, however, thought desirable to have a line to an Atlantic port that was independent of the USA, particularly as relations had not been entirely amicable since the War of Independence; and thus was born the concept of the "Intercolonial Railway", connecting Montreal with the maritime provinces of New Brunswick and Nova Scotia. After much discussion, extending over more than 20 years, the Intercolonial was authorized, and built by that great engineer Sandford Fleming, who later made the first surveys for the Canadian Pacific. The undertaking to build a railway connecting British Columbia with the eastern provinces was contained in an agreement signed in Ottawa in July 1870, and Fleming's first surveys led the federal government to decide that the line should pass through the main range of the Rockies by the Yellowhead Pass.

Although some contracts were let for the western end of the line, eastwards from Vancouver, progress of the work under government control was slow and unsatisfactory, and it was not until ten years after the signing of the Ottawa agreement of 1870 that the work was put on a sound business footing. An agreement was signed in England in September 1880 between the government and a syndicate of Canadian businessmen, the work of construction being handed over to a company to be formed by the syndicate. The "big four" of this arrangement were George Stephen, Donald A. Smith, afterwards Lord Strathcona, R. B. Angus, and a fiery entrepreneur named J. J. Hill. It was the last mentioned who made perhaps the greatest contribution of all, because he brought in, as general manager, that most outstanding of railwaymen, W. C. van Horne, then an American citizen. The line across Canada was completed in November 1885, with the driving of the last spike at Craigellachie, in the Rockies of British Columbia.

The success of the Canadian Pacific in developing the prairie regions, and as King George V, when Prince of Wales, said in a speech made in London in May 1908: ". . . helped to make a Nation", led to the building of competitive lines. Although when it came to the actual construction, the Canadian Pacific did not go through the Yellowhead Pass, but took the shorter, but far more difficult Kicking Horse Pass, its two rivals from Winnipeg to Pacific tidewater both went through the Yellowhead, abreast of each other, the Canadian Northern to come

abreast of the Canadian Pacific in the canyons west of Kamloops, and eventually to reach Vancouver, and the Grand Trunk Pacific to continue northwestwards through absolutely virgin country to Prince Rupert. Both these railroads, and the lines connecting with them from the east at Winnipeg, fell into financial difficulties, and were kept going during the First World War by substantial government loans. All these diverse lines were finally amalgamated with the Grand Trunk and the Intercolonial in 1922 to form the huge Canadian National Railways, publicly owned, and working alongside the privately owned Canadian Pacific.

The great majority of the powered coaching stock is diesel. A few are electric, and there are also 10 Turbotrain sets. The wagons total excludes 17,700 privately owned. The figures are for 1973, the latest available.

Canada

🍁

|||||||| 70,771 km (44,232 mls)

14
3,748
·130
2,175
·186,653

· see caption, right

## USA

In the USA railways began with projects to connect the Atlantic seaports with the rich valley of the Ohio River, between which lay densely wooded mountain ranges of the Alleghenies and the Appalachians. The Baltimore and Ohio, dating from 1827, and the Chesapeake and Ohio, by their names indicate the extent of their first activities. Another famous early line was the Pennsylvania, from Pittsburgh over the Alleghenies, to Atlantic tidewater at Philadelphia. West of the mountains a considerable network began to develop from Chicago and St Louis down the valley of the Mississippi. This was one of the main battle areas in the American Civil War, and the railways came to play a major part in the conflict. It was during the war that Abraham Lincoln realized the importance of having communication with the west coast, and ordered the hasty completion of the partly finished lines of the Union Pacific and Central Pacific, to meet in the famous "gold spike" ceremony at Promontory, Utah, in 1869. In the meantime the great proliferation of lines radiating from Chicago earned that city its title of the greatest railway centre in the world.

### Famous routes

In main lines alone, running southwest and west there are no fewer than four different routes to Kansas City and beyond — those of the Illinois Central Gulf, the Santa Fe, the Rock Island and the Burlington; while to Omaha, en route to the far west there are five routes, all covering different tracts of the intervening country. Due northwards, jockeying for position as it were beside the shores of Lake Michigan, are the Chicago North Western and the Chicago, Milwaukee, St Paul and Pacific, once steam rivals in a high-speed passenger service. From the east, crowding round the head of the lake, come the Baltimore and Ohio, the New York Central, the Pennsylvania and others — great names, some now merged in recent amalgamations — with the Wabash, the Monon, and the Illinois Central coming up from the south.

The discovery of gold in the Colorado Rockies, coupled with the extreme difficulty of the terrain, led to the building of a network of narrow gauge lines, weaving their ways through seemingly impossible mountain gorges. One of the most famous of these, remaining today as a major standard gauge artery through this region, is the Denver and Rio Grande Western. Two other routes to the west coast were the Atchison, Topeka and Santa Fe, from Chicago, through Kansas City and Albuquerque to Los Angeles, and the Great Northern, from St Paul running just south of the Canadian border, and rivalling the Canadian Pacific, to Spokane and Seattle. But the Great Northern did not have the territory south of the US border to itself. From Minneapolis westward there were two other routes, those of the Northern Pacific, and of the Chicago, Milwaukee, St Paul and Pacific. All three by diverse routes made their way to Spokane, and then through the highly picturesque Cascade Range to the west coast. Today the Great Northern and the Northern Pacific are included in the Burlington Northern Railroad, running in a degree of competition with the Milwaukee. Connecting the cities of the west coast, and continuing south and adjacent to the Mexican border was the Southern Pacific, to New Orleans.

### Into the twentieth century

Towards the end of the nineteenth century railways covered the entire United States, and the numerous private companies entered the new century on a great wave of confidence and prosperity. A huge manufacturing industry had grown up to supply the needs of the railways in locomotives, carriages, wagons, signalling and track equipment. Few of the railway companies built their own, though some, like the Pennsylvania, had extensive research facilities. Names like the New York Central, Union Pacific, Norfolk and Western, Erie, Louisville and Nashville, quite apart from the great pioneers, became household words in the world of transport. Delegations from celebrated railways in Europe travelled to the USA to study methods; and although exuberance and overconfidence sometimes led to bad accidents and serious loss of life, a tremendous "bank" of experience in operation was being built up, of which the benefit was reaped in later years.

*Below* Streaking through the Rockies.

*Bottom* Toronto sunset.

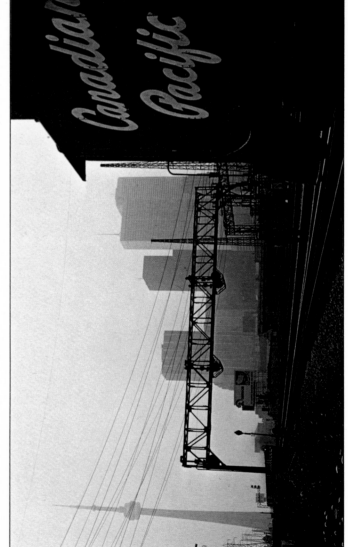

The railways of the USA, compared with those at the scene of conflict, were very little affected by the First World War, although in 1917, almost nine months after the USA declared war on the Axis powers, Woodrow Wilson put the whole system under government control — a measure that was to be enforced for over two years.

American railways entered on the period between the two world wars with renewed strength and for a short period were moderately successful. It was then that serious competition, from the increasing use of road haulage, began to strike, although because of the sometimes great distances involved it was at first not as serious a threat as that seen in such countries as Britain. But the period of the great slump of the 1930s struck hard, leading to a decline in equipment and manpower. Despite these setbacks many spectacular new services, using diesel power, were introduced.

The Second World War, on two fronts, made tremendous demands, particularly to the Pacific coast, and modern signalling technology was applied towards securing a greater throughput of trains on single-line sections. Both steam and diesel locomotives were called upon for outstanding feats, not only of power output but of aggregate distances travelled per month. In the immediate postwar era British engineers went to the USA to learn how it had been done. But the great recession soon started.

With the rapid development of internal airlines it became out of fashion to travel by train. Patronage of great express trains of international fame, such as The Twentieth Century Limited, languished; postal traffic was transferred to the air, and a train like the Fast Mail of the Santa Fe found itself with no business at all, and long-distance "trucking" on state subsidized highways began to supersede the freight train. Several famous railways went bankrupt. Others wished to discontinue altogether their unprofitable passenger business. This the federal government would not allow, and in 1971 the National Railroad Passenger Corporation (Amtrak) was set up, to support

the operation of inter-city passenger trains with federal funds. This provides a network of main line passenger services, while in the meantime, with greatly improved technology and immense drive, the railways themselves began to win back much of the freight traffic lost to the roads. There have been major amalgamations of companies, and much pruning of hitherto redundant services. The largest of the mergers has been that of Conrail, a grouping of six bankrupt eastern railways, supported by a large loan from the federal government. This group includes such previous giants as the Pennsylvania and the New York Central, the financial plight of which is enough to show the severity of the recession suffered by the American railways generally after the end of the Second World War.

Today, besides the activities of Amtrak, the principal accent is upon freight, in which the American railways have developed to an unparalleled extent the technology of handling huge loads at medium-high speed. At the points of traffic concentration all the latest marshalling yards are fully computerized, while the operations over entire railways, like the Southern at Atlanta, are visually controlled from a single operations centre, by remotely controlled colour light signalling, and radio communication with train crews. The art of handling such great trains at speed, and particularly on steep gradients, has become a highly developed science.

*Below left* Rio Grande — Durango loco 473 on turntable.

America's railways are divided into Class I and Class II 'roads'. Class I are those with annual operating revenues which exceed $10m. There were 52 in 1977, owning 96% of America's lines. Figures are for Class I only.

USA

Amtrak

319,058 km (199,411 mls)

216
27,350
1,590
230
1,331,705
6,471
482,882

* excluding cabooses

Mining and quarrying
Iron and steel production
Manufacturing centre
Oil refining
Chemical processing
Grain processing
Port
Rail depot/construction
Tourist centre

# Central America

## Mexico

17,262 km (10,789 mls)

1,305  54  1,611  33,669

NdeM carries only 82% of all rail traffic. Figures include other lines which own carriages. The last steam and only electric locos work mineral lines.

Central America may be divided into two parts: Mexico, and the rest, for Mexico alone has acquired a nationwide network, originally inspired by engineers and capital from the USA. In the rest of Central America, interest has concentrated on providing trans-isthmus routes and, with the exception of Mexico, none of these have been developed into adequate national rail systems. This can be attributed in part to the difficult terrain which makes railway construction so difficult, and in part to the climate which compounds these difficulties (the torrential rain leading to frequent washouts). But, generally speaking, the railways here, like those in Africa, have been built by outside interests for purposes of exploitation rather than national development.

The first Central American railway was built to provide transport across the isthmus. The Panama Railroad, which opened in 1855, saved so much time and money by cutting out the voyage around Cape Horn that it was able to charge passengers US$25 for the 77 km (48 mile) journey. Another proposal was for a "Ship Railway", with six lines of rails which would carry ships bodily across the isthmus. More recently, some banana-growing states have had lines built by the United Fruit Company of Boston and the Standard Fruit Company of New Orleans, as the best means of facilitating the immediate shipment that this kind of fruit requires.

**Map legend:**
- Mining and quarrying
- Iron and steel production
- Manufacturing centre
- Oil refining
- Chemical processing
- Grain processing
- Port
- Rail depot/construction

Map places: Mérida, Veracruz, Tampico, Ciudad Victoria, Monterrey, Ojinaga, Chihuaha, Gómez Palacio, Durango, Zacatecas, Aguascalientes, León, Guadalajara, Mexico City, Ciudad Juárez, Hermosillo, Ciudad Obregón, Culiacán, Nogales, Mexicali

km 0 200 400 600
mls 0 100 200 300

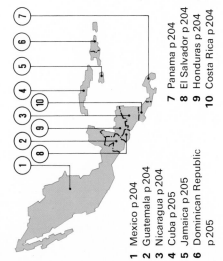

1  Mexico p204
2  Guatemala p204
3  Nicaragua p204
4  Cuba p205
5  Jamaica p205
6  Dominican Republic p205
7  Panama p204
8  El Salvador p204
9  Honduras p204
10 Costa Rica p204

## MEXICO FC Nacionales de Mexico (N de M)

Mexico's first train ran in 1850, but the bulk of the present, extensive, network was constructed in the 20 years after 1880. During that time, 12,300 km (7,687 miles) were built. Most lines are standard gauge, but the nationalized system N de M operates 450 km (280 miles) of 914 mm (3 ft) narrow gauge.

The creation of N de M began in 1908 with the amalgamation of the National Rail Road of Mexico with the Mexican Central Railway. Other railways have been acquired since, but at least two large lines remain independently managed and N de M can claim to comprise only 71 per cent of the Mexican railway system.

The largest of the independents is the FC del Pacifico, once a subsidiary of the USA's Southern Pacific. It stretches 2,140 km (1,330 miles) from Guadalajara to the US border. Incorporated in 1909, this company opened throughout only in 1927.

## Panama

441 km (263 mls)

29  51  49  1,817  880

Panama has 3 independent lines. The first opened in 1855, a predecessor of the Canal as a means of crossing the Isthmus. It is 1,524 mm gauge. In 1914 a line was begun from the Pacific port of Armuelles, intended to be part of an intercontinental Mexico-Argentina line. In the NW a line owned by an American company runs 48 km into Costa Rica.

## Costa Rica

757 km (473 mls)

1  34  14  81  135  1,881

figures exclude a 48 route-km plantation railway

The original concession for a Costa Rican railway was granted in 1871, but it was not finished until 1890. Running from the Caribbean port of Limón to San José, it connects with the electrified Pacific Railroad to form a route from sea to sea. The Pacific opened in 1910 and was electrified in 1930. Isolated in the south is the FC del Sur.

## Nicaragua

318 km (197 mls)

9  10  4*  820  194  1

no standard livery

* multiple unit sets: there are also 2 petrol railcars

The only railway of any importance in Nicaragua is the FC del Pacifico, both owned and operated by the government. The initial section, from Corinto to Chinandega, was opened in 1881. The line was finished in 1903, though Granada the inland terminus had been linked to the railhead since 1886 by a lake steamer service. The gauge is 1,067 mm.

## El Salvador

620 km (385 mls)

36  11  21  85  747

no standard livery

Ferrocarriles Nacional El Salvador were established in 1975 with the merger of 2 lines previously nationalized. The larger section was part of International Railways of Central America until 1974 (still operating in Guatemala). Steam locos may now not be working, as the government was hoping to upgrade the San Salvador-Acajutla line by mid-1976.

## Honduras

522 km (326 mls)

12  24  67  64  2,832

Honduras's route total is unreliable, because only one quarter of the lines are owned by the government: the others belong to American fruit-growing concerns (though all have passenger services). One of the private railways is built to 914 mm gauge, the rest (just over half of the total) to 1,067 mm. Honduras's first train ran in 1869.

## Guatemala

914 km (571 mls)

90  23  28  169  2,285

no standard livery

figures include privately-owned passenger carrying lines

The main rail network in Guatemala belongs to the International Railways of Central America, one of whose lines crosses into El Salvador (where it has been nationalized). This company formed in 1904, though Guatemala's first train had run in 1880. Totals include 95 km owned bu a subsidiary of the American United Fruit Co. Lines are 914 mm gauge.

Railway construction in South America started very late, as it was dependent upon the availability of foreign finance, and adversely affected by the lack of political stability. However, most of the network now existing was completed by 1930. Because many of the countries had closer ties with Europe and the USA than with each other, South America appears like a group of islands: the separate hinterlands of each port and their railway lines are often isolated from each other except by sea. One result has been that a profusion of gauges were used, at least nine existing in substantial route lengths being found on the continent. But much of South America's traffic is still of the mine-to-port pattern and the lack of inter-regional trade has not yet made the break-of-gauge the acute problem it has been in, for example, Australia. The decision of Paraguay to alter its gauge in 1911, to make through working with Argentina possible, was an isolated, early, example of a change which may become increasingly common in the next decade as South America progresses towards the creation of a standardized rail system that will eventually cover the whole of the continental land mass and become a major aid to economic growth.

## Jamaica

34
382
1,454

330 km (205 mls)

figures exclude 43 route-km of mineral railways

Jamaica's first train ran in 1845, on the first ever British colonial railway. Now the bauxite industry provides most traffic (and 2 mine companies own more wagons than the state). Jamaica's railways suffer from road competition: passenger services have ended and the narrow gauge government lines may have shut completely.

## Cuba

34
382
6
1,454

4,425 km (2,750 mls)*

*excludes 9,441 km sugar lines
**at least 11 route-km electric

Cuba has the densest system in the Caribbean, but information is sparse. The diesel loco total is a minimum, representing known orders only. The vast network of sugar industry lines is only used 100 days a year.

## Dominican Republic

28
1,800

560 km (348 mls)*

no standard livery
*no passenger services
*total track length

**COLOMBIA** *Ferrocarriles Nacionales de Colombia* (FCN) Although Colombia is the third most populous country in South America, its railway system is somewhat inadequate. Partly this is due to the mountains which divide the country into several regions between which transport of any kind has always been difficult. Partly it is due to political upheavals which culminated in civil war in 1899: foreign capital was difficult to attract, and the few lines which were built cost the government dear. As a result, a national rail system was a long time forming, and Bogotá, the capital was for long of secondary importance to the city of Cali, which was first in acquiring an outlet to the sea. To this day, the link between Bogotá and the Pacific port of Buenaventura is extremely circuitous and the missing 110 km (69 miles) of the direct route, from Ibagué to Armenia, is no more than a project: an attempt to build it started in 1913 but was finally abandoned in 1930. The Atlantic line was not completed until 1961.

## Colombia

FCN

no standard livery

336
7,664
11,291
146
32
30

3,460 km (2,135 mls)

The stock totals for Colombia must be treated with caution, for the sources are confused, particularly about the extent of dieselization. The long-drawn-out process of nationalization (it was started in 1901 and only completed in 1962) has enabled the gauge of Colombia's lines to be made uniform at 914mm.

## Venezuela

22
200
10

175 km (109 mls)*

*another 1,160 km scheduled to open in 1979

Venezuela's first line was begun in 1873. About 1,000 km of narrow gauge lines were built by 1894, but all have now closed, the last in 1967. The government is now building a standard gauge network, which should extend to 1,339 km in 1979. There are also 3 mineral lines totalling 96 route-km (and not included in the data panel figures).

**ECUADOR** *Empresa de Nacional de Ferrocarriles del Estado* Railways arrived in Ecuador in 1871, when the line from Guayaquil up to Quito, the capital, was begun. Geographical and financial difficulties ensured that it was not finished until 1908. Although its 3,609 m (11,841 ft) summit is not high by South American standards, it is one of the more dramatic Andean lines. The total curvature of the line amounts to 16,000 degrees, the equivalent of 45 complete circles; many have a radius of only 60.35 m (198 ft). Between Sibambe and Palmira, the line climbs 1,433 m (4,700 ft) in only 35 km (22 miles), on an actual gradient of 1 in 18; compensated for the curvature, this equals a straight 1 in 15. It is entirely adhesion worked. It accounts for 40 per cent of Ecuador's route length. Making a junction with it are two other 1,067 mm (3 ft 6 in) gauge lines, and there are also two isolated narrower-gauged lines on the coast, at Bahía and Puerto Bolívar. Much of the equipment in use on the G & Q is very old.

## Ecuador

46
499
14
53
39

1,120 km (696 mls)

The Ecuador totals are for the nationalized railways and exclude several sugar plantation lines. Included are four 1,067 mm gauge lines (one of which is an isolated 25 km at Puerto Bolívar) and two separate 750 mm lines totalling 96 km. The main system is under 3 divisional managements: Guayaquil-Quito, the Cuenca branch, and the San Lorenzo line.

## Surinam

22
58
8
3

86 km (53 mls)

totals refer only to the metre gauge government railway

no standard livery

The Dutch colonial government thought railways were unnecessary in Surinam, because of the waterways, but eventually opened a metre gauge line from Onverwacht to Brownsweg. It may close because of road competition (which has already happened in neighbouring Guyana), but 70 km of standard gauge will soon be open to exploit bauxite mines in the west.

1 Ecuador p 205
2 Columbia p 205
3 Venezuela p 205
4 Brazil p 207
5 Surinam p 205
6 Peru p 207
7 Bolivia p 207
8 Paraguay p 206
9 Uruguay p 206
10 Argentina p 206
11 Chile p 206

ECUADOR
Latacunga
Ambato
Riobamba
Quito
Guayaquil
Cali
Palmira
Popayán
Armenia
Manizales
Medellín
Bogotá
Tunja
Bucaramanga
Cúcuta
Puerto Berío
COLOMBIA

km
0 100 200 300
mls
0 200 400 600

# South America 11

**CHILE** *Empresa de Los Ferrocarriles del Estado (FFCCE)*

Chile claims that the line from Caldera to Copiapó, which opened in 1852, is the oldest in South America. It was not the first, however: that honour goes to a now-defunct railway in Guyana. The Caldera line was built by the American William Wheelwright to exploit the silver and copper ores of Atacama Province. Chile's mineral wealth stimulated many of the early railways. The government became involved from an early date, through having to step in to keep open lines whose economic justification (a mine) had closed. In 1873, the Organic Law for Railway Operation was passed. It established the state railway administration and a plan for a national railway construction policy. The plan envisaged a north-south trunk line through the Central Valley, with cross branches to the coast and to the foothills of the Andes. Today, Chile's rail system conforms very closely to the ideas established by this Law. When it was passed, there existed 950 km (594 miles) of government-owned, and 1,254 km (784 miles) of privately-owned, lines. However, it was not intended to be a vehicle for the nationalization of the railways, and today almost 1,900 km (1,187 miles) of line are still in private ownership. The largest such line is the Antofagasta (Chile) and Bolivia Railway, which operates a metre gauge line over the Andes with a weekly through train to the Bolivian capital, La Paz. It is one of the most financially successful of the Andean lines. Three other lines cross the Andes, including the Arica–La Paz Railway which is isolated from the rest of the Chilean system.

**PARAGUAY** *FC Presidente Carlos Antonio Lopez (PCAL)*

The first section of what is now the PCAL, from Asunción to Paraguarí, was built to a 1,676 mm (5 ft 6 in) broad gauge by British engineers employed by the government, and opened in 1861. Political upheavals delayed further construction until after 1889, when the Paraguay Central Railway Company was formed in London and continued construction under government guarantee. Rails finally reached Encarnación in 1911, across the River Paraná from the Argentine North Eastern Railway. To permit through traffic (carried on a train ferry), the Paraguayan system was converted to the Argentinian line's standard gauge in the same year. Little has changed since. The government bought out the British company in 1961 and it was given its present name in 1964. But the only sign of the modern era is the ten railcars purchased in 1971.

**URUGUAY** *Administración de Ferrocarriles del Estado*

Most of Uruguay consists of rolling plains. Even the hills in the north do not rise above 610 m (2,000 ft). In this easy countryside was built a comprehensive network, one of the densest national systems in South America, mostly by British interests and mostly between 1865 and 1915. The first line was opened in 1872 by a company which four years later became the Central Uruguay Railway and which grew into one of the three railway groups owning Uruguay's railways when all were nationalized in 1952. Projects are under way to extend the present system and three new lines are planned.

Uruguay's lines are all standard gauge, reducing the usefulness of the connections with railways in Brazil: all Brazil's lines at the border are metre.

**ARGENTINA** *Ferrocarriles Argentinos (FA)*

The construction of Argentina's first line began in 1855, built by the English engineer William Bragge using equipment originally destined for the Crimean War which was of the broad gauge of 1,676 mm (5 ft 6 in). The first section opened in 1857. The broad gauge, however accidentally established, was used for all early lines and almost 23,000 km (14,375 miles) now exist. But in 1872, the metre gauge was chosen for the line from Córdoba to Tucumán: it has grown into a system of 13,461 km (8,413 miles). In 1874, the East Argentina Railway chose the standard gauge, and the country now has 3,086 km (1,929 miles) of it. However, there are few problems with breaks of gauge: nearly all the lines were built to facilitate the export of agricultural produce, and nearly all the original railways, of whatever gauge, had access to the port of Buenos Aires, from which the Argentine system spreads like a gigantic fan. Much of the traffic still flows in this pattern, radiating from Buenos Aires. The British maintained their early interest in the development of Argentina's railways, and by the 1920s about 70 per cent were British owned. Much of the equipment is still very British in appearance. The railways were nationalized in 1947. Today the state system is divided into six "Lines", each named after an army general. Four of these "Lines" are 1,676 mm (5 ft 6 in) broad gauge, and there is one standard and one metre.

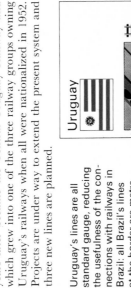

Paraguay

↧ 440 km (273 mls) *

no standard livery

22
10
915
196
13

* all figures exclude 613 km industrial lines

Paraguay has 4 separate railways, but only 1 caters for passengers, the PCAL (see right): so the totals are for this line only, although it operates only 42 % of the country's total railway route length.

Chile

▮▮▮ 9,100 km (5,687 mls)

341
17*
33*
307
157
956
16,544

Chile's figures include privately-owned, passenger carrying lines. Of the 5 gauges, the commonest are 1,676 mm and metre.

* multiple unit sets : excludes at least 22 diesel railcars

Uruguay

⊞ 3,008 km (1,866 mls)

156
31*
107
9,985
189*
3,569

* excludes 15 diesel multiple unit sets

Argentina

▮▮▮▮▮▮▮ 40,023 km (25,014 mls)

510
6
709
131
440
160,500
3,046
43,393

figures include only stock actually in service in 1976

A new, military, administration took over FA in April 1976 and discovered that half of the diesel-electric loco fleet was out of service due to a shortage of spares. The stock totals are for those in service at end 1976.

Mining and quarrying
Iron and steel production
Manufacturing centre
Oil refining
Chemical processing
Grain processing
Port
Rail depot/construction

km
800 600 400 300 200 100 0
mls
500 400 300 200 100 0

Paraguay — Villarrica, Asunción, Formosa, Corrientes, Resistencia, Paraná, Rosario, Junín

Salto, Paysandú, URUGUAY, Buenos Aires, La Plata, Montevideo, Mar del Plata, Coronel Dorrego, Bahía Blanca

Oran, Salta, Jujuy, Villazón, Tucumán, Santiago del Estero, Córdoba, San Luis, San Juan, Mendoza, Santiago, Rancagua, ARGENTINA, Comodoro Rivadavia

Arica, Pisagua, Iquique, Antofagasta, Taltal, Coquimbo, CHILE, Viña del Mar, Valparaíso, Talca, Chillán, Talcahuano, Concepción, Valdivia, Osorno, Puerto Montt

Argentina – traditional steam.

## PERU Empresa Nacional de Ferrocarriles del Perú (ENAFER-PERU)

The railways of Peru are lines running inland from ports, some to serve sugar plantations and two to assault the Andes. But however dramatic the achievement of operating over the Andes, Peru has nothing approaching a rail network. Since 1972, though, the railways have been nationalized, and present government plans would do much to remedy this. A coastal line from Nazca north through Lima to Chimbote, and the joining of the trans-Andean lines by building from Cuzco to Huancayo, are the major proposals. The latter is hardly new, as it was first surveyed in 1907. At present only the two Andean lines are of much importance. Both were built by the American engineer Henry Meiggs, though he died before the more spectacular, the Peru Central, was completed. It climbs 4,783 m (15,693 ft) with a ruling 1 in 23 gradient between stations on the upper section. It is adhesion worked throughout (see also page 19). A mineral siding off this line rises to the highest altitude ever achieved by a railway. At Oroya is the junction for the erstwhile Cerro de Pasco Railway, whose lowest point is 3,740 m (12,272 ft) above sea level and which advertised itself as "a railway on the roof of the world". Only just eclipsed by these achievements is Meiggs's other line, the Southern. It connects the coast with Lake Titicaca, where the railway runs a steamer service at 3,818 m (12,526 ft) – the highest navigation in the world. This single-line track depends on freight traffic for its survival, although the expanding tourist trade is giving it a new importance.

### Peru

Empresa Nacional de Ferrocarriles del Perú (ENAFER-PERU)

2,159 km (1,349 mls)

219
4,968
110
10
64

totals include passenger-carrying mineral lines

The trans-Andine lines are both standard gauge. 354 km of 914 mm gauge lines are also included in the figures but at least two mineral railways have been excluded. Also excluded is the 138 km Chimbote-Huallanca Railway, thought to be still closed after being badly damaged in an earthquake in 1970.

## BRAZIL Rede Ferroviária Federal SA (RFFSA)

The geography of Brazil has been a great obstacle to railway development, and this vast country of over 8 million sq km (3 million sq miles) has only 33,000 km (20,625 miles) of railway. Ninety per cent of the total is to be found within 480 km (300 miles) of the coast. This reluctance to penetrate the interior stems from the difficulty of ascending the steep scarp on to the interior plateau, and the neglect from which the Amazon basin has suffered until only very recently. The escarpment exercised the talents of several early engineers, including Robert Stephenson who produced a report for a projected line from Santos to the interior as early as 1839. The English engineer James Brunlees produced a spectacular solution in the 1850s: the São Paulo Railway ascended on an incline 8.5 km (5.3 miles) long, with cable haulage on a gradient of 1 in 10. In Amazonia, the first attempt to build a line, in 1878, was defeated by fever. It was promoted for a traditional nineteenth-century reason, to go around a set of rapids blocking navigation of the River Madeira. After the discovery of quinine it was retackled, successfully; this time, in 1908. This railway is the only one in the vast Amazonia region. Only recently has Brazil realized the economic potential of the interior. The government made a dramatic gesture to publicize the possibilities by creating a new capital 960 km (600 miles) inland in 1960. A new line was completed to Brasília in 1968, and during a Five Year Plan ending in 1979, the government is attempting to construct another 2,500 km (1,560 miles) of line and to some extent standardize gauges.

### Brazil

33,028 km (20,643 mls)

227
1,618
340
34
3,744
56,635
153,614

The RFFSA system owns less than 80% of Brazil's lines: the railways in the state of São Paulo are managed independently, and the totals also include 1,000 km of other independent passenger lines.

In the landlocked Andean state of Bolivia, below, railways are particularly important. There are two metre gauge systems, one linking with the Pacific ports of Antofagasta (see p 19), and Arica; the other connecting with Santos and Buenos Aires. The missing 300 km link, from Aiquile to Florida, is now being surveyed; its construction will complete a through, transcontinental, route of 3,784 km. Operating conditions are severe. The first diesels found the rarefied atmosphere indigestible, and had to be supercharged and have the brake compressors enlarged. The line down to La Paz is adhesion worked on a gradient of 1 in 14.

### Bolivia

3,581 km (2,238 mls)

14
60
16
80
149
1,578
7,900

* excludes 10 diesel multiple unit sets

# Australia and New Zealand

## Map legend

- Mining and quarrying
- Iron and steel production
- Manufacturing centre
- Oil refining
- Chemical processing
- Grain processing
- Port
- Rail depot/construction
- Tourist centre

### New Zealand

🚂 4,797 km (2,998 mls)*

*all figures exclude 23 km privately-owned railway

### Australia

🚂 42,033 km (26,271 mls)

Commonwealth Railways livery

* electric railcars and multiple units included with coaches

Christchurch to Greymouth railcar crossing Rough Creek just before arriving at Arthur's Pass.

The livery shown in the data panel is that of the Australian National Railways. There are 4 other major rail transport organizations, run by individual states. The totals exclude almost 1,000 km of standard gauge mineral lines, the largest of which, the 382 km Hamersley Iron Railway owns 47 diesel locos. There are 3 major track gauges: 1,600 mm gauge with 24% of the total route length; standard gauge with 34%; and 1,067 mm narrow gauge with 42%. Small amounts of narrower gauges remain, including the 762 mm gauge Puffing Billy Railway retained by the Victoria Government Railways for tourists.

## AUSTRALIA *Australian National Railways*

Railways in Australia began when the separate states were sparsely settled colonies in which matters of transport were controlled by the War Office in London. Work began with local enterprises in Melbourne (1854), Sydney (1855) and Adelaide (1855), but at an early date all were taken over by their respective state governments. In London concern was felt that all these independent projects should be built to the same gauge, but through intransigence and lack of communication New South Wales adopted the European standard while Victoria and South Australia adopted the Irish broad gauge standard of 1,600 mm (5 ft 3 in). In Queensland and Western Australia, which were thought at first to be beyond any unified state system, the 1,067 mm (3 ft 6 in) gauge was adopted to enable a greater length to be built for a given capital outlay. When the Commonwealth of Australia was set up in 1901 an inducement offered to Western Australia was that a line of railway would be built across the Nullarbor Plain to connect the state with those farther east. For this line, with a view to future standardization, the European standard gauge was chosen. It was not however until 1970, when the construction of further standard gauge lines was complete, that it became possible to travel without change of carriage from one side of the continent to the other, between Sydney and Perth, Western Australia.

The great conurbations of Sydney and Melbourne, with nearly half the total population of Australia concentrated around the two cities, led to the electrification of the suburban lines at an early date. In Sydney preparations had begun even before the First World War, but the system was greatly developed with the opening of the Sydney Harbour Bridge in 1932, and the opening in 1956 of the Circular Quay Loop on the underground line. In Melbourne, where at the great Flinders Street station all the passenger traffic is worked by multiple-unit electric trains, work is now in progress on a quadruple-tracked underground loop, which is planned to spread the traffic flow more evenly round the city centre. The new tracks will have a capacity of 24 trains an hour and the station will be able to handle up to 130,000 passengers an hour.

One of the most important recent developments in Australian railway working has been the establishment of a number of long single-purpose mineral hauls. Some of these, such as the iron ore run from Koolyanobbing, near Kalgoorlie, to the port of Kwinana, near Fremantle, and the coal runs in Queensland, are over state railway tracks; but in northwestern Australia great industrial organizations, such as Hamersley Iron, have built their own railways to act as a giant conveyor belt from the mines to the port of shipment. These special railways have been built to carry a clearly defined tonnage of mineral every day and the traffic regulation is thereby simplified from that necessary, for example, on the Western Australia main line, where the lengthy ore trains have to be accommodated amid an otherwise mixed traffic, including some prestige passenger trains like the transcontinental Indian-Pacific.

## NEW ZEALAND *New Zealand Government Railways*

Early local railway enterprises in New Zealand, all in the South Island, had resulted in the construction of no more than 74 km (46 miles) of line being opened to traffic by 1870; but in that year Julius Vogel, Colonial Treasurer, in a notable immigration and public works scheme, put forward proposals for construction of some 2,400 km (1,500 miles) of "cheap" railway to open up the country. The idea was that as the traffic grew so the railways would be improved. As a result, by 1880, 1,891 km (1,182 miles) of track had been laid and opened to traffic, including the 590 km (369 mile) South Island trunk line between Christchurch and Invercargill. In the North Island progress was slower, due to the central mountainous country; but by 1886 there was a 400 km (250 mile) line between Wellington and New Plymouth, run by the Manawatu Company. The North Island Main Trunk line, 682 km (426 miles) long between Wellington and Auckland, was not completed until 1908, including the famous Raurimu spiral, referred to in detail on page 98. In the South Island, the Otago Central line, providing a connection "over the garden wall", as it was jocularly described, between Dunedin, Alexandra and Cromwell, was a somewhat protracted enterprise running through very rugged mountain country. Begun in 1877, it was not finally opened throughout until 1921. In 1923 Westland was connected with Canterbury through the Otira Tunnel, but it was not until 1945 that the link between Christchurch and the present ferry port of Picton was completed. In the 1950s several new lines were built to tap large man-made forests in the North Island, and from 1968 onwards great improvements have been made in many areas to shorten distances, ease gradients and reduce curvature on the "cheap" railways built under the 1870 plan.

The 2 steam locos have been retained by NZR to operate passenger trains between Lumsden and Kingston as a tourist attraction. Most of the electrified lines are within the Wellington suburban area, but the 14 km over Arthur's Pass, from Otira, is electric too. NZR operates a train ferry between the islands.

208

# Reference

# Chronology

## Timeline 1800–1815

- **1801** Surrey Iron Railway incorporated and sanctioned by Parliament
- **1803** Surrey Iron Railway, first public goods line in world
- **1813** William Chapman patents
- **1815** First American railroa[d]
- **1814** George Stephenson
- **1800** Richard Trevithick constructs low-pressure steam engine
- **1806** Swansea and Mumbles Railway
- **1804** Oystermouth (Swansea and Mumbles) Railway incorporated
- **1803** Trevithick builds first steam rail locomotive for passengers
- **1807** Experiment with sail power on Swansea and Mumbles Railway
- **1807** Swansea and Mumbles Railway conveys first fare-paying passengers
- **1812** Scotland
- **1808** Wrought-iron rails introduced in Cumberland
- **1812** First commercial use of steam locomotive
- **1812** Introduction of spring-loaded safety valv[e]
- **1807** Abolition of slave trade in British Empire
- **1815** Humphry Davy invents
- **1815** Battle of Waterloo
- **1801** Trevithick constructs first steam-powered road vehicle for passengers
- **1801** First submarine *Nautilus* produced

### Legend
- Inaugurations
- Locomotive engineering landmarks
- Railway disasters
- Other railway events
- World events

# Who's Who

The biography section aims to be a concise guide to the originators of most of the more familiar features of railway practice as it has developed over the last 150 years. It does not claim to be a comprehensive "Who was who" of the whole world of railways. It only includes those who were innovators and pioneers, and an example may help to illustrate our intention. Charles Beyer is included, the man who founded the locomotive building firm of Beyer Peacock, because of the revolutionary design of engines for which the firm became famous (the Beyer Garratt double engine); but James Kitson, who founded a locomotive works at Leeds in 1839 which also exported worldwide, is not mentioned because there was nothing in any way novel about his enterprise – just good solid business acumen.

The majority of the people mentioned therefore belong to the latter half of the nineteenth century. Partly this is because many of the standard features of even a modern railway system had emerged by 1900; partly it is because the identity of individuals is nowadays often submerged in that of the vast corporations which supply most of the needs of the railway industry today. Today it is firms rather than individuals who tend to get the credit for a new achievement: identifying those individuals responsible for the technical developments incorporated in a modern diesel locomotive is almost impossible.

**ABT**, Roman (1850–1933) Swiss engineer, invented perhaps the most widely-used rack railway system: 1,695 km (1,059 miles) were installed 1884–1929.

**ADAMS**, Willia.n Bridges (1797–1872) Invented the steam railcar, founded the Fairchild Works, Bow, London, where he built them. His rail brake anticipated that developed later by Fell (q.v.).

**ALLPORT**, Sir James (1811–92) The champion of cheap travel in UK. As general manager, he had all Midland Railway trains carry third class passengers from 1872, in carriages which set new standards of accommodation. Until then, cheap travellers had been scorned, and carried only on some trains.

**ARROL**, Sir William (1839–1913) Scottish bridge contractor who founded the Dalmarnock Works and was knighted after his completion of the Forth Bridge in 1890.

**BAIRD**, Matthew (1817–77) Sole proprietor of the USA's Baldwin loco

*Arrol*

works after 1866. Pioneer of spark arresters and the firebrick arch.

**BAKER**, Sir Benjamin (1840–1907) English civil engineer who designed the cantilever system for the Forth Bridge. Engineered most of the early London Underground railways.

**BALDWIN**, Matthias William (1795–1866) Founder of the Baldwin loco works, Philadelphia, USA, which built almost 75,000 steam locos.

**BARLOW**, William Henry (1812–1902) Chief civil engineer to the Midland Railway (England) after 1844. He took out several patents for permanent way, including one in 1849 much used on the GWR. He designed the St Pancras station train shed, and the second Tay Bridge (the longest in Europe).

**BEHN-ESCHENBURG,** Hans (1864–1938) Electrical engineer who rose to be managing director of the Swiss firm Maschinenfabrik Oerlikon, which pioneered railway electrification. Introduced the first practical single-phase traction motor (1904).

**BELPAIRE,** Alfred Jules (1820–93) Belgian who introduced his famous firebox in 1860, achieving greater efficiency from low-grade fuels.

**BERKLEY,** James (1819–62) Englishman who in 1849 became chief engineer of the Great Indian Peninsula Railway, inventing the zig-zag technique to lessen the gradients on that company's two main lines over the Ghats.

**BEYER,** Charles Frederick (1813–76) A German who in 1843 became chief

*Baldwin*

designer of locos with the English firm Sharp Roberts & Co. In 1853 he was co-founder of the Beyer Peacock loco building firm at Gorton, Manchester.

**von BORRIES,** August (1852–1906) Pioneer of compound steam locos who was chief mechanical engineer to the Prussian State Railways (1875–1902).

**BOUCH,** Sir Thomas (1822–1880) English civil engineer with a reputation for paring costs to the bone: the first Tay Bridge, which he built, collapsed only a year after its opening.

## Timeline (1820–1845)

- locomotive bogie
- quarter granted
- constructs first practical steam locomotive
- ner's safety lamp
- Middleton colliery railway, England
- Leeds, England
- Austrian Empire **1827**
- Liverpool and Manchester Railway **1830**
- **1827** Marc Séguin constructs first locomotive with multi-tubular boiler
- France (St Etienne-Andrézieux) **1828**
- Stephenson's *Rocket* wins Rainhill trials **1829**
- Baltimore and Ohio Railway founded **1828**
- Delaware and Hudson's gravity railway **1829**
- **1820** Bedlington Iron Works granted patent for production of rolled rails
- **1825** Stockton and Darlington Railway, first public railway to use steam from outset
- Irish Republic **1834**
- **1833** Two killed in first passenger train accident in USA
- **1835** First attempts to propel railway cars by electric batteries
- Crampton introduces driving wheels behind firebox to support larger boiler **1845**
- First major disaster: 53 killed on Versailles-Paris express **1842**
- Walschaert develops his valve gear **1844**
- **1835** World's first nationalized railway system — Belgium
- Semaphore signals first used for railways at New Cross, England **1841**
- **1830** Baltimore and Ohio Railway, first passenger and freight railway in USA
- West Germany **1835**
- Pneumatic brake invented by James Nasmyth **1844**
- **1830** First regular steam passenger service in England (Canterbury)
- Compound steam engine developed by William M'Naught **1845**
- USSR **1836** — **1837** Cuba — **1842** Poland
- Denmark **1847** — **1846** Yugoslavia
- Canada **1836** — **1838** Austria — **1839** Netherlands — **1839** Czechoslovakia
- British Guiana **1848** — Spain **1848**
- **1839** East Germany — **1844** Switzerland — **1846** Hungary — **1845** Jamaica
- **1831** US fireman killed in boiler explosion
- Introduction of Morse telegraph between Baltimore and Washington **1844**
- **1839** Charles Goodyear discovers process of rubber vulcanization

## Biographical entries

**du BOUSQUET, Gaston** (1839–1910) Chief engineer to France's Northern Railway from 1890. His compound Atlantic loco of 1900 set the style for many subsequent French locos.

**BOVERI, Walter** (1865–1921) German engineer and co-founder of Brown Boveri & Co in 1891, the Swiss manufacturers of railway electrification equipment.

**BRADSHAW, George** (1801–53) Published a timetable for Britain's railways, 1839. From December 1841 it was *Bradshaw's Monthly Railway Guide* and was last published in June 1961.

**BRANDT, John** (1785–1860) Credited by many with the classic American 4-4-0 design.

**BRASSEY, Thomas** (1805–70) The greatest English railway contractor. He built lines in Europe, Canada, Australia, Argentina and India besides Britain. Brassey's contracts amounted to 3,820km (2,374 miles) altogether.

**BROWN, Charles** mechanical engineer of (1827–1905) English founder of the Swiss Locomotive and Machine Works (SLM) at Winterthur in 1871. His son, Charles E. L. Brown, became a pioneer of railway electrification and co-founder of the Swiss firm Brown Boveri & Co in 1891.

*Brunel*

**BRUNEL, Isambard Kingdom** (1806–59) Brilliant civil engineer whose excursions into the realms of mechanical engineering were either spectacular failures or touched with genius. When only twenty-seven he was appointed Engineer to the Great Western Railway. His controversial use of a 2,134 mm (7 ft) broad gauge, and a gradient profile that was compared to a billiard table, made the GWR by far the fastest of the early railways, though it was not until Brunel relinquished the design of the locos to Gooch (q.v.) that this was achieved.

**BULLEID, Oliver Vaughan Snell** (1881–1970) Born in New Zealand. Made chief mechanical engineer of the Southern Railway in 1937. He was a steam loco engineer in a world abandoning steam engines and many of his innovations did not have a chance to prove themselves.

**BURY, Edward** (1794–1858) Owner of an engineering workshop in Liverpool, where he built his first loco in 1829. Originated bar frames (much used in America) in 1830. His locos had a very distinctive large copper firebox.

engineer, designer of a loco valve gear first used in 1921.

**CHAPELON, André** (b 1892) Seen by many as the greatest loco designer ever. He rose to be head of the French Railways' Department of Steam Locomotive Studies. In 1926, he designed with Kylala the Kylchap double blast-pipe. His main achievement lay in vastly increasing the thermodynamic efficiency of his steam locos by streamlining the internal steam passages.

**CHURCHWARD, George Jackson** (1857–1933) Chief mechanical engineer to the Great Western Railway and perhaps the greatest British loco engineer. His design sources were international: the high boiler pressures were an idea of de Glehn (q.v.); from America came the front end design with the long travel valves and the tapered boiler; and he used Belpaire's (q.v.) firebox. In 1902 he built the first successful British 4-6-0.

**CONRAD, Frederik Willem** (1800–69) Appointed engineer director of the Dutch Railway Co in 1839 because his earlier work with waterways and dykes was considered an asset when building a railway through the Dutch countryside.

**COOK, Thomas** (1809–92) Founded the travel firm, the unlooked-for result of an excursion he ran in 1841. The firm was greatly-expanded by his son J. M. Cook, who was sole manager after 11878.

**CRAMPTON, Thomas Russell** (1816–88) Englishman who patented a loco design in 1843. Crampton locos were used more in France and Germany than in England.

**CROCKER, Charles** (1822–88) American in charge of the construction of the Central Pacific Railroad (1863–9). Responsible for merging the CP with the Southern Pacific in 1884.

**DALHOUSIE, Lord** (1812–60) Became President of the Board of Trade in 1845, during England's "Railway Mania," when he formed opinions about the desirability of government control of railway construction. Prime Minister Peel refused, but Dalhousie pursued such ideas in India when appointed Governor-General. His 1853 Minute on the railways of India, which was adopted, recommended a speedy introduction of railways throughout India, to be built by private enterprise under government supervision.

**DIESEL, Rudolph** (1858–1913) French born, German educated inventor. Did not in fact have much to do with the application of his engine unit to rail traction. The first diesel engines went into ships, starting 1903. The first diesel loco was built at the Swiss Sulzer works in 1913.

**DODGE, Grenville Mellen** (1831–1916) American civil engineer, surveyed nearly 97,000 km (60,000 miles) of rail routes. In 1866 became chief

**CAPROTTI, Arturo** (1881–1938) Italian

# Chronology

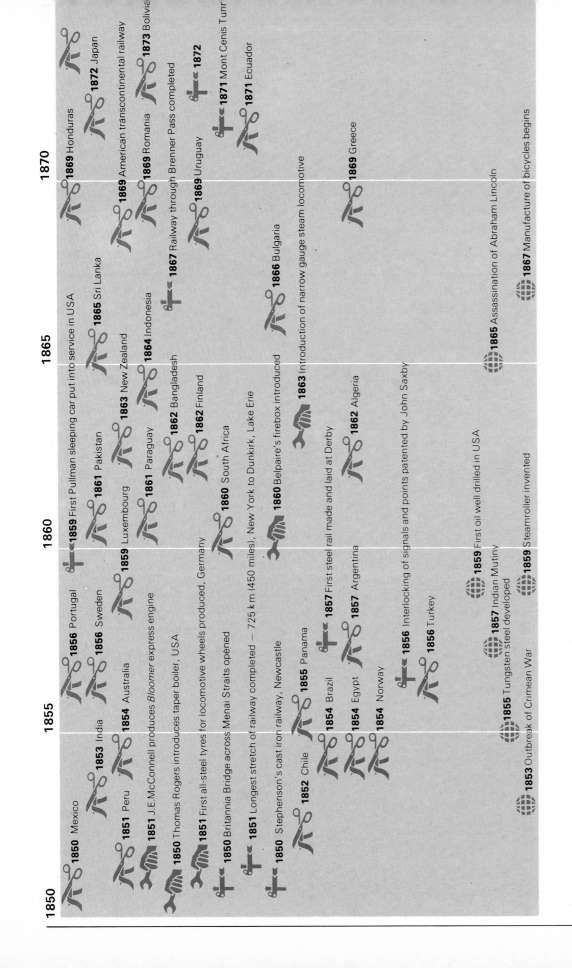

**1850** Mexico
**1851** Peru
**1852** Chile
**1853** India
**1854** Australia
**1854** Brazil
**1854** Egypt
**1854** Norway
**1855** Panama
**1856** Portugal
**1856** Sweden
**1857** Argentina
**1859** Luxembourg
**1860** South Africa
**1861** Pakistan
**1862** Algeria
**1862** Bangladesh
**1862** Finland
**1863** New Zealand
**1864** Indonesia
**1865** Sri Lanka
**1866** Bulgaria
**1869** American transcontinental railway
**1869** Honduras
**1869** Romania
**1869** Uruguay
**1869** Greece
**1871** Mont Cenis Tunnel
**1871** Ecuador
**1872** Japan
**1872**
**1873** Bolivia

**1850** J.E.McConnell produces *Bloomer* express engine
**1850** Stephenson's cast iron railway, Newcastle
**1850** Britannia Bridge across Menai Straits opened
**1851** Thomas Rogers introduces taper boiler, USA
**1851** First all-steel tyres for locomotive wheels produced, Germany
**1851** Longest stretch of railway completed – 725 km (450 miles), New York to Dunkirk, Lake Erie
**1856** Interlocking of signals and points patented by John Saxby
**1857** First steel rail made and laid at Derby
**1859** First Pullman sleeping car put into service in USA
**1860** Belpaire's firebox introduced
**1863** Introduction of narrow gauge steam locomotive
**1867** Railway through Brenner Pass completed

**1853** Outbreak of Crimean War
**1855** Tungsten steel developed
**1857** Indian Mutiny
**1859** First oil well drilled in USA
**1859** Steamroller invented
**1865** Assassination of Abraham Lincoln
**1867** Manufacture of bicycles begins

1850 1855 1860 1865 1870

# Who's Who

engineer to Union Pacific Railroad.

**DREW,** Daniel (1797–1879) American financier whose manipulation of railway stock brought disaster not riches: bankrupted himself by 1876.

**EDMONDSON,** Thomas (1792–1851) Englishman who in 1837 invented the card railway ticket and date press that have become standard throughout the world.

**EIFFEL,** Alexandre Gustave (1832–1923) French bridge builder whose wrought and cast iron constructions can be found in France, Spain and Portugal.

**FAIRBAIRN,** Sir William (1789–1874) Founder in 1817 of the firm which became Fairbairn & Sons, building in Manchester, England, almost 1,000 bridges and 400 locos.

**FAVRE,** Louis (1826–79) Swiss builder of the St Gotthard tunnel (inside which he died) and first to use spiral tunnels as a means of gaining height.

*Favre*

*Single Way* led to the introduction of block signalling.

**FOWLER,** Sir John (1817–98) English civil engineer of the Metropolitan Railway and the Forth Bridge.

**FOX,** Sir Douglas Charles (1810–74) Civil engineer and contractor who built many of the larger English train sheds. He pioneered narrow gauge railways in India.

**FELL,** John Barraclough (1815–1902) English inventor of a centre-rail friction drive system for extra adhesion. First in use 1868. Used on New Zealand's Rimutaka Incline, 1878–1955, it permitted a gradient of 1 in 14.

**FLEMING,** Sir Sandford (1827–1915) Born in Scotland, became engineer to the Canadian Pacific Railway in 1871.

**FOTHERGILL-COOKE,** Sir William (1806–79) Patented the railway electric telegraph in 1837. His 1842 publication *Telegraphic Railways or the*

Semmering Railway (1848–54).

**GARRATT,** Herbert William (1864–1913) Became loco superintendent to Central Argentina Railway, 1892. Worked on other railways in S. America, Cuba, Nigeria and Australia before returning to UK in 1906. In 1907 he patented his articulated loco design. Almost 2,000 were built by Beyer Peacock in Manchester.

**GHEGA,** Karl Ritter (1802–60) In 1836, made engineer on Austria's first steam-powered railway. His great achievement was the engineering of the fearsomely-graded

**GIFFARD,** Henri (1825–82) French inventor of the injector (to feed water into the boiler against pressure). First used in 1859.

**de GLEHN,** Alfred George (1848–1936) His work on compound locos while technical head of the French firm of Société Alsacienne was very influential. The first 4-cylinder de Glehn compound was made in 1886, and the last in 1929.

**GÖLSDORF,** Karl (1861–1916) Loco engineer to Austrian State

*de Glehn*

Railways from 1893. He introduced the 2-6-2 and 2-6-4 wheel arrangements into Europe and his loco numbering system was much copied. His most important innovation was a simple, reliable, starting gear for compound locos, widely used in Europe and America.

**GOOCH,** Sir Daniel (1816–89) First loco superintendent, and later the chairman, of England's Great Western Railway. Designer of the magnificent locos which came to symbolize the GWR in its broad gauge era.

**GOULD,** Jay (1836–92) One of the great American railroad magnates whose controversial activities were of much public interest in the era after the Civil War.

**GREATHEAD,** James Henry (1844–96) Inventor of the Greathead shield tunnelling device. Engineer to the world's first electric underground railway (the City and South London Railway, opened 1890).

**GRESLEY,** Sir Nigel (1876–1941) Became chief mechanical engineer of

*Gresley*

England's Great Northern Railway, 1911. As CME to its successor the London and North Eastern Railway, he designed the *Mallard*, the holder of the world speed record for a steam loco, 203 km/h (126 mph).

**HACKWORTH,** Timothy (1786–1850) Responsible for the establishment of the loco works of the Stockton and Darlington Railway, where he originated many of the features which became standard steam loco practice.

**HASWELL,** John (1812–97) Scottish engineer who settled in

Vienna where in 1837 he designed a loco works of which he became manager. In 1851 he produced the first European 8-coupled loco.

**HAWKSHAW, Sir John** (1811–91) Civil engineer, undertook many of the heaviest projects in nineteenth-century Britain. The first to prove that 1 in 50 was not the limit for adhesion worked inclines.

**HOWE, William** (1814–79) In 1842, invented the valve gear known as Stephenson's link motion.

**HUBER, Peter Emil** (1836–1915) Pioneer of Swiss railway electrification. The Bern-Lötschberg-Simplon line, which opened in 1913, was electrified from the outset to his specifications (15,000 volts AC at 16⅔ cycles per sec). This system was used on lines in Germany, Austria and Scandinavia.

**HUDSON, George** (1800–71) Early railway magnate who rose to be mayor of York and to control a network of 1,600 km (1,000 miles) of

*Jessop*

lines in the north of England. His questionable means of financing led to his downfall.

**HUNTINGTON, C. P.** (1821–1900) American railway magnate and unscrupulous financier. One of the four men who formed the Central Pacific Railroad Co in 1861 (and called the Big Four). To disguise the enormous profits made at the government's expense out of its construction, the CP's books were later burnt. In 1865, the same quartet formed the Southern Pacific Railroad by amalgamating lines they controlled in the south, Huntington becoming vice-president.

**JANNEY, Eli Hamilton** (1831–1912) Inventor of an automatic coupler made standard throughout the USA from 1888.

**JESSOP, William** (1745–1814) Civil engineer responsible for the Surrey Iron Railway, the horse-drawn line that was England's first public railway. He was the first to think of edge rails.

**KANDO, Kalman** (1869–1931) Became managing director of the Hungarian firm of Ganz and Partners. One of the few outstanding individuals (as opposed to firms) in the history of electric traction. From 1902, he electrified mountain lines in Italy. In 1915 he built the first loco to run on electricity at the industrial (high) frequency now used.

**KETTERING, Charles** (1876–1958) Chief engineer from 1922 of the firm later renamed General Motors. He and his son Eugene have done much to create the modern diesel loco.

**von KRAUSS, Georg** (1826–1906) In 1866, he founded his loco building firm at Munich, Germany. Another factory was later opened at Linz, Austria.

**LIST, Friedrich** (1789–1847) Engineer to the first German line (Furth-Nürnberg, 1835). His plans for a pan-Germanic rail network were ridiculed and he committed suicide.

**LOCKE, Joseph** (1805–60) English civil engineer, who built lines cheaply with heavy gradients and no tunnels. He introduced the bullhead rail, which became standard on all of Britain's railways for 100 years.

**LOMONOSSOF, George Vladimir** (1876–1952) Became chief mechanical engineer to the Tashkent Railway, 1908. Later deputy director-general of Russian Railways. As president of the Russian War Railway Mission to the USA, he was responsible for designing and ordering 2,000 locos.

**LOREE, Loener Fresnel** (1858–1940) Came to exert a strong influence on USA railway affairs due to his excellent management of the Delaware and Hudson Railroad during his 31-year presidency.

**MALLET, Anatole** (1837–1919) Swiss born, French educated engineer who patented his articulated loco in 1884. The design was particularly developed in the USA.

**MARSH, Sylvester** (1803–84) Built the first mountain rack railway (up Mt Washington, USA: opened 1869). Used a rack system like that patented by Riggenbach in 1863.

**MEIGGS, Henry** (1811–77) Moved from New York to Chile in 1854, where he started railway building. From 1867, engineer and contractor, Peru Central Railway; an extraordinary engineering feat which goes over the world's highest railway summit.

*Meiggs*

**MILHOLLAND, James** (1812–75) American loco engineer who developed a coal (as opposed to coke) burning firebox in 1855.

**MORGAN, John Pierpont** (1837–1913) US banker with an interest in railways. He and his partners controlled 29,000 km of lines in the south. This holding enabled him to induce many companies to agree to common rates and avoid ruinous competition.

**MURRAY, Matthew** (1765–1826) Built the first ever "commercially successful loco" for the Middleton Colliery line at Leeds (UK), in 1812.

### Timeline

- 1874 Colombia
- 1875 Sudan
- 1876 International Sleeping Car Company founded
- 1876 Tunisia
- 1877 Burma
- 1877 Venezuela
- 1878 Tay Bridge opened
- Alps opened
- Westinghouse perfects automatic railway air brake
- 1876 Bell invents telephone
- 1879 Zulu War
- 1879 Tay Bridge collapse in Scotland results in 78 deaths
- 1879 Electric locomotive exhibited in Berlin by E. W. von Siemens
- **1880**
- 1880 Guatemala
- 1881 Nicaragua
- 1881 Canadian Pacific Railway Company founded
- 1881 First public electric railway, Berlin
- 1882 El Salvador
- 1882 Gotthard Tunnel and railway opened
- 1883 Electric traction inaugurated on Giant's Causeway railway — first to use hydroelectric power
- 1883 China
- 1884 Parsons invents first practical steam turbine engine
- **1885**
- 1885 Malaysia
- 1885 Karl Benz builds single-cylinder engine for motor car
- 1885 Vietnam
- 1886 4-cylinder de Glehn compound locomotive introduced
- 1886 Angola
- 1886 Canadian Pacific Railway
- 1886 Senegal
- 1886 Mozambique
- 1887 Mallet's articulated locomotive constructed
- 1887 Severn Tunnel opened
- 1887 Present Tay Bridge opened
- 1888 Ethiopia
- 1888 Electric motor constructed
- 1889 British Railways Regulations alter signalling laws
- 1889 80 killed due to signalling error at Armagh, Ireland
- **1890**
- 1890 Costa Rica
- 1890 Israel
- 1890 Philippines
- 1891 Trans-Siberian Railway construction begins
- 1891 Taiwan
- 1892 Cape-Johannesburg railway
- 1892 British rail gauge size standardized
- 1893 Botswana
- 1893 Thailand
- 1893 Henry Ford builds his first car
- 1893 Diesel designs his internal combustion engine
- 1894 Tanzania
- **1895**
- 1895 Lebanon
- 1895 South West Africa
- 1895 Syria
- 1897 Kenya
- 1897 Rhodesia
- 1897 Multiple-unit train invented, USA
- 1897 Korea
- 1898 Uganda
- 1898 Zaire
- 1898 Schmidt's high-degree superheater developed
- 1898 Zeppelin builds airship
- 1899

# Chronology

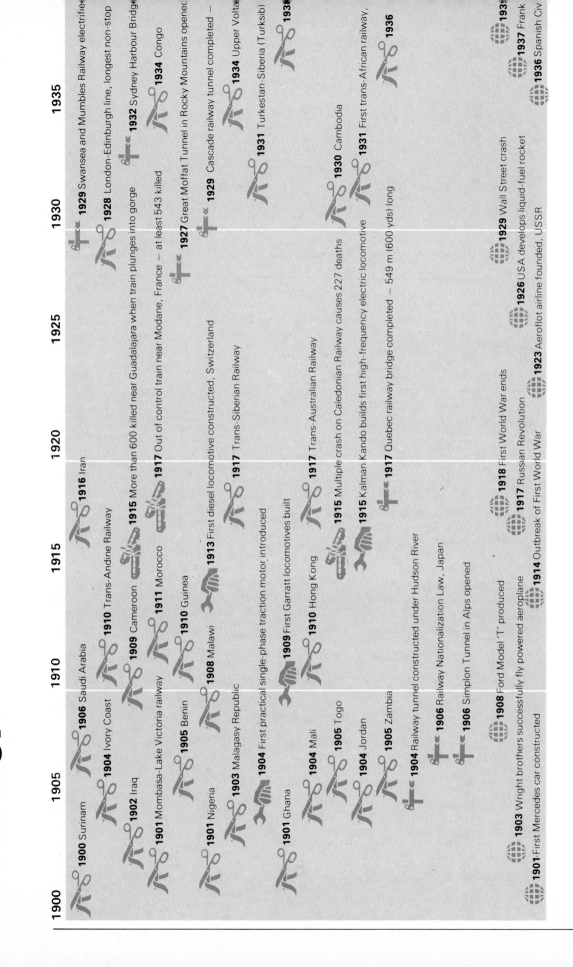

| 1900 | 1905 | 1910 | 1915 | 1920 | 1925 | 1930 | 1935 |
|---|---|---|---|---|---|---|---|

1900 Surinam

1906 Saudi Arabia

1904 Ivory Coast

1902 Iraq

1901 Mombasa-Lake Victoria railway

1910 Trans-Andine Railway

1909 Cameroon

1911 Morocco

1905 Benin

1910 Guinea

1908 Malawi

1913 First diesel locomotive constructed, Switzerland

1901 Nigeria

1903 Malagasy Republic

1904 First practical single-phase traction motor introduced

1917 Trans-Siberian Railway

1934 Upper Volta

1931 Turkestan-Siberia (Turksib)

1936

1904 Mali

1905 Togo

1909 First Garratt locomotives built

1910 Hong Kong

1917 Trans-Australian Railway

1901 Ghana

1905 Jordan

1905 Zambia

1915 Multiple crash on Caledonian Railway causes 227 deaths

1930 Cambodia

1915 Kalman Kando builds first high-frequency electric locomotive

1931 First trans-African railway,

1929 Swansea and Mumbles Railway electrified

1928 London-Edinburgh line, longest non-stop

1932 Sydney Harbour Bridge

1934 Congo

1936

1915 More than 600 killed near Guadalajara when train plunges into gorge

1917 Out of control train near Modane, France – at least 543 killed

1927 Great Moffat Tunnel in Rocky Mountains opened

1929 Cascade railway tunnel completed –

1917 Quebec railway bridge completed – 549 m (600 yds) long

1904 Railway tunnel constructed under Hudson River

1906 Railway Nationalization Law, Japan

1906 Simplon Tunnel in Alps opened

1918 First World War ends

1929 Wall Street crash

1926 Aeroflot airline founded, USSR

1908 Ford Model 'T' produced

1917 Russian Revolution

1923 Aeroflot airline founded, USSR

1903 Wright brothers successfully fly powered aeroplane

1914 Outbreak of First World War

1936 Spanish Civ

1937 Frank

1936 Congo

1916 Iran

1923 USA develops liquid-fuel rocket

1901-First Mercedes car constructed

---

# Who's Who

*Nagelmackers*

**NAGELMACKERS,** George (1845–1905) Belgian who founded the Wagons-Lits company in 1869 (Compagnie Internationale des Wagons-Lits et des Grands Express Européens): it inaugurated the Orient Express and other famous luxury expresses.

**NORRIS,** William (1802–67) Loco manufacturer in Philadelphia who refined and developed Jervis's 4-2-0 arrangement. Often called "Norris engines", they became an early American standard also used in Britain.

**PAGET,** Sir Cecil (1874–1933) Organizational genius who created the pattern of operating the London Midland and Scottish Railway after the Grouping in 1923, and applied by British Rail after the 1948 nationalization.

**PAULING,** George (1853–1919) Engineer and contractor often associated with lines promoted by Rhodes (q.v.) in southern Africa.

**PEASE,** Edward (1767–1858) The first man ever to invest a substantial amount of money in what today could be called a railway. He was the promoter of the Stockton and Darlington line, and appointed George Stephenson (q.v.) its chief engineer. Together, they founded the loco building firm of Robert Stephenson & Co.

**PULLMAN,** George Mortimer (1831–97) American who founded the Pullman Car Company in 1867. The crowded squalor of his American coaches caused Pullman's attempts

*Ramsbottom*

(1853–1902) English colonialist who in his struggles to gain control of southern Africa realized the unifying force of the railway. Railway promoter with a sense of the theatrical: proposed the Cape to Cairo route: wanted the Victoria Falls bridge built so that the spray would wet the coaches (which it does).

**ROGERS,** Thomas (1792–1856) American founder of Rogers Loco Works, 1837. Introduced the taper boiler in 1850.

**SAXBY,** John (1821–1913) English signalling pioneer who in 1871 invented his famous interlocking frame.

**SCHMIDT,** Wilhelm (1859–1924) German who developed a widely-used high-degree superheater first tried out on the Prussian State Railways in 1898.

**SEGUIN,** Marc (1786–1875) First to build a loco in France (1827), using the multi-tubular boiler he had patented in 1826.

to break into the European market to be defeated by consumer resistance and Nagelmackers' (q.v.) superior product.

**RAMSBOTTOM,** John (1814–92) Chief mechanical engineer of England's London and North Western Railway from 1862. Invented a safety valve named after him. Pioneered water troughs. Installed a Bessemer steel plant at Crewe in 1864, which led to the replacement of wrought iron by steel as the material for rails.

**RHODES,** Cecil John

*Von Siemens*

**SHAY,** Ephraim (1839–1916) Invented the Shay geared loco, the most popular of three geared loco designs produced in America for light temporary lines with steep gradients.

**von SIEMENS,** Ernst Werner (1816–92) German who exhibited what was really the world's first electric railway in Berlin in 1879. He built the electrified Giant's Causeway Tramway in Ireland (opened 1883).

**SPOONER,** Charles Easton (1818–89) Pioneered narrow gauge steam traction, which he introduced onto the Welsh

600 mm gauge Festiniog Railway in 1863.

**SPRAGUE,** F. J. (1857–1934) American pioneer of electric traction who invented the multiple-unit train in 1897.

**STANIER,** Sir William (1876–1965) As chief mechanical engineer to England's London Midland and Scottish Railway, he developed a new, remarkably standardized fleet of locos drawing on GWR practice, where he had been apprenticed under Churchward (q.v.). His 2-8-0 freight loco was adopted as a standard during the Second World War.

**STANLEY,** Albert, Lord Ashfield (1874–1948) After gaining experience in the USA (where he superintended Detroit's tramways, 1901–3), he returned to UK and was the man behind the establishment of the present London Transport system.

**STEPHENSON,** George (1781–1848) Son of a fireman at Wylam Colliery in the north of England

*George Stephenson*

who rose to become engineer to many early railways. His most important achievement was proving the capabilities of steam traction at the 1829 Rainhill Trial, which led to the choice of steam traction for the first major public railway, the Liverpool-Manchester line opened in 1830 (which Stephenson engineered).

**STEPHENSON, Robert** (1803–59) Really a civil engineer, but put in charge of his father George's (q.v.) loco works at Newcastle in 1823: the firm took his name. In 1833, he engineered the London and Birmingham Railway. Remembered for his tubular bridges, developed with Fairbairn (q.v.).

**STEVENS, Robert Livingston** (1787–1856) President and chief engineer of the USA's Camden and Amboy Railroad in 1830. Pioneer of much typical American railway practice, for example the cowcatcher.

**SYKES, William** (1840–1917) Englishman who patented the Lock & Block interlocking signal system in 1875. His son Joseph, who joined his signalling works in 1896, pioneered electric signalling.

*Trevithick*

**TREVITHICK, Richard** (1771–1833) Builder of pumping engines who was the first to use high-pressure steam. Built a loco in 1803, the first to haul a load on rails (on the Coalbrookdale wagon-way). Ruined financially by Peru's revolution (where he had gone in 1817 to install mine engines).

**TYER, Edward** (1830–1912) English inventor of the electric tablet system in 1878, for the safe working of single-line railways.

**VANDERBILT, Cornelius** (1794–1877) Made a fortune in steamboats. Sold out at age 67 and invested in railways. Gained control of the New York Central in 1867. When he died, he was worth US $100 million. The revelation of such wealth staggered America: his was the first modern-scale fortune.

*Van Horne*

**VAN HORNE, Sir William Cornelius** (1843–1915) operator with Illinois Central Railroad. Rose to be president of the Canadian Pacific in 1888 after having much to do with its construction.

**VAUCLAIN, Samuel Matthews** (1856–1940) Worked 51 years for Baldwins, the USA loco building firm, of which he became chairman in 1929. Invented the Vauclain system of loco compounding in 1889. Baldwins built 2,000 such locos.

**VIGNOLES, Charles Blacker** (1793–1875) Irish born early railway civil engineer. Built Ireland's first line (Dublin–Kingstown), 1832–4. In 1837 he introduced the flat-bottomed rail, now standard throughout the world. Later worked on lines in England, Russia, Switzerland and Poland.

**WALSCHAERT, Egide** (1820–1901) Belgian inventor of a valve gear, one of the most efficient ever, in 1844.

**WESTINGHOUSE, George** (1846–1914) American inventor of the compressed-air brake in 1868. He refined it in a further patent of 1871, making its application in an emergency automatic.

**WHISTLER, George Washington** (1800–49) American civil engineer responsible for Russia's 1,524 mm (5 ft) gauge. When working on the Moscow–St Petersburg line from 1842, he used the gauge then found on railways around his home in the USA.

**WHITTON, John** (1819–98) Englishman who was chief engineer to New South Wales Government Railways, 1856–1890. Responsible for the Great Zig-Zag Railway over the Blue Mountains.

**WINAN, Ross** (1796–1877) Originator of the American camel-back loco in the 1850s. The driver sat in a separate cab over the centre of the boiler.

**WORSDELL, Nathaniel** (1809–96) In 1837 invented an apparatus for picking up mailbags at speed, when he was carriage superintendent of the Liverpool and Manchester Railway.

*Walschaert*

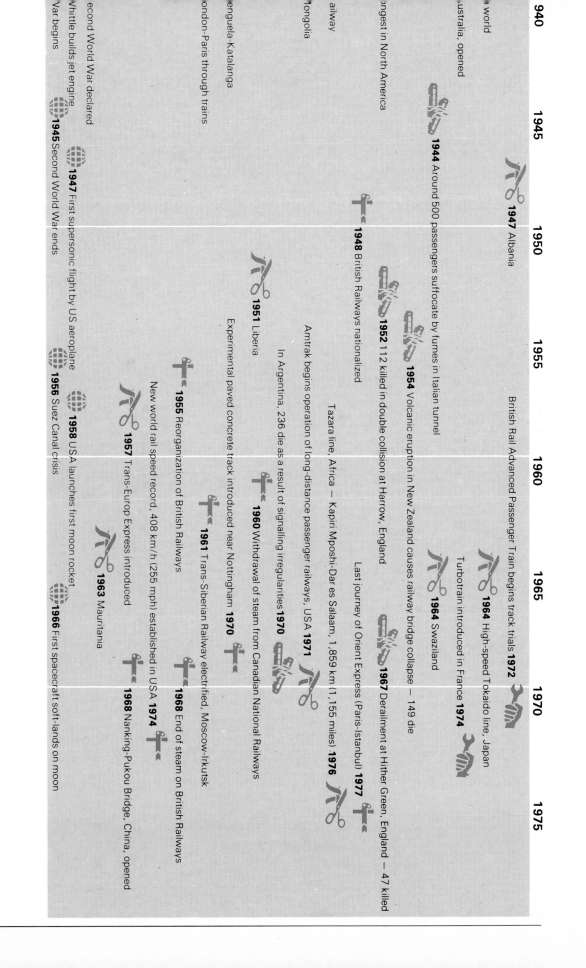

1940 · 1945 · 1950 · 1955 · 1960 · 1965 · 1970 · 1975

**World events**
- 1945 Second World War ends
- 1947 First supersonic flight by US aeroplane
- 1956 Suez Canal crisis
- 1958 USA launches first moon rocket
- 1966 First spacecraft soft-lands on moon
- 1947 Albania
- 1951 Liberia
- 1963 Mauritania
- 1968 Swaziland

**Railway events**
- 1944 Around 500 passengers suffocate by fumes in Italian tunnel
- 1948 British Railways nationalized
- 1952 112 killed in double collision at Harrow, England
- 1954 Volcanic eruption in New Zealand causes railway bridge collapse – 149 die
- British Rail Advanced Passenger Train begins track trials 1972
- Amtrak begins operation of long-distance passenger railways
- In Argentina, 236 die as a result of signalling irregularities, USA 1970
- Tazara line, Africa – Kapiri Mposhi–Dar es Salaam, 1,859 km (1,155 miles) 1976
- Last journey of Orient Express (Paris–Istanbul) 1977
- Turbotrain introduced in France 1974
- 1964 High-speed Tokaido line, Japan
- 1967 Derailment at Hither Green, England – 47 killed
- 1955 Reorganization of British Railways
- New world rail speed record, 408 km/h (255 mph) established in USA 1955
- Experimental paved concrete track introduced near Nottingham 1970
- 1960 Withdrawal of steam from Canadian National Railways 1971
- 1961 Trans-Siberian Railway electrified, Moscow-Irkutsk
- 1957 Trans-Europ Express introduced
- 1968 End of steam on British Railways 1974
- 1968 Nanking-Pukou Bridge, China, opened

# Glossary

## A

**Adhesion** Maintenance of contact between wheel and rail through friction.

**Air brake** Brake operated by compressed air.

**ALCO** (American Locomotive Company) US locomotive builders.

**Alternating current (ac)** Electric current whose direction is regularly reversed; in normal use in industry.

**Alternator** *Dynamo* producing *alternating* rather than *direct current.*

**Amtrak** (National Railroad Passenger Corporation) Nationalized, nationwide US passenger railway organization inaugurated in 1971.

**Anti-slide** Device which detects, and automatically corrects, sliding or skidding of the wheels when braking by momentarily reducing the braking force.

**Articulated locomotive** One which has two independent sets of frames, hinged or joined by a pivot, with independent groups of wheels driven by separate cylinders.

**ATC** (Automatic Train Control) Applied to any form of automatic driver assistance, including total automatic control.

**Atlantic locomotive** Steam *locomotive* with 4-4-2 wheel arrangement.

**ATO** (Automatic Train Operation) Automatic regulation or operation of trains as applied on certain single-track railways.

**Axle box** Metal box through which ends of axle pass, enclosing axle bearing and its lubrication system.

## B

**Ballast** Material, eg: crushed granite, slag, in which are bedded the *sleepers* carrying the track, to distribute the load of passing traffic, prevent track movement and provide drainage.

**Baseplate** Metal plate between flat-bottomed rail and *sleeper* whose purpose is to spread the weight of passing vehicles.

**Bellows** (US) Flexible connection between two carriages to provide access.

**Blade** The thinned rail at the actual place of junction in a pair of points.

**Blast pipe** Vertical pipe evacuating steam and waste products from the cylinders into the atmosphere, designed to create a partial vacuum in the *smokebox* and improve the draughting of the fire.

**Block signalling** System whereby only one train is permitted in each pre-determined section of line at a time.

**Bogie** Undercarriage with four or more wheels attached by a pivot under each end of long vehicles to facilitate negotiation of curves.

**Boiler** Part of *locomotive* in which steam is produced under pressure by the combustion of fuel in a *firebox* surrounded by water.

**Box car** (US) Covered freight wagon.

**Brake horsepower** Horsepower is a unit showing the rate at which work is done, as applied at the output shaft of an engine or motor, it is termed brake horsepower, indicating the power needed to stop the shaft turning.

**Brakeman** (US) Guard.

## C

**Cable railway** One on which trains are hauled by a cable attached to a stationary winding engine; usually used only on short, steeply graded sections of line.

**Caboose** (US) Guard's van or brake van on freight train.

**Camshaft** Rotating shaft on which shaped bodies (cams) are fixed to operate inlet and outlet valves of a *diesel engine* via a pushrod.

**Cant** *Superelevation.*

**Cardan shaft** Shaft with universal or cardan joint at one or both ends.

**Catenary** Cable in overhead electrification system which supports contact or conductor wire.

**Chaired track** Track on which rail is held in place on *sleepers* by iron or steel sockets (chair).

**Circuit breaker** Automatic switch to make or break an electric circuit.

**Clerestory roof** (1) Old-fashioned roof design with small windows and ventilators in slightly raised section running down centre of roof (2) (US) Bulbous glass roof of an observation coach ("dome car").

**Colour light signal** Fixed signal with red, yellow and green lights displayed as required – similar to road traffic signal.

**Commutator** Ring-shaped fitting connected to the *armature* of a *dynamo*, and bearing on to the brushes.

**Compounding** In steam *locomotives*: use of steam twice, first in a high-pressure cylinder, then in a larger, low-pressure cylinder, before exhausting it. Although intended as an economy measure, often necessitated more careful maintenance than "simple" locomotives.

**Compression stroke** Upward movement of piston into a cylinder which results in compression of air mixture in the cylinder.

**Compressor** Machine which increases air pressure by reducing the volume taken up by the air.

**Conrail** (Consolidated Rail Corporation) US railway organization formed in 1976 to operate seven bankrupt *railroads* in the northeast.

**Consist** (US) Composition or make-up of a train.

**Container** Large box, with or without roof, which can be easily lifted from a flat rail wagon and placed on a road transporter.

**Conversions** Metric to Imperial:

1 mm = 0.0393701 in
1 cm = 0.393701 in
1 m = 1.09361 yd
1 km = 0.621371 mile

Imperial to Metric:

1 in = 25.4 mm
1 in = 2.54 cm
1 ft = 0.3048 m
1 yd = 0.9144 m
1 mile = 1.609344 km

**Couchette** Passenger compartment whose seats convert into sleeping accommodation.

**Coupling** Means by which vehicles are linked together.

**Creep** Gradual forward movement of rails as a result of recurrent pressure from passing vehicles.

**Crosshead** Bar or metal block joining piston rod to connecting rod of a steam *locomotive.*

**Crossing** Intersection of two railway lines on the same level, enabling a vehicle to pass across another line.

**CTC** (Centralized Traffic Control) System of working signals from a central panel by remote control.

**Cut** (US) Group of cars coupled together in a *marshalling yard.*

**Cut and fill technique** (US) (*also* Cut and cover) Method of tunnelling where a trench is dug, lines laid and the whole then roofed over.

**Cut-off** (1) Short-cut or bypass route. (2) Point in the piston stroke when steam is stopped from entering the cylinder of a steam engine.

**Cutting** Open excavation for a railway through hilly terrain.

## D

**Dead man's handle** Automatic lever in electric *locomotive* kept depressed by driver. If released, ie, in the event of an accident to the driver, automatically cuts off power and applies brakes.

**Dead section** Part of conductor in electric railway circuit which is not supplied with power.

**Deck** (US) *Footplate.*

**Diesel engine** Internal combustion engine in which compressed air in a cylinder reaches a temperature high enough to ignite the fuel subsequently injected.

**Direct current (dc)** Electric current which always flows in one direction. Used in early railway electrification schemes, but now being superseded by *alternating current.*

**DMU** Diesel *multiple unit.*

**Double head** Two *locomotives* working in tandem to draw a train.

**Drawbar** Form of *coupling* connecting *locomotive* to unit or *tender.*

**Dump car** (US) Tipping wagon.

**Dynamo** Machine composed of rotating coils of copper wire in a magnetic field to produce a *direct current.* Used for lighting, etc.

**Dynamometer** Instrument for measuring energy. Used in a dynamometer car to test the performance of a *locomotive.*

## E

**Embankment** Man-made ridge built to raise natural ground level in order to carry railway over a valley, etc.

**EMU** Electric *multiple unit.*

**Entrance-exit (NX) signalling** Descriptive name for modern power signalling from large control panel in central cabin: once the signalman has indicated, on the panel, the entrance to, and exit from, the route which he wishes the train to take, the operation of intermediate points and signals is performed automatically.

**Expansion gap** Space traditionally left between one rail and the next to allow for expansion in hot weather. New track-laying techniques are making this unnecessary.

## F

**Firebox** Combustion chamber of a steam *boiler.*

**Firebrick** Material capable of withstanding great heat, used in the firebrick arch in a *firebox.*

**Fishplate** Metal plate used to join rail lengths.

**Flange** Projecting edge of rail or wheel to hold wheels on the rails.

**Fly-wheel** Wheel with heavy rim on revolving shaft used to keep revolutions constant and to accumulate power.

**Fog signal** Detonator placed on rail giving audible signal when vehicle passes overhead.

**Footplate** Platform on steam *locomotive* for driver and fireman.

**Frog** (US) *Nose.* Known as a movable frog where it occurs in *points.*

**Funicular** Railway found on steep gradients with ascending and descending vehicles counterbalanced; usually cable operated.

## G

**Gauge** (1) Dial indicating *boiler* pressure, etc, usually only in steam *locomotives.* (2) Distance between one rail and the other. Standard gauge is 1,435 mm (4 ft 8½ in), but several other gauges, broader and narrower, are in common use.

**Gondola car** (US) Flat, roofless car with low sides.

**Gradient** When the railway is not travelling horizontally. It is expressed as a unit rise or fall to the slope length, eg 1 in 50 down shows that the train descends 1 unit for every 50 units it travels. 1 in 50 is steep for a main line railway.

**Ground signal** Secondary signal fixed at low level to aid the driver.

## H

**Headstock** Lateral bar, part of the underframe of a wagon or coach, for the attachment of buffers or *coupling.*

**High-pressure steam** In locomotives, those designed to operate with a boiler pressure in excess of 14 kg/cm² (200 lb/in²).

**Home signal** Mandatory stop signal at entrance or exit of station, block section or junction to control movement of trains in that area.

**Hopper** Freight wagon with opening bottom doors through which the load is discharged.

**Hot box** Overheated *axle* box bearing as a result of insufficient lubrication.

**Hot box detector** Automatic device installed in track to detect over-heating in *axle box.*

**Hump** Artificial mound in *marshalling yard* over which vehicles are pushed before gravitating to their correct location.

**Hydraulic** Describes the control, usually mechanical, of water or other liquid flow through pipes, etc.

## I

**Induction** Production of an electric current in a conductor, either by changes in the magnetic field in which it lies, or by motion of a magnet nearby.

## L

**Light railway** Branch line or minor railway, often narrow gauge, constructed cheaply. Poorly laid track and steep gradients often necessitate slow speeds.

**Limit of shunt** Limit, marked by a board, beyond which *shunting* vehicles may not pass.

**Livery** Standard colours and design used for a particular railway company or line.

**Loading gauge** Maximum permitted height and width of a loaded train to ensure clearance of lineside structures.

**Lock and block** Refinement of the *block system* whereby it is physically impossible to signal a second train into a section of line until the first one has left it.

**Locking bar** Long bar along the inside of running rails and connected to the lock of mechanically operated *facing points* in order to hold the points in position while a train is passing.

**Locomotive** Steam, diesel or electric engine, one or more of which is used to draw a series of freight or passenger cars to form a train.

**Loop, passing** Short section of single-line railway which is double-tracked to allow trains going in opposite directions to pass.

**Low-pressure steam** (1) Pressure of exhaust steam from *compound locomotive*. (2) In a simple *locomotive*, *boiler* pressure below approximately 14 kg/cm² (200lb/in²).

## M

**Manganese rail** Steel rail toughened by the inclusion of more than 1% manganese.

**Manual block** Manually operated *block signalling* system.

**Marshalling yard** Large area devoted to multiple track siding network used for sorting wagons into complete trains. Particularly important in USA for high-load long distance running.

**Merry-go-round coal train** Permanently-coupled train of *hopper wagons* used for regular bulk traffic between colliery and power station. The train may load and unload without actually stopping, while negotiating a circular loop line.

**Mixed traffic** Steam locomotive designed to be able to work either fast passenger or heavy goods trains.

**Mixed train** Train which consists of both freight and passenger cars.

**Monorail** Railway system where only one running rail is needed. Most monorail trains run suspended beneath an elevated track.

**Multiple-aspect signal** System of *colour light signalling* in which each signal unit can display more than two colours.

**Multiple-unit train** Train drawn by two or more locomotives (or powered vehicles) coupled together and operated by one driver.

## N

**Net tonne kilometre** Commonly-used measurement of freight carried. Achieved by multiplying the *payload* of a freight train by the distance it has travelled.

**Nominal rating** Maximum efficient speed at which a machine may be driven without causing undue strain.

**Nose** Pointed part of a *crossing* or *points*, either fixed or movable. Also known as the angle.

## P

**Pacific** Steam locomotive with 4-6-2 wheel arrangement.

**Pallet** Movable flat base used for storage or transport of goods.

**Pantograph** Conductor transmitting power to the circuit of an electrically operated vehicle from an overhead contact wire.

**Passenger kilometre** Figure achieved by multiplying the number of passengers by the distance they travel. A more accurate indicator of the use made of the railways than merely counting the number of journeys undertaken.

**Payload** Weight of revenue-earning load of a train – ie. freight, etc.

**Piggyback operation** (US) Conveyance by rail of road vehicles on flat wagons.

**Platelayer** Track maintenance man.

**Point heater** Heater fitted to *points* to prevent seizure due to extreme cold.

**Point lock** Compulsory safety device fitted to *facing points* on passenger carrying lines, usually comprising a bolt which slots into the bar between the points and is operated from the signal box. A link to the relevant signals ensures that the points must be fully closed and locked before a signal is cleared.

**Points** Tapering, movable rails by which a train is directed from one line to another. "Facing" points are those presenting a forward moving train with a choice of direction, those over which a train has to reverse in order to switch tracks.

**Points, interlocking** Points whose operation is linked to corresponding signals to ensure synchronized movement, thus preventing accidents.

**Poppet valve** Independent, mushroom-shaped inlet and outlet valve operated by *camshaft* automatically to release excess steam and thus relieve pressure.

**Power to weight** Ratio of power generated by a *locomotive* to its total weight.

**Pullman car** Passenger carriage designed for luxury travel.

## R

**Rack system** System used in mountainous country whereby propulsion is effected, and slipping prevented, by interaction between a cog or pinion on the *locomotive* and a cogged or rack rail laid between the running rails.

**Rail, continuous welded** Any rail longer than 60 m (197 ft) formed by welding together standard or short lengths of rail.

**Rail, edge** The early name for modern style rails, which require vehicles to have flanged wheels. Used to distinguish this style from the original L-shaped "plate rails".

**Rail clip** Device for fastening rail to *sleeper*.

**Railcar** Self-powered passenger carrying vehicle.

**Railroad** (US) Railway.

**Rectifier** Instrument which converts *alternating current* to *direct current*.

**Regulator** Valve in a steam *locomotive* which controls steam flow from the *boiler* to the cylinder.

**Repeater signal** Advance warning signal used when normal signal is obstructed from driver's view.

**Retarder** Braking system used on a *hump* in *marshalling yard*.

**Roundhouse** Circular engine shed with central turntable. Now obsolete.

**Route indicator** Illuminated panel attached to a junction signal to indicate which of a number of possible routes is to be taken.

**Route length** Overall length of route run by a particular country or railway company over which journeys are made, excluding *sidings* and *shunting* areas, etc.

## S

**Safety valve** Valve in *boiler* which opens automatically to release excess steam and thus relieve pressure.

**Semaphore** Fixed signal with one or more movable arms which, when horizontal, or "on" indicate "stop".

**Servo** Denotes power-assisted device.

**Shinkansen** Japanese high-speed line.

**Shock absorber** Device linked to suspension to dampen vertical oscillation.

**Shoe brake** Standard braking system whereby a block is applied to the edge of a rotating drum or wheel.

**Shunt** Divert vehicles on to a subsidiary line or *siding*, or marshall them into a *siding*.

**Shunting, gravity** System of *shunting* or marshalling carried out on a gradient and relying on gravity to propel the wagons to their correct *siding*.

**Siding** Short track alongside main line for the purpose of *shunting* or stabling.

**Slab track** Experimental low maintenance track, the base of which is made up of a continuous stretch of concrete or asphalt, as opposed to *sleepers* and *ballast*, thus minimizing settlement and changes in alignment.

**Sleeper** (1) Wooden, steel or concrete beam laid transversely on *ballast* to support rails and spread load of passing vehicles. (2) Carriage on long-distance train which contains sleeping accommodation.

**Slide valve** Valve with sliding plate for opening and closing gap between steam chest and cylinder of a steam engine.

**Smokebox** Chamber in steam *boiler* located between chimney and flues.

**Spark arrester** Mesh or plate contained in the smokebox to prevent sparks and live coals issuing from the chimney.

**Spiral tunnel** Tunnel built in spiral formation rather than straight in order to gain height when crossing mountains, etc.

**Stephenson valve gear** Commonly-used *valve gear* designed in 1842 by an employee of Robert Stephenson & Company.

**Streamliner** Vehicle shaped so as to reduce air resistance and thus increase speed.

**Supercharger** Device supplying *diesel engine* with air at high pressure in order to increase efficiency.

**Superelevation** Amount of elevation of one rail above the other at a curve in the track.

**Superheater** Device used for raising temperature of steam as it leaves the *boiler*, in order to increase its pressure.

**Synchronous** Applied to an electric motor, the speed of which is directly proportionate to the supply frequency.

## T

**TEE** (Trans-Europe Express) Luxury trans-European passenger service containing first class accommodation exclusively.

**Tender** Vehicle coupled to a *locomotive* for the purpose of carrying fuel, water, etc.

**TGV** (Très grande vitesse) The French equivalent of England's APT (Advanced Passenger Train).

**Third rail system** System of carrying electric current along a third rail for supply to electric *locomotive* or train.

**Throttle** (US) *Regulator*.

**Thyristor control** Thyristors are a form of transistor used in the power regulator of modern electric and diesel-electric *locomotives* to give a smoother power control with a continuous current flow.

**Tie** (US) *Sleeper*.

**Track relay** Essential part of a track-circuited modern signalling system where a low voltage current is fed through the rails of each section. The presence of a train in that section short circuits the current and trips the relay, causing indicator lamps to light on the signal box control panel.

**Tractive effort** The nominal power capable of being developed by the cylinders of a steam *locomotive* at the moment of starting, calculated by multiplying the cylinder volume by the boiler pressure, and taking into consideration the diameter of the driving wheels (smaller wheels increase potential tractive effort).

**Turbine** Rotary engine driven by gas or steam flowing on to a series of vanes on a revolving disc or cylinder.

**Turbotrain** Train drawn by a *locomotive* powered by a *turbine*.

**Tyre** Steel band on outer edge of wheel.

## U

**UIC** (International Union of Railways) Organization founded in 1922 for the purpose of standardizing and improving railway equipment and operations.

**Underframe** Framework or supporting structure beneath a carriage or wagon.

## V

**Valve gear** Mechanism controlling steam distribution valve in the cylinder of a *locomotive*.

**Valve, reducing** Device whereby pressure of steam from the *boiler* is reduced to around 4kg/cm² (60lb/in²) for use in heating carriages.

**Variable gauge** Facility for operating on more than one track gauge. Applicable to vehicle or *wheel set* where wheel may be moved along axle and repositioned as required.

**Viaduct** Bridge resting on series of narrow arches, having high supporting piers, and carrying a railway over a valley or river.

## W

**Wagon-lit** (Fr) Luxury sleeping car run by Cie Internationale des Wagons Lits.

**Waist** Point immediately below window level of a carriage.

**Walschaert's valve gear** Widely-used steam *locomotive valve gear* designed by Edgie Walschaert in 1844.

**Wheel set** Pair of wheels secured to an axle.

**Whyte system** Classification of *locomotives* based on arrangement of wheels, eg: 2-4-2 — two leading wheels, four driving wheels and two trailing wheels. The continental system refers to wheel sets, thus 1-2-1.

**Working timetable** Timetable featuring all trains which are run over a specified route or area.

# Bibliography

### Historical

E. L. Ahrons, *Locomotive and train working in the latter part of the nineteenth century*, vols 1–5, Heffer, 1952.

James Buck, *Discovering Narrow Gauge Railways*, Shire, 1972.

Michael Conant, *Railroad Mergers and Abandonments*, California University Press, 1964.

Michael Darby, *Early Railway Prints*, V & A Museum Exhibition Catalogue, 1974.

W. J. K. Davies, *Light Railways: their rise and decline*, Ian Allan, 1964.

S. Kip Farrington, Jr, *Railroads at War (USA)*, Coward McCann, 1944.

Brian Haresnape, *Railway Design since 1830*, vols 1 & 2, Ian Allan, 1968 and 1969.

Paul Hastings, *Railroads: an international history*, Benn, 1972.

Edward Hungerford, *From Covered Waggon to Streamliner*, Greystones Press, 1941.

Henry Grote Lewin, *Railway Mania and its Aftermath, 1845–1852*, David & Charles, 1968.

M. J. T. Lewis, *Early Wooden Railways*, Routledge, 1970.

John Stewart Murphy and Charles Keeping, *Railways: How they were built*, Oxford University Press, 1964.

O. S. Nock, *Railways in the transition from steam 1940–1965*, Blandford, 1974.

O. S. Nock, *Railways Then and Now*, Paul Elek, 1975.

T. M. Simmons, *Railways 2: the 20th century*, HMSO, 1969.

J. B. Snell, *Early Railways*, Weidenfeld & Nicolson, 1964.

Gerard Vuillet, *Railway Reminiscences of Three Continents*, Nelson, 1968.

J. R. S. Whiting, *Coming of the Railways 1808–1892*, Evans, 1972.

### Engineering and architecture

E. F. Carter, *Famous Railway Stations of the World and their Traffic*, Muller, 1958.

Terry Coleman, *The Railway Navvies*, Penguin, 1968.

Philip Burtt, *Principal Factors in Freight Train Operating*, Allen & Unwin, 1924.

Peter Haining, *Eurotunnel: an illustrated history of the Channel Tunnel scheme*, New English Library, 1973.

John R. Day and Brian G. Wilson, *Unusual Railways*, Muller, 1957.

Alan A. Jackson, *London's Termini*, David & Charles, 1969.

Bryan Morgan, *Civil Engineering: Railways*, Longman, 1971.

John Prebble, *High Girders: the story of the Tay Bridge disaster*, Secker & Warburg, 1975 (new ed).

Jack Simmons, *St Pancras Station*, Allen & Unwin, 1968.

### Technical

Cecil J. Allen, *Modern Railways*, Faber & Faber, 1959.

O. S. Nock, *British Railway Signalling*, Allen & Unwin, 1969.

O. S. Nock, *50 Years of Railway Signalling*, Institution of Railway Signal Engineers, 1954.

Railway Clearing House, *Railway Junction Diagrams, 1915: a Reprint*, David & Charles, 1969.

Michael Robbins, *Points and Signals: A railway historian at work*, Allen & Unwin, 1967.

### Locomotives

E. L. Ahrons, *The British Railway Steam Locomotive 1825–1925*, Ian Allan, 1963.

Peter Allen and Robert Wheeler, *Steam on the Sierra: the narrow gauge in Spain and Portugal*, Cleaver-Hume, 1960.

*A Century Plus of Locomotives, New South Wales Railways 1855–1965*, Australian Railway Historical Society.

William Bay, *Danmarks Damp-Lokomotiver*, Herluf Andersens Forlag, 1977.

Alfred W. Bruce, *The Steam Locomotive in America*, Allen & Unwin, 1952.

W. J. K. Davies, *Diesel Rail Traction*, Almark, 1973.

*Diesel Traction: Manual for enginemen*, British Railways, 1962.

A. E. Durrant, *Garrett Locomotive*, David & Charles, 1969.

A. E. Durrant, *PNKA Power Parade: Indonesian steam locomotives*, Continental Railway Circle, 1974.

Graham Glover, *French Steam Locomotives 1840–1950*, Barry Rose, 1974.

D. W. and M. Hinde, *Electric and Diesel-Electric Locomotives*, Macmillan, 1948.

Ralph P. Johnson, *The Steam Locomotive*, Simmons-Boardman, 1942.

R. W. Kidner, *Development of the Railcar* (Locomotion papers No 12), Oakwood Press, 1958.

L. G. Marshall, *Steam on the RENFE: steam locomotive stock of the Spanish National Railways*, Macmillan, 1965.

O. S. Nock, *The British Railway Steam Locomotive 1925–1965*, Ian Allan, 1966.

O. S. Nock, *British Steam Locomotives at Work*, Allen & Unwin, 1967.

O. S. Nock, *Great Western Railway Stars, Castles and Kings*, vols 1 & 2, David & Charles, 1967 and 1970.

O. S. Nock, *Great Western Railway Steam*, David & Charles, 1972.

O. S. Nock, *Gresley Pacifics*, vols 1 & 2, David & Charles, 1973 and 1974.

O. S. Nock, *Historical Steam Locomotives*, A. & C. Black, 1959.

O. S. Nock, *Locomotion*, Routledge & Kegan Paul, 1975.

O. S. Nock, *London Midland and Scottish Steam*, David & Charles, 1971.

O. S. Nock, *London and North Eastern Railway Steam*, David & Charles, 1968.

O. S. Nock, *London and North Western Railway Locomotives of C. J. Bowen Cooke*, Bradford Barton, 1977.

O. S. Nock, *London and North Western Railway Precursor Family*, David & Charles, 1966.

O. S. Nock, *Railways of the World in Colour* (series), Blandford.

O. S. Nock, *Royal Scots and Patriots of the London Midland and Scottish*, David & Charles, 1978.

O. S. Nock, *Southern Steam*, David & Charles, 1966.

O. S. Nock, *Steam Locomotive*, Allen & Unwin, 1968.

A. N. Palmer and W. Stewart, *Cavalcade of New Zealand Locomotives 1863–1964*, Angus & Robertson, 1965.

P. Ransome-Wallis, *Last Steam Locomotives of British Railways*, Ian Allan, 1973.

P. Ransome-Wallis, *Last Steam Locomotives of Eastern Europe*, Ian Allan, 1974.

James G. Robins, *World Steam Locomotives*, Bartholomew, 1973.

Josef Otto Slezak, *Lokomotiven der Republik Österreich*, Verlag Slezak, 1973.

J. G. H. Warren, *A Century of Locomotive Building by Robert Stephenson and Co 1823–1923*, David & Charles, 1970.

Brian Webb, *British Internal Combustion Locomotives 1894–1940*, David & Charles, 1973.

G. F. Westcott, *The British Railway Locomotive*, HMSO, 1958.

D. W. Winkworth, *Bulleid's Pacifics*, Allen & Unwin, 1974.

### Great trains and train journeys

Cecil J. Allen, *Titled Trains of Great Britain*, Ian Allan, 1967.

Michael Barsley, *Orient Express*, Macdonald, 1966.

George Behrend, *Geschichte der Luxuszüge*, Orell Füssli, 1977.

George Behrend, *History of the Wagons-Lits 1875–1955*, Modern Transport, 1959.

George Behrend, *Pullman in Europe*, Ian Allan, 1962.

Geoffrey Blainey, *Across a Red World*, Macmillan, 1968.

E. F. Carter, *Famous Trains of the World*, Muller, 1959.

A. I. Dmitriev-Mamonov, *Guide to the Great Siberian Railway, 1900* (revised by John Marshall), David & Charles, 1971.

Garry Hogg, *Orient Express: Birth, life & death of a great train*, Hutchinson, 1968.

Kenneth Westcott Jones, *Exciting Journeys of the World*, Redman, 1967.

O. S. Nock, *"The Limited" – Cornish Riviera Express*, Allen & Unwin, 1978.

Martin Page, *The Lost Pleasures of the Great Trains*, Weidenfeld & Nicolson, 1975.

P. Ransome-Wallis, *On Railways at Home and Abroad*, Spring Books 1960.

Paul Theroux, *The Great Railway Bazaar*, Hamish Hamilton, 1975.

P. B. Whitehouse, *Great Trains of the World*, Hamlyn, 1975.

### Railways of Great Britain

Derek H. Aldcroft, *British Railways in Transition: the economic problems of Britain's railways since 1914*, Macmillan, 1968.

Cecil J. Allen, *Salute to the London Midland and Scottish*, Ian Allan, 1972.

J. I. C. Boyd, *Narrow Gauge Railways in South Caernarvonshire*, Oakwood Press, 1972.

British Railways Board, *Reshaping of British Railways*, parts 1 & 2, HMSO, 1963.

E. F. Carter, *Historical Geography of the Railways of the British Isles*, Cassell, 1959.

E. F. Carter, *Britain's Railway Liveries, 1825–1948*, H. Starke, 1963.

M. P. L. Caton and J. M. Stanier, *Railways in the Seventies*, Railway Invigoration Society, 1973.

Rex Christiansen, *West Midlands*, Regional History of the Railways of Great Britain, vol 7, David & Charles, 1973.

Edwin Course, *London Railways*, Batsford, 1962.

George Dow, *Great Central*, vols 1–3, Ian Allan, 1962, 1962 and 1965.

C. Hamilton Ellis, *Midland Railway*, Ian Allan, 1955.

C. Hamilton Ellis, *Railway Carriages in the British Isles 1830–1914*, Allen & Unwin, 1965.

R. J. Essery, D. P. Rowland and W. O. Steel, *British Goods Wagons from 1887 to the Present Day*, David & Charles, 1970.

G. F. Fiennes, *I Tried to Run a Railway*, Ian Allan, 1973 (revised ed).

D. I. Gordon, *Eastern Counties*, Regional History of the Railways of Great Britain, vol 5, David & Charles, 1968.

J. A. B. Hamilton, *Britain's Railways in World War One*, Allen & Unwin, 1967.

Campbell Highet, *Scottish Locomotive History 1831–1923*, Allen & Unwin, 1970.

Kenneth Hoole, *North East*, Regional History of the Railways of Great Britain, vol 4, David & Charles, 1974.

E. T. MacDermot, *History of the Great Western Railway*, vols 1 & 2, revised by C. R. Clinker, Ian Allan, 1964 and 1967.

C. F. Dendry Marshall, *History of British Railways down to the year 1830*, Oxford University Press, 1971.

G. T. Moody, *Southern Electric: the history of the world's largest suburban electrified system*, Ian Allan, 1968.

O. S. Nock, *Great Western Railway, 19th Century*, Ian Allan, 1962.

O. S. Nock, *Great Western Railway, 20th Century*, Ian Allan, 1964.

O. S. Nock, *Highland Railway*, Ian Allan, 1965.

O. S. Nock, *History of the Great Western Railway*, vol 3, Ian Allan, 1967.

O. S. Nock, *Lancashire and Yorkshire Railway*, Ian Allan, 1969.

O. S. Nock, *Caledonian Railway*, Ian Allan, 1962.

O. S. Nock, *Electric Euston to Glasgow*, Ian Allan, 1974.

O. S. Nock, *The Golden Age of Steam*, A. & C. Black, 1973.

O. S. Nock, *Great Northern Railway*, Ian Allan, 1958.

O. S. Nock, *Great Western Railway*, Ian Allan, 1966.

O. S. Nock, *Railway Race to the North*, Ian Allan, 1958.

O. S. Nock, *Scottish Railways*, Nelson, 1961.

O. S. Nock, *South Eastern and Chatham Railway*, Ian Allan, 1961.

O. S. Nock, *Steam Railways in Retrospect*, A. & C. Black, 1966.

B. Roberts, *Railways and Mineral Tramways of Rossendale*, Locomotion Papers No 76, Oakwood Press, 1974.

L. T. C. Rolt, *Railway Adventure*, David & Charles, 1961.

D. W. Ronald and R. J. Carter, *Longmoor Military Railway*, David & Charles, 1974.

Jack Simmons (ed), *Rail 150: The Stockton & Darlington Railway and what followed*, Methuen, 1975.

Roger Spear, *British Railways System*, Open University, 1975.

A. K. Steele, *Great Western Broad Gauge Album*, Oxford Publishing, 1972.

John Thomas, *Scotland*, Forgotten Railways Series, David & Charles, 1976.

David St. John Thomas, *West Country*, Regional History of the Railways of Great Britain, vol 1, David & Charles, 1973.

Norman W. Webster, *Britain's First Trunk Line: the Grand Junction Railway*, Adams, 1972.

Henry Patrick White, *Southern England*, Regional History of the Railways of Great Britain, vol 2, David & Charles, 1969.

## Railways of Europe

Cecil J. Allen, *Switzerland's Amazing Railways*, Nelson, 1965.

G. Freeman Allen, *Into the 125 m.p.h. Era on French Railways*, Ian Allan, 1972.

Michael H. C. Baker, *Irish Railways since 1916*, Ian Allan, 1972.

George Behrend, *Railway Holiday in France*, David & Charles, 1964.

H. C. Casserley, *Outline of Irish Railway History*, David & Charles, 1974.

W. J. K. Davies, *French Minor Railways*, David & Charles, 1965.

W. J. K. Davies, *Railway Holiday in Northern Germany*, Macdonald, 1965.

H. Fayle, *Narow-Gauge Railways of Ireland*, S. R. Publishers, 1970.

Claude Jeanmaire, *Elektrischen und Diesel-Triebfahrzeuge Schweizerischer Eisenbahnen*, vol 1, Basle Eisenbahn und Strassenbahnliteratur, 1970.

P. M. Kalla-Bishop, *Hungarian Railways*, David & Charles, 1973.

P. M. Kalla-Bishop, *Italian Railways*, David & Charles, 1971.

P. M. Kalla-Bishop, *Mediterranean Island Railways*, David & Charles, 1970.

Ole Winther Laursen, *Bygone Light Railways of Europe*, Oakwood Press, 1973.

John Marshall, *Metre Gauge Railways in South and East Switzerland*, David & Charles, 1974.

Franz Marti and Walter Trüb, *Gotthard Railway*, Ian Allan, 1971.

O. S. Nock, *Continental Main Lines: today and yesterday*, Allen & Unwin, 1963.

O. S. Nock, *Railway Holiday in Austria*, Macdonald, 1965.

O. S. Nock, *Railways of Western Europe*, A. & C. Black, 1977.

J. H. Price, *Railway Holiday in Bavaria*, David & Charles, 1967.

D. Trevor Rowe, *Railway Holiday in Spain*, David & Charles, 1966.

D. Trevor Rowe, *Spain and Portugal*, Ian Allan, 1970.

Ascanio Schneider, *Railways through the Mountains of Europe*, Ian Allan, 1967.

J. B. Snell, *France* (Continental Railway Handbook), Ian Allan, 1971.

H. A. Vallance, *Railway Holiday in Northern Norway and Sweden*, David & Charles, 1964.

D. W. Winkworth, *Railway Holiday in Portugal*, David & Charles, 1968.

## Railways outside Europe

George Behrend and Vincent Kelly, *Yaktit Vagon: Turkish steam travel*, Spearman, 1969.

P. S. A. Berridge, *Couplings to the Khyber*, David & Charles, 1969.

George S. Brady, *Railways of South America*, parts 1 & 2, US Dept of Commerce, 1926.

E. D. Brant, *Railways of North Africa*, David & Charles, 1971.

Robert B. Carson, *Main Line to Oblivion: the disintegration of New York railroads in the 20th century*, Kennikat Press, 1971.

Antony H. Croxton, *Railways of Rhodesia*, David & Charles, 1973.

John R. Day, *Railways of Northern Africa*, Arthur Barker, 1964.

John R. Day, *Railways of Southern Africa*, Arthur Barker, 1963.

Brian Fawcett, *Railways of the Andes*, Allen & Unwin, 1963.

John Murray Gibbon, *Steel of Empire: the romantic history of the Canadian Pacific*, Rich & Cowan, 1935.

Wesley S. Griswold, *Work of Giants: building the first transcontinental railroad*, Muller, 1963.

Richard Hall and Hugh Peyman, *The Great Uhuru Railway*, Gollancz, 1976.

Richard Hill, *Sudan Transport*, Oxford University Press, 1965.

Harold A. Innis, *History of the Canadian Pacific Railroad*, David & Charles, 1972.

S. E. Katzenellenbogen, *Railways and the Copper Mines of Katanga*, Oxford University Press, 1973.

D. B. Leitch, *Railways of New Zealand*, David & Charles, 1972.

W. Long, *Railways of South America*, vol III (Chile), US Dept of Commerce, 1926.

Norman Mackillop, *Western Rail Trail*, Nelson, 1962.

M. B. K. Malik, *Hundred Years of Pakistan Railways 1861–1961*, Ministry of Railways & Communications, Karachi, 1962.

S. M. Moir and H. Crittenden, *Namib Narow Gauge*, Oakwood Press, 1967.

O. S. Nock, *Railways of Australia*, A. & C. Black, 1971.

O. S. Nock, *Railways of Canada*, A. & C. Black, 1973.

O. S. Nock, *Railways of Southern Africa*, A. & C. Black, 1971.

O. S. Nock, *Railways in Asia and the Far East*, A. & C. Black, 1978.

David M. Pletcher, *Rails, Mines and Progress: seven American promoters in Mexico 1867–1911*, Kennikat Press, 1972.

Charles S. Small, *Rails to the Setting Sun*, Kigei, 1971.

Patsy Adam Smith, *Romance of Australian Railways*, Hale, 1974.

J. A. Stanistreet, *Keretapi Tanah Melayu: The Malayan Railway*, Oakwood Press, 1974.

Harmon Tupper, *To the Great Ocean: Siberia and the Trans-Siberian Railway*, Secker & Warburg, 1965.

H. J. von Lochow, *China's National Railways*, privately published, 1948.

Winthrop R. Wright, *British-owned Railways in Argentina: their effect on economic nationalism 1854–1948*, Texas University Press, 1974.

## Biography

H. A. V. Bulleid, *Bulleid of the Southern*, Ian Allan, 1977.

Richard S. Lambert, *Railway King: a study of George Hudson and the business morals of his time*, Allen & Unwin, 1934.

Oscar Lewis, *Big Four: the story of Huntington, Stanford, Hopkins, and Crocker, and the building of the Central Pacific*, Knopf, 1938.

John Marshall, *Lives of the Engineers*, David & Charles, 1978.

O. S. Nock, *William Stanier: an engineering biography*, Ian Allan, 1963.

E. M. S. Paine, *Two James's and two Stephensons*, Phoenix House, 1961.

Sir Alfred Pugsley (ed), *The Works of Isambard Kingdom Brunel*, Institution of Civil Engineers and University of Bristol, 1976.

L. T. C. Rolt, *Brunel*, Penguin, 1970.

L. T. C. Rolt, *George and Robert Stephenson*, Longman, 1960.

Charles Walker, *Thomas Brassey: Railway builder*, Muller, 1969.

N. W. Webster, *Joseph Locke: Railway revolutionary*, Allen & Unwin, 1970.

Archibald Williams, *Brunel and After*, Stephens, 1972.

## Reference

*British Railways Pre-Grouping Atlas and Gazetteer*, Ian Allan, 1965.

Robert C. Fisher (ed), *Fodor's Railways of the World*, Hodder & Stoughton, 1977.

Paul J. Goldsack (ed), *Jane's World Railways*, Jane's Yearbooks, annual.

John Marshall, *Guinness Book of Rail Facts and Feats*, Guinness Superlatives, 1971.

O. S. Nock (ed), *Encyclopedia of Railways*, Octopus, 1977.

O. S. Nock, *The Railway Enthusiast's Encyclopedia*, Hutchinson, 1968.

A. C. O'Dell and P. S. Richards, *Railways and Geography*, Hutchinson, 2nd ed, 1971.

J. H. Price (ed), *Thomas Cook International Timetable*, Thomas Cook Ltd, monthly.

*Railway Directory and Year Book*, Railway Gazette International, annual.

## Miscellaneous

George Dow, *Railway Heraldry*, David & Charles, 1973.

C. Hamilton Ellis, *Beauty of Railways*, Parrish, 1960.

G. H. I. Fairchild, *The World of Tickets*, published privately, 1972.

P. B. Whitehouse (ed), *Railway Relics and Regalia*, Hamlyn for Country Life, 1975.

Aalborg, 179
Aba, 199
Aberdeen, 17, 30, 35, 42, 180
Abidjan, 198
Acajutla, 204
Accra, 199
Achissi, 199
Adana, 193
Adapazari, 193
Addis Ababā, 197
Adelaide, 208
Advanced Passenger Train, (APT), 6, 9, 54-55, 89, 90
Agra, 194
Aguascalientes, 204
Ahmadābād, 194
Aiquile, 207
Air-brakes, continuous, 44
Air conditioning, 45
Airolo, 19
Ajaccio, 189
Ajmer, 194
Akahi, 197
Albacete, 188
Albania, 178, 190
Albany, 104, 208
Alberta, 126
Albula line, 84, 186
Albuquerque, 122, 202
Albury, 208
Aleppo, 193
Alexandria, 197
Alexandroupolis, 191
Algeciras, 188
Algeria, 198
Algiers, 198
Alicante, 188
Allāhābād, 194
Allegheny mountains, 13, 15, 104
Alma-Ata, 192
Alps, 82-85
Alsace-Lorraine railway, 189
Altels, 83
Altoona, 104
Amarillo, 203
Amato, 205
Ambrosiano, 86
American Railway Engineering Association, 56
Amersfoort, 183
Amherst, 203
Amman, 193
Amritsar, 194, 195
Amsterdam, 14, 86, 182, 183
Amtrak, (National Railroad Passenger Corporation), 24, 105, 106, 203
Anchorage, 203
Ancona, 190
Andalsnes, 179
Andalusian railway, 188
Andes, 19, 108-111
Ange, 178
Angola, 9, 199
Angoulême, 120, 121
Ankara, 94, 115, 193
Antofagasta, 19, 110, 206, 207
Antwerp, 182
Anyang, 95
Aomori, 101
Apache Canyon, 122
Apennine range, 190
  tunnel, 119
Apiscopia Bihor, 191
Appalachians, 15
Aqaba, 193
Aquitaine, 45, 120-121
Aracaja, 207
Arakan mountains, 94
Aranda, 188
Aran Pradet, 94
Architecture, 46
Arctic Circle, 178, 179
Arequipa, 207

Argentina, 108, 111, 204, 205, 206
Arhus, 179
Arica, 110, 200, 206, 207
Arizona, 104, 122
Arlberg line, 31
Arlon, 182
Armagh, 18
Armenia (Colombia), 205
Armuelles, 204
Arnhem, 183
Arthur's Pass, 98, 99, 208
Articulated locomotive, 32
Arusha, 200
Asia, 193
Asmara, 197
Astrachan, 192
Asunción, 206
Aswān, 197
Atchison Topeka and Sante Fe Railway, 69, 104, 122
Athens, 191
Athens Express, 115, 190
Atlanta, 203
Atlantic engines, 36
  compound, 120
Atmospheric railway, 28
Auckland, 98, 99, 208
Australia, 6, 9, 96, 100, 207, 208
Austria, 8, 82, 86, 114, 186, 187, 190
Austrian North Western railway, 186
Austrian Southern railway, 187
Austro-Hungarian State railway, 186, 187
Automatic air brakes, 18, 32, 42, 44, 185
  Westinghouse, 69
Automatic Car Identification, (ACI), 69
Avignon, 86, 87, 91, 189
Avila, 188

Bacau, 191
Badajoz, 188
Baghdād, 193, 194
Bahia Blanca, 206
Balclutha, 98
Balikesir, 193
Ballarat, 208
Ballasting, 56
Balmhorn, 83
Baltic, 185
Baltimore, 203
Baltimore & Ohio, 6, 13, 27, 202
Bamberg, 184
Bangalore, 194
Bangkok, 94
Bangladesh, 94, 194
Bangor, 116
Baotou, 95
Bar, 190
Barca d'Alva, 188
Barcelona, 87, 188
Bardonecchia, 82
Bareilly, 194
Bari, 190
Barlow, William Henry, 16, 47, 210
Barnaul, 192
Banoda, 194
Baron Hirsch railway, 114
Barrow, 180
Barstow, 78-79, 122
Basel, 47, 86, 183, 186
Basque coast, 120
Basra, 194
Basse Egypt railway, 197
Basti, 189
Bath, 180
Bathurst, 203
Baton Rouge, 203
Bauchi, 199
Bavaria, 184
Bay Area Rapid Transit (BART), 61

Bayonne, 189
Bayreuth, 184
Beaufort West, 124, 201
Beaver Hill, 107
Bebra, 184
Beira, 201
Beirut, 193
Bejaia, 198
Belém, 207
Belfast, 180
Belfast (NZ), 208
Belfort, 83
Belgaum, 194
Belgium, 8, 182, 184
Belgrade, 114, 115, 187, 190
Belo Horizonte, 207
Bengal-Assa, railway, 194
Benguela, 199
Benin, 199
Benoni, 201
Bergen, 179
Bergün, 84
Berlin, 184, 185, 194
  Charlottenburg, 185
  Friedrichstrasse, 185
  Ost, 185
  Zoo, 185
Bernese Oberland, 83, 112, 186
Bern-Lötschberg-Simplon railway, 19, 83, 186
Best Friend of Charleston, 13, 27
Beyer-Garratt, 19, 35, 37, 39
Béziers, 189
Bhopal, 194
Bialystok, 185
Biarritz, 120
Big Boy, 27, 37
Big Four, 181
Bilbao, 188
Birkinshaw, John, 11
Birmingham, 73, 90, 180, 181
Birmingham (USA), 203
Bizerte, 198
Black Five, 35
Black Sea, 114, 191
Blair Atholl (Aust), 208
Blaisy-Bas tunnel, 86
Blast pipe, 27
Blenkinsop, John, 11, 26
Block working, 18
Bloemfontein, 201
Bludenz, 186
Bluff, 98
Blue Train, 124-125
Boden, 178, 179
Bodö, 179
Boer War, 124
Bogie hopper wagon, 44
Bogotá, 205
Bolivia, 19, 108, 111, 207
Bologna, 119, 190
Bolzano, 190
Bombala, 208
Bombay, 128, 194
Bonate, Paul, 47
Bordeaux, 91, 120, 121, 189
Bosporus, 94, 115, 193
Boston, 203
Botswana, 201
Box car, 44
Box Hill tunnel, 14-15
Boxtel, 183
Braila, 191
Braithwaite, 27
Brasília, 207
Brasov, 191
Bratislava, 187
Brazil, 206, 207
Brazzaville, 199
Breda, 183
Bremen, 87, 184
Bremerhaven, 184
Brest, 189

Bridge construction, 60, 61
Bridge Stress Committee, 33
Brig, 84, 186
Brindisi, 190
Brisbane, 208
Bristol, 90, 180, 181
Britannia, 38
Britannia tubular bridge, 116
British Columbia, 106, 126
British Columbia Railway, 6, 107
British North Borneo Co., 196
British Rail, 69, 90, 117, 180, 181
  nationalisation, 38, 181
  Southern Region, 45
  Western Region, 118
Brno, 187
Broad gauge, 9, 19, 194
Broadway Limited, 104
Broken Hill, 96, 208
Brownsweg, 205
Brugge, 182
Brunel, Isambard, 14, 15, 19, 47, 116, 118, 188, 211
Brussels, 86, 118, 182
  Midi, 182
  Nord, 182
Bucaramanga, 205
Bucharest, 114, 191
Budapest, 114, 187, 191
Buenaventura, 205
Buenos Aires, 19, 206, 207
Buffalo, 203
Bugatti railcars, 35
Bulawayo, 200, 201
Bulgaria, 114, 115, 191
Bunbury, 208
Burgas, 191
Burgos, 188
Burlington, 105
Burlington Northern, 69, 105
Burma, 94, 194, 196
Butte, Montana, 105
Bydgoszcz, 185

Cab signalling, 90
Caceres, 188
Cadiz, 188
Cagliari, 190
Cairns, 208
Cairo, 197
Cajamarca, 207
Cajon Pass, 122
Calais, 118, 189
Calcutta, 94, 128, 194
Caledonian railway, 15
Calgary, 18, 78, 106, 126, 203
Cali, 205
California, 104, 122
California Limited, 122
Callao, 19, 207
Calvi, 189
Cambodia, 94, 196
Cambridge, 180
Cameroon, 199
Campos, 207
Canada, 8, 9, 15, 45, 104, 105, 106, 202
Canadian National Railways, 126
Canadian Northern, 107
Canadian Pacific Railway, 19, 105, 106, 126
Canadian, The, 126-127
Canberra, 208
Canton, 95, 195
Cape Government railway, 124
Cape Horn, 204
Cape of Good Hope, 124
Cape Province, 124
Cape-to-Cairo, 19, 197, 199, 200
Cape Town, 19, 124, 201
Capitole, Le, 45, 86

Cardiff, 9, 180
Čardžou, 192
Caribou Dayliner, 107
Carlisle, 23, 180, 181
Carregado, 188
Cartagena, 188
Casablanca, 198
Cascade Range, 106, 202
Caspian Sea, 194
Castle Class, 31
Catalan-Talgo, 86
Catania, 190
Catanzaro, 190
Cavour, Count Camillo, 82
Caxias do Sul, 207
Caxias Teresina, 207
Čel'abinsk, 92, 192
Central African Railway, 200
Central America, 204
Centralized Traffic Control, (CTC), 23, 99
Central Pacific Railway, 16, 105
Central Powers, 20
Central Railway of Peru, 19, 108
Central South African Railway, 124
Centre couplers, 44
Cerbère, 87
Cerro de Pasco, 109
České-Budějovice, 187
Chabarovsk, 192
Changchun, 95, 195
Chapelon, André, 35, 120, 211
Charleroi, 182
Charlottenberg, 178
Chat Moss, 6, 14
Cheb, 187
Cheltenham Flyer, 23
Chengdu, 195
Cherbourg, 189
Chesapeake and Ohio, 44
Chester, 116, 117
Chester & Holyhead railway, 116
Cheyenne, 105
Chiang Mai, 94
Chiba, 196
Chicago, 16, 39, 45, 104, 105, 122, 203
Chicago and Alton, 16
Chicago and North Western, 105
Chicago and Rock Island, 16
Chicago, Burlington and Quincy, 16, 106
Chicago, Milwaukee, St Paul and Pacific, 106
Chief, The, 104, 122-123
Chihuahua, 204
Chile, 108, 110, 111, 205, 206
Chillán, 206
Chimbote, 207
China, 94, 193, 195
Chinandega, 204
Chinese Eastern railway, 93, 95
Chita, 192
Chittagong, 94, 194
Choum, 198
Christchurch, 98, 208
Chuchou, 95
Chur, 186
Churchward, George J., 31, 32, 33, 211
Čierna, 187
Cincinnati, 203
Cisalpin, 86
Cisco, 107
Čita, 93, 192
Ciudad Juárez, 204
Ciudad Victoria, 204
Ciudad Obregón, 204
Class 25, 124
Clerestory roof, 124
Cloncurry, 208

Cluj, 191
Coaches, 62
Coalbrookdale Ironworks, 11
Coast Starlight, 105
Cochabamba, 207
Coimbatore, 194
Coimbra, 188
Cologne, 86, 87, 184
Colombia, 205
Colombo, 194
Colorado, 104, 122
Colorado Rockies, 105
Colour light signalling, 54, 88, 90, 179, 185
  multiaspect, 70
Commonwealth of Australia, 96
Como, 186
Comodoro Rivadavia, 206
Compound engines, 30, 31
Concepción, 206
Confederation class, 34
Congo, 19, 199
Conjugated valve gear, 34
Conrail (Consolidated Rail Corporation), 69, 80
Constantine, 198
Constantinople, 114, 187, 191, 193
Constanta, 191
Constantza, 191
Container, 44, 68
Continental Divide, 122
Cook, 96, 97
Cook Strait, 98
Cooma, 208
Copenhagen, 87, 178, 179, 185
Coquimbo, 206
Cordoba, 188
Cordoba (Arg), 206
Corinth, 191
Cork, 180
Corinto, 204
Corocoro, 207
Coronation Scot, 9, 36
Coronel Dorrego, 206
Corpus Christi, 203
Corridor carriage, 42
Corrientes, 206
Corunna, 188
Cossart valve gear, 34
Costa Rica, 204
Côte d'Azur, 86, 124
Cote d'Or mountains, 86
Cottbus, 185
Courbs la Ville, 91
Couplings, fish-eye, 66
Coutras, 120
Coventry, 180
Cox's Bāzār, 94
Craigellachie, 126
Craiova, 191
Crampton, Thomas Russell, 28, 211
Crewe, 180
Crow's Nest Pass, 107
Cuba, 8, 205
Cubitt, Lewis, 47
Cúcuta, 205
Culiacán, 204
Cumbre tunnel, 111
Curitiba, 207
Cuttack, 194
Cuxhaven, 184
Cuzco, 207
Czechoslovakia, 185-187

Dacca, 194
Dakar, 198
Dalhousie, Marquis of, 194, 211
Dallas, 203
Damascus, 193
Danube, 114, 187
Danzig, 185
Dar-es-Salaam, 200
Darjeeling, 194
Darlington, 181
Darmstadt, 47

Darwin, 208
De Aar Junction, 124, 201
Dashwood Pass, 99
Dawson Creek, 203
Debrecen, 187
Decapod, 32
Děčín, 187
Delft, 183
Delhi, 94, 194, 195
Den Haag-Zoetermeer, 183
Den Helder, 183
Denizli, 193
Denmark, 86, 178, 179
Denver, 105, 203
Denver & Rio Grande Western, 105
Denver and Salt Lake Railroad, 105
Dera, 193
Derby, 180, 181
Dessau, 185
Detroit, 203
De Witt Clinton, 27
Diamantina, 207
Dieppe, 189
Diesel electric, 37, 38, 128
  hydraulic, 51
  mechanical, 51
Dijon, 86, 91, 189
Dilolo, 199
Dimitrovgrad, 115, 190
Dinsdale, 12
Direct Orient, 114
Diré Dawa, 197
Direttissima, 119
Djibouti, 197
Dodge City, 122
Dondo, 199
Doncaster, 15
Doneck, 192
Dombas line, 179
Dome coach, 45, 126
Dominica, 205
Dominion, 126
Dortmund, 87, 184
Dotsero Cut-off line, 105
Dover, 180
Dragoman, 191
Dresden, 185
Driving wheels, 29
Drummond, Dugald, 31
Dublin, 116, 117, 180
Duchess class, 36
Duisburg, 184
Duluth, 203
Dundalk, 180
Dundee, 180
Dunedin, 98, 208
Dunkerque, 189
Dun Laoghaire, 116
Dunsmuir, 105
Durango, 204
Durban, 201
Dusseldorf, 87, 184
Dutch Rhenish railway, 33
Dynamometer cars, 33

Eaglescliffe, 12
East African Railways, 200
East Auburn, 105
East Germany, 184, 185, 187
Eastern Railway of France, 114
Ecuador, 108, 111, 205
Edelweiss, 86
Edge-rail, 11
Edinburgh, 15, 17, 23, 35, 119, 180, 181
Edirne, 115
Edmonton, 78, 107, 203
East London, 201
Egypt, 197
Egyptian Delta Light Railway, 197
Eiger, 112
Eindhoven, 183
Eismeer, 112
Eldoret, 200
Electric traction, 39, 52, 53, 120
Electrification, 22–24
El Ferrol, 188
Ellicott's Mills, 13
El Paso, 203
El Salvador, 204
Embankment, 101
Empire Builder, 105
Empire State Express, 31
English Channel, tunnel, 101
English Midland Railway, 180
Enter Rios, 201
Enugu, 199
Erfurt, 185
Ericsson, 27
Erie Canal, 13
Erstfeld, 19
Erzincan, 193
Erzurum, 193
Esbjerg, 179
Eskisehir, 94, 194
Essen, 87, 184
Étendard, 121
Ethiopia, 197
Étoile du Nord, 182
EEC, 86
Eugene, 105
Evening Star, 6
Exeter, 19, 180

Fairbanks, 203
Fairlie, Robert, 28–29
Faro, 188
Favre, Louis, 19, 212
Fdérik, 198
Fehmarn, 179
Ferrymead, 98
Festiniog Railway, 29
Finland, 178, 179
Firebox, Belpaire, 31
Firebrick arch, 29
First World War, 9, 20, 93, 98, 114, 117, 120, 181, 184, 186, 187, 190, 192, 193, 200
Fleming, Sir Sandford, 18, 107, 202, 212
Flensburg, 184
Florence, 47, 118, 119, 190
Florida, 207
Flushing, 183
Flying Hamburger, 23
Flying Scotsman, 6, 23, 119
Foggia, 190
Folkestone, 180, 181
Forguenot, M., 120
Formosa (Arg), 206
Forth Bridge, 61
Fortaleza, 207
Fort Madison, 122
Fort Morgan, 105
Fort Worth, 203
Fos, 91
France, 6, 8, 9, 13, 45, 82, 83, 86, 90, 94, 101, 121, 184, 188, 189, 196
Frankfurt am Main, 184
Fraser River, 106, 107
Fredericia, 179
Frederikshavn, 179
Freiburg, 184
Freight traffic, 66–69
Fremantle, 96
Friedrichshafen, 184
Frontier Mail, 128
Frýksta, 178
Fuchou, 195
Fukuoka, 196
Furness railway, 181
Fürth, 14, 184
Fushan, 95, 195

Gafsa, 198
Galera tunnel, 19, 109
Galitzin tunnel, 104
  summit, 15
Gallup, 122
Galway, 180
Galveston, 203
Ganges, 94, 128, 194
Gare de Lyon, 91, 114
Garibaldi, 82
Garrat, Herbert William, 2, 212
Gauhati, 194
Gavan, 192
Gavle, 178
Gdansk, 185
Gdesér, 179
Geelong, 208
Geneva, 86, 87, 91, 186, 208, Lake, 83, 86, 186
Genoa, 82, 86, 118, 190
Gent, 182
Geraldton, 208
Gerona, 87
Gezira Light Railway, 197
Ghana, 199
Ghega, Karl Ritter, 186, 212
Giovi Incline, 190
Gisbourne, 98
Giurgevo, 114
Giurgui, 191
Glacier National Park, 106
Glasgow, 15, 53, 89, 180, 181
de Glehn, Alfred George, 9, 31, 35, 120, 212
Glorieta Range, 122
Gloucester, 15
Gmünd, 187
Gobi Desert, 91
Goiânia, 207
Gölsdorf, Karl, 31, 212
Gómez Palacio, 204
Goppenstein, 83
Gore, 98
Gorky, 192
Gornergrat Railway, 112
Göschenen, 19
Goteborg, 178
Gothenburg, 178
Gottardo, 86
Gotthard line, 19, 118, 186
  tunnel, 83, 84, 86, 186
Gottingen, 184
Gowzow Wlkp, 185
Granada, 188
Granada (Nicaragua), 204
Grande Prairie, 203
Grand Russian Railway, 185
Grand Trunk Pacific, 107
Grängesberg-Oxelosund Railway, 178
Great Britain, 6, 9, 10, 20, 21, 23, 24, 29, 42, 43, 44, 101, 116, 121, 124, 178, 180, 181, 182, 184, 185, 188, 189
Great Northern Railway (GB), 15, 41
Great Northern Railway (Ireland), 18, 180
Great Western Railway, 14, 15, 19, 181
Greece, 114, 190, 191
Grena, 179
Grenoble, 189
Gresley, Sir Nigel, 34, 35, 36, 212
Greymouth, 98, 208
Grimsby, 180
Groningen, 183
Guana, 205
Guadalajara, 204
Guatemala, 204
Guayaquil, 205
Guinea, 198
Guiyang, 195
Gujranwala, 195
Gulf of Bothnia, 178
Gulf of Mexico, 105
Gweru, 201
Gwelo, 201
Györ, 187

Haarlem, 14, 183
Hackworth, Timothy, 15, 27, 192, 212
Haerbin, 95, 111, 195
Hague, The, 183
Haifa, 193
Hailung, 95
Hakata, 101
Hakodate, 101, 196
Hälsingborg, 179
Hama, 193
Hamburg, 47, 86, 87, 118, 178, 184
Hamersley Iron Railway, 6, 208
Hangchow, 95
Hangzhou, 195
Hanoi, 94, 195
Hanover, 86, 184
Hardwick, Philip, 47
Harrisburg, 104
Harwich, 180
Haydarpasa, 94, 115
Hedjaz railway, 20
Hedley, William, 11, 26
Helsingborg, 178, 179
Helsingør, 178, 179
Helsinki, 47, 179
Hengyang, 195
Hermosillo, 204
Hiawatha, 36, 106
High Speed Train (HST), 24, 39, 52, 54, 55, 62, 91
Hikari, 101
Hill, J.J., 105
Hiroshima, 101, 196
Hobart, 208
Honshū, 82, 100, 101
Ho Chi Minh City, 94
Hook of Holland, 183
Holyhead, 9, 116, 117, 120
Hokkaidō, 82, 101
Homs, 193
Hong Kong, 95, 195
Honduras, 204
Houston, 203
Howrah, 128
Howe Sound, 107
Horseshoe Bend, 104
Hradec Králové, 187
Huallanca, 207
Huancavelica, 108, 109, 207
Huancayo, 108, 109, 110, 207
Hubli, 194
Hudson, 34, 122
Hudson River, 104
Huelva, 188
Hull, 180
Hull and Barnsley, 181
Hungary, 187, 190
Husky Tower, 126
Hyderābad, 194, 195

Ibadan, 199
Ibagué, 205
Ica, 207
Illinois, 122
Illinois Central, 16
Imperial Indian Mail, 128
Imperial Japanese Railways, 100
Imperial Limited, 126
Imperial Royal Austrian State Railway, 186, 187
India, 45, 94, 128, 193, 194
Indianapolis, 203
Indian Ocean, 96
Indian-Pacific, 97
Indonesia, 9, 196
Indus, 94, 194, 195
Innsbruck, 186
Inter-city, 24, 90, 179
Interlaken, 112
International Railways of Central America, 204
International Sleeping Car Company, 114, 115
International Union of Railways (UIC), 44
Invercargill, 98, 208
Inverness, 180
Ipswich, 180
Ipswich (Aust), 208
Iquique, 206
Iran, 94, 194
Iraq, 194
Ireland, 117, 180, 181
Irish Mail, 29, 116–117
Irkutsk, 93, 192
Irrawaddy, 94
Irun, 188
Isalmi, 179
Iselle, 84
Iskenderah, 193
Islamabad, 195
Isle of Sheppey, 183
Israel, 193
Istanbul, 94, 114, 115, 190, 193
Italia, 118
Italy, 9, 82, 83, 86, 114, 118, 190, 196
Ivory Coast, 198
Izmir, 193
Izmit, 193

Jabalpur, 194
Jacksonville, 203
Jamaica, 8, 205
Jammagar, 194
Jamshedpur, 194
Japan, 6, 24, 45, 90, 91, 93, 99, 107, 118, 193, 195, 196
Jasper, 107
Java, 196
Jelenia Góra, 185
Jenny Lind, 29
Jequié, 207
Jerusalem, 193
Jessop, William, 11, 213
Jinja, 200
Jining, 95
João Belo, 201
João Pessoa, 207
Johannesburg, 124, 201
Johore Strait, 196
Jonkoping, 178
Jordan, 193
Jos, 199
Juiz de Fora, 207
Jujuy, 207
Juliaca, 207
Jungfrau, 112
Juniata River, 104
Junin, 206
Jura-Simplon Railway, 83, 186

Kaduna, 199
Kagoshima, 196
Kaitanguta, 208
Kalahari, 191
Kalama, 208
Kalani Valley Railway, 194
Kalemi, 199
Kalgan, 95
Kalgoorlie, 96, 208
Kamloops, 18, 107, 203
Kamon Strait, 101
Kampala, 200
Kananga, 199
Kandersteg, 83
Kandy, 194
Kankan, 198
Kankesanturai, 194
Kano, 199
Kānpur, 128, 194
Kansas City, 122, 202, 203
Kapikule, 115
Karāchi, 195
Karl-Marx-Stadt, 184
Kassel, 184
Katowice, 185
Kawasaki, 196
Kayes, 198
Kayseri, 94
Kelamayi, 95
Kelloselkä, 179
Kenya, 200
Kerma, 197
Kermân, 94, 194
Khairpur, 195
Khānewāl, 195
Khar'kov, 192
Khartoum, 197
Khulna, 194
Kicking Horse Pass, 18, 19, 202
Kiel, 184
Kiev, 192
Kigoma, 200
Killingworth Colliery, 11, 26
Kimberley, 59, 124, 201
King Class, 31
King's Messengers, 115
Kingston, 98, 208
Kingston Flyer, 98
Kingstown Ireland, 9
King Victor Emmanuel, 82
Kinshasa, 199
Kirikkale, 193
Kiruna, 178
Kisangani, 199
Kisumu, 200
Kitakyūshu, 196
Kitson, John, 210
Kitwe, 199
Klagenfurt, 186
Klarälven, 178
Klerksdorp, 124
Kōbe, 196
Koblenz, 87, 184
Kōchi, 196
Kodama, 101
Kokura, 101
Kolwezi, 199
Kompong Som, 196
Königsberg, 185
Kontiomaki, 179
Konya, 193
Korea, 195
Košice, 187
Kosti, 197
Kota, 128
Kotri, 194
Kotka, 179
Koulikoro, 198
Kowloon, 195
Krakow, 185
Krasnojarsk, 92, 192
Krasnovodsk, 192
Kriegslok, 37
Kristiansand, 179
Kuibyšev, 192
Kumasi, 199
Kumming, 195
Kure, 196
Kushiro, 197
Kwinana, 208
Kyōto, 101, 196
Kyūshū, 101

La Cima, 109
La Coruña, 188
La Crosse, 106
Lagos, 199
Lahore, 128, 194, 195
La Junta, 38, 104, 122
Lake Baykal, 92, 192
Lake Erie, 104
Lake Michigan, 106
Lake Nyasa, 200
Lake Superior, 18, 105, 126
Lake Lucerne, 112
Lake Titicaca, 110, 111, 207
Lake Tanganyika, 19, 201
Lake Urmia, 94
Lake Van, 94
Lake Wakatipu, 98
Lancaster and Carlisle Railway, 15
Lancaster, 29, 181
Lanchow, 195
Landen, 182
Lanzhou, 195
La Oroya, 109, 207
La Paz, 110, 206, 207
La Plata, 206
L'Arbalete, 86
La Rochelle, 189

Latacunya, 205
Las Vegas, 122, 203
Launceston, 208
Laurila, 179
Lausanne, 83, 91, 186
Le Cisalpin, 86
Leeds, 180, 181
Leganon, 193
Le Havre, 189
Leiden, 183
Leipzig, 185
Lemano, 86
Le Mans, 189
Leningrad, 93, 179, 185, 192
Leoben, 186
León, 204
Lerida, 188
L'Etendard, 86
Leuven, 182
Levitation, 55, 101
Liberec, 187
Liberia, 198
Libramont, 182
Liège, 182
Lille, 189
Lillehammer, 179
Lillooet, 107
Lilongwe, 200
Ligurean Riviera, 86
Likasi, 199
Lima, 108, 109, 207
Limerick, 180
Limoges, 189
Limón, 204
Linear motors, 55, 101
Linz, 186
Lisbon, 120, 188
Lismore, 208
List, Friedrich, 213
Livingstone, 200
Liverpool, 9, 90, 180, 181
Liverpool & Manchester Railway, 6, 8, 14, 27, 28, 40, 181
Livorno, 190
Ljubljana, 190
Llanfair, 116
Loading gauge, 44, 58
Lobito, 199
Locher, Edouard, 112
Locke, Joseph, 57, 88, 213
Locarno, 186
Locomotion, 12, 27
Lodz, 185
London, 9, 15, 16, 43, 45, 88, 90, 116, 117, 119, 180, 181, 184
Euston, 23, 25, 30, 53, 54, 55, 73, 88, 90, 116
King's Cross, 15, 23, 29, 30, 35, 36, 42, 47
London Bridge, 18
Paddington, 19, 23, 24, 47
St Pancras, 16, 47
Waterloo, 74
Londonderry, 181
London and Birmingham railway, 181
London and North Western railway, 15, 117, 181
London, Brighton and South Coast railway, 41
London Midland and Scottish railway, 9, 117
London Underground, 181
Londrina, 207
Long-boiler, 29
Lonza gorge, 83
Lord Nelson Class, 33
Lord of the Isles, 9
Los Andes, 111
Los Angeles, 38, 104, 105, 122, 123, 202, 203
Losh, William, 11
Lötschberg, 186
tunnel, 19, 83, 186
Loudima, 199
Louvain, 182
Lower Hutt, 208
Luanda, 199

Lübeck, 184
Lublin, 185
Lucerne, 186
Lucknow, 128
Lüda, 93, 95, 195
Ludwigsbahn, 14
Lugano, 86, 186
Luleå, 178
Lumsden, 98, 208
Lumumbashi, 199
Lüneburg, 184
Luoyang, 195
Lusaka, 200
Luxembourg, 86, 182
Luxor, 197
Luzon, 195
Lyallpur, 195
Lyntog, 179
Lyon, 45, 55, 82, 83, 86, 87, 90, 91, 114, 124, 189
Lyttleton, 98
Lytton, 107

Ma'an, 193
Maastricht, 183
Macau, 195
Maceió, 207
Mackay, 208
Mâcon, 91
Madras, 194
Madrid, 120, 188
Madurai, 194
Magdeburg, 185
Mainz, 87
Malagasy, 200
Malatya, 94
Malawi, 200, 201
Malaya, 195
Malaysia, 94, 196
Mali, 198
Mallard, 36, 39
Mallet locos, 23, 32, 33, 37
Mallet, Anatole, 30, 213
Malmö, 178, 179
Manakara, 200
Manchester, 90, 180, 181
Manchuria, 93, 95, 111
Mangalore, 194
Manizales, 205
Mannheim, 87, 184
Mansura, 197
Maputo, 201
Mar del Plata, 206
Marmara Express, 114, 115, 190
Marrakech, 198
Marsala, 190
Marseille, 86, 91, 189
Marsh, Sylvester, 112, 213
Marshalling, 44
yards, 23, 76, 78
Maryborough, 208
Massaua, 197
Matadi, 199
Mataro, 188
Matterhorn, 112
Maurienne valley, 82
Mauritania, 198
Mazabuka, 188
McConnell, J.E., 29
Mechelen, 182
Medecine Hat, 126
Medellin, 205
Medina, 193
Medina, del Campo, 188
Meiggs, Henry, 108, 109, 207, 213
Meknès, 198
Melbourne, 96, 208
Menai Strait, 116
Mendoza, 206
Mérida, 204
Merkur, 87
Merry-go-round, 44, 66
Messina, 190
Metz, 189
Mexicali, 204
Mexico City, 204
Miami, 203
Middlesbrough, 180

Middleton colliery, 11, 26
Midi railway, 120, 121
Midland Railway, 15, 16, 42
Milan, 83, 118, 119, 182, 186, 190
Lambrate station, 118
Mildura, 208
Milwaukee, 106, 203
Minna, 199
Minneapolis, 98, 202, 203
Minsk, 192
Mirjaveh, 94
Miskolc, 187
Mississippi River, 16, 104, 106
Missouri, 105, 122
Mistral, 45, 86
Mobile, 203
Moçambique, 201
Mocâmedes, 199
Modane, 82
Moffatt Tunnel, 105
Mohaka, viaduct, 98
Mollendo, 207
Mombasa, 200
Monorail, 103
Monrovia, 198
Mons, 182
Montana, 106
Montauban, 120
Mont Cenis Tunnel, 82, 91, 118
Monterrey, 204
Montevideo, 206
Montluçon, 189
Montpelier, 189
Montreal, 23, 45, 126, 202, 203
West, 126
Montreux, 186
Moose Jaw, 203
Morocco, 198
Moran, 196
Moscow, 92, 192
Moscow and Koorsk railway, 41
Moshi, 200
Mossel Bay, 201
Motorail train, 67
Mount Fuji, 101
Mount Isa, 208
Mount Pilatus, 112
Mount Rainier, 106
Mount Shasta, 105
Mount Washington, 112
Mozambique, 9, 200, 201
Mpwapwa, 200
Mughalserai, 128
Multan, 195
Munich, 86, 184
Murmansk, 192
Mussolini, 118
Mwanza, 200
Myingyan, 94

Nachodka, 192
Nagasaki, 196
Nagoya, 101, 196
Nägpur, 194
Nairobi, 50, 200
Nakuru, 200
Nampula, 201
Namur, 182
Nanchang, 195
Nancy, 84, 189
Nanjing, 195
Nanking, 95
Nankow Pass, 95
Nanning, 195
Nantes, 189
Napier, 98, 208
Naples, 86, 190
Narbonne, 87
Narvik, 178, 179
Natal, 124
Natal (Brazil), 207
National Coal Board, 181
National Union of Railwaymen, 11
Nebraska, 105
Needles, 122

Nelson, 208
Netherlands, 8, 14, 86, 183
Neuchâtel, 186
Neustrelitz, 185
Nevin, 116
Newcastle, 35, 180, 181, 208
Newcastle and Carlisle Railway, 181
New Delhi, 128
New Hampshire, 112
New Haven, 203
New Mexico, 104, 122
New Orleans, 105, 202, 203
New Plymouth, 98, 208
Newport News, 203
New South Wales, 96, 97
Newton, 122
New York, 13, 47, 104, 106, 203
New Zealand, 28, 66, 96, 98, 100, 208
Ngaounderé, 199
Nicaragua, 204
Nice, 86, 189
Niger, 198
Nigeria, 199
Niigata, 196
Niihama, 196
Nijmegen, 183
Nile, 19, 197
Nîmes, 189
Niš, 115
Nogales, 204
Norfolk and Western, 44
Norrkoping, 178
North Dakota, 106
Northern Ireland, 180
North Korea, 95
North Midland Railway, 181
North Platte, 105
North-West Frontier, 194
Norway, 178, 179
Noses, crossing, 59
Nottingham, 180
Novelty, 27
Novosibirsk, 92, 192
Nullarbor Plain, 96
'Straight', 97, 208
Nürnberg, 14, 184
Nyborg, 179

Oakland, 105
Oamaru, 206
Odense, 179
Odessa, 192
Ogden, 105
Ohio, 13
Ojinaga, 204
Okayama, 101
Olbio, 190
Olomouc, 187
Omaha, 105
Omdurman, 197
Omsk, 92, 192
Onverwacht, 205
Oostende, 182
Oporto, 188
Oradea, 191
Oran, 198
Oran (Arg), 206
Orebro, 178
Oregon, 105
Orense, 188
Orient Express, 114–115, 178, 187, 191, 193
Orléans, 35, 120, 121, 189
Oruro, 207
Osaka, 39, 100, 101, 196
Oshogbo, 199
Oslo, 179
Osorno, 206
Ostend, 182
Ostrava, 187
Otersund, 178
Otira tunnel, 98, 208
Ottawa, 203
Ouagadougou, 198
Oudtshoorn, 201

Oulu, 178

Pacific locomotives, 33, 34, 35, 36, 38, 50, 92, 98, 120
Pacific Railroad, 204
Pacific Railway, 185
Pakistan, 94, 194, 195
Palencia, 188
Palermo, 190
Palmira, 205
Pamplona, 188
Panama, 204
Panay, 195
Paöy Pêt, 94
Papapouli, 191
Paraguari, 206
Paraguay, 205, 206
Paraná, 206
Paris, 15, 45, 55, 82, 86, 90, 91, 114, 120, 121, 124, 182, 188, 189, 190
Paris-Orléans Railway, 189
Central Station, 47, 104
Parnaiba, 207
Parsifal, 86
Patentee, 28
Patna, 194
Patrai, 191
Pavlovsk, 15
Paysandú, 206
Pécs, 187
Peking, 95, 111, 195
Pelotas, 207
Pennsylvania Railroad Company, 15, 104
Pennsylvania Railway Station, 47
Pen-y-Darren, 11, 26
Penzance, 19, 180, 181
Peona, 194
Permanent way, 56–59
operating machine, 59
Perpignan, 189
Persian Gulf, 194
Perth, 97, 208
Peru, 19, 108, 109, 207
Pescare, 190
Peterborough, 15
Philadelphia, 13, 15, 203
Philippines, 195
Phividec Railway, 195
Phnum Pênh, 94
Phoenix, 203
Picton, 98, 99, 208
Piedmont, 82
Pieksämäki, 179
Pietermaritzburg, 201
Piggyback, 44, 67
Pimba, 97
Pingxiang, 94
Piraeus, 191
Piraeus, Athens and Peloponnesus railway, 191
Pisa, 118
Pisco, 207
Pittsburgh, 15, 104, 203
Platy, 191
PLM line, 86, 189
Ploesti, 191
Plovdiv, 191
Plymouth, 180, 181
Plzeň, 187
Point, 58, 59
Pointe Noire, 199
Poitiers, 120, 121
Poland, 8, 185
Polish Corridor, 185
Pontresina, 84
Popayán, 205
Port Arthur, 93
Port Augusta, 96, 208
Port Bou, 87
Port Elizabeth, 201
Port Harcourt, 199
Port Dinllaen, 116
Portland, 105, 203
Port Lincoln, 208
Porto, 188
Porto Alegre, 207
Porto Amboim, 199
Port Pirie, 96, 97, 208
Port Said, 197

Portsmouth, 180, 181
Port Sudan, 197
Portugal, 188
Potosi, 207
Poznam, 185
Prague, 94, 194, 195
Prairies, 126
Precedenze, 119
Přerov, 187
Pretoria, 124, 201
Prince George, 107
Prince Rupert, 203
Prinz Eugen, 86
Prior Park, 10
Promontory, 16, 105
Providence, 203
Pueblo, 105
Puerto Bolivar, 205
Puerto Berio, 205
Puerto Eten, 207
Puerto Montt, 206
Puffing Billy, 11, 26
Pullman, 86
Pullman car, 42
Puno, 111, 207
Punto Altobut, 110
Pwllheli, 116

Qom Junction, 94
Qotúr, 94
Quebec, 203
Queenborough, 183
Queenstown, (Ireland), 9
Queenstown, (SA), 201
Queen Victoria, 18
Que Que, 201
Quetta, 195
Quilon, 194
Quito, 111, 205

Rabat, 198
Rack and pinion, 112
Rack, centre rail, 98
Rahijkot, 194
Rail, bullhead, 57
continuous welded, 57
flat-bottomed, 57
gauge change, 68, 188
Railcars, 51
Rainhill trials, 27
Rajahmundry, 194
Rajdhani Express, 128
Rancagua, 206
Rangoon, 194
Rapidos, 118
Rapid transit, 45
Raton, 122
Raurimu spinal, 98, 208
Ravenna, 190
Rawalpindi, 195
Rawlinna, 96, 97
Recife, 207
Recordenze, 207
Red Sea, 197
Reefton, 208
Refrigerated vans, 42, 44
Regensburg, 184
Reggio di Calabria, 190
RENFE, 188
Rennes, 189
Resistencia, 206
Rhaetian Railway, 84, 186
Rheingold, 86, 183
Rhine, 183
Rhineland, 182
Rhodanien, 86
Rhodes, Cecil John, 9, 19, 201, 214
Rhodesia Railways Unitary System, 200
Rhône, 91, 186
Rhône valley, 84, 186
Riberão Prêto, 207
Richards Bay, 6
Riggenbach, Niklaus, 112
Riga, 192
Rigi, 112
Riksgransen Railway, 178
Rimini, 192
Rimutaka Incline, 98
Rimutaki tunnel, 98

Riobamba, 205
Rio de Janeiro, 207
Rio Grande, 207
Rio Grande Zephyr, 105
River Tees, 12
River Thames, 14
Roberts Bank, 6
Rocket, 9, 27, 28
Rockhampton, 208
Rockies, 15, 126
Rocky Mountains, 126
Rødby, 179
Rogers Pass, 18
Rohri, 94
Roissy Airport, 189
Rolling stock, 40–45
Roll-on roll-off, 98
Romania, 114, 191
Rome, 118, 119, 190
Rome Express, 82, 118
Rosario, 206
Rosenheim, 184
Roskilde, 179
Rostock, 185
Rostov-na-Donu, 192
Rotterdam, 14, 183
  Central Station, 46
Rouen, 189
Royal George, 27, 105
Royal Hudson locomotives, 107
Royal Scot, 33, 36
Ruhr, 10, 184
Ruling gradient, 112
Ruschuk, 191
Ruse, 191
Russia, 8, 15, 100, 121, 179

Saarbrücken, 184
Saarinen, Eliel, 47
Safi, 198
Sähiwäl, 195
Saigon, 195
Saint-Florentin, 91
Salamanca, 188
Salima, 200
Salisbury, 201
Salta, 206
Salto, 206
Salt Lake City, 105, 203
Salween River, 94
Salzburg, 186
Samsun, 193
San Antonio, 203
San Diego, 203
San Francisco, 105, 203
Sangre de Christo, range, 122
San José, 204
San Juan, 111, 206
San Lorenzo, 205
San Luis, 206
San Salvador, 204
San Sebastian, 188
Sans Pareil, 27
Santa Barbara, 105
Santa Cruz, 207
Santander, 188
Santiago, 206
Santiago del Estero, 206
Santos, 207
Sanyo, Shinkansen, 101
São Paulo, 207
Sapporo, 196
Sanyo, 190
Saskatoon, 106, 203
Sassari, 190
Sassnitz, 185
Santa-Mare, 191
Saudi Arabia, 194
Sault Ste Marie, 203
Savannah, 203
Savoy, 82
Scapa Flow, 20
Schipol Airport, 183
Scholer, F.E., 47
Scinde Railway, 61, 181

Scotland, 61, 181
Scott, Giles Gilbert, 16, 47
Seat reservation, computer, 45
Seattle, 18, 105, 202, 203
Second World War, 23, 24, 47, 50, 90, 100, 104, 105, 114, 118, 121, 122, 179, 181, 184, 185, 187, 189, 196, 197
Seikan tunnel, 101, 103
Sekondi, 199
Seligman, 122
Selkirk range, 126
Semmering Pass, 186, 187
Sendai, 196
Senegal, 198
Senegal River, 198
Serbia, 114
Serbian State Railways, 190
Setebello, 86, 118–119, 121
Seville, 188
Seward, 203
Sežana, 114
Sfax, 198
Shanghai, 95, 195
Shantung, 95
Sheffield, 180
Shenyang, 95, 195
Shildon, 12
Shimonoseki, 101
Shinkansen, 6, 45, 48, 55, 90, 91, 99, 100–103, 118, 193, 196
Shinyanga, 200
Sï'an, 195
Sidhiro Kastron, 191
Sierra Nevada, 105
Signalling, 70, 71
Silva Porto, 199
Silver Fern, 99
Silver Jubilee, 23, 35, 36
Silver Star, 99
Simplon, 186
Simplon Express, 190
Simplon-Orient Express, 114
Simplon tunnel, 82, 83, 114, 186
Sind desert, 95
Singapore, 196
Sirkeci, 115
Sittwe, 94
Skopje, 190
Skovorodino, 192
Sleepers, concrete, 57
Sleepers, wood, 57
Smith's Falls, 126
SNCF, 189
Sobral, 207
Sofia, 115, 191
Soldier Summit, 105
Soracaba, 207
Sorlands Express, 179
Sousse, 198
South Africa 9, 100, 201
South African railways, 59, 201
South America, 204
Southampton, 180
South Australia, 96
Southern Alps, 98
Southern Pacific, 105
Southerner, 98
Southern Railway of Peru, 110, 111
Southwest Limited 105, 123
Soviet Railways, 192
Spain, 86, 94, 178, 188
Spanish Sahara, 198
Spiez, 186
Spiral, 19, 98
Spokane, 106, 202
Squamish, 107
Sri Lanka, 194
Stadtbahn, 185
Standard gauge, 96, 190, 193

Stanier, Sir William, 35, 36, 214
Stanforth, John, 191
Stara Zagora, 191
Star Class, 33
Stavanger, 179
Stavanger Express, 179
Steam, demise of, 50
Stendal, 185
Stephenson, George, 6, 11, 12, 14, 26, 27, 82, 181, 214
Stephenson, Robert, 14, 15, 27, 28, 29, 116, 186, 192, 197, 207, 215
St Etienne and Andrézieux railway, 13
St Germain, 15
St Lawrence, 126
St Louis, 203
St Malo, 189
St Moritz, 84, 186
St Paul, 203
St Nazaire, 189
St Petersburg, 15, 185
St Paul, 18
St Pol-de-Léon, 189
St Pierre-des-Corps, Tours, 120, 121
Stockton and Darlington, 26, 27, 40, 181
Stockholm, 178, 185
Stockton, 181
Strängnäs, 185
Strasbourg, 86, 184, 189
Struer, 179
Stuttgart, 47, 87, 184
Styria, 185
Sucre, 207
Sud Express, 121
Sudan, 19, 197
Suez, 121
Sukkur, 195
Sumatra, 196
Sundsvall, 178
Super Chief, 104, 203
Super Continental, 107
Superheaters, 31
Surat, 194
Surinam, 205
Svendborg, 179
Sverdlovsk, 192
Svilengrad, 114, 115, 191
Swansea, 180
Swakopmund, 201
Swaziland, 201
Sweden, 178, 179
Swedish State Railways, 178
Swift Current, 126
Swindon, 23, 28, 180
Swiss Federal Railways, (SBB), 86, 186
Switzerland, 83, 86, 114, 186
Sydney, 96, 208
Sydney Harbour Bridge, 208
Syria, 193
Szczesin, 185
Szeged, 187
Székesfehérvár, 187

Tabriz, 94, 194
Taipei, 195
Taiwan, 195
Taiynan, 195
Taj Express, 50
Takamatsu, 196
Talara, 207
Talca, 206
Talcahuano, 206
Taigo train, 86, 87
Talien, 93
Tallinn, 192
Taltal, 206
Tampa, 203
Tampere, 179
Tamping machine, 58
Tampico, 204
Tanzania, 200
Tanger, 198
Tárábulus, 193
Taranto, 190
Tarbes, 189
Tarcoola, 96, 97
Tarnow, 185
Tarnów, 185
Taškent, 192
Tatvan, 94
Taunggyi, 94
Tauranga, 208
Taurus Express, 193
Tay Bridge disaster, 17
Tazara line, 19, 200
Tbilisi, 192
TEE, see Trans Europe Express
Tehran, 94
Teius, 191
Tel Aviv, 193
Telford, 116
Tennessee Pass, 105
Terni, 190
Texas, 105
TGV, 54, 55, 64, 90, 91, 189
Thailand, 94, 196
Thailand State Railways, 94
Thazi Junction, 94
Thessaloniki, 191
Thessaly Railway, 191
Thika, 200
Thompson River, 107
Thrace, 114
Thun, Lake of, 83, 186
Thunder Bay, 126
Thurso, 181
Thyristor controls, 53
Ticino canton, 186
Tientsin, 95, 195
Tilburg, 183
Timaru, 208
Timetabling, 72–75
Tiruchchirāppalli, 194
Tobruk, 197
Togo, 199
Tokaido line, 100
  New line, 24, 39, 101
  Old line, 100, 101
Tōkyō, 39, 100, 101, 196
Tom Thumb, 13, 27
Tornio, 179
Toronto, 23, 126, 202, 203
Tororu, 200
Toru, 185
Toulouse, 120, 189
Tours, 121, 189
Touwsrivier, 124
Townsville, 208
Track, concrete slab, 57
Track, concrete slab gauge, 124
Track maintenance, 57, 58
Trailing wheels, 29
Train Bleu, 124
Train ferry, 178
  Copenhagen–Malmö, 179
  Gedser-Warnemünde, 179
  Helsingør-Helsingborg, 179
  Rødby-Fehmarn, 179
Trans-alpine, 82–85
Trans-Andine railways, 79, 108
Trans-Asian Railway, 94
Trans-Australian line, 96
Trans-Europe Express (TEE), 86, 97, 118, 119, 121
Trans-Guinea Railway, 198
Trans-Iranian Railway, 194
Trans-Siberian Railway, 92–95, 192
Transvaal, 124
Trapani, 190
Treaty of Versailles, 187
Trevithick, Richard, 11, 26, 215
Triangulation, indirect, 82
Trieste, 114, 186, 190

Trikkala, 191
Trondheim, 178, 179
Troyes, 86, 189
Trujillo, 207
Truro, 19
Tsinan, 95
Tsingtao, 195
Tsuneb, 201
Tucumán, 206
Tulcea, 191
Tulsa, 203
Tumen, 95
Tunis, 198
Tunisia, 9, 198
Tunja, 205
Tunnel construction, 60–61
Tupiza, 207
Turbotrain, 202
Turin, 82, 91, 118, 190
Turkey, 94, 114, 190, 193
Turkish State Railways, 193
Turnu, 179
Turnouts, high-speed, 58
Twentieth Century Limited, 104, 203
Uberaba, 207
Udine, 190
Uganda, 19, 200
Ujjain, 194
Ulaan-baatar, 192
Ulan-ude, 93, 95, 111, 192
Ulm, 184
Umtali, 201
Ungeny, 191
Union Castle, 124
Union Limited, 124
Union Pacific Railroad, 16, 27, 36, 105
United Nations Committee for Asia and the Pacific (ESCAP), 94
Upper Engadine, 94
Upper Volta, 198
Uppsala, 178
Uruguay, 206
Urumchi, 95
USA, 6, 8, 9, 15, 23, 24, 42, 43, 45, 90, 98, 99, 104, 105, 121, 122, 178, 202, 203
USSR, 92, 178, 185, 192
Usti n.L., 187
Utah, 105
Utrecht, 183
Utrecht Transport Museum, 183
Uyuni, 207
Uzunköprü, 114

Vaasa, 179
Vadodora Junction (Baroda) 128
Valdivia, 206
Valence sur-Rhône, 189
Valencia, 188
Valladolid, 188
Vallorbe, 91
Valparaíso, 19, 111, 206
Vancouver, 18, 107, 126, 202, 203
Vancouver Island, 126
Van Horne, Sir William Cornelius, 18, 106, 202, 215
Väränäsi, 194
Varna, 114, 191
Venezuela, 205
Venice, 86, 190
Ventimiglia, 190
Veracruz, 204
Verona, 190
Vesuvio, 86, 119
Viaducts, 84, 101
Victoria, 96
Victoria Falls, 200, 201
Vienna, 114, 185, 186, 187
Vierzon, 120
Vietnam, 9, 94, 95, 195
Vila Cabral, 201
Vila Luso, 199
Vila Pery, 201

Vilar Formoso 188
Vilach, 186
Villa Montes, 207
Villarria, 206
Villazón, 206
Viña del Mar, 206
Visakhapatnam, 194
Vitória, 208
Vladivostock, 92, 93, 192
Vlissingen, 183
Volgograd, 192
Volos, 191
Vorkuta, 192
Wagons-Lit, 93
Wakkanai, 196
Wales, 116, 181
Walschaert, Egide, 215
  valve gear, 29
Walvis Bay, 201
Wanganui, 208
Wankie Colliery, 201
Warangal, 194
Warnemünde, 179, 185
Warsaw, 185, 186, 187
Washington, 13, 106, 203
Waterford, 180
Watt, James, 26
Webb, Francis William, 30
Weifang, 195
Wellington, 98, 99, 208
Western Australia, 96
Western Ghats, 194
West Germany, 8, 9, 10, 83, 86, 90, 121, 182, 184, 185, 187, 196
Westport, 98, 208
Wexford, 180
Wheeling, 13
Wick, 180, 181
Wicklow, 180
Williams Lake, 107
Windhoek, 201
Winnipeg, 18, 107, 126, 202, 203
Winslow, 122
Winterthur, 186
Witwatersrand, 201
Woomera, 97
Worcester, 116
Worcester (SA), 124, 201
Worth Valley Railway, 46
Wrocław, 185
Wuhan, 95, 195
Wuppertal, 184
Wurzburg, 184
Wyatt, 47
Wylam Colliery, 11, 26
Wylam Dilly, 26

Yato, 193
Yangtse, 95
Yantai, 195
Yaounde, 199
Yellowhead Pass, 18, 106, 107, 202
Yellow River, 95
Yingk'ou, 195
Yokkaichi, 196
Yokohama, 196
Yonago, 196
York, 180
Yugoslavia, 114, 190, 191
Yugoslav Railways, 190
Yumen, 195
Zacatecas, 204
Zagreb, 190
Zähedan, 94, 194
Zarand, 194
Zaria, 199
Zaire, 19, 199, 200, 201
Zambia, 200, 201
Zaribod, 114
Zermatt, 112
Zhengzhou, 195
Žilina, 187
Zimbabwe, 201
Zungeru, 199
Zürich, 86, 186
Zwolle, 183

# Acknowledgements

The Editor gratefully acknowledges help, advice and encouragement from the following.

Susie Ward, Paul Ekpenyong, Chris Milsome Ltd

Miss M Abbot, Dr J Davies, Birkbeck College, London
British Rail, BRB Press Office, Public Relations for Southern, London Midland, Eastern and Western Regions
British Rail Engineering Ltd, Works Manager Crewe, Public Relations Derby
Emmanuel Haussman, Carta, Jerusalem
Donald J Martin, Charles Laggan, E F Stefanovich, Conrail
J H Price, Cook's International Timetable
Messers Douglas, Ludlow, Middlehurst and Page, Crown Agents, London
Sarah Dale
Department of Trade and Industry, Export House Library
Diagram Ltd, London
Sally Foy
Railway Gazette International, Editorial Staff
J N Slater, Railway Magazine
Severn Valley Railway
Deborah Yates

## Photographs

Picture research was assisted by Helen Fayers, Annie Horton and Jonathan Moore.

Picture credits are by page number, additional numbers read in order from top to bottom and left to right, taken together; i.e. top left first, bottom right last.

Alco/O S Nock, 36/4
American History Picture Library, 13/1, 27/1, 38/1, 122/1, 122/2
Ann Ronan Picture Library, 30/1, 30/3, 41/3, 42/3, 43/3, 48/5
Arts Directors Library, 25/2, 86/4, 90/2, 94
ASEA, 53, 178/1
Barnabys Picture Library, 80/1, 105/2, 106
John Bennett/Chris Milsome Ltd, 25/3, 25/4, 40/2, 40/4, 42/2, 42/4, 42/5, 43/5, 45/5, 46/4, 47/3, 48/2, 68/2, 70/2, 82/2, 83, 84/1, 88/1, 182/2, 183/1, 189/1
Chris Bonington/Bruce Coleman Ltd, 112
British Rail/O S Nock, 42/1, 43/1
British Transport Films, 45/4, 45/6, 52/2, 52/3, 55/3, 55/4, 57/1, 57/4, 62, 63/2, 63/3, 64/5, 66/5, 67/4, 68/1, 116/2
Canadian National Railways, 67/4
Canadian Pacific Ltd, 126
Kenneth Cantlie, 95/1
Chicago N.W. Railway, 67/2
CIE, 180/1
Colour Library International Ltd, 61/2
Colourviews Publications, 14, P M Alexander, 117/4, J Dunn, 64/2, P J Howard, 44/1, 44/2, 45/3, 59/2, 66/4, 69/4, 69/5, 75, 127/1, C M Whitehouse, 65/1, 65/3, 206, P B Whitehouse, 35/2, 39/3, 66/2, 77/2, 115/5
Denver Rio Grande Western Railroad/O S Nock, 22/1
Derek Cross/O S Nock, 116/3
A P Dowley, 44/2, 44/3, 44/4
EBT Bahn, 32/1
Edito Service, 27/2
EMI Films Ltd, 115/4, 115/5, 115/6
Robert Estall, 45/1, 105/1, 202/2
Fox Photos Ltd, 6/1, 23/1, 54/1
Christopher Gammell, 95/2, 115/3, 125/1, 188, 189/2, 193, 203
Victor Goldberg, 115/1, 116/1
High Commissioner for New Zealand, London, 28/2
Michael Holford, 33
Ann Horton, 26/1
Alan Hutchinson, 50/2, 198
Illustrated London News, 82/3, 82/4

Intercontainer, 68/4
Italian Railways, 54/4, 54/5, 119/2
Japan Information Centre, 100/1, 100/3, 103/1, 103/2
Kiwi, 99/2
Mike Laye/Chris Milsome Ltd, 48/3, 48/4, 51/2, 58/2, 59/4, 63/1, 70/3, 71/1, 71/2, 71/3, 71/4, 73/2, 76/1, 88/2, 117/1, 117/2, 117/3, 118/1, 118/2, 119/1
R H Leach/O S Nock, 34/1
L G Marshall, 39/1, 61/1, 72/1, 128/2, 128/3
Mary Evans Picture Library, 17, 18/1, 18/2, 19, 20/2, 30/2, 40/1, 40/3, 40/5, 41/1, 41/2, 43/2, 43/4, 114
Ken Mills, 111/1
Jonathan Moore, 11/1, 109/2
National Railways Museum York, Crown Copyright, 6/2, 32/2
O S Nock, 32/3, 35/1, 100/2, 101, 128/1
Paul Forrester/Science Museum, London, 10/3, 11/3
Pictor, 60/2, 64/3, 77/1, 196
Picturepoint London/Kay Mander, 115/2
Popperfoto, 20/1, 21/1, 21/2, 21/3, 92
Roger Pring, 4, 5, 7, 48/1, 49, 81, 113, 129, 177, 209
Radio Times Hulton Picture Library, 16/1, 16/2, 22/2, 22/3, 22/4, 23/2, 36/3, 38/3, 82/2
Walter Rawlings, 36/3, 47/1, 56/2, 58/4, 59/2, 59/4, 66/6, 66/7, 67/3, 68/5, 69/2, 69/3, 80/2, 80/3
RENFE, 61/4
Rex Features, 39/2, 54/2, 54/3, 55/5
Robert Harding Associates, 127/2, 178/2, 191/2, 202/1
G R Roberts, 66/2, 96/1, 173/3
Santa Fe Railroad Company, 123
Santa Fe/J G Moore, 78/1, 78/2, 79
Science Museum, London, 10/1, 10/2, 11/4, 12, 13/2, 26/2, 43/6
Roy Sinclair, 98/1, 98/2, 99/1, 208
SNCF, 45/2, 55/1, 55/2, 91/1, 91/2, 120, 121/1, 121/2
South African Railways, Publicity and Travel Department, 60/1, 65/4, 124/1, 125/2
Spectrum Colour Library, 25/5, 37, 46/1, 46/2, 46/3, 47/4, 50/3, 51/1, 52/1, 61/3, 65/2, 67/1, 68/3, 70/1, 97, 103/3, 107/1, 108/2, 123/2, 180/2, 181/2
Brian Stephenson, 85/1, 85/2, 184/2, 185, 186/1, 186/2, 187/1, 187/2, 189/5
Tony Stone Associates, 25/1, 28/1, 31, 34/2, 102/1, 104, 108/1, 179, 192
Swiss Railways, 47/2, 84/2, 86/1
Syndication International, 36/2
P N Trotter, 39/4, 50/1, 56/1, 58/1, 58/3, 66/1
VIA Rail Canada, 127/5
J Winkley, 64/1, 64/4, 69/1, 86/3, 182
ZEFA, 51/3, 58/5, 86/2, 87, 90/1, 93, 109/1, 181/1, 183/2, 184, 204, front cover